To my wife Jane and our children
Esther, Sophia, Daniel and Joel

The IVP
Atlas
of Bible
History

PAUL LAWRENCE

IVP Academic

InterVarsity Press
P.O. Box 1400, Downers Grove, IL 60515-1426
Internet: www.ivpress.com
E-mail: email@ivpress.com

ISBN-10: 0-8308-2452-9
ISBN-13: 978-0-8308-2452-6

Printed and bound in China ∞

Library of Congress Cataloging-in-Publication Data

A catalog record for this book is available from the Library of Congress.

P	27	26	25	24	23	22	21	20	19	18	17	16	15	14	13	12	11	10	9	8	7	6	5	4	3	2	1
Y	27	26	25	24	23	22	21	20	19	18	17	16	15	14	13	12	11	10	09	08	07	06					

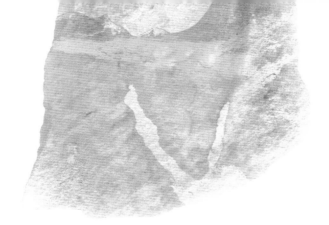

CONTENTS

INTRODUCTION

THE SCOPE OF THIS BOOK

The Lion Atlas of Bible History spans over two millennia of history from Abraham, placed approximately at 2000 BC, through to the Revelation seen by the apostle John, which closes the New Testament at the end of the first century AD. These limits are expanded by consideration of the biblical book of Genesis before Abraham, by surveys of Mesopotamia and Egypt, and by a look at the spread of Christianity in the first three centuries after the last book of the New Testament had been written.

Geographically this *Atlas* is not confined to the modern state of Israel and the West Bank, for about 40 per cent of the Bible is set outside this area or addresses people living outside it. In its widest sense the Bible world stretches from Spain to Iran, from Yemen (the Sheba/Saba of the Old Testament) to Philippi in northern Greece. Trade widens these horizons even further to encompass India and possibly China and the east coast of Africa.

The Bible is linked to all of these disparate historical periods and areas. In this *Atlas* the unfolding story of Bible history is presented as chronologically as is practically possible, supplemented by nine special features.

THE BIBLE AS HISTORY

The main purpose of this *Atlas* is to present the broad sweep of Bible history. To enter into academic controversies, unless they effect our understanding of the flow of Bible history, is beyond its scope. It is our contention that history should primarily be based on written sources and, although the writer is aware of a large body of critical scholarship connected with the Bible, theoretical reconstructions of the past based on minimal or no evidence have no place here. Ancient writers lived much closer to the events they described than we do, so it is our basic policy to show them healthy respect. This applies to the writers of the Bible just as much as to other ancient historians, whose work we sometimes also cite.

Since between two to four millennia separate us from the people and civilizations that produced the Bible, it should not surprise us that some of its details are obscure or difficult to understand; but it is our belief that such details do not obscure the much larger picture of the Bible that we are attempting to paint.

THE BIBLE AS GEOGRAPHY

Bible history is played out on a large geographical stage. The locations of political powers such as Israel, Moab and Rome are known, though the extent of territory they ruled varied historically. Many of the important locations of the biblical world are still significant today, such as Jerusalem, Damascus and Athens. Often, unless there is inscriptional evidence, the identity of a site remains uncertain. The exact locations of such sites as Libnah and Ziklag in the Old Testament and Emmaus and Arimathea in the New are unknown.

THE BIBLE AS THEOLOGY

The broad flow of Bible history provides the setting for the main message of the Bible: how God provided in Jesus a saviour for rebellious humankind. The God of the Bible is the Bible's greatest unifying theme. For the Hebrew prophet Isaiah (c. 700 BC), there is a graphic contrast between God and his creation. The people of the world are like grasshoppers, but the living God of the Bible 'sits enthroned above the circle of the earth' (Isaiah 40:22). To the biblical writers he alone, it would seem, has the true perspective on Bible history. It would seem arrogance on our part to suppose otherwise.

CHRONOLOGY OF THE EVENTS OF THE BIBLE AND THE ANCIENT NEAR EAST

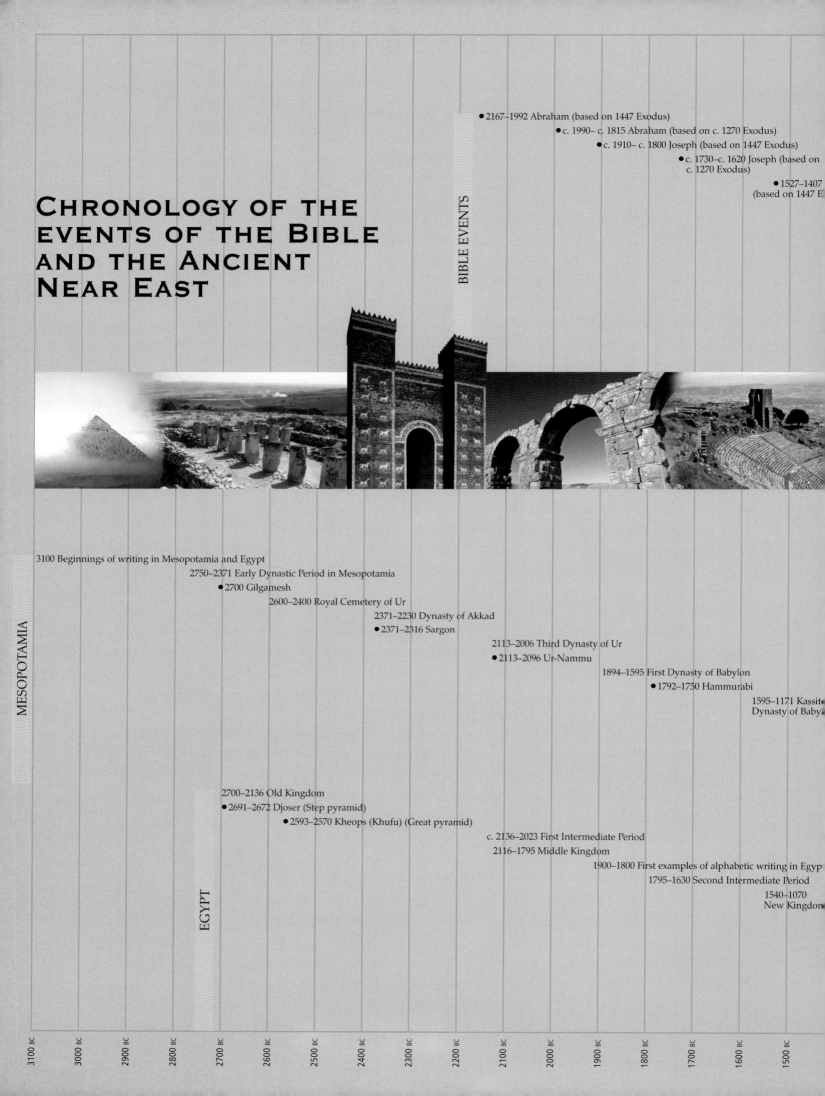

BIBLE EVENTS

- 2167–1992 Abraham (based on 1447 Exodus)
- c. 1990– c. 1815 Abraham (based on c. 1270 Exodus)
- c. 1910– c. 1800 Joseph (based on 1447 Exodus)
- c. 1730–c. 1620 Joseph (based on c. 1270 Exodus)
- 1527–1407 (based on 1447 E

MESOPOTAMIA

- 3100 Beginnings of writing in Mesopotamia and Egypt
- 2750–2371 Early Dynastic Period in Mesopotamia
- 2700 Gilgamesh
- 2600–2400 Royal Cemetery of Ur
- 2371–2230 Dynasty of Akkad
- 2371–2316 Sargon
- 2113–2006 Third Dynasty of Ur
- 2113–2096 Ur-Nammu
- 1894–1595 First Dynasty of Babylon
- 1792–1750 Hammurabi
- 1595–1171 Kassite Dynasty of Baby

EGYPT

- 2700–2136 Old Kingdom
- 2691–2672 Djoser (Step pyramid)
- 2593–2570 Kheops (Khufu) (Great pyramid)
- c. 2136–2023 First Intermediate Period
- 2116–1795 Middle Kingdom
- 1900–1800 First examples of alphabetic writing in Egypt
- 1795–1630 Second Intermediate Period
- 1540–1070 New Kingdom

3100 BC 3000 BC 2900 BC 2800 BC 2700 BC 2600 BC 2500 BC 2400 BC 2300 BC 2200 BC 2100 BC 2000 BC 1900 BC 1800 BC 1700 BC 1600 BC 1500 BC

JUDAH

• 930–913 Rehoboam
926 Shishak (Shoshenq 945–924) of Egypt invades Judah and Israel
• 910–869 Asa of Judah   538 Cyrus issues decree authorising the Jews to return from exile in Babylon to Jerusalem
• 869–848 Jehoshaphat (of Judah)   536 Foundations laid for a new Temple at Jerusalem
• 841–835 Athaliah (queen of Judah) Haggai and Zechariah (520–518)
• 767–752 Uzziah (of Judah) (sole reign)
Isaiah (740–681)   516 Zerubbabel finishes rebuilding the Temple at Jerusalem
• 735–715 Ahaz (of Judah)   479 Esther becomes Xerxes' queen and saves the Jews from extinction (474)
• 715–686 Hezekiah (of Judah)
701 Sennacherib invades Judah
• 686–641 Manasseh (of Judah)
Nahum (663)   458 Ezra returns to Jerusalem
• 639–609 Josiah (of Judah)
Zephaniah (reign of Josiah)
Jeremiah (626–586)
Habakkuk (c. 610) 445 Nehemiah rebuilds the wall of Jerusalem
605 First deportation – Daniel and friends
Daniel (605–536) Malachi (late 5th century)
597 Second deportation – Jehoiachin and leading men
Ezekiel (593–573)   198 Antiochus III of Syria gains control of Palestine
586 Nebuchadnezzar exiles Judah to Babylon – Jerusalem and Temple destroyed (Third deportation)
582 Fourth deportation – some of remaining Jews

Exodus – earlier placement
–1400 Conquest of Canaan – earlier placement
1380–1050 Period of Judges (based on 1407 conquest)
• c. 1350– c. 1230 Moses (based on c. 1270 Exodus)
c. 1270 Exodus – later placement
c. 1230–1223 Conquest of Canaan – later placement
c. 1200–1050 Period of Judges (based on c. 1230 conquest)
c. 1050–930 United Israelite Monarchy
• c. 1050–1010 Saul
• 1010–970 David
• 970–930 Solomon   • 175–164 Antiochus IV (Epiphanes) of Syria
967–960 Solomon builds Temple of the Lord at Jerusalem   168 Antiochus IV desecrates the Temple at Jerusalem
165 Following victories by the Maccabees the Temple at Jerusalem is rededicated
930 Division of the Kingdom into Israel (north) – Judah (south, around Jerusalem)

ISRAEL

• 930–909 Jeroboam I   63 Roman general Pompey captures Jerusalem and enters the Most Holy Place in Temple
• 880–873 Omri (of Israel)   • 40–4 Herod the Great
• 873–853 Ahab (of Israel)   19 Herod the Great begins rebuilding of the Temple at Jerusalem
Elijah (starts ministry in reign of Ahab)   5 BC Jesus is born
• 841–813 Jehu (of Israel)   30–33 Public ministry of Jesus
Jonah (c. 800–780)   33 Jesus dies and rises again, Day of Pentecost – beginning of the church
Elisha (dies in reign of Jehoash of Israel 798–782)
781–753 Jeroboam II (of Israel)   47 The apostle Paul sets out on his first journey
Amos (reign of Jeroboam II)   49 Council of Jerusalem, Paul at Athens
Hosea (mid 8th century)   60 Paul arrives in Rome
722 Israel exiled to Assyria   60–62 Paul's house arrest in Rome
• 1115–1077 Tiglath-pileser I (of Assyria)   63–65 Paul's final journey
• 884–859 Ashurnasirpal (of Assyria)   66–67 Paul's final imprisonment and execution under emperor Nero
• 859–824 Shalmaneser III (of Assyria)
853 Battle of Qarqar Shalmaneser v Ahab and allies   81–96 Persecution of church under emperor Domitian, apostle John sees Revelation on island of Patmos
763 Solar eclipse in Assyria
• 746–727 Tiglath-pileser III (of Assyria)
• 722–705 Sargon II (of Assyria)
• 705–681 Sennacherib (of Assyria)
• 681–669 Esarhaddon (of Assyria)
• 669–627 Ashurbanipal (of Assyria)
612 Fall of Nineveh
605 Battle of Carchemish Crown Prince Nebuchadnezzar v Egyptians
• 605–562 Nebuchadnezzar (of Babylon)
• 556–539 Nabonidus (of Babylon) with Belshazzar as regent
539–530 Cyrus (of Persia), as king of Babylon
539 Fall of Babylon to Persians

PERSIA

• 522–486 Darius (of Persia)
490 Darius' campaign against Greece, battle of Marathon
• 486–465 Xerxes (of Persia)
483–479 Xerxes' campaign against Greece, battles of Thermopylae and Salamis (480)
• 465–424 Artaxerxes (of Persia)

JESUS AND THE EARLY CHURCH

THE GENTILE RULERS

• 336–323 Alexander the Great conquers the Persian Empire
• 285–246 Ptolemy II of Egypt commissions Old Testament translation into Greek (Septuagint)
30 Egypt becomes a Roman province
27 Octavian becomes the first Roman emperor Augustus (27 BC – AD 14)

–1425 Tuthmosis III
• 1353–1337 Amenophis IV (Akhenaten)   • AD 14–37 Tiberius
• 1336–1327 Tutankhamun   • 41–54 Claudius
• 1279–1213 Ramesses II   • 54–68 Nero
1275 Battle of Qadesh Ramesses II v Hittites   70 Jerusalem falls to the Romans
• 1213–1203 Merenptah
1209 Israel stela of Merenptah attests Israel in Canaan
1180 Ramesses III defeats the Sea Peoples

1300 BC   1200 BC   1100 BC   1000 BC   900 BC   800 BC   700 BC   600 BC   500 BC   400 BC   300 BC   200 BC   100 BC   0   AD 100

Israel in Old and New Testament Times

Modern political boundaries are marked in grey

Legend:
- town mentioned in OT
- town mentioned in NT
- town mentioned in OT and NT
- town not mentioned in the Bible
- (QUMRAN) site mentioned in OT and/or NT but with change of name

0   60 km
0   40 miles

LEBANON

SYRIA

Damascus

Helam

Rehob?

Edrei

Sidon

Caesarea Philippi

Dan (Laish, Tell el-Qadi)

Lake Huleh

Ashtaroth

Golan

Dion?

Ramoth in Gilead

Rabbah

Gerasa

Jabbok

Mahanaim

Abel Beth Maacah

Hazor

Bethsaida (Julias)

Gamala

Yarmuk

Jogbehah

Kedesh

Jordan

Chorazin

Gennesaret

Sea of Kinnereth

Gergesa (Kursi)

Sennabris

Beth Yerah

Gadara

Pella

Jabesh Gilead

Tishbe

Penuel

Livias

Heshbon

Gischala

Capernaum

Tiberias

Magdala

Beth Shan (SCYTHOPOLIS)

Zarethan

Succoth (Tell Deir Alla)

Adam

Archelais

Tyre

Cana

Rimmon

Gath Hepher

Nazareth

Endor

Jezreel

GILBOA MTS

Abel Meholah

Tirzah

Sychar

Coreae

Sartaba (Alexandrium)

Jordan

Gilgal

Jericho

Aczib

Jotapata

Sepphoris

Shimron

Nain

Shunem

Ophrah

Ginae

Baddan

Shechem

SAMARIAN HILLS

Shiloh

Ephraim

Michmash

Gibeah

Anathoth

Acshaph?

Galilee

Acco (PTOLEMAIS)

Jokneam

Megiddo

Taanach

Dothan

Shamir

Samaria (SEBASTE)

Pirathon

Kanah

Ai

Bethel

Mizpah

Ramah

Gibeon

Nob

MT CARMEL

Dor

Hepher

Socoh

Aphek (ANTIPATRIS)

Gophna

Modin

Shaalbim

Ramah

Aijalon

Kriath

Caesarea

PLAIN OF SHARON

Lod (LYDDA)

Ebenezer (Izbet Sarteh)

Gezer

Timnah

Joppa

Gibbethon

Makaz

Ekron

JORDAN

Medeba
Jahaz
Beth Baal Meon
Beth Diblathaim
Ataroth
Machaerus
Dibon
Aroer
Arnon
Kir Hareseth
(Kerak)
Zered
Zara
(CALLIRHOE)
(QUMRAN)
Hyrcana
Murabba'at
Sela
(Petra)
Bethlehem
En Gedi
Salt
Sea
Herodium
Nahal Hever
Tekoa
Ziph
Horesh
Maon
Masada
THE ARABAH
Hebron
Makkedah?
Adullam
Keilah
Hereth
Arad
Socoh
Debir
Hormah?
Jarmuth
Azekah
Moresheth
Beersheba
Libnah?
Mareshah
Eglon?
Lachish
THE NEGEV
I S R A E L
Ashkelon
Ziklag?
Gaza
WILDERNESS
OF ZIN
Besor
Raphia
Kadesh Barnea
E G Y P T

WHAT IS THE BIBLE?

ONE BIBLE, TWO TESTAMENTS

The word 'Bible' is derived from a Greek word *'biblia'* meaning 'books'. Essentially the Bible is a collection of sixty-six books, divided into two sections of unequal length, which Christians call the Old and New Testaments. 'Testament' in biblical terminology means 'covenant', an agreement made between God and his people.

The Old Testament claims to be a record of God's revelation to his people, Israel. It was written by some thirty different writers over a period of approximately a thousand years. Its primary language was Hebrew, the language of the Israelites, although a few short portions were written in Aramaic, a Semitic language related to Hebrew that the Jews learned during their exile in Babylon.[1]

The New Testament purports to be a record of Jesus' life and ministry and the establishment of the church. It was written in Greek by some nine different writers in the second half of the first century AD. Whereas the Old Testament was God's message to Israel communicated 'at many times and in various ways',[2] the New Testament records God's word made flesh in the person of his son Jesus.[3]

The term 'Bible' is used differently by Jews and Christians. Jews use the term 'Bible' for what Christians call the 'Old Testament'. Christians use the term 'Bible' for both Old and New Testaments. The latter is the use in this book.

A SACRED BOOK IN A HISTORICAL SETTING

The Old Testament owes its preservation to the fact that it was perceived by Jewish scribes and priests to be a sacred book. Similarly, the New Testament was viewed by the fathers of the early Christian church as sacred – sacred because in the pages of the Bible the living God claims to reveal himself to humankind. Most of the Bible is not however written in the form of a theological treatise. It is an account of how God revealed himself to many different

men and women over many centuries, real men and real women each living in a particular place at a particular time. The events described in the Bible are rooted in history – the history of the ancient Near East and the Greco-Roman world, to be precise. This *Atlas* sets the main events of Bible history in their wider historical setting.

THE GEOGRAPHICAL SETTING

We should not forget that nearly two thousand years have elapsed since the last events described in the Bible. Many of the cities mentioned in the Bible have been destroyed, much of the countryside has been subject to the ravages of war and general neglect. As a result the geographical settings given by scholars to many of the incidents described in the Bible are general rather than specific.

ARCHAEOLOGICAL AND HISTORICAL EVIDENCE

Archaeological discoveries over the past two hundred years have enabled a number of places mentioned in the Bible to be pinpointed; King Hezekiah's water tunnel at Jerusalem and the theatre at Ephesus in Turkey are good examples.[4] However, archaeology has done more than identify sites. We can see buildings and artefacts used by people from Bible times: city walls, weapons, cooking utensils and pottery, to name but four examples. Since precise dates cannot always be given, such evidence may be difficult to interpret. Archaeology has also revealed many written documents. Many of these are simply lists of commodities or receipts, but some record historical events. Historical texts from the peoples of the ancient Near East and the literature of Greece and Rome are regularly used in this work to shed further light on Bible history.

Some of the incidents that occur in the Bible can be illuminated to some extent by material evidence, but the vast majority cannot. So, when all is said and done, the role of archaeology is limited; it cannot bring to life people's personal experiences of the God of the Bible. If we want to

Silver amulet from Ketef Hinnom on the western edge of Jerusalem. When unrolled this text was only about 9cm (3½ in) long. It contained many of the words of the priestly blessing from the Old Testament book of Numbers 6:24–26 as well as other words not found in the Bible. The writing suggests a date in the seventh or sixth century BC.

The books of the Old Testament

Genesis	Ezra	Joel
Exodus	Nehemiah	Amos
Leviticus	Esther	Obadiah
Numbers	Job	Jonah
Deuteronomy	Psalms	Micah
Joshua	Proverbs	Nahum
Judges	Ecclesiastes	Habakkuk
Ruth	Song of Songs	Zephaniah
1 Samuel	Isaiah	Haggai
2 Samuel	Jeremiah	Zechariah
1 Kings	Lamentations	Malachi
2 Kings	Ezekiel	*The following books from the Apocrypha are also cited*
1 Chronicles	Daniel	1 Maccabees
2 Chronicles	Hosea	2 Maccabees

The Elizabeth Hay Bechtel Psalms scroll from cave 11 at Qumran. Apart from a few minor variations this scroll agrees with the later Masoretic or traditional Hebrew text of the Old Testament. However, it has some additional psalms not found in the Bible. It is dated c. AD 30–50.

The Ten Commandments (Exodus 20) from one of the earliest examples of a complete Old Testament in Hebrew. The so-called St Petersburg Codex of the Masoretic text of the Old Testament dates from AD 1008.

KEY

[1] Ezra 4:8 – 6:18; 7:12–26; Jeremiah 10:11; Daniel 2:4–7:28

[2] Hebrews 1:1–2

[3] John 1:14

[4] 2 Kings 20:20; 2 Chronicles 32:30; Acts 19:29

[5] Matthew 7:12; 22:40

The books of the New Testament

Matthew	1 Timothy
Mark	2 Timothy
Luke	Titus
John	Philemon
Acts	Hebrews
Romans	James
1 Corinthians	1 Peter
2 Corinthians	2 Peter
Galatians	1 John
Ephesians	2 John
Philippians	3 John
Colossians	Jude
1 Thessalonians	Revelation
2 Thessalonians	

know what happened when God gave the Law to Moses at Sinai or what happened at the empty tomb of Jesus (to cite examples that are fundamental to Judaism and Christianity respectively) we have to trust the biblical record; there is nothing else beside.

THE OLD TESTAMENT

The Old Testament itself consists of three main parts, called the Law, the Prophets and the Writings in Jewish terminology. The 'Law' is the first five books attributed to Moses. The 'Prophets' consists of all the prophets except Daniel, but includes the books of Joshua, Judges, Samuel and Kings. The 'Writings' is everything else. This is further reduced to 'the Law and the Prophets' in the New Testament.[5] In the Christian Bible the order of the historical books is somewhat more chronological. The wisdom literature is placed after the histories, with the prophets at the end.

THE NEW TESTAMENT

The New Testament consists of two main parts: the four Gospels and the letters of Paul and other leaders of the early church. Between the Gospels and the letters is Luke's account of the growth of the early church called 'The Acts of the Apostles'. The New Testament concludes with the 'Revelation', a glimpse into heaven and the future as seen by the apostle John.

THE APOCRYPHA

The books of the Apocrypha (a Greek term meaning 'hidden') were written by Jewish religious writers in the period between the Old and New Testaments. Some Apocryphal books, such as Ecclesiasticus and Tobit, turned up among the 'Dead Sea Scrolls' at Qumran. Later Jewish and Protestant Christian opinion did not regard the Apocrypha as authoritative or 'canonical'. The Catholic and Orthodox Churches accord the Apocrypha 'canonical' status, but there is not complete agreement as to which writings should be included. Of the Apocryphal books we quote only 1 and 2 Maccabees; they are valuable historical sources.

CREATION

IN THE BEGINNING

'In the beginning God created the heavens and the earth.' So begins the book of Genesis, the first book of the Bible. The Bible nowhere attempts to prove the existence of God; it simply states that he was there 'In the beginning'. Incidentally, the title of the Bible's first book, Genesis, comes from its title in Greek meaning 'origin'. The words 'the heavens and the earth' mean the universe. For the Bible writers nothing (except God) existed before, so everything in the universe was created out of nothing by God.

Although the Bible tells us that God made the heavens and the earth it does not give precise details of *how* he did it. The Lord's question to Job 'Where were you when I laid the earth's foundation? Tell me if you understand'[1] applies just as much to modern people with all their scientific knowledge as it did to Job perhaps 3,500 years ago. We have to face the fact that no human being was a witness to creation. Whether we accept it or not, Genesis claims to be God's own account. It is this account that gave birth to the biblical world-view, a view we must attempt to understand if we are to understand the Bible.

The account of creation in Genesis 1:1 – 2:3 enables us to make the following observations:

1. The Genesis 1 account is structured in terms of six days, which are further defined by the oft repeated phrase 'and there was evening, and there was morning'. The pattern of six days of work followed by a day of rest was to provide a model for the sabbath principle later to be taught in Exodus 20:8–11.

2. The account was not written by someone with modern scientific understanding. Light is called into being on the first day,[2] yet the sun, moon and stars which give light to our planet are not made until the fourth day. The moon is called the 'lesser light'. That it simply reflects the sun's light was almost certainly unknown to the author.

3. The Bible's account of creation is earth-centred; the emphasis is not on space. Indeed the creation of the stars is dismissed with less than half a verse in Genesis 1:16 ('and also the stars'). Some six thousand stars are visible to the naked eye, yet within the observable universe, according to modern estimates, there are some 100 billion stars in our galaxy alone, and a 100 billion galaxies.

4. The writer avoids mentioning the sun and moon by name, maybe because of the widespread worship of celestial bodies in the nations around.

5. God was pleased with his creation. Six times we read 'God saw that it was good.' Genesis 1 concludes: 'God saw all that he had made and it was very good.'

6. God is the creator. He is separate from his creation, not part of it.

7. Human beings are viewed as the climax of God's creation. Of all God's creatures human beings alone are

KEY
[1] Job 38:4
[2] Genesis 1:3
[3] Genesis 1:26–27
[4] Genesis 2:16–17, 3:17; Romans 5:12
[5] Matthew 1:1–17
[6] 1 Chronicles 3:11–12
[7] *Atrahasis Epic* 1.223–26
[8] *Enuma elish* 6.32–36

RIGHT: **The location of the rivers mentioned in Genesis 2**
This is a possible solution based on the identification of the river and place names that are known from antiquity. Some consider that the geography was later sufficiently changed by Noah's flood to invalidate direct comparison with modern geographical features.

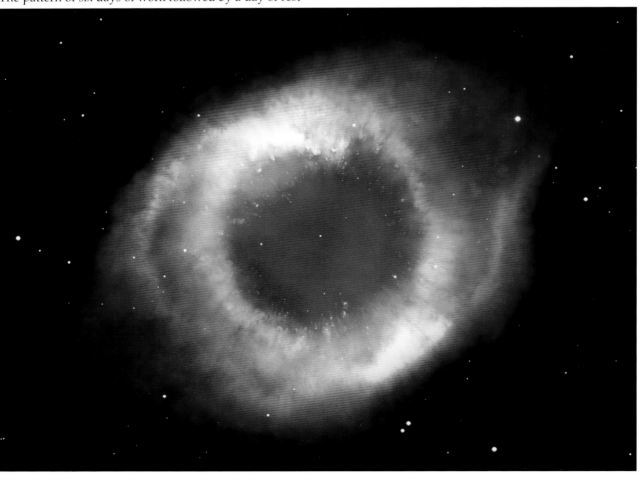

One of the nearest nebulae to Earth, the coil shaped Helix Nebula, as viewed through the NASA Hubble Space Telescope. NASA has nicknamed it 'the eye of God'.

made in God's image, in his likeness.[3] In Genesis 2:4–25 more details of the direct, special and personal creation of the first humans are given. The man is made 'from the dust of the ground' and the woman from man.

Chapter 3 of Genesis states that it was the sin of the first humans that brought death into the world.[4]

CHRONOLOGICAL CONSIDERATIONS

The question of *when* God created the world is not directly stated by the biblical writers (contrast the date given to the exodus in 1 Kings 6:1). Throughout the centuries scholars have added up the figures given in the genealogical lists in the book of Genesis and advanced their own dates. Most famous was that of 4004 BC, published by James Ussher (1581–1656), the Archbishop of Armagh, in his *Annales Veteris et Novi Testamenti* (1650–54). Such a method can be criticized on a number of counts, three of which are worthy of note here:

1. The writer of Genesis has two lists showing the line of descent from Adam to Noah (Genesis 5) and from Noah to Terah, the father of Abraham (Genesis 11). Both lists give ten generations, with the final patriarch in each list producing three sons (Shem, Ham and Japheth in the case of Noah in Genesis 5:32 and Abram, Nahor and Haran in the case of Terah in Genesis 11:26). The writer seems to have schematic as well as chronological considerations in mind, as is clearly the case with Matthew's division of the genealogy of Jesus into three sets of fourteen generations at the beginning of his Gospel.[5]

2. A strict chronological approach to the data would mean that all the patriarchs of the Genesis 11 list would still have been living when Abram was fifty years old, and Eber would have been a contemporary of Jacob.

3. We know that the term 'was the father of' is sometimes used for ancestral relationships. A classic case in point is Matthew 1:8 where Jehoram, 'father' of Uzziah, was actually his great-great grandfather.[6]

THE GARDEN OF EDEN

Genesis 2:8 states that the original home of Adam and Eve was 'a garden in the east, in Eden'. Genesis 2:10–14 locates it where four rivers rose. From elsewhere in the Bible we know that the third and fourth rivers are the Tigris and Euphrates, which rise in eastern Turkey and flow through Iraq into the Persian Gulf. Cush, in the Old Testament, normally denotes Egypt south of Aswan and Sudan as far south as Khartoum, which would make the Gihon River, which winds through Cush, the Nile. The Pishon River, which ran through Havilah, could be a prehistoric river of Arabia flowing into the Persian Gulf. Havilah was famous for its gold. Hawlan, a gold-bearing region in western Arabia, may be Havilah. It is strange how the river that flowed through Eden could separate into four headwaters comprising such diverse rivers as suggested above. Perhaps the geography was later sufficiently changed by Noah's flood to invalidate direct comparison with modern geographical features.

MESOPOTAMIAN CREATION STORIES

The account of creation in Genesis is sometimes compared to creation stories from ancient Mesopotamia (modern Iraq). In the *Atrahasis Epic* of c. 1635 BC the mother goddess Mami (or Nintu), with the help of the wise god Ea, created humans out of clay mixed with the blood of a slain god named Aw-ilu.[7]

Enuma elish ('When on high'), a Babylonian epic composed c. 1200 BC from older sources, narrates how the god Marduk used the blood of Qingu, the evil leader of the enemy gods whom he had slain, to create humankind with the help of Ea.[8] The only similarities between the *Enuma elish* and Genesis are the mention of 'the deep', the separation of heaven and earth, the divine element in humans, divine rest after creation and the task given to humans of working the soil. Much closer parallels exist between Genesis and various flood stories from Mesopotamia.

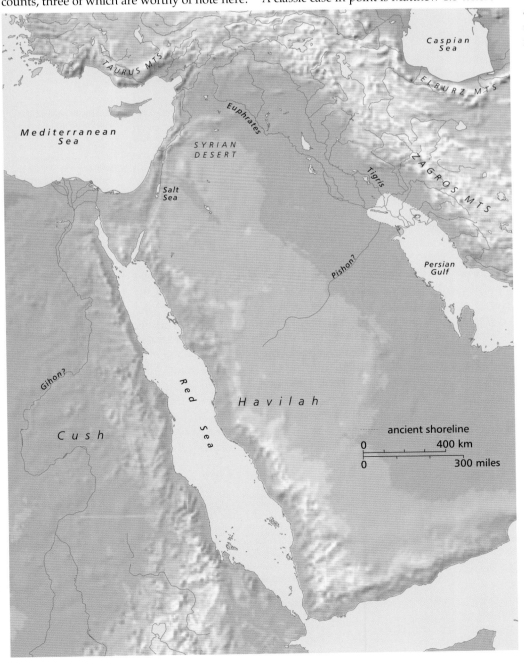

Caspian Sea

TAURUS MTS

ELBURZ MTS

Euphrates

Mediterranean Sea

SYRIAN DESERT

ZAGROS MTS

Salt Sea

Tigris

Pishon?

Persian Gulf

Gihon?

Red Sea

Havilah

Cush

ancient shoreline

0   400 km

0   300 miles

THE FLOOD

FROM ADAM TO NOAH

The book of Genesis tells how Adam and Eve disobeyed God and were expelled from the Garden of Eden. Their descendants are credited with several aspects of civilization: 'a city', 'harp and flute' and 'tools of bronze and iron'.[1] Their descendants are recorded as being very long-lived, 969 years in the case of Methuselah.[2] Long, to many impossibly long, but almost nothing compared to figures in the famous list of kings from Mesopotamia, known as the 'Sumerian King List'. The record there is held by a certain Enmenluanna: 43,200 years. Their descendants' wickedness was the cause of great grief to the Lord who resolved to wipe humankind from the face of the earth.

NOAH'S FLOOD

The Lord chose Noah, 'a righteous man, blameless among the people of his time, and he walked with God'[3] and told him to build a huge wooden box (traditionally translated 'ark') 300 cubits long, 50 cubits wide and 30 cubits high – in modern measurements approximately 133.5 m by 22.3 m by 13.4 m (roughly 438 ft by 72 ft by 45 ft), probably indicating a weight in excess of 10,000 tons. Noah was to take into the ark, with him and his family, seven pairs of all clean animals and birds and a pair of all unclean animals. Forty days of rain would wipe off from the face of the earth every living creature.

Adding up the figures given between Genesis 7:11–12 and 8:14 a total of 371 days is obtained for the duration of the flood, unless we assume that some of the periods were simultaneous rather than sequential. Statements such as 'all the high mountains under the entire heavens were covered',[4] 'the waters rose and covered the mountains to a depth of fifteen cubits' (approximately 7 m or 23 ft),[5] and 'every living thing that moved on the earth perished – birds, livestock, wild animals, all the creatures that swarm over the earth, and all mankind'[6] arguably show the writer's belief in the universality of the flood. From the author's perspective the destruction was total: 'Everything on the face of the earth was wiped out; men and animals and the creatures that move along the ground and the birds of the air were wiped from the earth. Only Noah was left, and those with him in the ark'.[7] Some substitute 'land' for earth in the above verses and argue that the flood was localized.

The ark came to rest on 'one of the mountains of Ararat'[8] and after sending out a raven, then a dove to see if the waters had receded Noah, his family and the animals left the ark. The Lord promised never again to destroy all living creatures and gave a rainbow as a sign of his covenant-promise.

COMPARISON WITH MESOPOTAMIAN FLOOD STORIES

Parallels between the flood story in Genesis are to be found in the Mesopotamian stories of the flood. These exist in three versions: the *Atrahasis Epic* (c. 1635 BC), the *Epic of Ziusudra* (c. 1600 BC), and the *Epic of Gilgamesh*, which is known from copies made at Nineveh and other cities in the first millennium BC. It adapted the flood story from the

The majestic snow-covered peak of Turkey's highest mountain, Ağrı Dağı, which is sometimes called 'Mount Ararat'. A view from near the Turkish town of Doğubeyazıt, with the palace of Ishakpasha in the foreground.

RIGHT: The map shows the places associated with the Genesis and Mesopotamian flood stories.

Atrahasis Epic. The similarities between the accounts of the flood given in Genesis and the *Epic of Gilgamesh* are shown in the table opposite.

Although aspects of the Gilgamesh story appear to be legendary, Gilgamesh himself is not to be dismissed as a mythological figure. Gilgamesh was a king of Uruk, in southern Mesopotamia (Erech of Genesis 10:10). In all probability he was a real king living about 2700 BC.

In his search for immortality Gilgamesh travels to meet the only immortal human beings, Utnapishtim and his wife. Utnapishtim (whose name means 'he who found life') explains how the gods gave him immortality because he survived the flood, and he tells Gilgamesh his history. He was living in Shurruppak (now Fara) by the Euphrates when the gods decided to send a great flood upon humankind. The god Ea was a friend of humans and warned Utnapishtim of the approaching disaster. He was instructed to build a ship that seems to have been a cube with dimensions of 120 cubits (approximately 60 m or 200 ft),

A comparison of the flood stories

The story of the flood is preserved in the biblical book of Genesis and in a number of texts from the Ancient Near East. The table opposite compares the flood stories recorded in the eleventh tablet of the *Epic of Gilgamesh* and in Genesis 6–9. The figures in brackets refer to the lines of the eleventh tablet of the *Epic of Gilgamesh* and to the verses of Genesis.

A fragment of the *Epic of Gilgamesh* found near the gate at Megiddo. Fifteenth century BC.

Utnapishtim describes the end of the storm:

'For six days and seven nights the wind came, the flood and storm ravaged the land. On the seventh day the storm and flood, which had struggled like a woman in labour, stopped. The sea became calm, the storm abated, the flood ceased. I looked at the weather, silence was established, and all mankind had turned to clay. The flood water was level like a roof. I opened the hatch and sunlight fell upon my cheeks. I bowed down, sat down and wept. My tears flowed continually over my face.'

GILGAMESH 11.127–37

consisting of seven storeys, in turn divided into nine sections. He was to load the ship with gold, silver, cattle, animals and beasts. Utnapishtim boarded the ship with his family and craftsmen. For six days and seven nights the skies were black and the storm raged. The boat came to rest on Mount Nimush. Utnapishtim sent out a dove, which returned after finding no resting place, then a swallow, which also returned, then finally a raven, which did not return. Utnapishtim disembarked from the boat and offered a sacrifice to the gods. For his services in saving humankind the gods granted Utnapishtim and his wife eternal life.

A comparison between the flood stories in Genesis and Gilgamesh 11, summarized in the table below, reveals significant differences. If Utnapishtim's boat were a cube it would have spun round and round, and doubtless the animals inside would have become ill. Noah's boat had very stable proportions of 6:1. Utnapishtim sends out the weakest bird (the dove) first. Not so Noah, who sends out the stronger raven first.

The resting place of the ark has aroused much passion. All that Genesis 8:4 says is: 'on (one of) the mountains of Ararat'. Note the plural. Ararat is simply the Hebrew name of the kingdom of Urartu, which in the eighth century BC encompassed much of what is now Eastern Turkey. Turkey's highest mountain Ağrı Dağı (5,137 m or 16,854 ft) is sometimes called 'Mount Ararat', but Genesis need not be limited to such a specific location.

Flood stories are found in the mythologies of many peoples from the Pacific, the Americas and South Asia as well as the Near East. Of all these Gilgamesh 11 is the closest to the biblical account, which is hardly surprising given the relative proximity of Mesopotamia to the 'Ararat' region and the great age of the Mesopotamian flood tradition.

EVIDENCE FOR THE FLOOD?

What is the evidence for the flood? Flood level strata at the ancient southern Iraqi cities of Ur, Kish and Fara (formerly Shurruppak) do not correlate, neither do they even cover the whole of each city. Perhaps we are to look for the flood in an era of greater antiquity, and in the geological rather than archaeological record.

	GILGAMESH 11	GENESIS 6–9
Date	Copies date to the first millennium BC, but it adopted the story from the earlier *Atrahasis Epic* c. 1635 BC.	Ostensibly written by Moses, perhaps 15th or 13th century BC, who probably had access to earlier source material.
Boat	*eleppu* 'ship' (24). Utnapishtim's boat was a 120-cubit cube with seven storeys divided vertically into nine sections (60–62). Pitch used to waterproof (65).	*tebah* (6:14) traditionally 'ark'. Noah's ark had dimensions of 300 cubits by 50 by 30 (6:15). It had three decks (6:16). Pitch used to waterproof (6:14).
Occupants	Seed of all living creatures, all his family and relations, domestic and wild animals, craftsmen (83–86).	Noah, his wife, their three sons and their wives, a pair of all living creatures, seven pairs of clean animals (6:18–19; 7:2)
Duration of the flood	6 days and 7 nights (127); after an unspecified time Utnapishtim and those with him left the boat.	40 days and nights of rain (7:12); total time in the ark 371 days.
Resting place	Nimush (140)	'on (one of) the mountains of Ararat' (8:4)
Birds released	1 dove (146) 2 swallow (149) 3 raven (152)	1 raven (8:7) 2 dove (8:8) and again (8:10) and again (8:12).
Sacrifice	'cane, cedar, myrtle' (158)	'some of all the clean animals and birds' (8:20)

NATIONS AND LANGUAGES

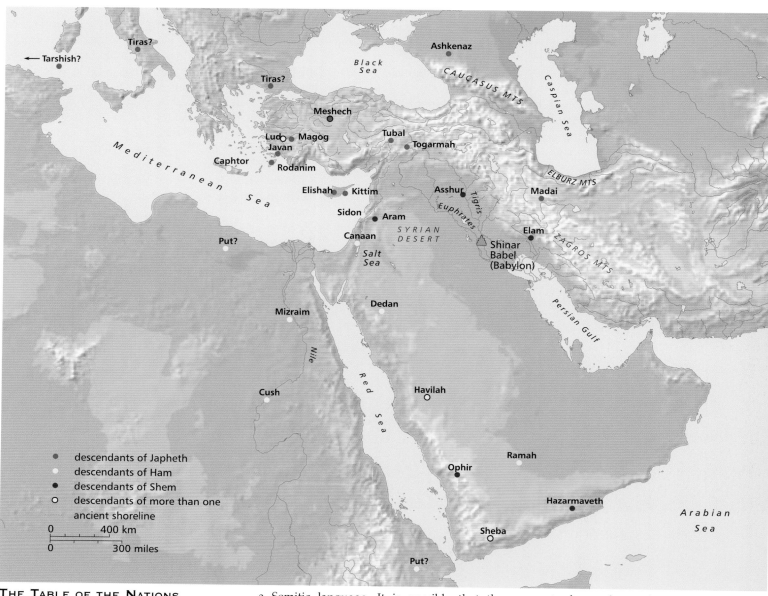

THE TABLE OF THE NATIONS

Genesis 10 is often called the 'Table of the Nations'. Nations within the world-view of the writer are listed as descendants of one of Noah's three sons, Shem, Ham and Japheth. The relationships represent the perceptions of the writer's time and probably involve geographical, political and linguistic associations, not all understandable today.

In very general terms their names are applied on the basis of their language groups to the 'Semitic' peoples of the Near East and the 'Hamitic' inhabitants of Africa, while Japheth covers the 'Indo-European' peoples. However the correlation is only approximate, witness Elam, a descendant of Shem, ancestor of the Elamites of southern Iran, whose language is neither Semitic nor Indo-European, but perhaps akin to the Dravidian languages of southern India. Canaan is listed as a descendant of Ham, although Canaanite is

a Semitic language. It is possible that the compiler of the list lived at a time when Elam was ruled by the 'Semitic' Babylonians and Canaan by the 'Hamitic' Egyptians. Furthermore Sheba is listed under both Shem and Ham, a reminder that ethnic origins are often complex.

We should note that not all the peoples can be identified with equal certainty. Tiras is variously identified with Thrace (northern Greece) or the Etruscans of central Italy. Certain peoples make a datable appearance on the stage of world history. For example, Meshech are the Mushki, an Anatolian tribe first mentioned in 1115 BC in the Annals of the Assyrian king Tiglath-pileser I. The Madai are the Medes, first attested in Assyrian records in 836 BC.

Some would use such evidence to date the 'Table of the Nations', but at best this gives us a date only for the final form of the document. We

cannot deny that other names are of considerable antiquity; Togarmah is attested in Old Assyrian texts from their colony at Kanesh (Kültepe) in central Turkey, destroyed about 1780 BC and reoccupied centuries later.

Even though a number of identifications remain uncertain we can, however approximately, use the 'Table of the Nations' to delimit the author's world: from Javan (the Ionian Greeks of western Turkey) to Elam in south-west Iran and to Sheba (modern Yemen). The 'Table of the Nations' was essentially a verbal map of the Old Testament world; very few Old Testament events take place outside it.

THE TOWER OF BABEL

The story of the Tower of Babel in Genesis 11:1–9 is the author's explanation for linguistic diversity. We shall limit ourselves to the following observations.

1. Originally there was just one universal language.[1]

2. When, as a punishment for building the Tower of Babel, the Lord confused the language of the people, mutually unintelligible new languages were generated.[2] What and how many these new languages were is unknown, but the result of the Lord's action was clear – confusion. The people were unable to understand each other and so scattered over the face of the whole earth.

3. This incident is placed in Shinar, the land inhabited by the Sumerians, i.e. southern Iraq. The city of which the tower was a part was Babel, the Hebrew name for Babylon. Indeed the writer employs a word play between Babel and the Hebrew verb *balal* 'to confuse'.[3]

4. Stepped towers built of bricks bonded with bitumen, 'ziggurats', have been found at a number of Mesopotamian cities. But the rise in the water table at Babylon since antiquity means that the original Tower of Babel may never be found.

THE ORIGIN OF LANGUAGE

In the modern world there are 7,148 known languages. The vast majority can be categorized into between ten and twenty distinct language families.

'Indo-European' is a language family that is represented from the west coast of Ireland, by Irish, to Chinese Turkestan, where Tocharian was once spoken. Its representatives in the biblical period are Hittite, Philistine, Old Persian, Greek and Latin. All the Indo-European languages from Portuguese to Punjabi, from Spanish to Sanskrit, ultimately derive from an original language, termed 'proto-Indo-European'.

The Semitic languages of which Hebrew, Aramaic, Akkadian, Ugaritic and Phoenician, Amorite, Canaanite, Moabite, Ammonite and South Arabic are represented in the biblical period, and of which Arabic and Amharic are modern examples, originally stemmed from a single tongue, termed 'proto-Semitic'. It should be noted however, that proto-languages remain hypothetical, no direct written evidence of them has survived.

What is clear is that, whereas there are major similarities between languages of the same family, there are, except for the odd word, virtually no clear similarities between languages of different families. Some languages, such as Sumerian and Basque, cannot be related to any family.

Connections between proto-Indo-European and other groups such as proto-Afro-Asiatic (which gave birth to the Semitic family, Berber, Ancient Egyptian and other languages of Saharan Africa) are sometimes advanced. Indeed a proto-language, ancestor to an even wider group, termed 'Nostratic' is sometimes postulated. And from there a 'proto-world' language is even postulated, but the nature of such a language remains hypothetical in the extreme. However, according to the writer of the Tower of Babel story in Genesis there was a 'proto-world' language. The origin of the various proto-languages at the Tower of Babel is at least an explanation of why there are, surprisingly, so few clear similarities between them.

The 'Table of the Nations' according to Genesis 10
The possible distribution of groups of people descended from Noah's three sons, Shem, Ham and Japheth, are shown on the map.

A Babylonian map of the world. Clay tablet, c. 600 BC.

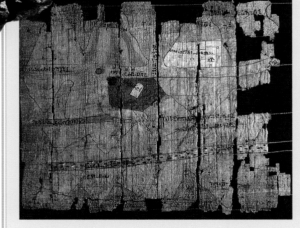

A map of the gold mines in the Wadi Hammamat, Egypt. Papyrus, c. 1150 BC.

Maps from the period of the Old Testament

Apart from the 'Table of the Nations' the Old Testament writers give other detailed geographical information in the form of lists. For example:
● the journey of the Israelites through the desert (Numbers 33:2–49)
● Canaan, the promised land as divided between the twelve tribes (Joshua 13:8–21:42)
● the restored Israel (Ezekiel 47:13–48:29).

To modern readers this information is more easily understood in the form of a map, but we have to make do with the 'verbal maps' of the biblical writers. That is not to say that maps never existed in ancient Israel, simply that none have survived. We do know of a number that have survived from ancient Mesopotamia and Egypt, however.

The earliest known example comes from the site of Nuzi (Yorghan Tepe, near Kirkuk in northern Iraq) dating to c. 2300 BC. The cardinal points are clearly indicated on the clay tablet, east being at the top. The map shows a district bounded by two ranges of hills and bisected by a watercourse.

Another tablet from Babylon dates to c. 600 BC. Babylon is marked by a rectangle bisected by the two parallel lines of the River Euphrates. An arm of the sea (Persian Gulf) touches these lines. Assyria and Urartu (Ararat) are marked by ovals and a circular band represents the salt sea which encircles the known world. The accompanying text names legendary beasts reputed to live in regions beyond the sea.

The Egyptian papyrus called the 'Turin map' dating from c. 1150 BC shows the gold-bearing mountains between the Nile and the coast of the Red Sea. It shows part of the route from Coptos (Qift) on the Nile through Wadi al-Hammamat to the port of Quseir on the Red Sea, though its orientation is uncertain.

LANGUAGES OF THE BIBLE

PEOPLES AND LANGUAGES

In the Bible, as in our world today, we meet an ethnic mix. Peoples with a very local base such as the Jebusites, the original inhabitants of Jerusalem, are listed alongside much larger ethnic groups such as the Canaanites, Hittites and Amorites.[1] Although the kingdoms of Israel and Judah both spoke Hebrew, Judah had its own dialect[2] and Israel did too, traces of which are preserved in the book of Kings. The Moabite language as preserved on the Moabite Stone is very similar to Hebrew; indeed features of the Moabite language are preserved in the book of Ruth. A simple equation of people and language, as in the modern world, cannot always be made.

In the Bible reference is made to languages with a very localized base, witness Ashdodite in the time of Nehemiah and Paul's encounter with the Lycaonian language at Lystra,[3] but we also meet prestige international languages – Aramaic, Greek and Latin. Languages develop and change with time; some are also adopted in new geographical areas. The changing kaleidoscope of languages in the world of the Bible is summarized briefly below.

LANGUAGES C. 1200 BC

In c. 1180 BC two events of major international significance occurred. The Hittite empire in central Turkey collapsed and Egypt was attacked by the so-called Sea Peoples, many of whom came from the Aegean and what is now Turkey. Reasons for the collapse of the Hittite empire are complex. Internal and economic disorder, famine and pressure from the Phrygians, themselves displaced by the so-called Sea Peoples, played their part. What is clearer, however, is that the arrival of the Sea Peoples triggered events that dramatically changed the ethnic and linguistic map of the Near East.

In c. 1200 BC Hittite and two other Indo-European languages, Palaic and Luwian, were spoken in what is now modern Turkey. Greece was inhabited by Mycenaean Greeks (also Indo-European), but soon to succumb to the Dorian Greeks.

The main language of Canaan was Canaanite, with perhaps the first traces of Hebrew if the 'Song of Deborah' is that early.[4] Akkadian, the language of Mesopotamia, served as the language of diplomacy in the mid-second millennium BC. The 382 so-called Amarna letters from Tell el-Amarna, the abandoned capital of Amenophis IV (Akhenaten) (1353–1337 BC) in Middle Egypt, were written in Akkadian, albeit at times heavily tainted with a Canaanite dialect.

LANGUAGES C. 800 BC

A language map of c. 800 BC graphically reflects the changes in the preceding centuries. In south-east Turkey Hittite had been replaced by East Luwian, sometimes called Neo-Hittite. Aramaic, a Semitic language originating in Syria, was spoken from Zincirli (ancient Sam'al) in south-east Turkey as far south as Tell Deir 'Alla in modern Jordan (Succoth of the Old Testament) where an Aramaic text mentioning the prophet Balaam has been

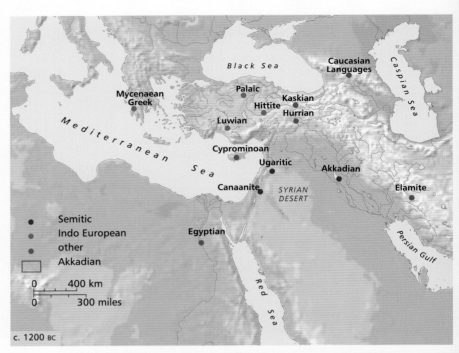

c. 1200 BC

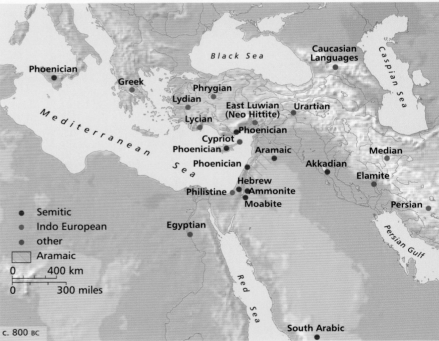

c. 800 BC

found. Hebrew was well established in Palestine, Phoenician was spoken along the coast of Lebanon, in Cyprus and at Karatepe in south-east Turkey. In Transjordan other Semitic languages, Ammonite and Moabite, are attested. In the area around Van in eastern Turkey Urartian, a descendant of the earlier Hurrian, was spoken.

LANGUAGES C. 400 BC

In 400 BC the Persian empire had passed its zenith, its rule in Egypt was weakening, but it still ruled from the Aegean eastwards to Persia and beyond. The language known as Old Persian is attested in a number of places, most notably on the famous rock-cut inscription of Darius I (522–486 BC)

KEY
[1] Joshua 3:10
[2] 2 Kings 18:26
[3] Nehemiah 13:24; Acts 14:11
[4] Judges 5:1–31
[5] Ezra 4:8–6:18; 7:12–26; Daniel 2:4–7:28
[6] Esther 8:9
[7] Herodotus, *Histories* 5.49; 7.73
[8] Jerome, *Commentary on Galatians* 2:3

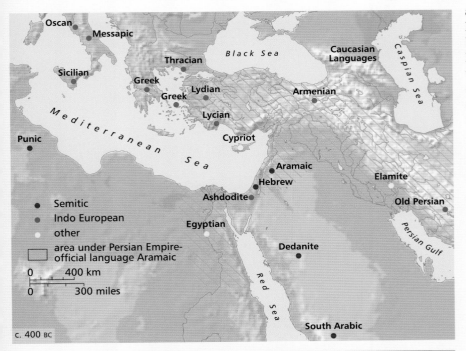

Oscan
Messapic
Thracian
Black Sea
Caucasian Languages
Caspian Sea
Sicilian
Greek
Lydian
Armenian
Greek
Lycian
Punic
Cypriot
Mediterranean Sea
Aramaic
Hebrew
Elamite
Ashdodite
Old Persian
Egyptian
Persian Gulf
Dedanite

- Semitic
- Indo European
- other
- area under Persian Empire- official language Aramaic

0   400 km
0   300 miles

Red Sea

South Arabic

c. 400 BC

Illyrian
Latin
Black Sea
Caucasian Languages
Caspian Sea
Galatian
Armenian
Greek
Lycaonian
Eastern Aramaic
Palmyrene
Hatrene
Mediterranean Sea
Hebrew/ Aramaic
Parthian
Greek
Nabataean

- Semitic
- Indo European
- other
- eastern half of Roman Empire- official language Greek

0   400 km
0   300 miles

Dedanite

Red Sea
Persian Gulf

South Arabic

c. 5 BC

Languages spoken in the biblical world were constantly changing. Four maps, each four hundred years apart, show these changes.

RIGHT: Aramaic inscription from Dascylium (Ergili), north-west Turkey, fifth century BC.

at Behistun (or Bisitun) some 30 km (19 miles) east of Kermanshah in Iran, an inscription which also carries Babylonian and Elamite versions. The administrative language of the Persian empire however was Aramaic, which was used for portions of the Old Testament books of Ezra and Daniel.[5] An Aramaic text from Sardis also exists in a Lydian version. An inscription set up at Letoon near Xanthus in south-west Turkey is in Aramaic, Greek and Lycian. A calcite vase found at Halicarnassus, (modern Bodrum) was inscribed in Old Persian, Babylonian, Elamite and Egyptian. Clearly, under the Persians multilingualism was the order of the day as is further evidenced in the book of Esther.[6] Under the Persian empire the Indo-European Armenians make their first appearance, being mentioned in the Behistun inscription and by the Greek historian Herodotus.[7]

Classical Greek was spoken in five major dialects with much regional variation. At one time there were 158 Greek city states, yet the Greeks regarded themselves as one people, the language being seen as the unifying factor.

LANGUAGES C. 5 BC

The conquests of Alexander the Great (336–323 BC) resulted in Greek displacing a number of languages as the official language. In Egypt Greek replaced Egyptian, but this was later to survive in a modified form known as Coptic. In Syria Greek replaced Aramaic and relegated Akkadian in Mesopotamia mainly to the recording of astronomical observations. Thus, by the birth of Christ in about 5 BC, Greek was the official language of the eastern half of the Roman empire, with Latin being used in the west and among the army. The Greek of the New Testament was considerably different from the Classical Greek of Athens in the fifth century BC. Following the conquests of Alexander the Great, the so-called *koiné* or common Greek fused together several of the main dialects into a common language.

The Galatians of the New Testament were perhaps the descendants of Gauls who had invaded in the third century BC. Jerome (b. AD 347) notes that the Galatians spoke a language very similar to the language of Trier in Gaul, modern France.[8] Several Semitic languages make their appearance in the vicinity of Palestine at this time. Nabataean was spoken around Petra in Jordan; Palmyrene in the Syrian oasis of Palmyra. A note in Palmyrene, added to a Latin inscription found at South Shields in north-east England, bears eloquent testimony to the multilingualism of the Roman empire.

Mesopotamia

(From fourth millennium to ninth century BC)

The Tigris and Euphrates

The term Mesopotamia can be equated with modern Iraq and eastern Syria, the land of the twin rivers Tigris and Euphrates. Both rivers rise in the mountains of eastern Turkey. The Euphrates, following a more winding course through Turkey and making a huge bend in Syria, is the longer of the two at 2,850 km (1,771 miles). The Tigris strikes a faster and more direct course southwards and is 1,840 km (1,143 miles) long. The two rivers converge to within 30 km (18½ miles) of each other near modern Baghdad, then diverge as they meander across the wide alluvial plain of southern Iraq. There, irrigation produced a fertile land, the main crops being barley and dates. Although today both rivers join to form the Shatt el-Arab, in antiquity they discharged separately into the Persian Gulf, the coastline of which moved southwards over the millennia.

The beginnings of civilization

Archaeologists have been able to trace a number of prehistoric village cultures in Mesopotamia. The site of Uruk (the Erech of Genesis 10:10) in southern Mesopotamia illustrates the transition from village to city. A temple 78 by 33 m (256 by 108 ft) was found, decorated with terracotta cones some 10 cm (4 in) long, which had been painted in black, red and white and then stuck into mud-plaster. It is dated to the late fourth millennium BC. At this general time wheel-made pottery first appears, but even more significant are the first examples of writing dating from c. 3100 BC. Clay tablets record the transfer of commodities such as grain, beer and livestock. Since they employ some seven hundred separate pictorial signs, they are evidently too complex to be the first attempts of people to preserve their thoughts. Clearly there must have been an earlier stage in the development of writing which is as yet unknown. The language of these texts is unknown, but since the script is largely pictographic they can at least be partially understood.

The Early Dynastic period

During the so-called Early Dynastic period, 2750–2371 BC, a number of city states – Sippar, Kish, Lagash, Uruk, Larsa, Umma, Ur and Eridu – emerged in the south of Mesopotamia. This period produced brief inscriptions in Sumerian, the world's first recorded language. The origin of the Sumerians remains obscure. Some argue that they came from outside Mesopotamia, perhaps from the mountains of Iran, others that they were aboriginally

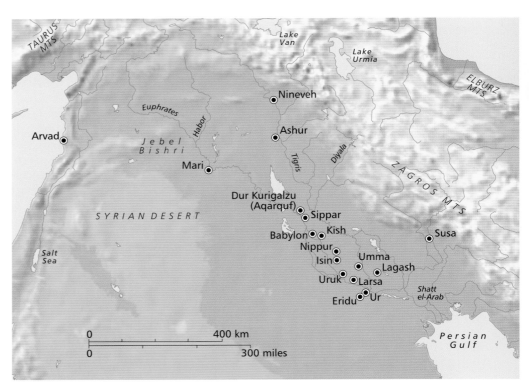

Mesopotamian. Their language gives few clues since it has few if any connections with any known language. By 2500 BC the Sumerian 'cuneiform' (wedge-shaped) writing system was also being used to record another language known as Akkadian,[1] a Semitic language related to both Hebrew and Arabic.

Excavations at Ur (Tell el-Muqayyar) conducted by C.L. Woolley in 1927 came across the Royal Cemetery of the later Early Dynastic period (2600–2400 BC). In some of the Royal Tombs there was evidence of human sacrifice, with as many as seventy-four servants being drugged and killed in the Great Death Pit. Holes produced by the decomposition of the wooden parts of nine lyres and three harps were filled with plaster of Paris and melted paraffin wax to enable reconstructions to be made. The so-called 'Standard of Ur', nearly 22 cm (8½ in) long, was probably the sounding box of a musical instrument. The inlay of shell on a background of lapis lazuli, red limestone and bitumen depicts a war scene on one side and a peace scene on the other with shaven-headed men in fleecy kilts feasting. A musician plays an eleven-stringed lyre, which is of great value in reconstructing the lyres found at Ur. Incidentally, lapis lazuli was imported from Badakshan in north-east Afghanistan. Other finds included the magnificent gold head-dress of queen Pu-abi, a dagger with a gold blade and lapis lazuli handle, gold vessels and an inlaid, rectangular board game having twenty-two squares and two sets of seven counters. Its rules are unknown.

The Dynasty of Akkad

In 2371 BC the cupbearer of the king of Kish overthrew his master and took the Akkadian throne name of Sharrum-kin, meaning 'legitimate king'. He is more commonly known as Sargon, the Old Testament form of his name, borne by a later king of Assyria. Sargon attacked the cities of Umma, Ur and Lagash. Everywhere he was victorious, he tore down the walls of every town, and washed his weapons in the Lower Sea (Persian Gulf). He founded a new capital, Agade, whose location is still unknown. His official inscriptions are in Akkadian. The dynasty he founded is known as the Dynasty of Akkad, which in 2230 BC fell to the Gutians, whose origins remain obscure.

The Third Dynasty of Ur

In 2113 BC Ur-Nammu became king of Ur and ruled most of southern Mesopotamia. The dynasty he established is known as the Third Dynasty of Ur; its official language was Sumerian. Ur-Nammu promulgated the most ancient collection of laws yet discovered and erected brick-built ziggurats (or temple-towers) at Ur, Uruk, Eridu and Nippur. The ziggurat at Ur, 60 m by 45 m at the base (197 ft by 148 ft), is the best preserved. Only the first and part of the second storeys have survived. An astonishing impression of lightness was created through the use of 'entasis', slightly curved lines, as on the Parthenon in Athens.

Ur-Nammu's contemporary at Lagash, Gudea (2141–2122 BC), is known from statues in polished black diorite from Magan (Oman).

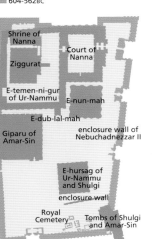

Bronze head often attributed to Sargon of Akkad (2371–2316 BC).

Ancient Mesopotamia
Mesopotamia, broadly speaking modern Iraq, was the home of a succession of sophisticated civilizations, the main centres of which are shown on the map.

KEY
[1] Genesis 10:10
[2] Genesis 11:28

Plan of Ur
Ur, the birth place of Abram (later known as Abraham), is also famous for its Royal Cemetery and the ziggurat of Ur-Nammu.

In 2006 BC Ur fell to the Amorites, a Semitic group from the western desert.

THE AMORITES

After the fall of Ur several small Amorite kingdoms ruled in southern Mesopotamia. Lipit-Ishtar (1934–1924 BC), king of Isin, was the author of a collection of laws. Another Amorite kingdom was established at Larsa.

THE FIRST DYNASTY OF BABYLON

In 1894 BC the Amorite chieftain Samuabum chose Babylon for his capital. He founded a dynasty that was to rule Babylon for about 300 years, the most famous ruler of which was Hammurabi (1792–1750 BC). By the end of his reign Hammurabi had defeated the kings of all the neighbouring states to unite Mesopotamia under Babylonian rule. Towards the end of his reign Hammurabi drew up his famous collection of laws. The most famous copy, a stela of polished basalt 2.7 m (9 ft) high found in Susa in south-west Iran in 1901 and now exhibited in the Louvre Museum, Paris, shows Hammurabi in an attitude of prayer facing the sun-god Shamash seated on his throne. The rest of the stela, front and back, is covered with horizontal columns of text beautifully engraved and written in the purest Babylonian language consisting of at least 282 laws, preceded by a lengthy prologue enumerating the religious deeds of the king, and followed by a lengthy epilogue calling for divine punishments against those who would deface the monument or alter the laws.

THE KASSITES

In 1595 BC Babylon fell to a surprise attack from a Hittite king, Mursilis I, from central Turkey. The main beneficiaries of this attack were a group called the Kassites, who eventually took control over Babylonia. The Kassites originated in the central part of the Zagros range known as Luristan, immediately to the south of Hamadan (Ecbatana).

The use of the horse as a draft animal became more common during the Kassite period. The Kassites were the first to breed horses systematically and successfully.

Mastery of the horse in turn led to the use of chariots in warfare and easier and faster commercial transport.

The Kassites built a new capital, Dur Kurigalzu (Aqarquf), 32 km (20 miles) west of Baghdad, which they graced with a ziggurat. Layers of bitumen-soaked reed matting and plaited ropes which served as bonding can still be seen in the 57-metre-high (187-ft) core. The Kassites also introduced inscribed boundary stones, which were records of the king's granting of land, sometimes very extensive, to favoured subjects.

Kassite rule over Babylonia came to an end in 1171 BC with the conquest of Babylon by Shutruk-nahhunte of Elam in south-west Iran.

ASSYRIA

In the thirteenth and twelfth centuries BC the north of Mesopotamia, the area known as Assyria, eclipsed its southern neighbours.

Tukulti-Ninurta I (1244–1208 BC) claimed that his conquests extended as far as the shore of the Upper Sea, probably Lake Van, in eastern Turkey. He also attacked Babylon, occupying and sacking the city.

Tiglath-pileser I (1115–1077 BC) campaigned in eastern Turkey, and crossed the Euphrates in pursuit of the Arameans, Semitic tribes originating in the Jebel Bishri in Syria. In his inscriptions Tiglath-pileser boasts of killing four wild bulls (the now extinct aurochs), ten mighty bull elephants and 920 lions. On a 20-km (13-mile) boat trip on the Mediterranean from Arvad he boasts of killing a *nahiru*, which they call a 'sea-horse'. Scholarly opinion is divided as to whether a swordfish, dolphin or a narwhal whale is in view here. His zoological interests were furthered when he was presented with a crocodile and a large female ape. Perhaps these were presents from the Egyptian king. His inscriptions are the first to record the foundation of botanical gardens stocked with specimens collected during his widespread expeditions.

THE ARAMEANS AND CHALDEANS

Because of increased Aramean pressure after Tiglath-pileser I's death Assyria went into decline, from which it was not to recover until the ninth century BC. The Chaldeans, a people with close links to the Arameans, settled in southern Mesopotamia. They were to add their name to the city of Ur as designated in the Old Testament: Ur of the Chaldeans.[2]

■ 2500–2400 BC
■ 2112–2004 BC
■ 604–562 BC

0   50 m
0   150 ft

Shrine of Nanna
Court of Nanna
Ziggurat
E-temen-ni-gur of Ur-Nammu
E-nun-mah
E-dub-lal-mah
Giparu of Amar-Sin
enclosure wall of Nebuchadnezzar II
E-hursag of Ur-Nammu and Shulgi
enclosure wall
Royal Cemetery
Tombs of Shulgi and Amar-Sin

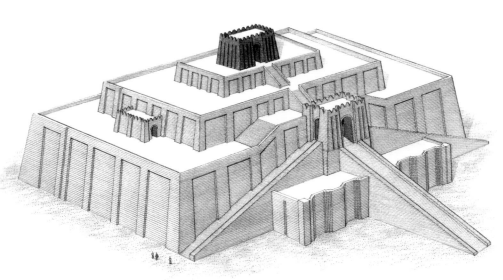

The ziggurat (temple-tower) of Ur-Nammu (2113–2096 BC).

THE PATRIARCHS: THE BIBLICAL EVIDENCE

(Early second millennium BC)

A CHRONOLOGICAL SETTING

Genesis 12–50 is concerned with God's dealings with one man, Abraham, and his descendants: Isaac, Jacob (Israel) and his twelve sons, of whom Joseph was the most important. It is difficult to place these 'Patriarchs', as they are often called, into a precise historical period. Much depends on the date given to a later event in Bible history, the exodus, for which there are two main placements (as we shall see in detail later).

- One placement of the exodus is in 1447 BC[1]. When allowance is made for the 430-year Israelite stay in Egypt[2], a date of 1877 BC results for the arrival of Jacob and his sons in Egypt. By this scheme Abraham would have been born in the middle of the twenty-second century BC.
- Taking the other placement of the exodus in c. 1270 BC and accepting the remaining data as the same, the birth of Abraham is placed around 2000 BC.

There are also scholars who, shortening the Israelite stay in Egypt, place the Patriarchs later (that is, closer to our time), between the twentieth and sixteenth centuries BC, the so-called Middle Bronze II period.

ABRAM TRAVELS FROM UR TO HARAN

Terah, the father of Abram (as he was then known), left 'Ur of the Chaldeans'[3] and settled in Haran on the northern fringes of Mesopotamia, 32 km (20 miles) south-east of the modern Turkish city of Urfa. Some have equated Ur with Urfa, but such an identification would require Abram

retracing his steps before setting out for Canaan. The designation of Ur as 'Ur of the Chaldeans' in fact settles the issue. The Chaldeans were a people who lived in southern Iraq from the late second millennium onwards. Ur of the Chaldeans is thus to be identified with the famous city of Ur in southern Iraq now known as Tell el-Muqayyar. Ur was a centre of a sophisticated civilization several centuries before Abraham, witness the Royal Cemetery of Ur and the ziggurat (temple-tower) of Ur-Nammu, dated respectively at c. 2500 BC and 2113–2096 BC.

The so-called 'Standard of Ur' from the Royal Cemetery of Ur, c. 2500 BC. Nearly 22 cm (8½ in) long, it was probably used as a sounding box for a musical instrument. Having an inlay of shell on a background of lapis lazuli, red limestone and bitumen, it depicts war (shown partly above) and peace (shown in total below) on its two longest sides.

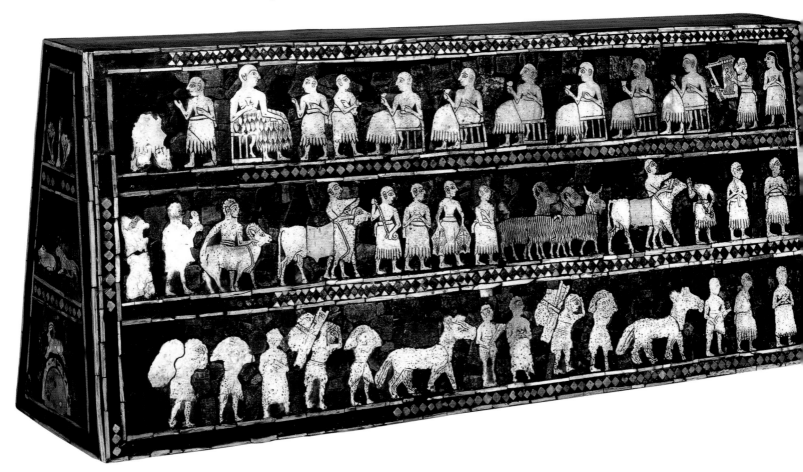

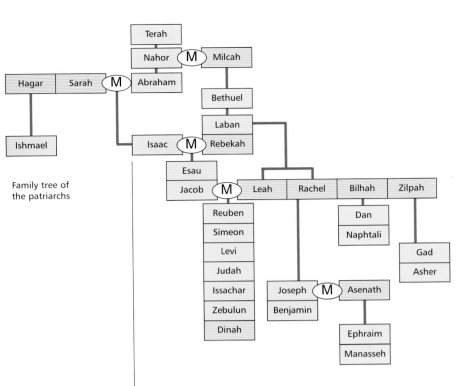

Family tree of the patriarchs

ABRAM TRAVELS TO CANAAN AND EGYPT

When Abram was 75 years old he responded to the Lord's call to leave his country, people and father's household and go to the land that the Lord would show him.[4] Abram made his way to Canaan, the promised land, but because of a famine sought temporary refuge in Egypt. There his wife Sarai (later to be known as Sarah) aroused the interest of none other than the Pharaoh himself.[5]

IN CANAAN

Back in Canaan Abram became very wealthy in livestock, silver and gold.[6] He had so many flocks and herds he had to separate from his nephew Lot, who chose to pitch his tents near Sodom, whose inhabitants were a byword for

wickedness. According to Genesis 19:24–25 'the Lord rained down burning sulphur on Sodom and Gomorrah and… overthrew those cities and the entire plain.' There is no doubt that Sodom and Gomorrah were in the vicinity of, perhaps under, the present Dead Sea, but precise locations cannot be made. The extraordinary salt content (25 per cent) of the Dead Sea may be evidence of this disaster.

Abram (Exalted father) was to become Abraham (Father of many).[7] He fathered Ishmael by his wife Sarah's maidservant, Hagar, and Isaac (the child of the promise).[8] When Sarah died at Kiriath Arba (modern Hebron) Abraham bought a field containing a cave from Ephron the Hittite as a burial place for her. In due time Abraham, his son Isaac, Isaac's wife Rebekah, their son Jacob and his wife Leah were to be buried there too.

Isaac reopened wells that had been dug in the time of his father Abraham in the Valley of Gerar. Jacob is credited (in John 4:5–6) with digging a well at Sychar near Shechem.

The patriarchs were clearly men of wealth and influence within Canaan. Abram had three hundred and eighteen 'trained men' at his disposal.[9] Incidentally the word 'trained men' is of considerable antiquity, since it also occurs in Egyptian execration (curse) texts from the late nineteenth century BC. The patriarchs married within their wider family, Isaac marrying his father's grand-niece Rebekah and Jacob his cousins Leah and Rachel. All the women in question were from the vicinity of Haran, also called Aram-Naharaim and Paddan Aram.

BELOW: The possible location of Sodom and Gomorrah
According to Genesis 19:24 the cities of Sodom and Gomorrah were destroyed by burning sulphur raining out of the sky. It is commonly supposed that these cities lay at the southern end of what is now the Dead Sea.

RIGHT: Abram's journeys
Abram travelled from Ur in southern Iraq to Haran in south-eastern Turkey, and then to the promised land of Canaan (Palestine). He also made a brief visit to Egypt.

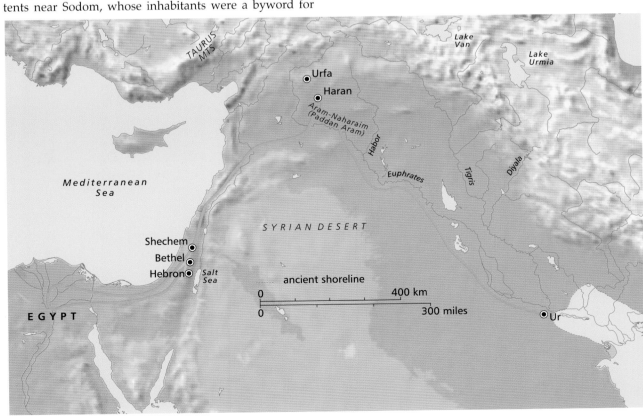

ARCHAEOLOGICAL EVIDENCE FOR THE PATRIARCHS

(Early second millennium BC).

EVIDENCE FROM SYRIA

No direct archaeological evidence confirms the existence of the patriarchs, but several personal names found in the Bible also appear in texts from two important sites in Syria:

1. Ebla (modern Tell Mardikh), which lies 70 km (44 miles) south of Aleppo, was the site of an important kingdom of the third millennium BC. An archive of some 3,000 cuneiform tablets dated to c. 2300 BC was found between 1974 and 1976. The texts were in Sumerian and a hitherto unknown Semitic language, which was given the name 'Eblaite'. Personal names similar to Abraham, Ishmael and Israel have been found, but this is evidence only of the names being used at that time rather than of the patriarchs themselves.

2. Mari (modern Tell Khariri) on the Euphrates in south-east Syria was the site of an Amorite kingdom in the early second millennium, conquered by Hammurabi of Babylon in c. 1760 BC. An archive of over 22,000 cuneiform tablets was deposited in this period. These texts mention prophets (of a sort!) and the place names Haran and Hazor. Personal names similar to Arioch,[1] Abraham and Jacob occur.

THE PROBLEM OF THE PATRIARCHS' CAMELS

References to camels[2] in the stories of the patriarchs are often dismissed as anachronistic, since according to most archaeologists the camel was not domesticated until the twelfth century BC. Camels in the story of Job,[3] which probably also took place in the patriarchal period, receive

the same treatment. The camels in question are the one-humped, dromedary variety, the so-called Arabian camel.

Evidence for the pre-twelfth century use of camels is scanty, but this should not surprise us. The camel is not a city animal; it is kept outside settlements and is primarily used in the desert. Even so, there is some evidence, recorded on the map.

Thus the biblical narratives themselves should also be treated as evidence of pre-twelfth century camel domestication, not simply dismissed as 'anachronistic'.

THE PROBLEM OF PHILISTINES AND HITTITES

Philistines in the stories of the patriarchs (for example, Genesis 26:1) are likewise sometimes dismissed as anachronistic, since the Philistines are not mentioned

Domestication of the camel before the 12th century BC

It is often claimed that camels were not domesticated before the 12th century BC. The map shows a substantial body of evidence that negates this claim.

1) Models of camels pulling carts, Namazga, Turkmenistan, 3000–2600 BC

2) Camel bones, hair and dung, Shahr-i-Sokhta, west Afghanistan, 2700 BC

3) Camel bones have been found at Mari in pre-Sargonid levels, 25–24th century BC

4) Fragmentary ceramic relief from Tell Asmar (Eshnunna), 21st century BC

5) Old Babylonian lexical texts 19th–17th centuries BC attest domestication

6) Sumerian text from Nippur 19th–17th centuries BC refers to camel's milk

7) Seal from northern Syria showing two men riding a Bactrian camel, 18th century BC

8) Fragmentary camel bones, Bir Resisim, Negev, c. 1900 BC

9) Camel jaw bone has been found in a tomb at Tell el Farah North, Palestine, c. 1900–1550 BC

10) Seal showing camel with rider, Syria, 17th century BC

11) Kneeling camel figure from Byblos, 18th century BC

12) Camel skull from Fayûm, Egypt, 19th–13th centuries BC

13) Camel bones from Bedouin sites in South Arabia, mid-second millennium BC

14) Figure of a camel carrying two jars from Rifeh near Memphis in Egypt, 13th century BC

15) Camel figure on potsherd from Pi-Ramesse, Egypt, 13th century BC

16) Camel figure on potsherd, Qurraya, northern Arabia, 13th-12th century BC

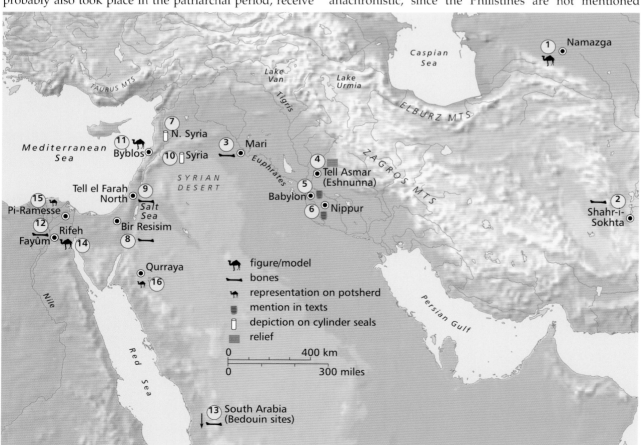

figure/model
bones
representation on potsherd
mention in texts
depiction on cylinder seals
relief

0   400 km
0   300 miles

An offering stand of gold, silver and lapis lazuli in the form of a male goat standing by a sacred tree. Royal Cemetery of Ur, c. 2500 BC.

elsewhere until the Egyptian Pharaoh Ramesses III encountered them in his fifth year (1180 BC). Ramesses III records his defeat of the Philistines on his temple at Medinet Habu in Egypt. The Philistines, who had distinctive feathered head-dresses, were part of a wider group called the 'Sea Peoples'. It is known the Philistines were an Aegean people (Caphtor in Amos 9:7 is Crete) and there is clear evidence of trade between the Aegean and Syria–Palestine in the period c. 1900–1700 BC. There is no reason why small groups of 'Philistines' could not have been among these early Aegean traders when they settled along the Mediterranean coast of Palestine. Alternatively it is possible that the term 'Philistine' in the book of Genesis represents an updating revision by either the author of Genesis or a later reviser.

In Genesis (for example, Genesis 23) we also encounter Hittites, a name given to the Indo-European group who formed an empire in Anatolia, central Turkey, in the middle of the second millennium BC. It is uncertain what, if any, was the relationship between the Hittites of Anatolia and the Palestinian 'Hittites' of Genesis. The 'Hittites' of Genesis bear Semitic names.

KEY
[1] Genesis 14:1
[2] Genesis 12:16; 24:14, 19, 20, 35; 30:43; 32:7, 15
[3] Job 1:3, 17; 42:12

Trade routes in the fertile crescent and beyond in the early second millennium BC
By the time of the Patriarchs (early second millennium BC), a network of trade routes was well established throughout the fertile crescent – Palestine, Syria and Mesopotamia – and beyond.

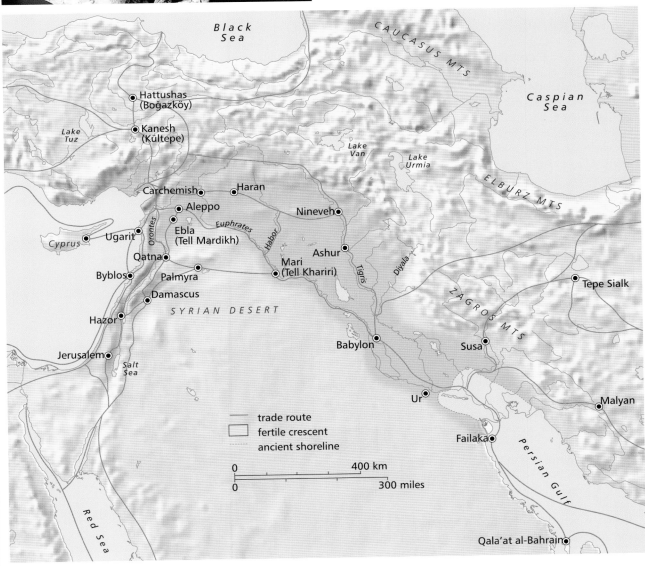

EGYPT

(From the fourth millennium to 332 BC)

THE GIFT OF THE NILE

Egypt, in the words of the Greek historian Herodotus (*Histories*, 2.5), is a 'gift of the river'. Certainly, if there were no Nile, Egypt would be virtually all desert and would not have given birth to one of the world's earliest civilizations. At 6,670 km (4,145 miles) the Nile is the world's longest river. Its ultimate source can be traced to streams such as the Kagera that flow into Lake Victoria in Tanzania. It is joined in Sudan by its principal tributaries, the Blue Nile and the Atbara from the highlands of Ethiopia. Some 20 km (13 miles) north of modern Cairo the Nile divides into two main branches. Between them stretches the flat, swampy Delta. Before the completion of the Aswan High Dam in 1968 the Nile was at its lowest in May. Swollen by melting highland snows and African monsoon rains, it rose until September, depositing some 100 million tons of sediment over the land. Seed sown after the annual inundation produced a harvest in March.

The Nile acted as a natural clock, dividing the year into three four-month seasons: inundation, 'coming forth' (when the land emerged from the receding waters) and the baking heat of summer. The Nile also provided a natural highway, the current taking boats downstream and the prevailing wind taking them upstream. The desert increased the protection of the country from foreign invaders.

THE ARCHAIC PERIOD

At about 3100 BC a succession of prehistoric cultures gave way to unified rule over the whole land. Greek sources attribute this to Menes. The double-sided stone from Hierakonpolis known as the 'Narmer Palette' appears to show the amalgamation of Upper and Lower Egypt under a single ruler. One side shows the king wearing the red crown of Lower Egypt preceded by his standards going out to inspect the enemy dead. Below are two entwined, long-necked felines and the king as a wild ox battering down the door of a fortified settlement. The other side shows the king wearing the tall conical white crown of Upper Egypt striking a kneeling enemy. It is at this time that the first written texts – short labels on stone and pottery – appear. This is roughly contemporary with the appearance of cuneiform (wedge-shaped) writing in Mesopotamia. The relationship, if any, between the two is debated. The form of writing that emerged in Egypt is called hieroglyphics, a Greek term meaning 'sacred writing'.

THE OLD KINGDOM

The kings of the so-called Old Kingdom are best remembered for their construction of pyramids, huge tetrahedrons of stone into which their mummified bodies were placed. The earliest pyramid is that of Djoser (2691–2672 BC), a Third Dynasty king, at Saqqara. Traditionally attributed to the architect Imhotep, it is 124 m by 107 m at the base (407 ft by 351 ft) and 60 m (197 ft) high. It has six unequal stages, hence its name 'the Step Pyramid'.

In the Fourth Dynasty three huge pyramids, the best preserved of the Seven Wonders of the Ancient World, were built at Giza. These were not stepped constructions, but had sloping sides. Largest of all is the Great Pyramid of Kheops (or Khufu) (2593–2570 BC), 230 m (750 ft) on each side of the base and 146 m (480 ft) high. Its area is 5.3 hectares (13 acres), and its sides slope at an angle of nearly 52 degrees. It is estimated to contain 2.5 million blocks weighing an average of 2.5 tons, but some blocks are as heavy as 15 tons. The original polished limestone facing blocks have all disappeared as have the top 9 metres (30 feet).

The pyramid of Khephren (Khafre) (2562–2537 BC) is almost as big at 143 m (469 ft) high. The third pyramid, that of Mycerinus (Menkaure) (2537–2519 BC), is much smaller at 66 m (217 ft) high. Nearby is the famous sphinx, a knoll of rock fashioned by Khephren's craftsmen into a recumbent lion with a human head. It is 73 m (240 ft) long and 23 m (76 ft) high. The maximum width of the face is just over 4 m (13 ft).

THE FIRST INTERMEDIATE PERIOD

Between c. 2136 and 2023 BC Egypt had its first so-called 'Intermediate' period, a period of social upheaval and infiltration by Asiatics. It is possible that this was triggered by famine caused by a series of low Niles.

THE MIDDLE KINGDOM

From 1973 to 1795 BC Egypt was ruled by the powerful Twelfth Dynasty of the Middle Kingdom. Four kings called Amenemhet (Ammenemes) and three called Sesostris brought great prosperity to the land. Their capital was Memphis and its adjoining suburb Ithet-Tawy. The pyramids of the Twelfth Dynasty were all made of mud-brick faced with limestone. That of Sesostris I at Lisht was 105 m (345 ft) square and 61 m (200 ft) high, sloping at 49 degrees.

THE SECOND INTERMEDIATE PERIOD

Between 1795 and 1540 BC Egypt was again in an 'Intermediate' period, being ruled by the Asiatic Hyksos from Avaris in the eastern Delta.

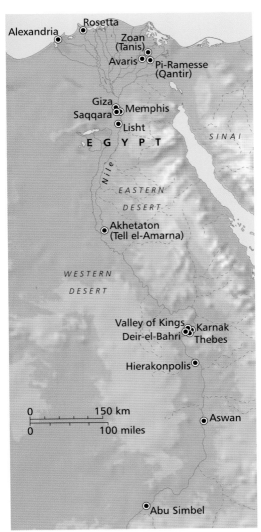

THE NEW KINGDOM

In 1540 BC Ahmose expelled the Hyksos and established the Eighteenth Dynasty. Tuthmosis III (1479–1425 BC) mounted eighteen campaigns in Syria–Palestine. The capital of Egypt under the Eighteenth Dynasty was Thebes, in Upper Egypt. Huge temples were built, such as the huge mortuary temple of Tuthmosis' co-regent Queen Hatshepsut (1479–1457 BC) among the hills west of Thebes at Deir-el-Bahri.

Amenophis IV (1353–1337 BC), also called Akhenaten, has aroused much interest for his new monotheistic faith, symbolized by the worship of the sun-disc (Aten). He also established a new capital Akhetaten, today called Tell el-Amarna, whose art is characterized by realism as the old conventions were abandoned. But after his death Amarna and the cult of Aten were abandoned and the traditional gods and conventions and the supremacy of Thebes were restored.

Kings of the New Kingdom were buried in the Valley of the Kings, situated in hills to the west of Thebes on the west bank of the Nile. All but one of the tombs were robbed in antiquity, but the tomb of the comparatively minor pharaoh Tutankhamun (1336–1327 BC) was found intact by the British archaeologist Howard Carter in 1922. It contained a fabulous assemblage of chests, chariots, statues, funerary beds, vases, jewellery, a gold dagger, bows, a trumpet and three gaming boards. Arguably the most spectacular were several wooden shrines, overlaid with gold, the solid gold coffin and the gold funeral mask of the deceased king himself, inlaid with blue glass and semi-precious stones.

The Nineteenth Dynasty was dominated by Ramesses II (1279–1213 BC). He campaigned in Syria against the Hittites of central Turkey for twenty years, including the inconclusive battle of Qadesh (Tell Nebi Mend) in 1275 BC. This was eventually followed by a peace treaty with the Hittites in 1259 BC. Ramesses' capital was Pi-Ramesse, modern Qantir, in the Delta, of which little survives *in situ*, but many of the stones were reused in the construction of Tanis (the Zoan of the Old Testament) some 20 km (13 miles) to the north. His huge mortuary temple at Thebes, popularly known as the Ramesseum, and his hypostyle hall at Karnak bear eloquent witness to the magnificence of his building projects.

At Abu Simbel, 280 km (174 miles) south of Aswan, Ramesses II had four huge stone statues, each more than 20 m (66 ft) high, carved out of the solid rock. Behind them a funerary temple with complex of halls and chambers was carved out of the rock. Because of the construction of the Aswan High Dam to create Lake Nasser, between 1964 and 1968 the temple was cut into more than two thousand huge blocks and relocated on ground 210 m (689 ft) away from and 65 m (230 ft) higher than the now flooded original site.

THE LATE PERIOD (THIRD INTERMEDIATE)

The New Kingdom came to an end with the death of Ramesses XI in 1070 BC. Thereafter Egypt went into another 'Intermediate' period, ruled among others by Libyans, Cushites (from northern Sudan) and Assyrians (from northern Iraq).

LATER DEVELOPMENTS

In 525 BC Egypt was conquered by the Persians under Cambyses II. In 332 BC Egypt was conquered by Alexander the Great, who founded the city of Alexandria at the mouth of the Nile. A Greek-speaking dynasty, the Ptolemies, ruled until Egypt became part of the Roman empire in 30 BC. Greek became the language of administration. The Rosetta stone, a decree of Ptolemy V (196 BC) in hieroglyphics and Greek, provided the key to the decipherment of hieroglyphics by J. F. Champollion in 1822.

JOSEPH

(Early to mid-second millennium BC)

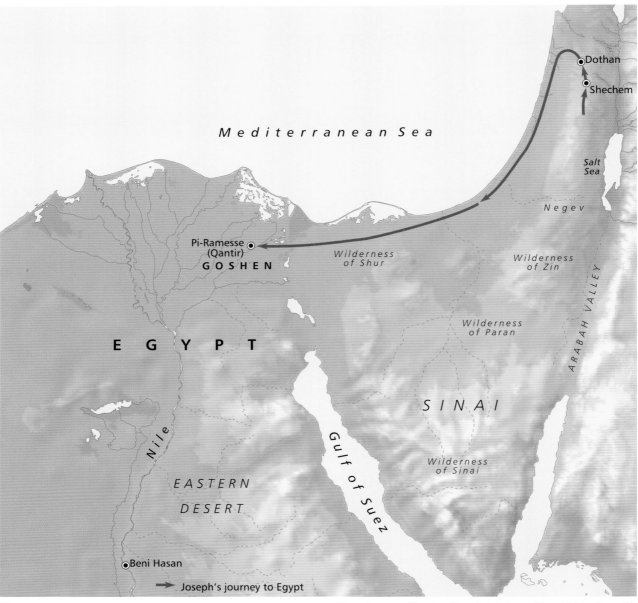

Mediterranean Sea

Dothan
Shechem

Salt Sea

Negev

Pi-Ramesse (Qantir)
GOSHEN

Wilderness of Shur

Wilderness of Zin

E G Y P T

Wilderness of Paran

ARABAH VALLEY

Wilderness of Sinai

S I N A I

Nile

EASTERN DESERT

Gulf of Suez

Beni Hasan

→ Joseph's journey to Egypt

RIGHT: Egyptian cattle census. Painting from the tomb of Nebamun, Thebes, c. 1400 BC.

Joseph's route to Egypt
Joseph was sold as a slave to Egypt, where he became a trusted servant of the Pharaoh. As a result of a severe famine in Canaan, Joseph's brothers were later to follow the same route to Egypt in search of food, only to discover eventually that Pharaoh's trusted servant in charge of food distribution was none other than their brother Joseph.

RIGHT: This old photograph shows a distant view of the pyramids from the banks of the Nile in flood.

KEY
[1] Genesis 37:27
[2] Genesis 37:28
[3] Genesis 39:1
[4] Genesis 41:14
[5] Genesis 42:1–7
[6] Genesis 46:6, 26–27
[7] Genesis 46:34; 47:6
[8] Genesis 50:26

RIGHT: A painting of a caravan of Semites applying for entry into Egypt, as depicted on the tomb of Prince Khnumhotep at Beni Hasan. Many Near Eastern nomads regarded the Nile Delta as a place of refuge in time of need, and it was to Egypt that Jacob sent his sons when famine struck their own land.

THE FAVOURITE SON

Genesis 37, 39–50 tell the story of Jacob's favourite son, Joseph. It is a story of great pathos and drama. Joseph received a robe from his father as a mark of his favour. What exactly was special about this robe is uncertain. Traditionally it has been translated as a 'coat of many colours', as plausible a guess as any, but a guess all the same.

Joseph further aroused his brothers' anger by describing two dreams in which his brothers, father and mother bowed down to him. Joseph, aged seventeen, was sent by his father to visit his older brothers, who were grazing their flocks near Shechem. Joseph's jealous brothers sold him to some passing Ishmaelites,[1] also called Midianites.[2] He was sold for twenty shekels of silver, which was the average price for slaves during the first half of the second millennium BC. By the second half of the second millennium BC it was thirty shekels and by the first millennium BC it was fifty or sixty, so this price can be taken as evidence that the story accurately reflects prices of the early second millennium BC. The brothers' staining of Joseph's robe with blood allowed Jacob to make the false inference that Joseph was dead.

JOSEPH IN EGYPT

In Egypt Joseph was sold to Potiphar, captain of the king's bodyguard.[3] Finding favour with Potiphar, Joseph was put in charge of his household. Falling foul of Potiphar's wife, Joseph found himself languishing in prison. But even there he prospered and found himself interpreting the dreams of Pharaoh's chief cupbearer and baker.

Two years later Joseph's God-given gift of interpreting dreams was sought by Pharaoh himself.[4] Joseph's interpretation of seven years of abundance followed by seven years of famine convinced the king, who put Joseph in charge of gathering the surplus food and storage.

Pharaoh placed his own signet ring on Joseph's finger. He dressed him in robes of fine linen and put a gold chain around his neck. As Joseph sped by in his chariot men were encouraged to shout '*abrek*', a word of uncertain meaning.

orchestrated events to ensure that his younger brother, Benjamin, was also present when he eventually made himself known. Eventually the entire family, the stunned Jacob included, journeyed to Egypt.[6]

THE ISRAELITES SETTLE IN EGYPT

Other people of Semitic, Palestinian origin are known to have travelled to Middle Kingdom Egypt. The tomb of Khnumhotep (c. 1900 BC) from Beni Hasan in Middle Egypt shows thirty-seven Asiatics, led by a Semite named Absha, coming to Egypt. They are engaging in trade, probably transporting to Egypt the raw materials for making eye paint or kohl.

The Israelites settled in the region of Goshen.[7] Exactly where Goshen was is unknown, but it was certainly in the eastern Delta and regarded as the best part of the land. According to Genesis 47:11 they were given property 'in the best part of the land, the district of Rameses'. The city of Rameses is the huge site now known as Qantir, covering about 1,000 hectares (2,471 acres) in the eastern Delta. The name Rameses doubtless refers to the great Egyptian pharaoh Ramesses II (1279–1213 BC). So it seems likely that the name Rameses was placed in the text in Ramesses' time or later.

Joseph died at the age of 110 and was embalmed.[8] This was the Egyptian ideal age, attested in texts from the late Old Kingdom to the Ptolemaic period. It is considerably longer than the Israelite ideal age, which was seventy according to Psalm 90:10. Thus the Bible's first book, that began 'In the beginning God created the heavens and the earth', ends describing the death and embalming of Joseph, who was placed in a coffin in Egypt.

'Make way!' or 'Bow down!' are sometimes suggested.

Of the seven years of abundance and seven years of famine there is no direct archaeological evidence, but it was clearly a famine that effected more than just Egypt, since Joseph's older brothers made their way from Canaan to Egypt in search of food.[5] Dressed as an Egyptian, and using an interpreter, Joseph was not recognized by his brothers. Realizing that he had plenty of time to test his brothers' true intentions, Joseph

MOSES

(Fifteenth or thirteenth century BC)

THE ISRAELITES ARE OPPRESSED

Joseph had ensured that Jacob's family were given good land. Their descendants, the Israelites, 'multiplied greatly and became exceedingly numerous, so that the land was filled with them'.[1] A new pharaoh, who did not know about Joseph, declared that such a large community posed a threat to his country's security.[2] This unnamed king began treating the Israelites ruthlessly, forcing them to build the store cities Pithom and Rameses with sun-baked bricks and to labour in the fields. But the more they were oppressed, the more the Israelites multiplied.

On the walls of the tomb chapel of Rekhmire, vizier of Tuthmosis III (c. 1450 BC), at Thebes a mixed group of workers – Syrians, Cushites and Egyptians – is shown in various stages of brick making: scooping water in jars from a pool, mixing the water and soil to make mud, forming row upon row of bricks with a hollow rectangular brick mould and carrying the dried bricks to the building site. Egyptian overseers, each armed with a slim baton, keep vigil over the work. There is no specific evidence that these workers are Israelites, but the tomb of Rekhmire does show the kind of conditions endured by the Israelites in their forced labour for the Egyptians.

MOSES IS RESCUED

Not content with mere oppression, the pharaoh ordered that all baby Israelite boys were to be thrown into the Nile. One boy was hidden for three months, but doubtless as he grew more wakeful and made ever more noise his parents found it increasingly difficult to keep his existence secret. They then hit on a plan of putting him in a papyrus basket, coated with tar and pitch, and placing this among the reeds along the bank of the Nile. Their daughter kept watch on her baby brother from a distance.[3]

Who should find the baby in the reeds but an unnamed daughter of Pharaoh who had come to the river to bathe? The baby's big sister went to get her mother who was officially sanctioned by Pharaoh's daughter to nurse her own baby.

Pharaoh's daughter named the boy Moses, an Egyptian name evident in the names of pharaohs such as Ahmose and Tuthmosis, meaning 'child', but also sounding like the Hebrew for 'draw out'. Pharaoh's daughter adopted Moses and he went to live in the palace. Here he would have received an education, not only mastering the complexities of the hieroglyphic script, but perhaps also Akkadian, the language of Mesopotamia and the language used in diplomacy with Asia.

MOSES FLEES TO MIDIAN

Moses lived at the palace until he was forty.[4] One day he saw an Egyptian beating one of his own people. Seeing no

RIGHT: **The main places associated with the life of Moses**

Workers making bricks. Painting from the tomb of Rekhmire, vizier of Tuthmosis III (c. 1450 BC), Thebes.

KEY
[1] Exodus 1:7
[2] Exodus 1:9
[3] Exodus 2:1–4
[4] Acts 7:23
[5] Exodus 2:11–14
[6] Acts 7:30; Exodus 7:7
[7] Exodus 4:27

Fishermen on the River Nile.

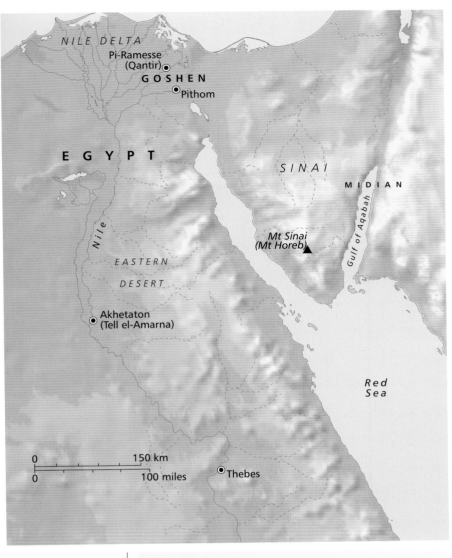

NILE DELTA
Pi-Ramesse (Qantir)
GOSHEN
Pithom

EGYPT

Nile

SINAI

MIDIAN

Gulf of Aqabah

Mt Sinai (Mt Horeb) ▲

EASTERN

DESERT

Akhetaton (Tell el-Amarna)

Red Sea

0 ____ 150 km
0 ____ 100 miles

Thebes

The Desert of Midian, where Moses found refuge after killing the Egyptian.

one around, he killed the Egyptian and hid his body in the sand. The next day he saw two of his own people fighting and tried to separate them. One of them already knew that Moses had killed the Egyptian the previous day.[5] Realizing that Pharaoh too would know, Moses thought it wise to leave Egypt. He fled to Midian, a land that flanked both sides of the eastern arm of the Red Sea, the modern Gulf of Aqabah. It was here that he married Zipporah, the daughter of Reuel (also called Jethro), a priest of Midian, and had two sons.

THE LORD CALLS MOSES
Forty years after fleeing to Midian, while tending his father-in-law's sheep, Moses, now aged eighty,[6] came to Horeb, the mountain of God. This was either an alterative name for Mount Sinai, where Moses was later to receive

the Ten Commandments, or another mountain in the vicinity. Here the Lord appeared to Moses in a burning bush, which was not consumed. The Lord had taken note of the misery of the Israelites and was going to rescue them, bringing them out of Egypt and into the land of Canaan, a fertile land flowing with milk and honey. The shock to Moses was that God was going to use him to bring it about: 'So now, go, I am sending you to Pharaoh to bring my people, the Israelites, out of Egypt' (Exodus 3:10).

Not surprisingly, Moses wanted to know the name of the God of his fathers who was sending him back to Egypt to rescue his people. 'God said to Moses: "I AM WHO I AM. This is what you are to say to the Israelites: I AM has sent me to you"' (Exodus 3:14).

His name is then revealed as 'the LORD' – or this is how it is widely rendered in English versions of the Bible. Actually, in the Hebrew text, it is composed of four consonants and no vowels: YHWH. Several centuries before Jesus the Jews stopped using this name in everyday speech because they considered it too holy to pronounce. Consequently its original pronunciation is not certain.

In the translation of the Old Testament into Greek, the so-called Septuagint translation, and in the New Testament, the four consonants YHWH are rendered by the Greek word *Kurios* meaning 'Lord'. Later the Jews added vowels from the Hebrew word *Adonay* (meaning 'lord' or 'master') to produce a hybrid form, traditionally rendered in English as 'Jehovah'. More modern scholarship favours the term 'Yahweh', which was the Samaritan pronunciation of the divine name as recorded by the church father Origen in a note on Exodus 6:3, but this too is disputed. What is clear is that the name is some form of the verb 'to be'. 'I am who I am' is thus a good explanation, if not an exact translation.

MOSES RETURNS TO EGYPT
Despite his protests Moses agreed to return to Egypt, God assuring him that all the men wanting to kill him were dead. Moses' older brother, Aaron, was also summoned to the mountain of God.[7] He was to be Moses' spokesman. Moses and Aaron brought together the elders of the Israelites. When they saw Moses' staff become a snake and his hand become white with a skin disease, they believed.

BRICKS WITHOUT STRAW
Moses and Aaron approached the unnamed pharaoh to ask him to let the Israelites go. He refused point blank. 'Who is the Lord that I should obey him and let Israel go? I do not know the Lord and will not let Israel go' (Exodus 5:2).

Things then went from bad to worse for the Israelites. They were no longer to be supplied with straw for their bricks: they would have to supply their own. (Straw contained an acid that made the clay more plastic to work and stopped the bricks from shrinking.) The Israelites scattered throughout Egypt looking for straw but were required to produce the same quota of bricks. The Israelite foremen complained to Moses and Aaron.

Moses appealed to the Lord for help. The Lord said he would harden Pharaoh's heart so he would not let the Israelites go, but he promised to multiply miraculous signs and wonders in Egypt and bring his people out of Egypt. It took a sequence of ten devastating plagues to accomplish it.

THE TEN PLAGUES

(Fifteenth or thirteenth century BC)

The book of Exodus tells us that the Lord sent Moses and his older brother Aaron to Pharaoh. Aaron threw his staff in front of Pharaoh and it became a snake.[1] The Egyptian sorcerers and magicians were able to reproduce this by their magic arts, but Aaron's staff swallowed theirs. The Lord then unleashed a series of devastating plagues culminating in the slaying of the firstborn Egyptians. The writer of Exodus describes plagues that show the Lord's control over many areas of his creation and, by implied contrast, the impotence of the Egyptian gods and magic. Indeed the writer records God's stated purpose that 'the Egyptians will know that I am the Lord, when I stretch out my hand against Egypt and bring the Israelites out of it' (Exodus 7:5). With the exception of the last plague it is possible to advance natural explanations for the plagues; the 'miracle' is in their devastating sequence and the fact that half of them (4, 5, 7, 9 and 10) specifically do not affect the Israelites.

1. Blood

The Nile rises in July and August, crests in September, and is usually reddish in appearance owing to particles of soil suspended in the water, but clearly something unusual was occurring here. It is suggested that millions of microscopic organisms known as flagellates, probably originating in Lake Tana, Ethiopia, produced the blood-red water. The fish died, there was a foul smell and the water was undrinkable. During the night the flagellates would require higher amounts of oxygen, whereas during the day they would give off oxygen. This fluctuation would cause the death of the fish, which need constant amounts of oxygen.

2. Frogs

Frogs are known to invade land towards the end of the inundation September–October. Polluted water would have given them an extra reason to leave the river and over-run the land (even as far as Pharaoh's bedroom). The sudden death of frogs might have been caused by contamination from decomposing fish.[2]

3. Gnats

Humans and animals were afflicted by gnats (perhaps a type of mosquito), which would have bred in pools and puddles left by the retreating Nile.

4. Flies

Dense swarms of flies (perhaps horse-flies) ruined the land. They too would have bred in the pools and puddles.

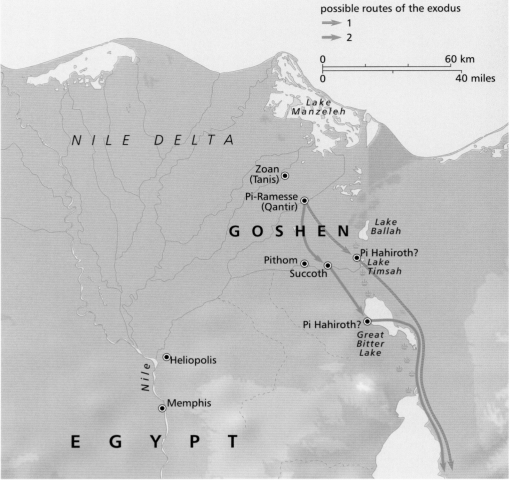

5. Animal sickness

The fifth plague, possibly anthrax spread by the frogs, wiped out the Egyptians' livestock.

6. Boils

Festering boils broke out on both humans and animals throughout the land.

7. Hail

Hail is uncommon in a hot land like Egypt. This hailstorm was clearly out of the ordinary. It beat down everything growing in the fields and stripped bare every tree. Exodus 9:31 records that flax and barley were in flower and were ruined by the hail, but the wheat and emmer-wheat had not yet germinated. This enables us to place the devastating hailstorm in January or February.

8. Locusts

In March or April the prevailing east winds would bring in, perhaps from Sudan, hordes of migratory locusts in their immature, most voracious stage. They covered the ground until it was black and consumed all the vegetation that had survived the hail.

9. Darkness

The three days of darkness were perhaps the *hamsin*, a desert sandstorm common in March. There was doubtless more dust to fuel the sandstorm after the locusts had denuded the land.

10. Death of the firstborn

The tenth plague occurred in March–April, now celebrated by Jews as the time of Passover. This is the one plague for which a natural explanation cannot be offered. It is clearly and unequivocally supernatural. 'At midnight the Lord struck down all the firstborn of Egypt, from the firstborn of Pharaoh, who sat on the throne, to the firstborn of the prisoner, who was at the dungeon, and the firstborn of all the livestock as well' (Exodus 12:29).

THE CROSSING OF THE SEA

The Egyptians urged the Israelites to escape. Exodus 12:37 records their numbers as 600,000 men, besides women and children. Taking the Hebrew term *eleph* (commonly translated as 'thousand') as 'family groups', some suggest a considerably lower figure. Pharaoh, however, changed his mind and pursued his escaping slave labour force. During the night a strong

KEY
[1] Exodus 7:9–10
[2] Exodus 8:13
[3] Acts 7:36; Hebrews 11:29

east wind drove the sea back and turned the sea into dry land. The Israelites crossed the sea to safety. The sea then closed over the pursuing Egyptians, who were drowned. This dramatic deliverance was viewed in Israel's subsequent history as the constitutive event that called Israel into being as a people.

In the English Bible it is the waters of the 'Red Sea' that part and then engulf the pursuing Egyptians. The Hebrew term *yam suph* actually means 'reed sea' and was perhaps one of the shallow lakes to the north of the Gulf of Suez, rather than what we would call the Red Sea, the Gulf of Suez itself. Geographic, oceanographic and archaeological evidence suggests that the Gulf of Suez stretched further north than it does today and the southern Bitter Lake extended further south, the two could have been connected during the second millennium BC. Alternative crossing sites are Lakes Timsah and Ballah, further to the north.

The objection is sometimes raised that a salt-water marsh cannot support reeds. But salt-tolerating reeds and rushes called halophytes are known to thrive in salt-marsh areas. Incidentally, the eleventh-century Jewish scholar Rashi (Rabbi Solomon ben Isaac) and the sixteenth-century reformers Martin Luther and John Calvin all adopted 'Reed Sea'. But the term 'Red Sea' has been solidified in modern English parlance by its adoption in the Septuagint (the Greek translation of the Old Testament) and the New Testament.[3]

Black granite statue of Ramesses II (1290–1224 BC). Height 194 cm (6 ft 4 in). Probably from Karnak.

THE EXODUS

(Fifteenth or thirteenth century BC)

If the exodus was the pivotal event of the Old Testament, surely we should expect clear and abundant extra-biblical evidence of it. Unfortunately this is not so. The scholarly world is so divided over whether there was an exodus or not and when it might have happened that the exodus is without doubt the biggest problem in the whole of biblical archaeology. Two main views are held – one which places the exodus at 1447 BC or thereabouts, and one which places the exodus at about 1270 BC.

THE 1447 BC PLACEMENT

The book of Kings provides a date for the exodus: 'In the four hundred and eightieth year after the Israelites had come out of Egypt, in the fourth year of Solomon's reign over Israel… he began to build the temple of the Lord.'[1] Since we know that the fourth year of Solomon was 967 BC, the date of the exodus, being 480 years earlier, would be 1447 BC, which in Egyptian history falls during the reign of

Landscape of the Sinai Desert.

possible route of the exodus
trade route

0 ————— 80 km
0 ————— 60 miles

KEY
[1] 1 Kings 6:1
[2] Judges 11:26
[3] Numbers 14:33–34; Deuteronomy 1:3
[4] Exodus 1:11
[5] Exodus 8:22
[6] 1 Kings 11:40
[7] Censorinus, *De die natali* 18.10; 21:10, 11

The route of the Exodus
The red arrow marks a possible route taken by the Israelites from Egypt to Mount Sinai.

LEFT: Grey granite bust of Merenptah (1213–1203 BC), the son and successor of Ramesses II. Height 91 cm (36 in). From the second court of the funerary temple of Merenptah, western Thebes.

RIGHT: The black granite 'Israel' stela of Merenptah (1213–1203 BC). Height 2.3 m (7.5 ft). From the Mortuary Temple of Amenophis III, Thebes.

Tuthmosis III (1479–1425 BC), a pharaoh of the Eighteenth Dynasty. Tuthmosis III was a strong warrior king who is known to have conducted eighteen campaigns in Syria–Palestine.

A date in the early fifteenth century is also produced by a remark of the judge Jephthah, who towards the end of the Judges' period, arguably c. 1070 BC, refers to the Israelite occupation of Heshbon and the neighbouring settlements east of the Jordan as being three hundred years.[2] Although Jephthah may be speaking in round figures, by adding his three hundred years to the forty years of the Israelites' wandering in the desert,[3] we arrive at a date for the exodus of around 1410 BC.

THE 1270 BC PLACEMENT

Many scholars consider that the Egyptian evidence does not fit with an exodus in the reign of Tuthmosis III and so have advanced a more recent exodus at about 1270 BC. Taking as their primary source the book of Exodus itself, they advance the following reasons in support of a later exodus:

1. The Israelite slaves built store cities for the pharaoh, which were named Pithom and Rameses.[4] The name Rameses doubtless refers to the great Egyptian pharaoh Ramesses II (1279–1213 BC). He was the greatest pharaoh of Egypt's Nineteenth Dynasty.

2. The Israelites lived in the land of Goshen,[5] that is, somewhere in the eastern Delta region.

Exodus 7:23 implies that Pharaoh had a palace near this region. Ramesses' capital was at Pi-Ramesse, a site now known as Qantir, which is in the Delta, whereas the capital of the Eighteenth Dynasty was Thebes, several hundred kilometres up the Nile from the Delta.

3. We should note that the pharaoh is unnamed. The title 'pharaoh' used throughout Genesis and Exodus is derived from an Egyptian term meaning 'great house'. As an epithet for the monarch it does not occur until the Eighteenth Dynasty, sometime before the reign of Tuthmosis III (1479–1425 BC). From its inception until tenth century BC the term 'pharaoh' stood alone without a juxtaposed personal name in ordinary documents. This is precisely what we find in the Old Testament: 'pharaoh' occurs alone until a named king of Egypt appears with Shishak in 926 BC.[6] In the exodus story the pharaoh's name may ultimately be withheld for theological reasons, because the Bible is not trying to answer the question: 'Who was the pharaoh of the exodus?' Rather it was clarifying for Israel who the God of the exodus was.

MERENPTAH'S STELA

The latest possible date for the exodus is imposed by an Egyptian source. The pharaoh Merenptah (1213–1203 BC) recorded on a stela in his fifth year, 1209 BC: 'Israel lies desolate, its seed is no more.' The precise significance of this remark need not concern us here, but this is the earliest mention of Israel in the extra-biblical record. Thus there is evidence for Israel being in Canaan at least by 1209 BC, and we should add forty years to cover the wanderings in the Sinai Desert to obtain a latest possible date for the exodus of 1249 BC.

EGYPTIAN CHRONOLOGY

Some who have maintained a 1447 BC date for the exodus, but have struggled to accept a placement in Egyptian history of that time, have questioned the reliability of the Egyptian chronological system. However, it should be pointed out that chronological systems have to be proven to work as a whole, not just in isolated details. Furthermore there is an undeniable fact about Egyptian chronology. As the Egyptian calendar year was only 365 days long, it gained a day ahead of the true season every four years and after 1460 years had advanced a full 365 days. We know the calendar matched the true

seasons in AD 139.[7] Thus the previous match fell about 1317/21 BC and the one before that c. 2800 BC.

A text known as Graffito 862 from Western Thebes is apposite here.

'Year 1, third month of Akhet (Inundation) Day 3, this day of the descent made by the waters of the great Nile-flood of the King of South and North Egypt, Baienre (Merenptah) Life, Prosperity and Health!'

The date 'Third month of Inundation, Year 1 of Merenptah' can be computed to 12 August 1213 BC. This date fits with the season of the Nile-flood exactly, which occurs between July and early September. Thus the dates in the early thirteenth century BC are very close to the true seasons, which is what we would expect if there were an alignment of the Egyptian calendar with the real calendar in 1317 BC or thereabouts.

It is also undeniable that Egyptian chronology provides many synchronisms with the Aegean, Anatolia, Mesopotamia, Syria and Palestine. Thus any change to Egyptian dates results in changes elsewhere too. In Assyria the king list gives reliable dates for kings stretching back to Ninurta-apal-ekur at the end of the twelfth century BC and there are many synchronisms with Babylonia; so Mesopotamian chronology cannot be shortened and neither, we would argue, can those of any of the other areas mentioned above.

IN RETROSPECT

In summary, the evidence from the book of Exodus points towards a Nineteenth Dynasty exodus, arguably at c. 1270 BC. The reference in 1 Kings 6:1 stating that there were four hundred and eighty years between the foundation of Solomon's Temple and the exodus points to a date of 1447 BC in the Eighteenth Dynasty. Proponents of the more recent, c. 1270 BC exodus view this figure as an ancient chronological calculation, with the figure four hundred and eighty perhaps representing twelve generations, calculated at forty years each, which in reality were significantly shorter, or overlapped.

The date of the exodus is far from being a merely academic question, since it affects all Bible chronology before the exodus. It is an issue that will come to the fore again when we consider the conquest of Canaan under Joshua some forty years later.

THE GIVING OF THE LAW

(Fifteenth or thirteenth century BC)

MOUNT SINAI

The Israelites continued their journey south-eastwards, roughly parallel to the Gulf of Suez. It is impossible to pinpoint the locations of their stopping places, but even so the general course of their journey through what is now called the Sinai Peninsula can be traced.

In the third month after leaving Egypt the Israelites came to the Desert of Sinai. It was here that the Lord appeared to Moses saying, 'I am the Lord your God, who brought you out of Egypt, out of the land of slavery,' and revealing a series of laws, initially the Ten Commandments,[1] but ultimately a vast body of law, which now constitutes the rest of Exodus, the whole of Leviticus, and Numbers 1:1–10:10. The people camped at the base of the mountain while its top was covered in fire when the Lord descended.

The precise location of Mount Sinai is today uncertain. Two candidates are favoured:

1. the traditional site, Jebel Musa, at 2,244 m (7,362 ft), an identification going back to the Byzantine emperor Justinian (AD 527–565)

2. Ras es-Safsafeh, less high at 1,993 m (6,539 ft), but having a considerable plain at its foot, large enough for six hundred thousand men and their dependents to keep their distance.[2] Jebal Serbal, 2,070 m (6,793 ft) to the north-west, is sometimes also advanced.

Modern attempts to locate Mount Sinai elsewhere – for example, east of the Gulf of Aqabah in Arabia – involve a radical redrawing of the route through the desert. That Paul located Mount Sinai in Arabia[3] can hardly be cited as evidence, since in Roman times the area known as Arabia included what is now known as the Sinai Peninsula.

TREATY AND COVENANT

The text of the covenant (or agreement) that the Lord made with his people Israel on Mount Sinai is now preserved in the second half of Exodus and Leviticus. Other material describing the building of the worship tent (or tabernacle) and priestly rituals was added into this framework. This covenant was renewed nearly forty years later when Moses was about to die and when Israel was about to go into the promised land. The text of this covenant is preserved in the book of Deuteronomy (a Greek term meaning 'repeated law'). Both covenants follow a similar pattern, outlined on page 39.

We are fortunate to have a number of treaties (agreements between rulers and their vassal states) from the Hittite Empire, which came to an end c. 1180 BC. These treaties follow a format virtually identical to that of the covenants preserved in the Pentateuch, the major difference being that in the Hittite treaties curses precede blessings. In the Old Testament covenants the stipulations are the various laws that the Lord gives his people.

By contrast the treaties made in the first half of the first millennium BC, when many think the Pentateuch was compiled from a pastiche of sources, follow a substantially different pattern. There is no historical prologue, a list of witnesses precedes the stipulations, which are followed by the curses on those who violate the treaty. Significantly there are no blessings on those who keep the treaty.

ANCIENT COLLECTIONS OF LAWS

The Law that the Lord gave to Moses was not the only collection of laws that has survived from the ancient Near East. Several others are worthy of mention here:

- the 60 laws from the central Mesopotamian city-state of Eshnunna, dating from c. 1800 BC
- the celebrated 282 or so Laws of Hammurabi, king of Babylon (1792–1750 BC), engraved on a 2.7-metre-high (9 ft) polished basalt stela, taken as booty to Susa in south-west Iran and now in the Louvre Museum, Paris

KEY
[1] Exodus 20:1–17
[2] Exodus 12:37; 20:18
[3] Galatians 4:25
[4] Mark 7:10

The Laws of Moses and ancient Near Eastern law collections
The book of Exodus records that the Lord gave Moses a collection of laws at Mount Sinai. This was not however the only collection of laws from the ancient Near East. The places of origin of other ancient Near Eastern laws are shown on the map.

RIGHT: The Sinai peninsula
This map shows the favoured locations for Mount Sinai.

LEFT: The view from Mount Sinai (Jebel Musa)

RIGHT: The top of the stela of Hammurabi, king of Babylon (1792–1750 BC). It shows Hammurabi receiving a sceptre and ring from the sun god Shamash. The basalt stela, 2.7 m (9 ft) high, contains the 282 or so Laws of Hammurabi. From Susa, south-west Iran.

FAR RIGHT: Collections of laws in the ancient Near East
The form of two covenants preserved in the Old Testament books of Exodus/Leviticus and Deuteronomy, is compared to a treaty between Shattiwaza, king of Mitanni and the Hittite king Suppiluliuma I, mid-14th century BC.

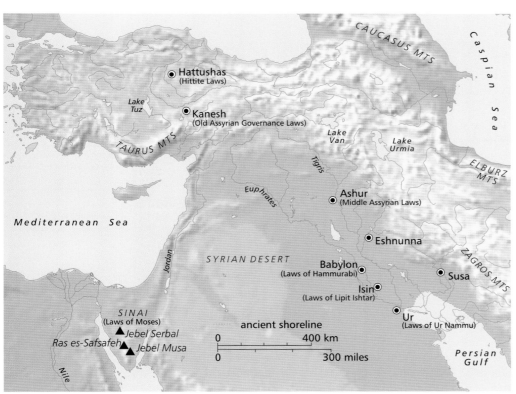

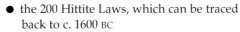

Leviticus arguably having 138 and Deuteronomy 101.

THE COMPILER OF THE PENTATEUCH

That Moses could have put together such a document as the Pentateuch using earlier sources is hardly to be questioned, given our knowledge of ancient scribal practices. Moses would certainly have been familiar with the Egyptian hieroglyphic writing system; maybe he had also learned Akkadian, the language of the Babylonians and the language of diplomacy at the time. Alphabetic writing was known by Moses' time. Interestingly, some of the earliest known examples of an alphabet are from the Egyptian turquoise mines of Serabit el-Khadim in the Sinai Peninsula. These were done by Semite miners and date to c. 1700 BC. The similarity of the biblical covenants – Exodus–Leviticus and Deuteronomy – to contemporary treaties suggests that they were compiled by someone with a diplomatic background. Moses fits the bill well, but the many biblical scholars reject the traditional view, espoused by Jesus,[4] that Moses was the compiler of the Pentateuch or at least a very substantial part of it. The language of the Pentateuch, it is argued, is that of the Hebrew monarchy several centuries after Moses' death. But even if the text of the Pentateuch were 'modernized' at some later date, Moses' authorship is not necessarily invalidated. The account of Moses' death, in Deuteronomy 34, is a clear exception.

- the 200 Hittite Laws, which can be traced back to c. 1600 BC
- the 128 so-called Middle Assyrian Laws, which can be dated to the reign of Tiglath-pileser I (1115–1077 BC).

The differences between the Laws of Eshnunna and Hammurabi, for example, and the Laws of Moses are far too large to suggest a direct relationship between them. Each collection of laws, when they are similar, merely reflects a common set of values that was present throughout much of the ancient Near East at that general time. We should note that, in terms of the number of legal stipulations, the Laws of Moses are in the same order as those mentioned above, Exodus and

Section	Exodus–Leviticus	Deuteronomy	Hittite treaty between Shattiwaza of Mitanni and Suppululiuma I of the Hittites
1 Title	Exodus 20:1	1:1–5	Title
2 Historical prologue	Exodus 20:2	1:6–3:29	Historical prologue
3 Stipulations	Exodus 20:3–23:33; 25:1–35:19; Leviticus 11:1 – 26:2	4:1–26:19	Stipulations
4 Deposit and reading of covenant document	Exodus 24:1–14	27:1–26	Deposit and reading of covenant document
5 Witnesses	Exodus 24:4b–6	31:14–32:47	Witnesses
6 Blessings	Leviticus 26:3–13	28:1–14	Curses
7 Curses	Leviticus 26:14–39	28:15–68	Blessings

The Tabernacle

(Fifteenth or thirteenth century BC)

What was the tabernacle?

While encamped in the desert by Mount Sinai the Lord gave Moses detailed instructions for the construction of a worship-tent.[1] It was variously called the 'sanctuary', 'tabernacle' or 'tent of meeting'.

The term 'tabernacle' (from *tabernaculum*, the Latin word for tent) was both the central worship-tent and the courtyard that surrounded it. The central tent itself consisted of a Holy Place 20 cubits by 10 (about 9 m by 4.5 m or 30 ft by 15 ft) and the Most Holy Place, the so-called 'Holy of Holies' 10 cubits (4.5 m or 15 ft) square, where the 'ark of the covenant' was kept. The two parts of the sanctuary were separated by a curtain of blue, purple and scarlet yarn. The central worship-tent was surrounded by a rectangular courtyard, enclosed by a wall of curtains 100 cubits by 50 (45m by 22.5 m or 148 ft by 74 ft).

The frame of the structure was made of acacia wood, which is avoided by wood-eating insects and common in the Sinai Peninsula. Over this, skins of rams and goats were stretched as well as the skin of an animal whose precise identification remains uncertain.[2] The dugong or sea cow is sometimes advanced, which is certainly more probable than the 'badger' of the Authorised Version.

Portable shrines from Egypt and Sinai

Moses and his workmen could draw on long-established Egyptian technology for portable shrines. The earliest known example is the gold-plated canopy-frame of Queen Hetepheres (c. 2600 BC), the mother of Khufu (Kheops), who built the great pyramid. Several gold-plated portable shrines were found in the tomb of the Egyptian king Tutankhamun (1336–1327 BC).

Moses spent the forty years prior to the exodus living in the Sinai Peninsula with his Midianite in-laws.[3] A tented shrine, dated to c. 1100 BC, from the copper-mining site of Timnah (Khirbet Tibneh) in the Arabah Valley south of the Dead Sea, may be Midianite work. Wooden poles with traces of red and yellow woollen curtains were found there. Maybe Moses called on Midianite as well as Egyptian experience in constructing the tabernacle.

The tabernacle furnishings

A number of items that were deposited in the tabernacle are described in detail in Exodus 25:10–40; 27:1–8.

Pride of place is given to the 'ark of the covenant'[4] – a gold-plated chest of acacia wood 2½ cubits (1.1 m or about 3 ft 6 in) long and 1½ cubits (0.7 m or 2 ft 4 in) wide and high. This contained the two stone tablets on which the Ten Commandments were

engraved. The lid of this chest was a slab of pure gold with two cherubim with outspread wings facing each other. The name of this lid, traditionally translated 'mercy seat', is derived from the Hebrew verb 'to atone'. Attached to the feet of the 'ark' were four gold rings. Poles of acacia wood overlaid with gold were inserted into these rings to carry the 'ark'. This carrying arrangement is similar to that on a box from the tomb of Tutankhamun.

A view of the inside of the gold-plated canopy frame of Queen Hetepheres (c. 2600 BC) as reconstructed in the Egyptian Museum, Cairo.

KEY
[1] Exodus 26:1–37
[2] Exodus 26:7, 14–15
[3] Exodus 2:15–21
[4] Exodus 25:10–22
[5] Exodus 25:31–39

Reconstruction of the tabernacle. The ark of the covenant and the golden lampstand can be seen inside the central worship-tent.

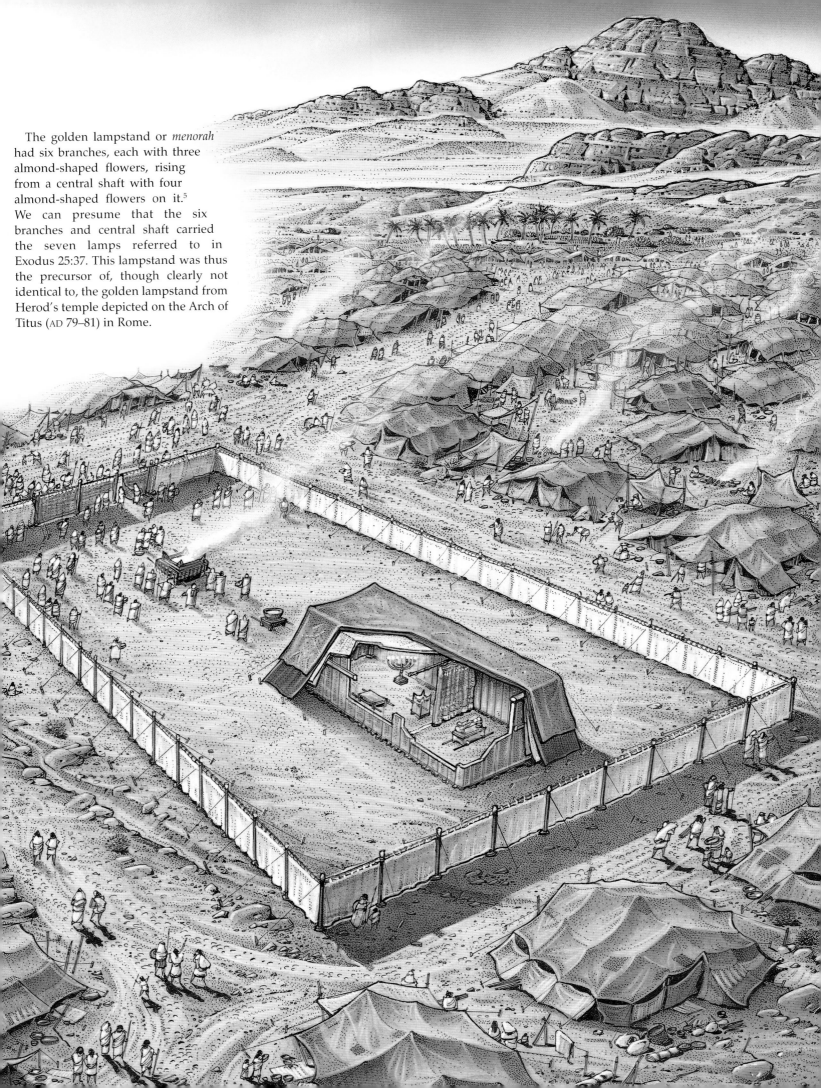

The golden lampstand or *menorah* had six branches, each with three almond-shaped flowers, rising from a central shaft with four almond-shaped flowers on it.[5] We can presume that the six branches and central shaft carried the seven lamps referred to in Exodus 25:37. This lampstand was thus the precursor of, though clearly not identical to, the golden lampstand from Herod's temple depicted on the Arch of Titus (AD 79–81) in Rome.

THE CONQUEST OF TRANSJORDAN

(Fifteenth or thirteenth century BC)

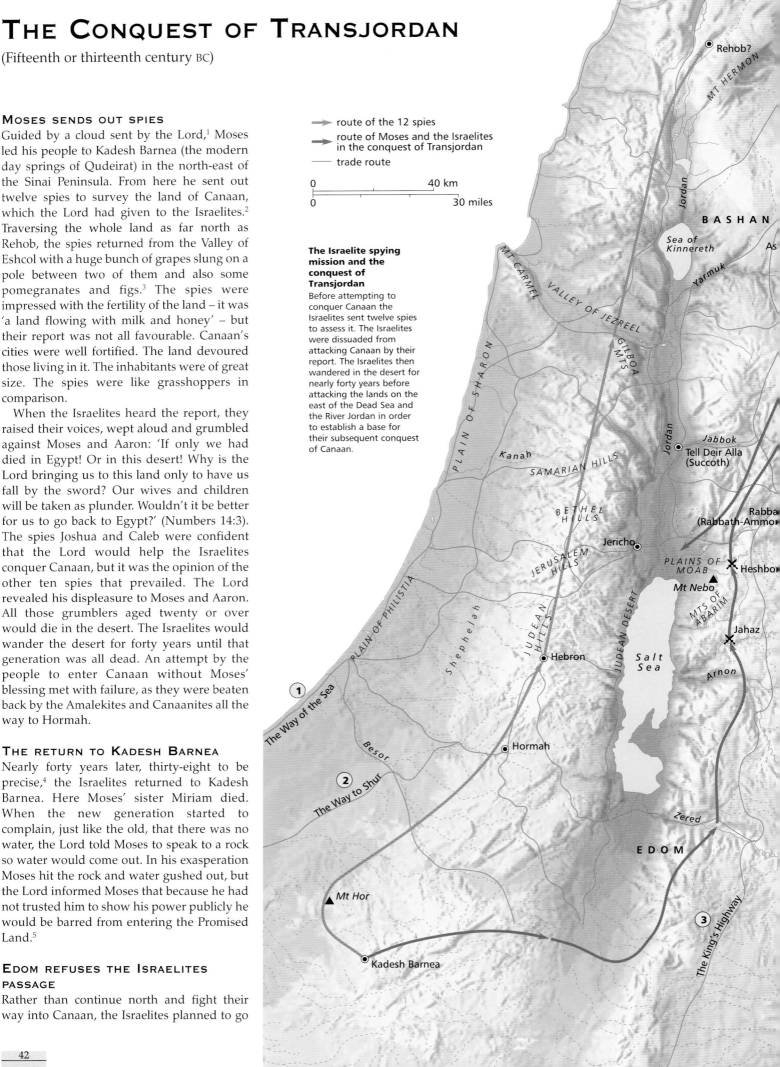

MOSES SENDS OUT SPIES

Guided by a cloud sent by the Lord,[1] Moses led his people to Kadesh Barnea (the modern day springs of Qudeirat) in the north-east of the Sinai Peninsula. From here he sent out twelve spies to survey the land of Canaan, which the Lord had given to the Israelites.[2] Traversing the whole land as far north as Rehob, the spies returned from the Valley of Eshcol with a huge bunch of grapes slung on a pole between two of them and also some pomegranates and figs.[3] The spies were impressed with the fertility of the land – it was 'a land flowing with milk and honey' – but their report was not all favourable. Canaan's cities were well fortified. The land devoured those living in it. The inhabitants were of great size. The spies were like grasshoppers in comparison.

When the Israelites heard the report, they raised their voices, wept aloud and grumbled against Moses and Aaron: 'If only we had died in Egypt! Or in this desert! Why is the Lord bringing us to this land only to have us fall by the sword? Our wives and children will be taken as plunder. Wouldn't it be better for us to go back to Egypt?' (Numbers 14:3). The spies Joshua and Caleb were confident that the Lord would help the Israelites conquer Canaan, but it was the opinion of the other ten spies that prevailed. The Lord revealed his displeasure to Moses and Aaron. All those grumblers aged twenty or over would die in the desert. The Israelites would wander the desert for forty years until that generation was all dead. An attempt by the people to enter Canaan without Moses' blessing met with failure, as they were beaten back by the Amalekites and Canaanites all the way to Hormah.

THE RETURN TO KADESH BARNEA

Nearly forty years later, thirty-eight to be precise,[4] the Israelites returned to Kadesh Barnea. Here Moses' sister Miriam died. When the new generation started to complain, just like the old, that there was no water, the Lord told Moses to speak to a rock so water would come out. In his exasperation Moses hit the rock and water gushed out, but the Lord informed Moses that because he had not trusted him to show his power publicly he would be barred from entering the Promised Land.[5]

EDOM REFUSES THE ISRAELITES PASSAGE

Rather than continue north and fight their way into Canaan, the Israelites planned to go

→ route of the 12 spies

→ route of Moses and the Israelites in the conquest of Transjordan

— trade route

0   40 km

0   30 miles

The Israelite spying mission and the conquest of Transjordan

Before attempting to conquer Canaan the Israelites sent twelve spies to assess it. The Israelites were dissuaded from attacking Canaan by their report. The Israelites then wandered in the desert for nearly forty years before attacking the lands on the east of the Dead Sea and the River Jordan in order to establish a base for their subsequent conquest of Canaan.

The view from Mount Nebo into the Promised Land.

KEY

[1] Numbers 9:15–23
[2] Numbers 13:2
[3] Numbers 13:23
[4] Deuteronomy 2:14
[5] Numbers 20:12
[6] Numbers 21:21–26;
   Deuteronomy
   2:32–34
[7] Numbers 21:33–35;
   Deuteronomy 3:1–6
[8] Deuteronomy 3:11
[9] Numbers 25:1–3; 31:8

The life of Balaam
The map illustrates places associated with the life of Balaam, a diviner hired to bring curses on the Israelites.

via the lands east of the Dead Sea and the River Jordan and enter Canaan from the east. More immediately the Edomites, the descendants of Jacob's twin brother Esau, stood in the way. Moses sent messengers requesting passage through Edomite territory, but Edom's king refused. The Israelites had no option but to bypass Edom. At Mount Hor, Moses' brother Aaron died, aged 123.

SIHON IS DEFEATED

The Israelites crossed the Zered Valley and made their way to the Arnon Valley to the border of Moab. At that time much of Moab was ruled by an Amorite king named Sihon. Refusing Israel's request for passage through his territory, Sihon attacked the Israelites at Jahaz. The Old Testament books of Numbers and Deuteronomy that deal with this campaign record events from a marked Israelite perspective and state that the Israelites then occupied Sihon's capital of Heshbon, completely destroying his towns with all their inhabitants.[6]

OG IS DEFEATED

As Moses marched his people northward towards Bashan, the region to the north-east of Lake Galilee, Og, king of Bashan, who reigned in Ashtaroth, marched out to do battle at Edrei (Der'a) in Syria. Og was comprehensively defeated and sixty of his cities, fortified with high walls, gates and bars, came under Israelite control. Once again the Israelites completely destroyed the king's towns with all their inhabitants.[7]

There is a curious note in the book of Deuteronomy about Og's bed,[8] which at the time of writing could still be seen at Rabbah of the Ammonites, modern Amman. The 4-metre-long (13-foot) bed is described as a 'bed of iron'. The meaning 'decorated with iron' seems preferable; but, given the fact that several basalt sarcophagi have been found in Bashan, an alternative rendering of 'basalt sarcophagus' is sometimes advanced.

The Israelite victories over Sihon and Og secured a large swathe of land to the east of the River Jordan that was to provide them with a secure base to mount an attack across the Jordan into Canaan. The tribes of Reuben and Gad and half the tribe of Manasseh were promised land on the east side of the Jordan provided they joined the rest of the Israelite tribes in conquering Canaan.

BALAAM

The Israelites then camped in the Plains of Moab (also called Shittim) across the Jordan from Jericho. Balak, king of Moab, hired a diviner named Balaam to pronounce curses on the Israelites. Balaam was summoned from Pethor in the land of Amaw. This is the Sajur Valley between Aleppo and Carchemish on the Euphrates, in what is now northern Syria. In fact all of Balaam's oracles recorded in the book of Numbers are blessings, not curses. Having failed to curse the Israelites, Balaam seduced them into committing sexual immorality with Moabite women and worshipping Baal. Later he was to pay for this with his life.[9] Balaam, whose chief claim to fame in the Bible is that he was addressed by a donkey, was also the subject of an Aramaic inscription written in ink on plaster from Tell Deir Alla (biblical Succoth) in modern Jordan and dating about 800 BC. This text clearly shows Balaam's wider fame.

DEUTERONOMY

Perhaps because of the Israelites' immorality and idolatry in the Plains of Moab, Moses thought it necessary to repeat the Law to the new generation about to go into the Promised Land. Moses' words on this occasion form the book now known as Deuteronomy (a Greek term meaning 'second or repeated law'). The latter definition is to be preferred, as the book is a reiteration of the existing law rather than a second instalment of that same law.

Deuteronomy follows Exodus–Leviticus in its basic form. It concludes with a song Moses taught the people, so that they would obey the Lord's words, and with his blessing on each of the twelve tribes of Israel.

THE DEATH OF MOSES

Moses was ordered to climb Mount Nebo across from Jericho and view the Promised Land of Canaan. Because of his disobedience at Kadesh Barnea he was not allowed to enter the land in person. From the top of Mount Nebo (probably the modern Jebel en-Neba, 835 m or 2,740 ft) Moses was able to see much of the Promised Land, from the glistening white peak of Mount Hermon to the north of Lake Galilee to Zoar at the southern end of the Dead Sea, shimmering away over 1,000 metres (3,300 ft) below him. The sites of Jericho, Jerusalem and Bethlehem would have been clearly visible.

There at the age of 120 he died, still in possession of all his faculties. The author of the postscript to Deuteronomy records that the Lord buried Moses in Moab, in the valley opposite Beth Peor. 'To this day no one knows where his grave is. [...] Since then no prophet has risen in Israel like Moses, whom the Lord knew face to face, who did all those miraculous signs and wonders the Lord sent him to do in Egypt – to Pharaoh and to all his officials and to his whole land. For no one has ever shown the mighty power or performed the awesome deeds that Moses did in the sight of all Israel' (Deuteronomy 34:6b, 10–12).

THE CONQUEST OF CANAAN: JERICHO AND AI

(Late fifteenth or thirteenth century BC)

MOSES' CHOSEN SUCCESSOR

Joshua was Moses' trusted assistant, who had fought the Amalekites shortly after the exodus from Egypt and had been one of the original twelve spies sent to explore Canaan.[1] Shortly before his death, Moses let it be known that Joshua was to be his successor.[2]

JOSHUA TAKES CHARGE

After the death of Moses it fell to Joshua to lead the Israelites into Canaan, the Promised Land. The Lord gave Joshua the words of reassurance that he needed: 'As I was with Moses, so I will be with you; I will never leave you, nor forsake you. Be strong and courageous, because you will lead these people to inherit the land I swore to your forefathers to give them. Be strong and very courageous' (Joshua 1:5b–7a).

CROSSING THE JORDAN

Across the Jordan lay the strong walled city of Jericho. Joshua sent two of his men as spies into Jericho, where they stayed in the house of a woman named Rahab. Traditionally she has been considered to be a prostitute, but perhaps she was an innkeeper. Rahab confirmed that the inhabitants of Canaan were all terrified because of the Israelites. Promising to spare Rahab and her family when they conquered the city, the men returned to Joshua greatly encouraged.

Between Joshua and Jericho lay the River Jordan, which was in flood. It was harvest time, that is April or May. Through a miraculous intervention Joshua led the Israelites across the dried-up Jordan and into Canaan, the Promised Land.

The book of Joshua states that the river was blocked at Adam (modern ed-Damieh) some 30 km (19 miles) upstream. Blockings of the Jordan have been recorded there at least twice since. The Arab historian an-Nawairi

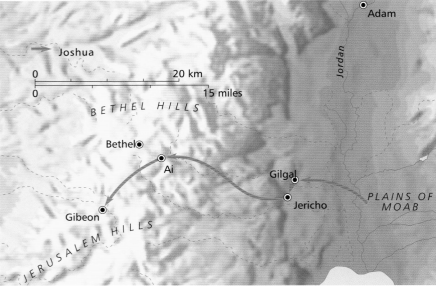

states that on the night of 7 December AD 1267 the Jordan was dammed at ed-Damieh for sixteen hours. A similar blocking was recorded for twenty-one and a half hours on 11 July 1927. The undermining of the soft, perpendicular river bank by a flood or a local earthquake is advanced as a possible cause.

THE CONQUEST OF JERICHO

The conquest of the first city, Jericho, is undoubtedly the most famous incident in the whole campaign. The book of Joshua records it from an overtly Israelite perspective. Following the Lord's orders Joshua had his army march around the city once a day for six days. Seven priests blowing seven trumpets marched before the ark of the covenant. Armed men went ahead of them and a rearguard followed the ark, while the trumpets kept sounding. Then they returned to the camp.

Joshua conquers Jericho and Ai
Joshua's campaign against the Canaanite cities of Jericho and Ai is illustrated on the map above.

KEY
[1] Exodus 17:10; Numbers 13:8, 16
[2] Numbers 27:18–23; Deuteronomy 3:28; 31:23; 34:9
[3] Deuteronomy 20:16–18; Joshua 6:17
[4] Joshua 7:3–5
[5] Joshua 7:25–26a

LEFT: Old Testament Jericho (Tell es-Sultan) and its surroundings.

RIGHT: Neve Kedem, a Samaritan village on Mount Gerizim. Mount Ebal is in the background (right). Shechem (modern Nablus) is in the valley in between.

On the seventh day they got up at daybreak and marched around the city seven times. The seventh time around, when the trumpets sounded, the people shouted, and the city wall collapsed. Maybe there was another earthquake. Every man charged straight in and they took the city. The Lord had told them that the people, like all the others in Canaan, were so idolatrous they were to be destroyed.[3] This included every living thing in the city – men and women, young and old, cattle, sheep and donkeys. The Israelites burned the city, sparing only Rahab and her family.

SET-BACK AND EVENTUAL VICTORY AT AI

Joshua then moved his army some 24 km (15 miles) up into the hills away from the Jordan Valley. They came upon a town called Ai, a Hebrew term meaning 'ruin'. The biblical account says that, selecting three thousand men to attack the town, Joshua suffered a reverse, losing about thirty-six men and being chased from the city.[4] A reason for the defeat was advanced: a certain Achan had taken some of the spoils of Jericho against the Lord's specific orders to destroy everything in the wicked city. To regain the Lord's favour, Achan and his family were stoned to death and burned[5] and Joshua tried again to attack Ai, this time with different tactics.

At night Joshua set an ambush behind Ai to the west, between Bethel and Ai. Early the next morning Joshua marched his main force to the north of Ai. The men of Ai attacked Joshua's main army, who let themselves be driven back so as to lure the men of Ai away from the city. Then the ambushing force rushed forward to capture the city and set it on fire. Joshua's main force then turned round and attacked the men of Ai, who were also set upon by the ambushing force who came out of the city. The city of Ai was burned, its twelve thousand inhabitants were killed and its king hung on a tree.

The battle for Ai   JOSHUA 8:1–29
possible reconstruction

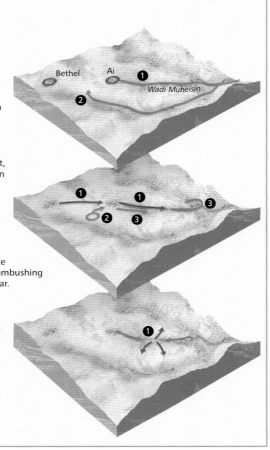

PHASE ONE

1 The Israelite main force moves (blue arrows) from Jericho to attack Ai.

2 Another force advances under cover of darkness and conceals itself between Ai and Bethel.

PHASE TWO

1 The Israelite main force feigns retreat, and all the men of Ai and Bethel (brown arrows) break out in pursuit.

2 After receiving a signal from Joshua, the concealed force attacks and burns the undefended town.

3 As the men of Ai see the smoke rising from their town, the main Israelite force turns to face their pursuers. The ambushing force attacks the men of Ai from the rear.

PHASE THREE

1 Joshua's army inflicts total defeat on the enemy.

THE CONQUEST OF CANAAN: THE DEFEAT OF THE KINGS

(Late fifteenth or thirteenth century BC)

THE PACT WITH THE GIBEONITES

As news of the Israelite victories at Jericho and Ai spread, all the Canaanite cities grew worried. Doubtless they had heard of the Lord's command to Moses to wipe out all the inhabitants of the land.[1] To the Israelite base camp at Gilgal near the River Jordan came the Gibeonites wearing old clothes and carrying dry and mouldy bread, pretending they had come on a long journey. Without enquiring of the Lord, Joshua made a peace treaty with them. Three days later the Israelites found out that, in fact, the Gibeonites were near neighbours, living only some 35 km (22 miles) away. Having sworn an oath, they were obliged not to attack them; so they let them live in their midst as household servants.

THE DEFEAT OF THE SOUTHERN KINGS

When Adoni-Zedek, the Amorite king of Jerusalem, heard that Gibeon (modern el-Jib) had concluded a peace treaty with the Israelites, he persuaded his allies, the Amorite kings of Hebron, Jarmuth, Lachish and Eglon to attack Gibeon. The Gibeonites appealed to Joshua for help in his base camp at Gilgal. Marching his men all night some 32 km (20 miles) up into the hills, Joshua attacked the army of the five kings, eventually winning a great victory. A hailstorm lashed down on the fleeing confederates and, mysteriously, the book of Joshua records: 'So the sun stood still and the moon stopped... The sun stopped in the middle of the sky and delayed going down about a full day' (Joshua 10:13). With only this statement it is hazardous to guess at the physical processes that occasioned this event, but as far as the writer of the book of Joshua is concerned it was a unique event which showed that the Lord was fighting for Israel. Joshua then returned to his base camp at Gilgal.

The five Amorite kings fled to a cave at Makkedah. On hearing this Joshua had the mouth of the cave blocked with large rocks. Later he brought the kings out of the cave and put them to death, hanging their bodies on trees until sunset. Anxious to follow up his victory Joshua put to the sword the inhabitants of the nearby cities of Libnah and Lachish. He defeated the king of Gezer who had come to help Lachish and massacred the inhabitants of Eglon, Hebron and Debir. Having subdued a broad swathe of territory across southern Palestine, fulfilling the Lord's command to leave no survivors,[2] Joshua again returned to his base camp at Gilgal.

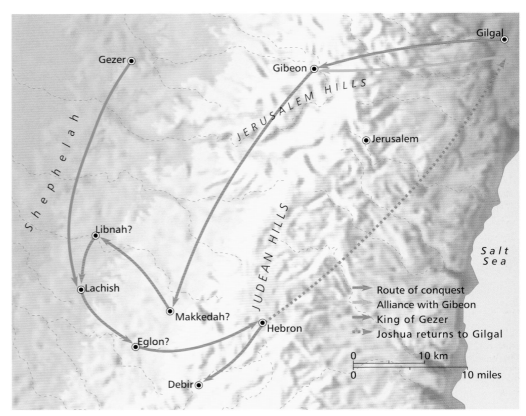

THE DEFEAT OF THE NORTHERN KINGS

Jabin, the king of the northern city of Hazor, sent word to his allies the kings of Madon, Shimron and Acshaph and other northern kings. They gathered at the Waters of Merom, the precise site of which is uncertain. Joshua attacked them suddenly and defeated them. His men then gave chase in several different directions, hamstringing their horses and burning their chariots. Joshua then captured Hazor, a city of 71 hectares (175 acres), and the most important northern city, massacring its inhabitants. He put its king to the sword and burned the city. Once again Joshua returned to Gilgal, this time to divide up the land between the twelve tribes.

LEFT: **Joshua defeats the southern kings**
Joshua continued his campaign, overthrowing the southern Canaanite kings.

RIGHT: The citadel of Hazor, with a total area of 71 hectares (175 acres), was the largest of the Canaanite cities.

KEY
[1] Joshua 9:24
[2] Joshua 10:40
[3] Deuteronomy 2:14
[4] Joshua 17:16, 18
[5] Joshua 23:12–13; Judges 2:3
[6] Judges 1:1–21; 2 Samuel 5:6–7

RIGHT: **Joshua defeats the northern kings**
Joshua's campaign against the northern Canaanite kings.

Canaanite cult mask from Hazor.

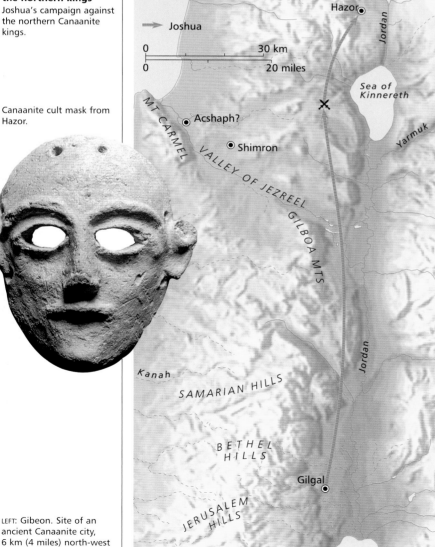

LEFT: Gibeon. Site of an ancient Canaanite city, 6 km (4 miles) north-west of Jerusalem.

A LIGHTNING CONQUEST?

In Joshua 14:10 Caleb, who is about to take up his inheritance, speaks of the promise that the Lord had made forty-five years earlier that he would inherit the land. If we take off thirty-eight years for the wanderings in the desert,[3] a period of seven years results, into which the whole conquest of Canaan is to be placed.

At first glace the book of Joshua, on which our account of the conquest of Canaan is based, seems to suggest that Joshua swept all before him in those seven years of lightning conquest. A reader might be carried away by the upbeat rhetoric and miss clues that may help us to come to a fairer assessment of that conquest. After each campaign Joshua and his army return to base camp at Gilgal. Inhabitants and kings are killed, but no attempt is made to occupy territory. These campaigns were essentially disabling raids, rather than territorial conquests followed by immediate occupation. When the tribes went to possess their inheritances, Canaanites were still there, even possessing chariots partly reinforced with iron.[4] At the end of Joshua's life he warned the people not to intermarry with the survivors of the Canaanites. They would become snares and traps for them, whips on their backs and thorns in their eyes.[5]

The book of Judges, which follows the book of Joshua, begins with the Israelites fighting the Canaanites in their midst. The most famous enclave of all, that of the Jebusites in Jerusalem, did not fall until it was captured by David.[6]

EVIDENCE OF THE CONQUEST OF CANAAN

(Late fifteenth or thirteenth century BC)

TWO PLACEMENTS

In our consideration of the date of the exodus we saw that there are two main placements, one in 1447 BC and another in c. 1270 BC. Both of these placements occasion different dates for the Israelite conquest under Joshua, which, allowing for the period of wandering in the desert, is some forty years later at either 1407 BC or so or c. 1230 BC. In terms of the archaeology of Palestine the former date corresponds to a period known as Late Bronze IB (c. 1450–1400 BC) and the latter to a period known as Late Bronze IIB (c. 1300–1200 BC). What is also clear is that the Israelites must have been in the land by 1209 BC when the Egyptian pharaoh Merenptah met a people called Israel in Canaan.

JERICHO: A KEY SITE

When the British archaeologist John Garstang excavated Jericho (Tell es-Sultan) between 1930 and 1936 and found evidence of the whole city having been destroyed by fire,[1] and of part of the city wall having fallen in an earthquake, it seemed that there was conclusive evidence in favour of the earlier placement c. 1400 BC. However, when another British archaeologist, Kathleen Kenyon, recommenced excavations at Jericho between 1952 and 1958, she showed that Garstang's dating of City IV at Jericho (the so-called Middle Bronze city) to c. 1400 BC was in fact to be dated to c. 1550 BC. Historically, this action was linked to the Egyptian war of retaliation against the expelled Hyksos, not to Joshua's armies. Attempts have been made to

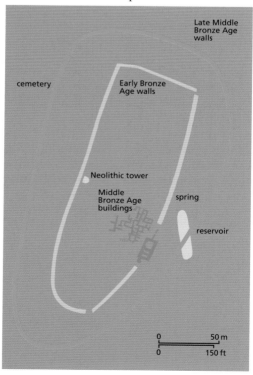

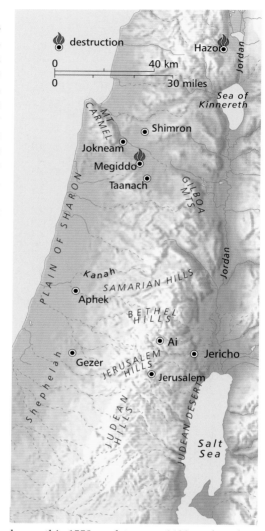

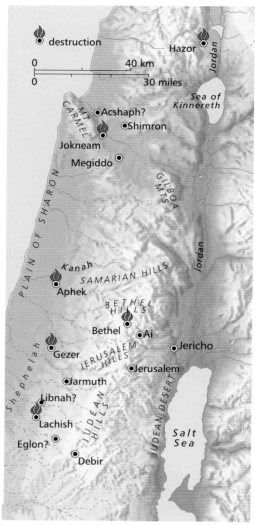

lower this 1550 BC date to c. 1400 BC, but they have not met with widespread acceptance. The problem has to be faced that there is little archaeological evidence for the Israelite conquest of Jericho either in the c. 1400 BC Late Bronze IB placement or the c. 1230 BC Late Bronze IIB placement.

Some have argued that, if anything did survive of Joshua's city, it simply fell victim to subsequent erosion. Certainly much of the Middle Bronze city, destroyed by fire in c. 1550 BC, was removed by erosion. As for the walls, we know that Rahab's house was part of the city wall.[2] The fortifications may have consisted of a continuous ring of perimeter buildings rather than a classic city wall.

An analogy provided by the Egyptian king Tuthmosis III (1479–1425 BC) may be apposite here. He conducted eighteen campaigns in Syria–Palestine, yet very few of those cities show related destruction levels. He describes Megiddo as a fortified city, to which he laid siege for seven months. Yet no trace of a wall has been found in the Late Bronze IA level there.

CORRECT IDENTIFICATION OF SITES

Joshua 12:9–24 lists thirty-one defeated kings. This does not necessarily mean that Joshua's armies personally defeated all thirty-one of these kings in their own home towns. The king of Gezer was defeated at Lachish when he came to help its king.[3] We should not assume either that all thirty-one cities were destroyed, although it was common for citizens to be totally destroyed. Of all the towns mentioned only Jericho, Ai and Hazor were burned.[4]

About ten of these thirty-one cities cannot be securely identified. Perhaps the most significant case is that of Ai. The traditional identification with et-Tell is based on the fact that both Ai and et-Tell mean 'ruin'. Of the remaining identifiable sites four – Geder, Adullam, Tappuah and Hepher – have not been excavated.

THE CITIES OF CANAAN VIEWED AS A WHOLE

If the problem is to be solved, the evidence from all the cities of Canaan not just Jericho needs to be considered. It is possible to list sites that were inhabited and destroyed in either one or in both of these placements. However, it should be noted that no site has been fully excavated. Many sites have been excavated only 5 per cent or so at the relevant level, as in the case of Gibeon.

Where destructions are evident, there is no conclusive proof that the Israelites were responsible. For the c. 1400 BC Late Bronze IB placement, settlement is attested at eight of the definitely identifiable sites, namely Jerusalem, Gezer, Aphek, Hazor, Shimron, Taanach, Megiddo and Jokneam. Destruction, however, is only attested at two sites: Hazor (Tell el-Qadeh) and Megiddo (Tell el-Mutesellim).

For the c. 1230 BC Late Bronze IIB placement, settlement is attested at fourteen of the definitely identifiable sites, namely Jerusalem, Jarmuth, Lachish, Eglon, Gezer, Debir, Libnah, Bethel, Aphek, Hazor, Shimron, Achshaph, Megiddo and Jokneam. Destruction is attested at six sites, namely Lachish, Gezer, Bethel, Aphek, Hazor and Jokneam. Thus the c. 1230 BC Late Bronze IIB placement fares better, but it has to be admitted that it is not a comprehensive match.

TRANSJORDAN

In Transjordan no fortified cities dated to either Late Bronze placement have yet been found. In the case of Heshbon, the traditional identification with Tell Hesban may be in error. The nearby sites of Tell el-Jalul or Tell el-Umeiri may be better candidates, as they have evidence of Late Bronze occupation.

IN RETROSPECT

As the Israelites re-occupied the towns after their 'lightning conquest', they would not have destroyed them. Even though they were newcomers, they would not necessarily have brought a wholly different material culture, so their sites would show continuity with the previous occupants. An archaeological picture of the whole of Joshua's conquest involves the interpretation of evidence over a large number of partially excavated and sometimes not conclusively identified archaeological sites. It is therefore understandable why conclusions are so varied and why a consensus may never clearly emerge.

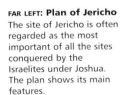

KEY
[1] Joshua 6:24
[2] Joshua 2:15
[3] Joshua 10:33
[4] Joshua 6:2; 8:28; 11:11

THE GEOGRAPHY OF CANAAN

NAMES FOR THE REGION

The name of the Promised Land west of the Jordan was Canaan, the name also given to the son of Noah's son Ham.[1] The people who inhabited the land before the Israelite conquest are called Canaanites and are first found in an inscription of Idrimi of Alalakh (Atçana) in south-east Turkey, dating from the mid-fifteenth century BC.

The term 'land of Israel' is an Old Testament one, much loved by the prophet Ezekiel, but today has become too highly politicized to be universally accepted as a designation for the land itself. The term Palestine, a term ironically derived from Israel's traditional enemies the Philistines and the name of the Roman province, is, like Canaan, used commonly to designate the land between the River Jordan and the Mediterranean Sea. This latter is the usage of this *Atlas*, but should not be interpreted in a modern, political sense. Terms such as 'Israel' and 'Judah' are used to denote the historic nation states that emerged in the region. The term 'holy land', although an Old Testament one, is limited to a single occurrence.[2]

THE MAIN FEATURES

Parallel to the Mediterranean coast run two ranges with the valley of the Jordan between them. There is thus a five-fold division of the land from west to east:

1. coastal plain
2. the western hills
3. the Jordan Valley
4. the eastern hills of Transjordan
5. the eastern desert.

In reality this scheme is a little more complex. South of Gaza on the Mediterranean Sea and Beersheba, and continuing east to the Dead Sea, is a barren steppe called the Negev. The coastal plain is pierced by the Carmel range, which is a spur from the western hills. On the east side of Carmel the coastal plain continues inland. This is sometimes called the Valley of Esdraelon or the Plain of Megiddo. Beyond the watershed another valley, the Valley of Jezreel joins the Jordan Valley. The western hills are effectively bisected by this lowland. A further discernible region is the Shephelah, a range of low hills between the coastal plain and the Judean hills.

1. The coastal plain of Palestine, which was often outside of Israel's control, lacks natural harbours. Israelite inexperience in seafaring is thus easily understood.

2. The western hills rise to 1,200 m (3,950 ft) in northern Galilee and 1,115 m (3,660 ft) near Bethel. Mountains on this range include Tabor (587 m or 1,926 ft), Gilboa (496 m or 1,627 ft), Ebal (939 m or 3,081 ft), Gerizim (881 m or 2,890 ft) and the Mount of Olives (816 m or 2,677 ft).

3. The Jordan Valley is the deepest depression on the earth's land surface, forming part of the Great Rift Valley which continues south along the Red Sea into east Africa. The Jordan Valley has three lakes.

a) Lake Huleh (now drained) is 70 m (230 ft) above sea level.

b) Lake Galilee, variously called Kinnereth (harp) and the Sea of Tiberias, is 210 m (689 ft) below sea level. It is 20 km (13 miles) long, and 13 km (8 miles) across at its widest, having a surface area of 170 square km (66 square miles). Its maximum depth is 48 m (157 ft). South of Lake Galilee the River Jordan winds along the valley floor through lush thickets of tamarisk and thorn scrub, once inhabited by lions.[3]

c) The Dead Sea, variously called the Salt Sea, the Eastern Sea and the Sea of Arabah, is 403 m (1,322 ft) below sea level. It is the lowest point on earth, its maximum depth being a further 433 m (1,420 ft). It is 75 km (47 miles) long and 16 km (10 miles) across at its widest. The Dead Sea is 25 per cent salt, whereas the Atlantic Ocean is only 6 per cent. To the south of the Dead Sea is the Arabah Valley. This rises to a height of 230 m (755 ft) above sea level, before sinking again to the Gulf of Aqabah.

The highest point in the eastern hills is Mount Hermon (2,814 m or 9,232 ft) whose snow capped peak is visible from over 100 km (62 miles) away. From Mount Nebo (835 m or 2,740 ft) Moses was allowed to view the Promised Land.

There is no clearly defined natural boundary between the eastern Transjordanian hills and the desert further to the west, from where came marauding desert tribes such as the Amalekites and Midianites.

NATURAL RESOURCES

The central highlands and Galilee are largely limestone, which provided the Israelites with good building stone. Copper was mined at Timnah in the Arabah and cast into bronze in the Jordan Valley between Succoth and Zarethan. The Israelites had access to an unlimited supply of salt on the shores of the Dead Sea. The 'City of Salt' mentioned in Joshua 15:62 is perhaps Qumran, the later

home of the Essene sect at the northern end of the Dead Sea.

EARTHQUAKES AND GEOTHERMAL ACTIVITY

From time to time Palestine suffers from disturbances in the earth's crust. Earthquakes may have contributed to Joshua's army crossing the Jordan and taking Jericho. The great earthquake in the days of Judah's king Uzziah was remembered nearly two and a half centuries later.[4] At the moment of Jesus' death the earth shook and the rocks split.[5] The El-Aksa mosque which stands on the Temple Mount in Jerusalem has been damaged by earthquake several times in its history. The last serious earthquake was in 1927. Volcanoes south-east of the Gulf of Aqabah were active as late as the eighth and thirteenth centuries. Evidence of geothermal activity is provided by the hot springs near En Gedi on the west side and at Zara (Callirhoe) on the east side of the Dead Sea. Anah, the Edomite, apparently discovered some hot springs in the desert east of the Jordan.[6]

A GOOD LAND

The Promised Land of Canaan is frequently presented as a good land, a land worth possessing: 'For the Lord, your God, is bringing you into a good land – a land with streams and pools of water, with springs flowing in the valleys and hills; a land with wheat and barley, vines and fig trees, pomegranates, olive oil and honey; a land where bread will not be scarce and you will lack nothing; a land where the rocks are iron and you can dig copper out of the hills' (Deuteronomy 8:7–9).

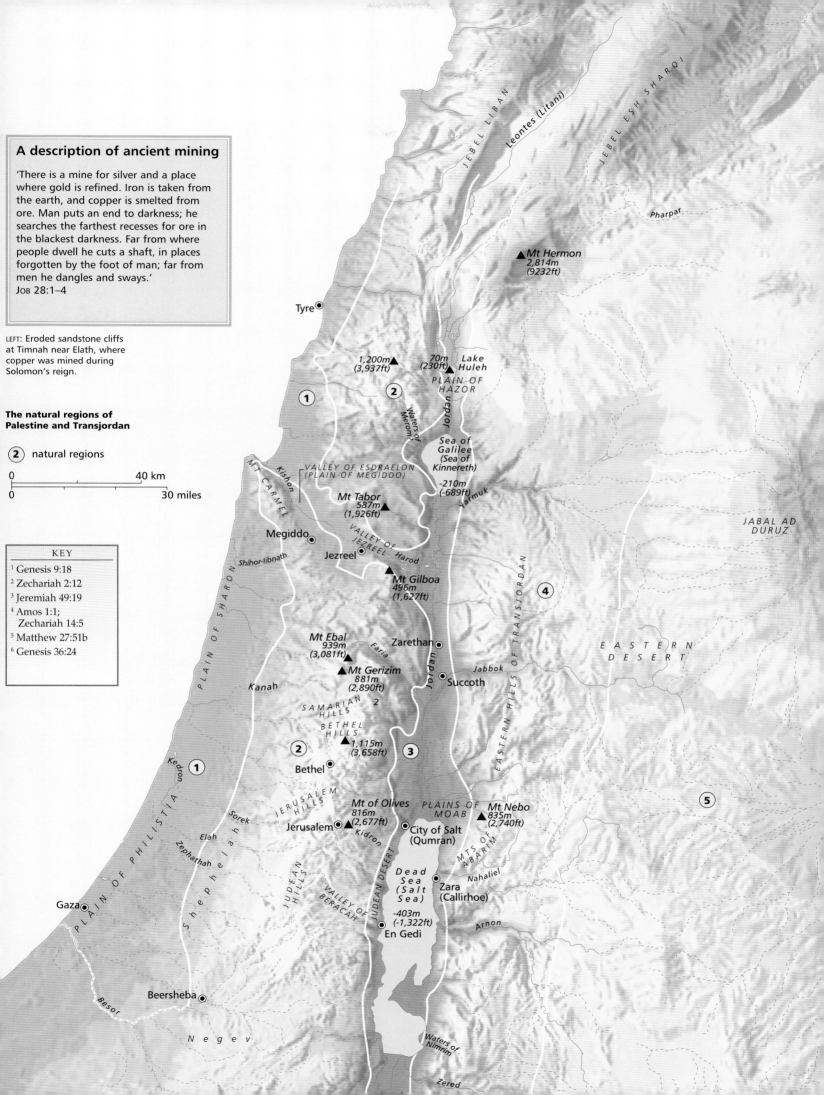

A description of ancient mining

'There is a mine for silver and a place where gold is refined. Iron is taken from the earth, and copper is smelted from ore. Man puts an end to darkness; he searches the farthest recesses for ore in the blackest darkness. Far from where people dwell he cuts a shaft, in places forgotten by the foot of man; far from men he dangles and sways.'
JOB 28:1–4

LEFT: Eroded sandstone cliffs at Timnah near Elath, where copper was mined during Solomon's reign.

The natural regions of Palestine and Transjordan

② natural regions

0 — 40 km
0 — 30 miles

KEY
[1] Genesis 9:18
[2] Zechariah 2:12
[3] Jeremiah 49:19
[4] Amos 1:1;
Zechariah 14:5
[5] Matthew 27:51b
[6] Genesis 36:24

JEBEL LIBAN

Leontes (Litani)

JEBEL ESH SHARQI

Pharpar

▲ Mt Hermon
2,814m
(9232ft)

Tyre ◉

1,200m ▲
(3,937ft)

70m ▲
(230ft)

Lake Huleh

PLAIN OF HAZOR

② ①

Waters of Merom

Jordan

Sea of Galilee
(Sea of Kinnereth)

-210m
(-689ft)

Yarmuk

JABAL AD DURUZ

MT CARMEL

Kishon

VALLEY OF ESDRAELON
(PLAIN OF MEGIDDO)

Mt Tabor
587m
(1,926ft) ▲

VALLEY OF JEZREEL

Valley of Harod

④

Megiddo ◉

Shihor-libnath

Jezreel ◉

Mt Gilboa
496m
(1,627ft) ▲

EASTERN HILLS OF TRANSJORDAN

EASTERN DESERT

PLAIN OF SHARON

Mt Ebal
939m
(3,081ft) ▲

Faria

Zarethan ◉

Mt Gerizim
881m
(2,890ft) ▲

Jabbok

Jordan

Succoth ◉

Kanah

SAMARIAN HILLS

2

BETHEL HILLS

1,115m
(3,658ft) ▲

② ③

Bethel ◉

JERUSALEM HILLS

Mt of Olives
816m
(2,677ft) ▲

PLAINS OF MOAB

Mt Nebo
835m
(2,740ft) ▲

⑤

Kedron

①

Sorek

Jerusalem ◉ ▲

Kidron

City of Salt
(Qumran) ◉

MTS OF ABARIM

Elah

Zephathath

JUDEAN HILLS

Dead Sea
(Salt Sea)

-403m
(-1,322ft)

Zara
(Callirhoe) ◉

Nahaliel

PLAIN OF PHILISTIA

Shephelah

JUDEAN DESERT

VALLEY OF BERACAH

En Gedi

Arnon

Gaza ◉

Besor

Beersheba ◉

Negev

Waters of Nimrim

Zered

THE CLIMATE OF CANAAN

RAIN

In the time of Moses and Joshua, as today, rain was crucial to the climate of Canaan: 'The land you are entering to take over is not like the land of Egypt, from which you have come, where you planted your seed and irrigated it by foot as in a vegetable garden. But the land you are crossing the Jordan to take possession of is a land of mountains and valleys that drinks rain from heaven' (Deuteronomy 11:10–11).

The prevailing moisture-bearing winds come from the Mediterranean Sea, and are forced to rise upwards by the western hills, over which they lose their moisture in the form of rain. Once over the watershed there is a rain shadow. The rainfall drops dramatically and in a few kilometres the land becomes a desert. This is graphically illustrated by comparing the annual rainfall of modern Jerusalem, some 600 mm (24 in), with that of Jericho (only 20 km or 13 miles away), some 160 mm (6½ in).

The annual rainfall of Jerusalem is virtually the same as London's, but in Jerusalem the rain is concentrated into some fifty rain days a year, whereas London has some three hundred. In general the rainfall increases the further north one goes; thus the hills of Upper Galilee can have up to 1,000 mm (40 in) of rain a year. In the south and east of Palestine there is less than 300 mm (12 in) of rain. In such conditions agriculture is not normally possible.

CLIMATE CHANGE?

The land of Canaan as described in the Old Testament appears to be more fertile than its

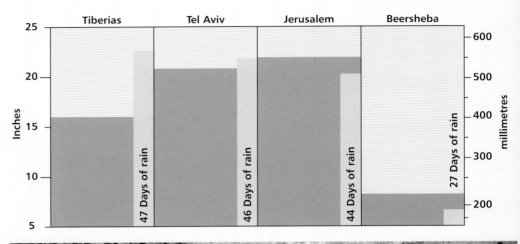

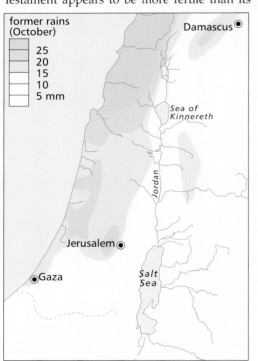

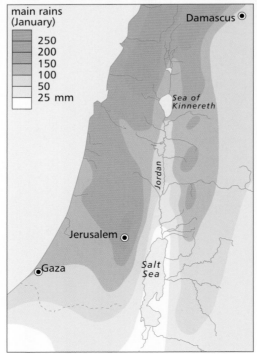

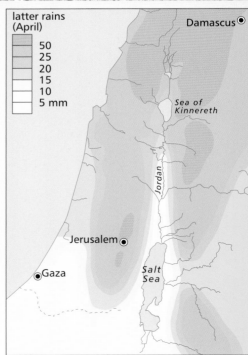

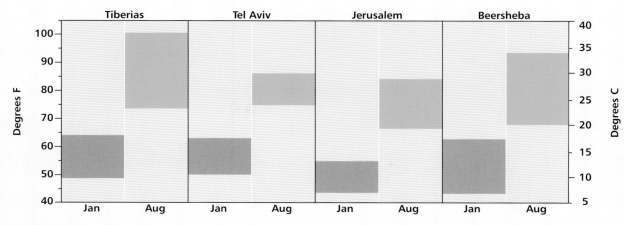

RIGHT: The maximum and minimum temperatures of modern-day Palestine

KEY

1 Deuteronomy 20:19
2 Ruth 1:22
3 2 Samuel 23:20; 1 Chronicles 11:22
4 Joshua 10:11
5 Ezra 10:9
6 Jeremiah 36:23
7 John 18:18
8 1 Kings 18:2b

LEFT: Cultivated fields in the Dothan Valley.

RIGHT: **Temperatures in Palestine**

LEFT: **Rainfall**
Rainfall in Canaan was concentrated in the months October to April. The three maps show the extent of the former rains of October, the main rains of January, and the latter rains of April.

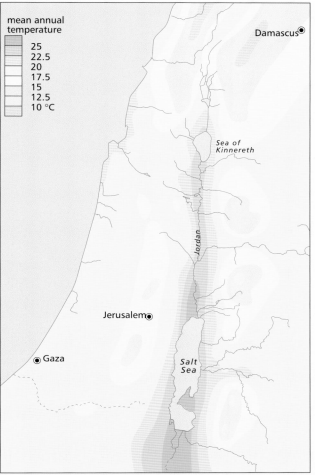

culminating with the latter rains in April or early May, which represent the last showers of the rainy season. These cause the grain to swell just before the harvest. Barley was less valuable than wheat, but had the advantage of growing on poorer soils and being harvested earlier. The barley harvest[2] coincided with the Festival of Passover in late March or April and the wheat harvest with the Feast of Pentecost seven weeks later. Grapes, olives, figs and other fruits were harvested in autumn.

Winters can be cold, sometimes snowy and certainly wet. Heavy snow falls in Jerusalem about once every fifteen years. Snow is mentioned a number of times in the Old Testament. For example a certain Benaiah went into a pit and killed a lion on a snowy day.[3] A freak hailstorm killed more Canaanites than the Israelites killed with their swords.[4] Rain in the ninth month (December) greatly distressed the people who were sitting in the square in Jerusalem.[5] In the same month Judah's king, Jehoiakim, was sitting in his winter apartment with a fire burning in a brazier in front of him.[6] Fires at night were required as late as early April, as the story of Peter's denial clearly shows.[7] A problem associated with the rainy season, particularly along the coast and by Lake Galilee, was mildew. It was common in garments and dwellings and was to be eradicated. It also plagued crops.

DROUGHTS
Sometimes the normal pattern of rainfall ceased and drought gripped the land. The three-and-a-half-year drought in the time of Elijah is the most famous and arguably the most devastating. Severe famine ensued.[8] Such events were foreseen by the writer of Deuteronomy. Disobedience to the Lord's laws would bring about the Lord's curse of drought: 'The sky over your head will be bronze, the ground beneath you iron. The Lord will turn the rain of your country into dust and powder; it will come down from the skies until you are destroyed' (Deuteronomy 28:23–24).

modern counterpart. Overgrazing especially by goats has led to soil erosion and loss of fertility. Undoubtedly the land is less forested, witness the use of wood for building and fuel and the devastation caused by numerous wars and sieges.[1] However, there is no evidence that modern levels of rain are substantially different from those of biblical times, simply that erosion of hillsides has increased water run-off and decreased their usefulness.

THE CALENDAR OF CANAAN
Usually there is no rain from mid-May to mid-October. From mid-June to mid-September vegetation dries out in the stifling heat of summer. The highest temperature recorded was 51° C (124° F) at the southern end of the Dead Sea.

The former (or early) rains normally begin in mid-October, but may sometimes be delayed until January. These soften the ground so ploughing can begin. The principal crops of wheat and barley would have been sown then. Rain continues periodically throughout the winter

THE AGRICULTURE OF CANAAN

NATURAL VEGETATION

Palestine has a number of climatic zones from alpine to desert and tropical. Consequently it has a great variety of vegetation with 2,780 species of plants recorded. Over twenty species of tree are mentioned in the Bible, from the date palms of tropical Jericho to the cedar and conifer forests of Lebanon. Not all the trees can be identified with botanical accuracy; some terms may have spanned a number of different species. For example, the Hebrew term for apple may also have included apricot.[1] Some, such as the carob, whose pods the prodigal son ate,[2] are unfamiliar to those living outside the lands of the Mediterranean basin. Not all the trees mentioned in the Bible actually grew in Canaan. Frankincense and myrrh from south Arabia and cedar from Lebanon are the classic cases, but algum, perhaps a species of juniper, was also imported from Lebanon.[3] Other trees were introduced to Canaan from distant lands, as is the case of the mulberry,[4] the white variety coming from China and the black from Iran. The spring months see a profusion of wild flowers, the 'lilies of the field' of Jesus' sermon on the mount (Matthew 6:28) carpeting the land.

THE ANIMAL KINGDOM

Palestine is home to 113 species of mammals, 348 species of birds and 68 species of fish. It has 4,700 species of insects, of which some two thousand are beetles and one thousand butterflies. The reader of the Old Testament is struck by a wide variety of animals, birds and insects known to the ancient inhabitants of the land. David killed a lion and a bear.[5] Certainly most modern inhabitants are grateful that lions and bears no longer inhabit the land. Other animals, such as apes and baboons, were imported from distant lands.[6] A bewildering variety of 'unclean' birds was forbidden to be eaten.[7] But who in his right mind would eat a vulture anyway? Some of these 'unclean' birds could have been migrants rather than regular residents of Canaan. The migratory habits of some birds were known, if not understood.[8] Certain flying insects were 'clean' and could thus be eaten.[9] John the Baptist, it seems, developed a taste for 'locusts and wild honey' (Mark 1:6).

CROPS

Wheat and barley were used to make bread. Lentils and beans were grown. Herbs such as mint, dill and cummin, which the Pharisees of Jesus' day tithed so assiduously,[10] added taste to an otherwise rather bland diet. When Moses sent the spies into Canaan, they brought back a huge bunch of grapes, plus pomegranates and figs. Grapes were made into wine that 'gladdens the heart of man' (Psalm 104:15) and 'sacred raisin cakes' (Hosea 3:1). Olive trees produced oil which, as well as being burned in lamps to provide light, was used in food, as a medicine and in the anointing of kings and priests. Flax was grown to provide linen for clothes. Nut trees included almonds, pistachios and walnuts.

ANIMAL HUSBANDRY

Canaan was envisaged as 'a land flowing with milk and honey' (Exodus 3:8) and described thus in the Old Testament fourteen times before the Israelites set foot in the

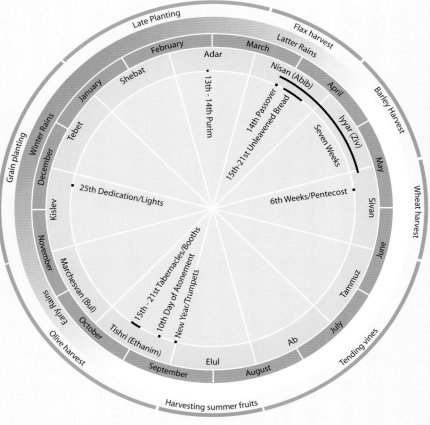

LEFT: The agricultural cycle of ancient Israel and its main festivals.

land. The milk was that of sheep and goats as well as cows. These animals also provided wool, hair and skins respectively. Their meat was eaten too but, as far as most people were concerned, mainly at the special festivals such as Passover, when every Israelite family was required to sacrifice a lamb.[11] The regulations of the sacrificial system for the entire Israelite community, if followed to the letter, required the annual offering of more than two tons of flour, over 1,300 litres (344 gallons) of olive oil and wine and 113 bulls, 32 rams, 1,086 lambs and 97 goats.

The size of cattle and their need of good pastures limited the areas where they could be kept. They did best in the hilly country of northern Galilee. The bulls of Bashan, a fertile area east of Lake Galilee, were renowned for their strength.[12] In addition to cattle, sheep and goats Solomon's daily provisions included deer, gazelles, roebucks and choice fowl.[13] The exact nature of the last item is uncertain: chickens are possible, since they were known in Egypt as early as the fifteenth century BC. Camels, rabbits and pigs were among the animals classed as 'unclean' and thus not to be eaten.

KEY
[1] Proverbs 25:11
[2] Luke 15:16
[3] 2 Chronicles 2:8
[4] Luke 17:6
[5] 1 Samuel 17:34
[6] 1 Kings 10:22; 2 Chronicles 9:21
[7] Leviticus 11:13–19; Deuteronomy 14:12–18
[8] Jeremiah 8:7
[9] Leviticus 11:21–22; Deuteronomy 14:20
[10] Matthew 23:23
[11] Exodus 12:3
[12] Psalm 22:12
[13] 1 Kings 4:23

A description of Canaan

'He makes springs pour water into the ravines; it flows between the mountains. They give water to all the beasts of the field; the wild donkeys quench their thirst. The birds of the sky nest by the waters; they sing among the branches. He waters the mountains from his upper chambers; the earth is satisfied by the fruit of his work. He makes grass grow for the cattle, and plants for people to cultivate – bringing forth food from the earth; wine that gladdens human hearts, oil to make their faces shine, and bread that sustains their hearts. The trees of the Lord are well watered, the cedars of Lebanon that he planted. There the birds make their nests; the stork has its home in the junipers. The high mountains belong to the wild goats; the crags are a refuge for the hyrax.'

Psalm 104:10–18

Legend:
- barley
- cattle
- cedars
- wheat
- cultivated land
- grazing land
- fishing
- salt
- important route

0 — 40 km
0 — 30 miles

The main agricultural products and natural resources of Palestine and Transjordan

JEBEL ESH SHARQI

JEBEL LIBAN

Litani

Sidon

Damascus

Tyre

Lake Huleh

Hazor

Jordan

Acco

VALLEY OF ZEBULUN

Galilee

Sea of Kinnereth

BASHAN

MT CARMEL

PLAIN OF MEGIDDO

VALLEY OF JEZREEL

JABAL AD DURUZ

Megiddo

GILBOA MTS

Beth Shan

Yarmuk

PLAIN OF SHARON

EASTERN HILLS OF TRANSJORDAN

EASTERN DESERT

Shechem

Kanah

SAMARIAN HILLS

Jabbok

Succoth

Joppa

Aphek

BETHEL HILLS

Bethel

Jericho

Jordan

PLAINS OF MOAB

JERUSALEM HILLS

Jerusalem

City of Salt (Qumran)

MTS OF ABARIM

Shephelah

JUDEAN HILLS

JUDEAN DESERT

Salt Sea

Gaza

PLAIN OF PHILISTIA

Hebron

En Gedi

Arnon

Besor

Beersheba

Negev

Zered

Arabah

THE TWELVE TRIBES OF ISRAEL

THE TWELVE TRIBES

The people led by Joshua in their newly conquered territory consisted of twelve tribes, based on the sons of Jacob (who was also named Israel):

- the sons of Leah: Reuben, Simeon, Levi, Judah, Issachar and Zebulun
- the sons of Rachel: Joseph and Benjamin
- the sons of Rachel's maidservant, Bilhah: Dan and Naphtali
- the sons of Leah's maidservant, Zilpah: Gad and Asher.

Jacob had given each of the tribes an oral blessing shortly before his death, and Moses had similarly blessed all the tribes apart from Simeon.[1] In effect there were thirteen tribes, as the tribe of Joseph was divided into two, named after Joseph's two sons, Ephraim and Manasseh. As promised by God to Abraham, Jacob and Moses,[2] they had taken possession of a land and could divide it up amongst themselves.

THE TWO AND A HALF TRIBES EAST OF THE JORDAN

The book of Joshua gives a detailed 'verbal map' of the parcels of territory allotted to each of the tribes.[3] Before the Israelites crossed the River Jordan to begin their conquest of Canaan, the tribes of Reuben and Gad and half the tribe of Manesseh asked for and were allotted territory east of the Jordan. The tribes of Reuben and Gad took over the former kingdom of Sihon, king of the Amorites; and half the tribe of Manasseh took over the former kingdom of Og, king of Bashan, to the north.

THE TRIBES WEST OF THE JORDAN

The allotment for Judah was a large tract of land in the southernmost point of the Promised Land, stretching from the Dead Sea to the Mediterranean, its southern boundary running from the Wadi of Egypt (Wadi el-Arish) to south of Kadesh Barnea. The tribe of Ephraim and the rest of the tribe of Manasseh received land further north, stretching from the River Jordan to the Mediterranean. The portions for the remaining seven tribes were assigned by lot. These were, in general, smaller allotments.

The land allotted to Benjamin formed a buffer, in places barely 10 km (6 miles) wide, between the territory of Judah and that of Ephraim. It included the Jebusite city, an enclave of Jebusites, that was later to be conquered by David and to be known as Jerusalem. The allotment given to Dan continued this buffer to the Mediterranean Sea in the east. The portion given to Judah was considered too big, so an area around Beersheba was marked out and assigned to Simeon. Eventually Simeon was absorbed into Judah.

The remaining tribes were assigned portions of land to the north of Manasseh. That of Asher stretched along the Mediterranean coast as far north as Sidon, which marked the northernmost point of the Promised Land. But the books of Joshua and Judges state that these tribes were prevented from taking up their full territorial allotment by substantial pockets of Canaanites.[4]

THE LEVITES AND 'CITIES OF REFUGE'

The tribe of Levi had already been assigned to priestly duties and so was not to inherit a portion of land in the Promised Land. Instead the Levites were assigned forty-eight towns throughout the land together with their adjoining pasture-lands.

Six cities assigned to the Levites were designated as 'cities of refuge'. People who had accidentally and unintentionally killed someone might flee there and find protection from those seeking vengeance. In an era when blood feuds were common this was an important provision. Fugitives could stay in the city until their trial or until the death of the high priest, which was thought to bring in some kind of amnesty. Three cities were designated east of the Jordan: Bezer, Ramoth in Gilead and Golan in Bashan. Three were to the west: Kedesh in the territory assigned to Naphtali in the north, Shechem in the hill country of Ephraim and Hebron in Judah.

CANAANITE ENCLAVES

The books of Joshua and Judges hint that several of the envisaged allotments were never wholly taken up. Although Gezer was assigned to the Ephraimites, they did not dislodge the Canaanites living there.[5] Canaanites having chariots are recorded as living in Beth Shan, Megiddo and the Valley of Jezreel. The Danites had difficulty in taking up their territory. This led to a part of the tribe's migrating north to Laish and capturing it, naming it Dan[6].

Despite a raid on the cities of Gaza, Ashkelon and Ekron, Judah never extended east to the Mediterranean as envisaged in her allotment, since, as archaeological evidence shows, the Philistines were later to occupy the coastal area.

After the death of Joshua the tribes of Judah and Simeon were to fight the Canaanites within their allotted territory. The men of Judah took possession of the hill country but were unable to drive the Canaanites from the plains. A Canaanite king of Hazor named Jabin opposed the Israelites.[7] The Canaanites, it seemed, possessed superior military equipment, their chariots being partly reinforced with iron.[8] To the Israelites the Canaanite enclaves had become a barb in the eye and a thorn in the side, just as Moses had foreseen.[9]

KEY
[1] Genesis 49:3–27; Deuteronomy 33:6–25
[2] Genesis 12:7; 35:12; Exodus 3:17
[3] Joshua 13:1–19:48
[4] Judges 1:30–33
[5] Joshua 16:10; Judges 1:29
[6] Judges 18:1–29
[7] Judges 4:2–3
[8] Judges 4:13
[9] Numbers 33:55

The Canaanite high place (site of worship and sacrifice) at Megiddo, built in the third millennium BC.

tribal boundary

areas outside of permanent Israelite control

city of refuge

| 0 | | 40 km |
| 0 | | 30 miles |

The Promised Land as divided between the twelve tribes of Israel

Although extensive tracts of land were allotted to the twelve tribes, the continued presence of Canaanites meant that the tribes were unable to take up all their allotments to their full extent.

Sidon

Tyre

ASHER

Dan (Laish)

Kedesh

NAPHTALI

Lake Huleh

Hazor

Aphek

Galilee

Rimmon

Sea of Kinnereth

Golan

Mt. CARMEL

ZEBULUN

Dor

Shunem

ISSACHAR

Megiddo

Jezreel

Beth Shan

MANASSEH

Taanach

Ramoth in Gilead

JABAL AD DURUZ

Jordan

Yarmuk

Jordan

EASTERN DESERT

MANASSEH

PLAIN OF SHARON

Shechem

Kanah

Jabbok

Succoth

Joppa

Shiloh

EPHRAIM

GAD

EASTERN HILLS OF TRANSJORDAN

Jericho

DAN

Gezer

BENJAMIN

Ekron

Jerusalem

Heshbon

Bezer

Gath

MTS OF ABARIM

Ashkelon

PLAIN OF PHILISTIA

REUBEN

Salt Sea

JUDEAN DESERT

Gaza

Shephelah

JUDEAN HILLS

Hebron

Arnon

Aroer

JUDAH

SIMEON

Beersheba

Besor

Negev

Zered

Arabah

Kadesh Barnea

THE JUDGES

(Fourteenth to eleventh centuries BC)

After the death of Joshua the Israelites were ruled by 'shophetim' a word which has traditionally been translated 'judges', although judging was only part of their function. 'Rulers' might be a better translation. The book of Judges tells of periods when Israel was oppressed by foreign powers, followed by times when the Lord raised up 'judges' to deliver his people. The recurring theme of the book of Judges is summarized in the refrain 'In those days Israel had no king, everyone did as he saw fit' (Judges 17:6; 21:25).

A CHRONOLOGY OF THE JUDGES

If we add up the totals the book of Judges gives for the rule of the named judges and all the periods of peace and foreign oppression, a total of 410 years results, from the start of the oppression by Cushan-Rishathaim to the death of Samson. Even if we adopt a 1447 BC date for the exodus, based on the statement that the year that Solomon began to build the temple (967 BC) was 480 years after the exodus,[1] it is clear that the remaining seventy years cannot accommodate the forty years of wandering in the desert and the somewhat notional eighty-six years covering the reigns of Saul, David and the first four years of Solomon, let alone several unknowns such as the length of the rule of Joshua, of the elders who followed him and of Samuel. We must therefore assume that at least some of the judgeships and the oppressions were contemporary. Such a requirement becomes even more necessary if we shorten the whole period by placing the exodus later, in c. 1270 BC.

LOCALIZED SPHERES OF OPERATIONS

The book of Judges shows that the judges had localized spheres of operations. This is certain in the cases of the 'minor' judges such Tola, Jair, Ibzan, Elon and Abdon. Even the more famous judges such as Deborah did not command national respect. Deborah was from the hill country of Ephraim. In her defeat of Jabin, the Canaanite king of Hazor, the tribes of Ephraim, Manasseh, Benjamin, Zebulun, Naphtali and Issachar rallied to her cause, but Reuben, Dan and Asher were rebuked for not helping. The account in the book of Judges indicates no expectation that the southern tribes of Judah and Simeon should have helped. Similarly Gideon's defeat of the Midianites involved men from Manasseh, Naphtali, Asher and Ephraim, but not from the southern tribes.

DEBORAH

The Israelites fell victim to the oppression of Jabin, the local Canaanite king of Hazor. His army commander, Sisera, possessed nine hundred chariots, partly reinforced with iron. The Israelite commander Barak gathered together his army on Mount Tabor. At Deborah's orders Barak and his ten thousand men swept down the steep slopes of the mountain, losing over 400 m (1,312 ft) in height. Sisera's chariots were routed. The River Kishon, apparently swollen by sudden rain, seems to have impeded the chariots.[2] Local Canaanite kings trying to aid Sisera were also defeated. Barak pursued the fleeing chariots; not a man was left of Sisera's army. But Sisera managed to flee on foot only to be killed by a local woman named Jael with a

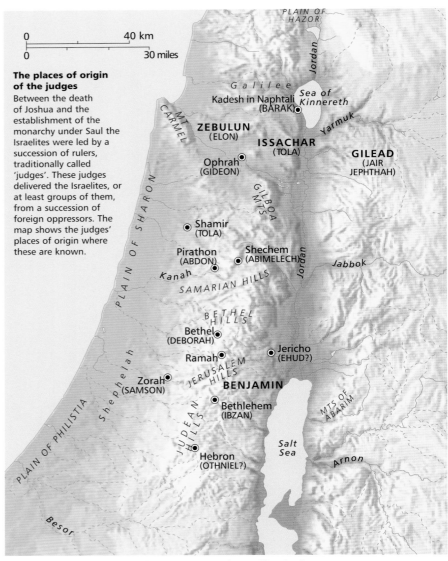

The places of origin of the judges

Between the death of Joshua and the establishment of the monarchy under Saul the Israelites were led by a succession of rulers, traditionally called 'judges'. These judges delivered the Israelites, or at least groups of them, from a succession of foreign oppressors. The map shows the judges' places of origin where these are known.

tent-peg and hammer as he, supposing himself safe, lay asleep in her tent.

FAR RIGHT: The Plain of Jezreel, scene of Gideon's pursuit of the Midianites.

GIDEON

According to the book of Judges, the camel-riding Midianites and Amalekites swarmed across the Jordan into northern Israel in vast numbers, forcing the Israelites into caves. The invaders encamped in the Valley of Jezreel.[3] Twenty-two thousand Israelites rallied to the Lord's chosen deliverer, Gideon, but at the Lord's insistence he reduced his force to a mere three hundred. At night, armed only with trumpets and torches hidden in jars, Gideon's men approached the Midianite camp from the Hill of Moreh. Blowing their trumpets and smashing their jars, they surprised the Midianites. The panic-stricken Midianites fled and were prevented from crossing the Jordan by the Ephraimites who had seized the crossing at Beth Barah.

THE MIGRATION OF THE DANITES

The tribe of Dan were unable to take up their allotment.[4] As already noted, they attacked the town of Laish, far to the north, by the headwaters of the River Jordan. They slaughtered the inhabitants, burned the city, rebuilt it and

KEY
[1] 1 Kings 6:1
[2] Judges 5:21
[3] Judges 6:33
[4] Judges 18:1
[5] Judges 18:27–29
[6] Ruth 1:1
[7] Leviticus 23:22; Deuteronomy 24:19
[8] Judges 20:47

Deborah and Barak's defeat of Sisera JUDGES 4:12–5:27

PHASE ONE

1 The tribes of Naphtali and Zebulun (shown in blue), assisted by other Israelites, gather on Mount Tabor under the command of Deborah and Barak.

2 Sisera's army (shown in brown) moves from Harosheth Haggoyim to the Kishon Valley.

PHASE TWO (possible scenario)

1 An Israelite force moves from Mount Ephraim to divert Sisera, but is intercepted by villagers near Taanach.

2 Sisera turns from Mount Tabor to assist the villagers.

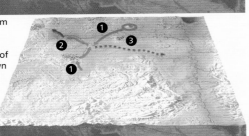

PHASE THREE

1 Barak leads the main Israelite army from Mount Tabor in pursuit of Sisera.

2 Sisera's army is defeated, the chariots of the Canaanites are probably bogged down by the River Kishon after heavy rain, and they are pursued as far as Harosheth Haggoyim.

3 Sisera escapes on foot, only to be murdered as he sleeps in Jael's tent.

Gideon's defeat of the Midianites JUDGES 7:1–8:21

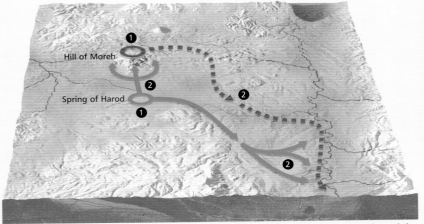

1 The Midianite army of 135,000 men is camped north of the Hill of Moreh. Gideon's force is based at the Spring of Harod. He selects 300 men and divides them into three groups to attack the enemy by night. The main part of his army moves south.

2 The three-pronged attack succeeds, and the Midianites rush towards the Jordan Valley, where the main Israelite force hampers their retreat.

3 The remnants of the Midianite army cross the River Jordan. With help from the tribes of Naphtali, Asher, Manasseh and Ephraim, Gideon pursues them as far as Succoth and Penuel, but the inhabitants refuse to feed his men. Gideon continues the chase as far as Karkor, where the remaining 15,000 Midianites are resting. They are taken by surprise and routed.

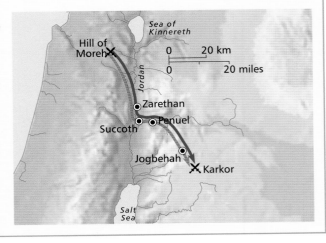

named it Dan after their forefather.[5] The site of Dan (Tell el-Qadi) has been excavated. Archaeologically the city the Danites destroyed corresponds to Level VIIA, dated to c. 1200 BC. Level VI, a mere encampment with a large number of deep storage pits, probably represents the Danites' immediate occupation after capturing the city and Level V the rebuilt town.

RUTH THE MOABITESS

The book of Ruth is set in the period of the Judges.[6] It tells the story of Naomi, from Bethlehem in Judah, who because of a famine went to live across the Dead Sea in Moab. Eventually, widowed Naomi returned to Bethlehem with Ruth, her widowed Moabite daughter-in-law. The Law of Moses[7] allowed the poor and aliens to glean leftover grain from a harvested field. Ruth's gleaning catches the eye of Boaz, a wealthy landowner and a relative of Naomi's deceased husband. Boaz marries Ruth and provides for the widowed Naomi. The significance of this story is doubtless in the fact that Ruth and Boaz were later to become great-grandparents of none other than King David.

CIVIL WAR

Arguably the lowest point in the story of Israel under the judges is saved for an appendix at the end of the book of Judges.

A Levite is journeying home through the region controlled by the tribe of Benjamin when some Israelites from the town of Gibeah, just north of what is now

Jerusalem, rape his concubine. The Levite cuts up his concubine into twelve and sends the parts to the other Israelite tribes, who are shocked into taking action. When the Benjamites refuse to hand over the rapists, the other tribes swear not to give any of their daughters in marriage to a Benjamite and launch an attack, some 400,000 swordsmen, the report says, ranged against 26,700 Benjamites. The Benjamites are initially successful, but the tables are turned and only six hundred are left alive.[8] The virtual extermination of a tribe galls the other Israelites. Ironically this leads to further bloodshed, as they feel obliged to attack the town of Jabesh Gilead (which had not joined in the action against the Benjamites) to carry off wives for some of the surviving Benjamites. Perhaps not surprisingly, after narrating this sad sequence of events, the writer of the book of Judges closes his work with the refrain: 'In those days Israel had no king, everyone did as he saw fit' (Judges 21:25).

THE PHILISTINE THREAT

(Twelfth to eleventh centuries BC)

WHO WERE THE PHILISTINES?

Arguably the most serious threat posed to Israel came from the Philistines. In his fifth year – 1180 BC – Ramesses III, king of Egypt, defeated the so-called 'Sea Peoples' in a naval battle which probably took place at the mouth of the Nile. His actions were recorded on carved reliefs on the walls of his temple dedicated to Amun at Medinet Habu, on the west bank of the Nile near Thebes. They show the Sea Peoples arriving in Egypt by wagon and ship with their families and belongings. (Some of the people alternatively moved overland, down the coast of the Levant.) Among the Sea Peoples are a group called *Pereset*, who are depicted wearing head-dresses of feathers or possibly reeds rising vertically from a horizontal band. These are the Philistines of the Old Testament.

One of the pictographic signs on a clay disk found at Phaistos in Crete and usually dated to the seventeenth century BC shows a head-dress very similar to those from Medinet Habu. This and Amos's reference that the Philistines came from Caphtor[1] point to the Philistines' Cretan origin. Caphtor is equated with the Egyptian *Keftyw* ('Crete'). The Philistines were probably driven out of Crete by some of the other Sea Peoples. The identity of the other 'Sea Peoples' need not concern us here. But studies of European tree rings and level changes in peat-bogs and lakes suggest there was a crisis in the climate of Europe in c. 1200 BC which could have triggered the migrations.

The Egyptians claimed a great victory in their battle with the Sea Peoples. The 40-metre-long (131-ft) Great Harris Papyrus of Ramesses IV (1153–1147 BC) recording the events of the reign of Ramesses III notes: 'I overthrew all who transgressed the boundaries of Egypt, coming from their lands. I slew the Danuna from their isles, the Tjekker and the Pereset (Philistines)... the Sherden and

the Weshwesh of the Sea were made as if non-existent.' The defeated Philistines then settled along the coastal plain of southern Palestine, hence its name.

PHILISTINE CULTURE

The Philistines' arrival in Palestine is marked archaeologically by their distinctive pottery (Mycenaean IIIC1b), which is very similar to Aegean examples. The Philistines were the first people to use iron in Palestine, so archaeologically their arrival is marked by the transition from the Bronze Age to the Iron Age. Because of the Philistines' monopoly on iron, the Israelites became dependent on Philistine smiths to sharpen their tools.[2] Five main Philistine cities emerged on or near the Mediterranean coast: Gaza, Ashkelon, Ashdod, Ekron and Gath. Each was ruled by a ruler known in Hebrew as *seren*, a word only used of Philistine rulers, and connected, through Greek, with the term 'tyrant'.

LEFT: A Philistine beer jug with built-in strainer to remove barley husks. Ashdod, twelfth century BC.

MIDDLE RIGHT: The map shows Samuel's circuit as a judge in the hills to the north of Jerusalem.

The arrival of the Philistines
The arrival of the Philistines on the Mediterranean coast of Palestine was part of a wider migration of a group called the Sea Peoples, whom the Egyptian king Ramesses III defeated in a naval battle at the mouth of the Nile in 1180 BC.

SAMSON

The judge Shamgar delivered Israel from the Philistines, but a more famous case is that of Samson, who possessed superhuman strength – shown by his killing a thousand men with a donkey's jaw-bone and his carrying the city gate of Gaza up a hill[3] – and who led or judged Israel for twenty years.[4] His weakness for women ultimately led to the loss of his hair, his strength and his sight. His exploits, though dramatic, were unable to deliver Israel from Philistine oppression.

SAMUEL

The Philistines posed a threat to Israel unlike any other. They were disciplined soldiers, possessing superior weapons to those of the Israelites. Not content with mere raids, the Philistines aimed at conquest. Moving inland from the coastal plain, they occupied much of the central mountains.

Against such a background a young lad named Samuel was growing up at Shiloh in the hill country of Ephraim. It was here that

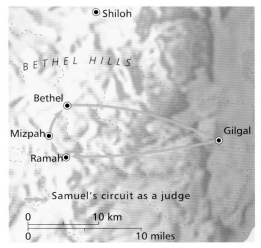

Shiloh

BETHEL HILLS

Bethel

Mizpah

Ramah

Gilgal

Samuel's circuit as a judge

0   10 km

0   10 miles

LEFT: A Philistine anthropoid clay coffin from Beth Shan, Twelfth to eleventh century BC.

the tabernacle had been pitched. Permanent buildings had been added[5] to create a complex called the 'Temple of the Lord'.[6] Samuel spent his youth here as the protégé of the old priest Eli. As he grew up, all Israel from Dan to Beersheba recognized Samuel as a prophet of the Lord. He also functioned as a judge, going on a circuit from Bethel to Gilgal to Mizpah and to his home at Ramah.[7]

THE PHILISTINES CAPTURE THE ARK

The book of Samuel records that, after four thousand Israelites were killed by the Philistines on the battlefield at Aphek, the people sent to Shiloh and brought the ark of the covenant to the Israelite camp at Ebenezer (perhaps the site of Izbet Sarteh). As the Israelites cheered enthusiastically, the Philistines thought a god had come into the camp. In the resulting battle the Israelites were resoundingly defeated. Thirty thousand Israelite foot soldiers perished, among them Eli's two wayward sons, and the ark of the covenant was captured. On hearing this, the aged Eli fell off his chair, broke his neck and died. Eli's daughter-in-law also died in childbirth, exclaiming: 'The glory has departed from Israel' (1 Samuel 4:22).

BELOW: The naval battle between Ramesses III and the Sea Peoples (1180 BC), from the temple of Amun at Medinet Habu, Egypt. The Philistine fighters are shown wearing their characteristic head-dresses.

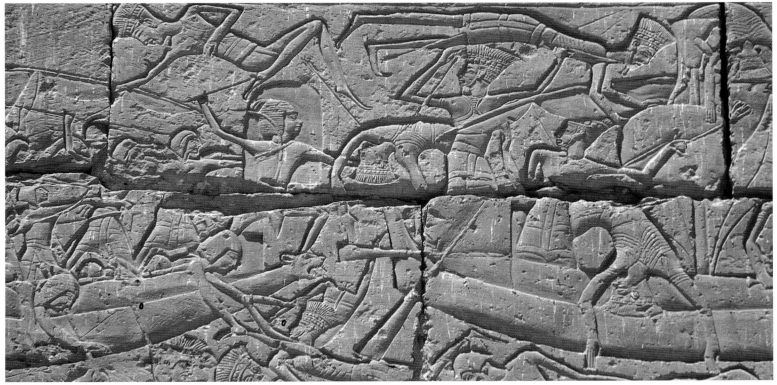

THE ESTABLISHMENT OF THE HEBREW MONARCHY

(c. 1050–970 BC)

ISRAEL DEMANDS A KING

The Philistine defeat of Israel at Aphek was a pivotal event in Israel's history. Not only did the Philistines capture the ark of the covenant, but it seems they also destroyed the Lord's sanctuary at Shiloh.[1] Archaeological excavations at Shiloh (modern Seilun) show that parts of the city were destroyed in c. 1050 BC and this could well be the result of Philistine action.

The elders of Israel pressed Samuel to appoint a king to lead them, like all the other nations.[2] Samuel warned them of the oppression a king could bring. They refused to listen. The need to have a permanent military commander dominated their thinking. 'We want a king over us. Then we shall be like all the other nations, with a king to lead us and to go out before us and fight our battles' (1 Samuel 8:19b–20).

SAUL BECOMES KING

Samuel's great reluctance to establish a monarchy is not surprising, since monarchy was an institution utterly alien to Israel's tradition. The Lord let it be known that it was primarily his kingship over Israel that they were rejecting. But even so, since the Lord had made it clear that Israel should have a king, Samuel reluctantly bowed to the people's request. So when a young Benjamite named Saul, who was a head taller than anyone else, appeared before him looking for his father's lost donkeys, Samuel took a flask of olive oil and anointed him king. Saul's subsequent victory over the Ammonites who were besieging Jabesh Gilead won him much popular acclaim. The people then went to Gilgal and confirmed Saul as king in the presence of the Lord.

THE REIGN OF SAUL

The length of Saul's reign over Israel is uncertain, because the figure in the verse stating this information appears to be incomplete.[3] A forty-two year reign is sometimes postulated on the basis of the figure forty cited in Acts 13:21. Saul and his son Jonathan saw some success in battle against the Philistines, but Saul could not deliver the knock-out blow required to end their menace. Worse still was his loss of the prophet Samuel's endorsement. Under pressure from the Philistines, facing the desertion of his own men and having waited for Samuel for a whole week, Saul usurped the priestly function by offering sacrifices. He also failed to carry out to the letter Samuel's divinely ordained instruction to *totally* destroy the Amalekites,[4] in

---

The Battle of Michmash 1 SAMUEL 13:16–14:23
possible reconstruction

PHASE ONE

1 While Saul and Jonathan are staying at Gibeah of Benjamin, the Philistines gather at Michmash. They send out three raiding parties to provoke an Israelite response.

2 Saul moves to Migron, opposite the Philistine position. The Philistines have a small forward outpost on the edge of the gorge of the Wadi Suweinit.

PHASE TWO

1 Jonathan and his armour-bearer attract the attention of the Philistines in the outpost and disappear into the gorge. Climbing the steep side of the gorge, they come up behind the Philistine outpost.

2 Jonathan and his armour-bearer kill some twenty Philistines, capture the outpost and send the rest running.

PHASE THREE

1 The main Philistine force mistake their companions running towards them for an Israelite attack and start to retreat.

2 Saul takes advantage of the confusion and attacks with his main force, pursuing the Philistines beyond Bethel.

---

that he spared their king and the best of their sheep and cattle. Samuel delivered the Lord's verdict: he had rejected Saul as king.[5]

THE RISE OF DAVID

The Lord commissioned Samuel to anoint a successor to Saul. He made his way to the Judean town of Bethlehem and anointed a young shepherd lad, ruddy and handsome, named David. David's bravery as a warrior and skill with the harp landed him a job in Saul's court at Gibeah. Saul's volatile temperament was soothed by David's harp-playing.

When the Philistines camped between Socoh and Azekah in Judah, Saul's army drew up lines against them in the Valley of Elah (modern Wadi es-Sunt). The Israelites were terrified of the Philistine champion named Goliath, who for forty days challenged the Israelites to provide a warrior who would take him on in single combat. Goliath was six cubits and a span tall (c. 2.9 m or 9½ ft).[6] Saul, despite being a head taller than anyone else, would not take Goliath on. But David, who was visiting his older brothers at the front line, was willing. Trusting in the Lord, David approached Goliath armed with only a sling and stones. A single shot hit Goliath on the forehead. David then used Goliath's own sword to cut off his head. The Philistines fled and the Israelites pursued them as far as Gath and Ekron.

Not surprisingly, it was David who was fêted by the Israelite women singing and dancing as news of the victory spread: 'Saul has slain his

thousands, and David his tens of thousands.'[7] Insanely jealous, Saul hurled a spear at David as he was playing his harp. It went into the wall.

SAUL PURSUES DAVID

Even though David had strong ties to Saul's family – he was a close friend of Saul's son Jonathan, and had married Michal, Saul's daughter – he was frequently hounded by Saul, who seemed obsessed with hunting him down. The steep, wooded hills of Judah and the ravines of the Judean Desert offered ideal refuge for David. On one occasion at Nob, north-east of Jerusalem, Saul had eighty-five of the Lord's priests killed because they had given assistance to David.

Disadvantaged and discontented men rallied around David, who lived the precarious existence of a bandit chief, striking the Philistines as opportunity offered, while continually being on the run from Saul. On one occasion Saul went into a cave in the Desert of En Gedi to relieve himself. Unknown to him David and his men were in the back of the cave. David's men urged David to kill Saul, but all David did was to creep up and cut off a corner of Saul's robe. He refused to harm Saul, who for all his faults was still 'the Lord's anointed'. David was determined not to wrest the kingship from Saul, but to leave his eventual succession to the Lord. He did however use the incident to point out to Saul the wrongness of his pursuit. A similar opportunity presented itself to David when he came across the sleeping Saul encamped in the

Desert of Ziph. Again David resisted calls to finish Saul off and merely took a spear and water jug that were near the head of the sleeping king.[8]

SAUL'S DEATH

Saul's hounding of David drove him twice to seek refuge in Ziklag, a city of Achish, the Philistine king of Gath. Asylum, however, carried with it the condition of military service, potentially against his own people. David was no traitor at heart and he convinced Achish by false reports that he was conducting raids against Judah while actually he was harrying the Amalekites and other tribes of the southern desert. The other Philistine rulers persuaded Achish not to take the risk of taking David on a campaign against Israel.

The Philistines fought against Saul at Mount Gilboa on the edge of the Valley of Jezreel. There the Israelite forces were cut to pieces. Saul's three sons, including David's close friend Jonathan, were killed. Saul himself, severely wounded, took his own life.[9]

Mount Gilboa, scene of Saul's death in battle.

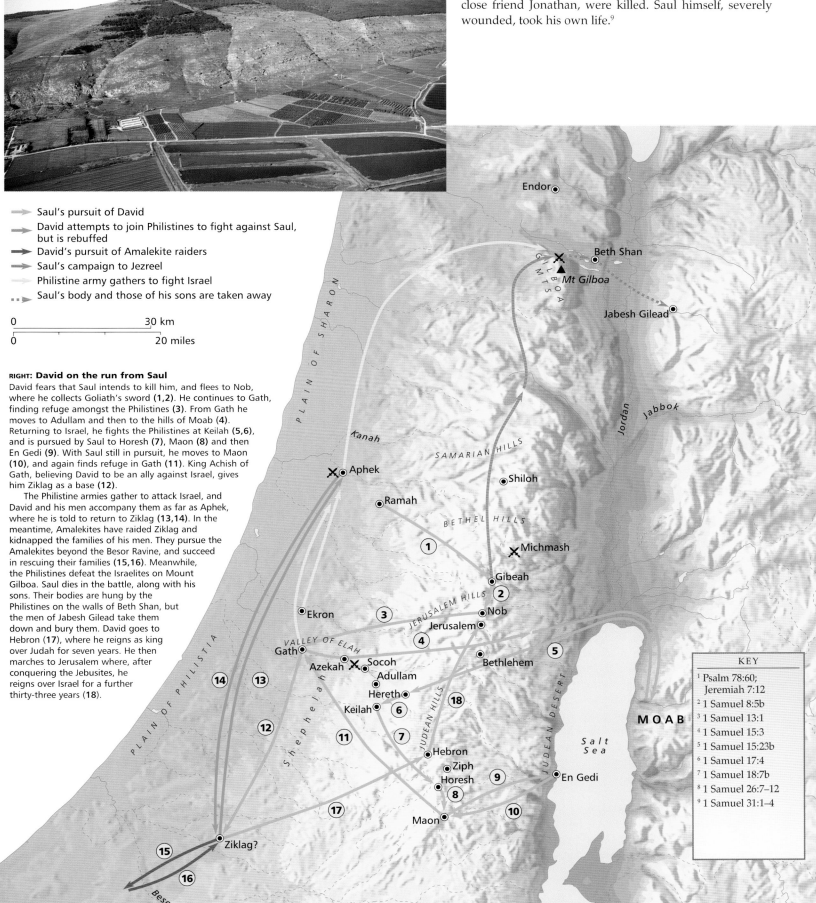

Saul's pursuit of David

David attempts to join Philistines to fight against Saul, but is rebuffed

David's pursuit of Amalekite raiders

Saul's campaign to Jezreel

Philistine army gathers to fight Israel

Saul's body and those of his sons are taken away

0   30 km

0   20 miles

RIGHT: David on the run from Saul
David fears that Saul intends to kill him, and flees to Nob, where he collects Goliath's sword (1,2). He continues to Gath, finding refuge amongst the Philistines (3). From Gath he moves to Adullam and then to the hills of Moab (4). Returning to Israel, he fights the Philistines at Keilah (5,6), and is pursued by Saul to Horesh (7), Maon (8) and then En Gedi (9). With Saul still in pursuit, he moves to Maon (10), and again finds refuge in Gath (11). King Achish of Gath, believing David to be an ally against Israel, gives him Ziklag as a base (12).

The Philistine armies gather to attack Israel, and David and his men accompany them as far as Aphek, where he is told to return to Ziklag (13,14). In the meantime, Amalekites have raided Ziklag and kidnapped the families of his men. They pursue the Amalekites beyond the Besor Ravine, and succeed in rescuing their families (15,16). Meanwhile, the Philistines defeat the Israelites on Mount Gilboa. Saul dies in the battle, along with his sons. Their bodies are hung by the Philistines on the walls of Beth Shan, but the men of Jabesh Gilead take them down and bury them. David goes to Hebron (17), where he reigns as king over Judah for seven years. He then marches to Jerusalem where, after conquering the Jebusites, he reigns over Israel for a further thirty-three years (18).

KEY
[1] Psalm 78:60; Jeremiah 7:12
[2] 1 Samuel 8:5b
[3] 1 Samuel 13:1
[4] 1 Samuel 15:3
[5] 1 Samuel 15:23b
[6] 1 Samuel 17:4
[7] 1 Samuel 18:7b
[8] 1 Samuel 26:7–12
[9] 1 Samuel 31:1–4

DAVID'S CONQUESTS

(1010–970 BC)

DAVID BECOMES KING OF JUDAH

David was devastated to hear news of the death of King Saul and his son Jonathan on Mount Gilboa. When he learned from an Amalekite that he had assisted in Saul's suicide, he had the Amalekite put to death. He thus made it abundantly clear that he had no personal satisfaction in Saul's death and that he held the Amalekite guilty of murdering the Lord's anointed. David then went to Hebron, where he was anointed king of Judah. He was thirty years old.[1] Here he reigned for seven and a half years.[2]

ISH-BOSHETH BECOMES KING OF ISRAEL

Saul's army commander Abner did not recognize David. Instead he took Saul's surviving son and made him king over Israel. This was the territory occupied by the northern tribes and Benjamin, although, given the Philistine victory, how much of it was under Israelite control is uncertain. In 2 Samuel the son is called Ish-Bosheth, meaning 'man of shame', which can hardly have been his real name! 1 Chronicles 8:33 gives his real name Esh-Baal, meaning 'man of Baal', which was changed by the scribes of Samuel.

Ish-Bosheth is credited with a two-year reign. There were clashes between Ish-Bosheth's men and those of David; but when Abner defected to David, Ish-Bosheth's power was fatally weakened. Ish-Bosheth was murdered by two of his officers. Again David, anxious to clear himself of complicity, had them executed. The tribes of Israel then came to him at Hebron. Acknowledging him now, they anointed David king over Israel.

DAVID DEALS WITH THE PHILISTINE THREAT

The existence of the rival regimes of Ish-Bosheth and David had suited Philistine interests, but a single Israelite regime under David's rule posed a greater threat. So a Philistine force came to the Valley of Rephaim, near Jerusalem, which as a Jebusite enclave was still in Canaanite hands. Their aim was to cut David off from his new northern allies at his most vulnerable point. David defeated the Philistines there, not once but twice. After the second occasion he struck down the Philistines all the way from Gibeon to Gezer. The Philistine hold over Israel has been decisively broken.

DAVID CONQUERS JERUSALEM

The Jebusite enclave later to be known as Jerusalem effectively divided David's territory into two: Israel to the north and Judah to the south. Surrounded on three sides by deep valleys and having a good source of water, it had great defensive potential. Hence it had eluded capture by the Israelites until then. It would provide David with an excellent, central site for a national capital, acceptable to both Israel and Judah.

David captured Jerusalem using his personal troops, although the details are obscure. Reference to a water shaft suggests that David knew of a secret tunnel, perhaps that running from the Gihon spring outside the city walls into the city.[3] David then took up residence in the city. That it was his personal holding is evidenced by its name, 'the City of David'.

THE ARK OF THE COVENANT COMES TO JERUSALEM

After its capture by the Philistines the ark of the covenant had been taken to the Philistine cities of Ashdod, Gath and Ekron. Following an outbreak of plague it had been sent back on a cart pulled by two cows and without a driver to Beth Shemesh in Israelite territory. From there it was taken to Kiriath Jearim.[4]

David decided to bring the ark up to Jerusalem. It was not without mishap, when Uzzah was killed reaching out to steady the ark, but it was an immensely joyous occasion, amid the music of harps, lyres, frame-drums, sistrums and cymbals; David danced with all his might. A tent was erected to receive the ark and priests were appointed to officiate at the required sacrifices. Jerusalem thus became the religious as well as the political capital of David's kingdom, although through the prophet Nathan the Lord made it clear that it would be one of David's sons who would build a permanent temple to house the ark.

DAVID'S WARS

David embarked on aggressive action against his neighbours. An exact chronological sequence is difficult to ascertain, but in the end David was the ruler of a sizeable empire.

When David's ambassadors were humiliated by having half of their beards shaved and their garments cut, David's army commander Joab laid siege to the Ammonite capital of Rabbah (modern Amman). The Ammonites hired mercenaries from the Aramean states of Beth Rehob, Zobah and Tob to the north. Joab routed the Arameans, but they regrouped and came with a new army. David moved his army to Helam (perhaps modern Alma in southern Syria) and defeated the Arameans, striking down Shobach their commander. While Joab resumed the siege of Rabbah, David returned to Jerusalem. Here he committed adultery with Bathsheba and had her husband, Uriah the Hittite, murdered – an event that was to blacken his name and earn him a stinging rebuke from the prophet Nathan.

Eventually Rabbah was taken, the people were put to forced labour and the bejewelled gold Ammonite crown, weighing some 34 kg (75 lb), was placed, probably only momentarily, on David's head.

David defeated the Moabites, sparing a third of them, but killing two-thirds. David – or perhaps more precisely his generals, Joab and Abishai – struck down twelve thousand Edomites in the Valley of Salt, in the Arabah south of the Dead Sea.[5] David then placed garrisons throughout Edom.

David turned his attention to Hadadezer, the king of the Aramean kingdom of Zobah, capturing a thousand of his chariots. Since he hamstrung all but a hundred of the chariot horses, it seems David did not see the value of chariots for his own forces. The Israelites still fought mainly on foot. When the Arameans of Damascus came to help Hadadezer of Zobah, David resoundingly defeated them and placed garrisons in Damascus. David's rule stretched from the River of Egypt (the Wadi el-Arish) right through (though somewhat loosely) to the Euphrates.

ISRAEL GROWS RICHER

As spoils of war David took gold shields and a great quantity of bronze from Hadadezer. Tou, the Aramean king of Hamath, doubtless pleased to see Zobah defeated and anxious to court good relations with David, sent his son Joram to congratulate him, bearing gold, silver and bronze. Talmai, the Aramean king of Geshur, gave his daughter Maacah in marriage to David. Hiram, the ruler of the Phoenician coastal city of Tyre, also wanted good relations with David. Along with cedar logs he sent carpenters and stonemasons, who built a palace for David at Jerusalem.

View of a tenth-century BC
supporting wall, 'City of
David' excavations, Jerusalem.

Judah and Israel
conquered kingdom
route of the ark of the covenant

0 ———————————— 40 km
0 ———————————— 30 miles

David's conquests
On becoming king, David
embarked on an extensive
series of foreign
conquests. Into his new
capital of Jerusalem he
brought the ark of the
covenant.

BETH REHOB

Sidon

Damascus

Tyre

Dan

PLAIN OF
HAZOR

Lake
Huleh

Jordan

Acco

GESHUR

Galilee

Sea of
Kinnereth

Helam

MT CARMEL

Yarmuk

Megiddo

Beth Shan

GILBOA
MTS

Ramoth in Gilead

Jordan

Jabbok

EASTERN
HILLS OF TRANSJORDAN

EASTERN
DESERT

Shechem

Kanah

SAMARIAN
HILLS

PLAIN OF SHARON

Aphek

Ebenezer

BETHEL
HILLS

AMMON

Joppa

ISRAEL

Rabbah
(Rabbath-Ammon)

Gezer

Gibeon

JERUSALEM
HILLS

Ekron

Jerusalem

PLAINS OF
MOAB

Ashdod

Gath

Kiriath
Jearim

Valley of
Rephaim

MTS OF
ABARIM

PLAIN OF PHILISTIA

Beth
Shemesh

JUDAH

Salt
Sea

Gaza

Hebron

JUDEAN DESERT

Arnon

Aroer

VALLEY OF SALT

MOAB

Besor

Negev

Zered

Arabah

Brook of Egypt
(Wadi el-Arish)

Kadesh Barnea

EDOM

KEY
[1] 2 Samuel 5:4a
[2] 2 Samuel 5:5
[3] 2 Samuel 5:8
[4] 1 Samuel 5:1–7:2
[5] 2 Samuel 8:13;
1 Chronicles 18:12;
Psalm 60 (title)

DAVID'S LATTER YEARS

(c. 980–970 BC)

THE ADMINISTRATION OF DAVID'S KINGDOM

We know little of the administrative practices David employed during his forty-year reign. His rule saw the introduction of an official who was in charge of forced labour.[1] This was imposed on Canaanites and conquered foreigners, not on Israelites. David's census that so aroused the anger of the prophet Gad[2] was probably done in preparation for a sweeping fiscal reorganization and possibly, too, for conscription. Ironically, it was his family that David found hardest to control. It was his family that was to give him a whole host of problems in his latter years.

DAVID'S FAMILY

From the perspective of the writer of the book of Samuel the infighting and sexual misconduct that beset David's family were divine punishment for his adultery with Bathsheba and his murder by proxy of her husband, Uriah the Hittite.[3] David had two wives at his accession to the throne, he took four more during his seven and a half years at Hebron, and he took more wives and concubines when he became king in Jerusalem.[4]

ABSALOM'S REBELLION

Two of David's children began a tragic series of events that ended in his temporarily losing his throne. David's eldest son fell in love with his half-sister Tamar. Pretending to be ill, Amnon requested that Tamar prepare him some bread and bring it to him, while he was alone in his bedroom. Amnon then raped Tamar. Two years later, Tamar's full brother Absalom murdered Amnon and fled to his mother's family in Geshur on the east of Lake Galilee. After three years Absalom was brought back to Jerusalem, where he curried support by endorsing the people's grievances. Then, going to Hebron, he had himself proclaimed king.

On hearing this David, now in his early sixties, immediately fled from Jerusalem and crossed the Jordan to Mahanaim. Absalom entered Jerusalem and lay with his father's concubines in full view of the people. Not only was this a fulfilment of Nathan's prophecy,[5] it was a claim of royal power.

Absalom pursued David across the River Jordan. Battle was joined in the Forest of Ephraim. Absalom's army was defeated and Absalom, riding a mule, was left hanging in mid-air from a terebinth tree, caught by his long hair. Joab, David's army commander, against David's explicit instructions plunged three javelins into Absalom's heart as he hung from the tree. The rebellion then fell apart.

The Psalms

A SONG WRITER

Even in his formative years David's reputation as a harpist went before him; indeed this was how he had first entered King Saul's service. Several of David's songs are preserved in the historical books of the Old Testament,[8] but seventy-three psalms attributed to David are preserved in the book of Psalms. Some have argued that the term 'of David' means, 'about David' or 'dedicated to David', not 'written by David'. We cannot be dogmatic, yet the extra information given by some of the psalm headings aptly places these psalms into the framework of David's life, as given by the historical books.[9] Later Bible writers remembered David's direction of musical worship, his invention and skill in playing musical instruments and his composition.[10]

NON-DAVIDIC PSALMS

Many psalms have no title and are thus undatable, but occasionally a historical context is clear, as in the case of Psalm 137 which describes the suffering of the Jews in exile in Babylon.

MUSICAL INSTRUMENTS

It is evident that the psalms were written to be sung, to what tunes we know not, though we do know some of their names.[11] Neither can we be certain what David's musical instruments looked like. However, we are fortunate to have representations of musicians from various places in the ancient Near East.

Very occasionally actual musical instruments have been found, as in the case of the lyre from the death pit of Ur c. 2500 BC. Reconstructions remain conjectural, however, especially in the details.

ABOVE: Terracotta relief showing a musician with a seven-stringed harp. Height 12 cm (4³/4 in). Early second millennium BC. From Eshnunna, Iraq.

BELOW: Clay figurine of a girl playing a double flute.

BELOW: Relief showing two frame drum players, a harpist and a lyre player from the palace of Barrakab, the Neo-Hittite king of Sam'al, Zincirli in south-east Turkey c. 730 BC. Incidentally, this relief enables us to see clearly the essential difference between a lyre and a harp. In a lyre the strings are all of the same length and meet the sounding board at right angles. In a harp the plane of the strings is at an angle, not parallel with the sounding board.

David was devastated to hear of Absalom's death, wishing that he had died in place of his son. Eventually David returned to Jerusalem to popular, but not universal, acclaim. A further rebellion of a Benjamite named Sheba fizzled out when the inhabitants of Abel Beth Maacah in the extreme north of the country threw his head over the wall of their besieged city.

David had supposedly promised Bathsheba that her son Solomon would succeed him.[6] As David grew increasingly old and feeble, Adonijah, the oldest of his surviving sons, made a bid for the throne. He too curried popular support and received the endorsement of Joab, David's army commander. When Nathan the prophet brought news to David that Adonijah had proclaimed himself king during a great feast at En Rogel, just outside Jerusalem, David was prompted to take action and have Solomon proclaimed king. Zadok the priest and Nathan the prophet anointed Solomon at the spring of Gihon just outside Jerusalem. Adonijah's bid to be king collapsed and Solomon acceded to the throne. David then died, after a forty-year reign, at the age of seventy.[7]

ARCHAEOLOGICAL EVIDENCE

Since David is not mentioned in any contemporary inscriptions, he has sometimes been dismissed as fictitious. However, in July 1993 a fragmentary basalt stela was found at Tell el-Qadi (ancient Dan in the north of Israel). It was set up by an Aramean king, probably Hazael of Damascus (843–796 BC), and was written in Aramaic. Its chief claim to fame is that it mentions 'the house of David'. The term 'house' here refers to a 'dynasty' or 'state founded by', and was also adopted by a number of other states in the ancient Near East. Thus, just a hundred and thirty or so years after David's death he was clearly regarded as a historical figure.

It has also been proposed that there is a mention of David in an Egyptian inscription from Karnak of the Pharaoh Shoshenq (945–924 BC) and on a restoration to line 31 of the Moabite Stone from Dibon in modern Jordan (an inscription written by King Mesha of Moab in c. 830 BC), although neither proposal has received much scholarly endorsement.

Rebellions against David in his latter years

In the latter years of his reign David faced a number of rebellions. David's own son Absalom laid claim to the throne and David was forced to flee from Jerusalem. Absalom pursued David across the River Jordan to the Forest of Ephraim. Here Absalom was killed and the rebellion fell apart.

KEY
[1] 2 Samuel 20:24
[2] 2 Samuel 24:11–14
[3] 2 Samuel 12:10–12
[4] 2 Samuel 2:2; 3:2–5; 5:13–14
[5] 2 Samuel 12:11–12
[6] 1 Kings 1:13, 17
[7] 2 Samuel 5:4; 1 Kings 2:10–11
[8] 2 Samuel 1:19–27; 22:2–51; 1 Chronicles 16:8–36
[9] Psalms 18; 24; 51; 52
[10] Amos 6:5; Nehemiah 12:24, 36, 45
[11] Psalms 9; 22; 45

WRITING

THE EARLIEST WRITING

We have already seen how writing emerged more or less simultaneously in both Egypt and Mesopotamia c. 3100 BC. In both places pictures were used to represent words. The script used in Egypt was later called 'hieroglyphics' (a Greek term meaning 'sacred writing'). In its classic form, that of Middle Egyptian (2116–1795 BC), some seven hundred signs were in use. This was the script used for monuments and religious texts, and it could be written left to right or right to left. By 2500 BC hieroglyphics had spawned a simplified, cursive script (known as 'hieratic', from a Greek term meaning 'priestly'). This was used for administrative and business purposes, written with ink on papyrus, from right to left.

In Mesopotamia the pictures quickly became stylized, as it was impossible to render curves using a stylus on a clay tablet, the predominant writing material. The writing system that developed is called 'cuneiform' meaning 'wedge-shaped', which was used to record both the Sumerian and Akkadian languages. It was written left to right.

With such complex writing systems in both Egypt and Mesopotamia, writing remained the monopoly of a scribal élite. Whereas hieroglyphics were confined to Egypt, the cuneiform script was exported outside of Mesopotamia to record languages such as Eblaite in Syria, Elamite in south-west Iran, and Hittite, Hurrian and Urartian in Turkey. Cuneiform tablets have also been discovered at several sites in Palestine. Megiddo has yielded part of the *Epic of Gilgamesh* for example.

THE FIRST ALPHABET

In 1999 at Wadi el-Hol in Upper Egypt archaeologists found what may be the earliest alphabetic inscriptions. Dating between 1900 and 1800 BC they are a couple of centuries earlier than any previously known alphabetic inscriptions and were apparently the work of Semitic-speaking mercenaries or migrant

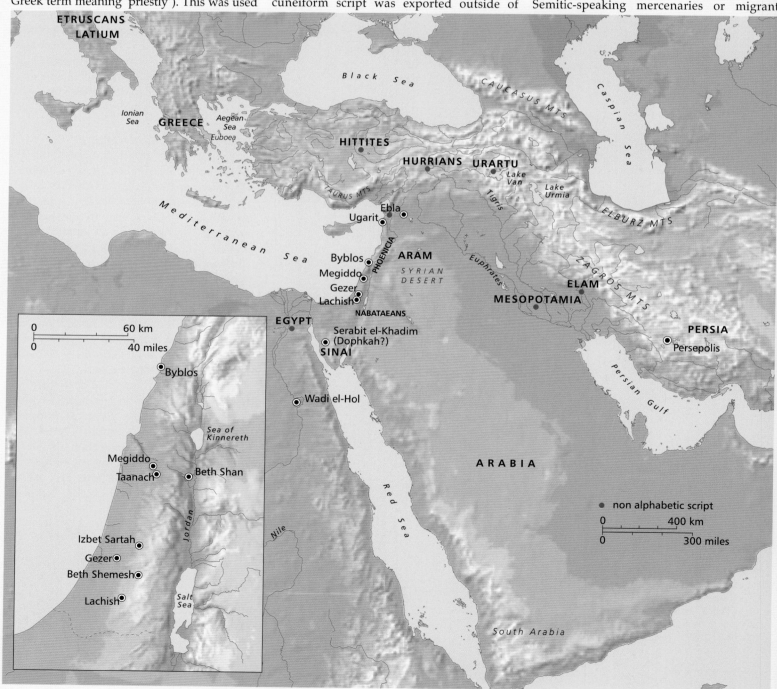

labour miners. These Semites used pictures to record single sounds, all of them consonants.

Until 1999 the earliest known examples of an alphabet were from the Egyptian turquoise mines of Serabit el-Khadim (perhaps the Dophkah of Numbers 33:13) in the Sinai Peninsula. These were again done by Semite miners and date to c. 1700 BC. At least twenty-three separate characters were used, nearly half of which were clearly borrowed from Egyptian.

Our word alphabet is derived from the first two letters of the Greek alphabet, alpha and beta, words which are meaningless in Greek. They themselves were derived from Semitic. The first two letters of the twenty-two letter Hebrew alphabet, aleph and beth mean 'ox' and 'house' respectively. Thus a picture of a house was used to represent the consonant *b*. The significance of the alphabet cannot be underestimated. An alphabet could be mastered by almost anyone with a day or two's concentrated effort. Writing, in theory at any rate, no longer remained in the hands of the privileged few.

WRITING IN THE OLD TESTAMENT

It is interesting to note that the earliest evidence for the alphabet is earlier than either placement of the exodus and that it comes from the two places – Egypt and Sinai – that were closely associated with the life of Moses. There is thus no reason to doubt that Moses could have recorded the Law in an alphabetic script. Moses is several times instructed to write,[1] Joshua asks for a description of the unpossessed portions of the Promised Land to be written[2] and a young man writes down for Gideon the names of seventy-seven officials of the town of Succoth.[3] Ordinary Israelites were commanded to write the Lord's commands on the door frames of their houses and on their gates.[4]

WRITING IN EARLY ISRAEL

Four inscribed potsherds from Lachish are dated to c. 1250 BC. Some of the letters are recognizable, but as the sherds are damaged they cannot be understood fully. An *ostracon* (pottery sherd with writing) dating from the twelfth century BC was found in 1976 at Izbet Sartah, (perhaps biblical Ebenezer). Measuring 8.8 cm by 15 cm (3½ in by 6 in), with 83 letters in five faint lines, it defies decipherment, although its fifth and last line appears to be an exercise in writing the alphabet left to right.

The so-called 'Gezer Calendar', 11 cm by 7 cm (4¼ in by 2¾ in), found in Gezer in 1908 and now in the Istanbul Archaeological Museum, dates from c. 925 BC, perhaps a little after the division of the Israelite monarchy, following the death of Solomon. Written from right to left it appears to be a schoolboy exercise written on limestone describing the agricultural year, beginning with the autumn.

Two months of gathering.
Two months of sowing.
Two months of spring growth.
A month of pulling flax.
A month of barley harvest.
A month of (harvesting) everything else.
A month of pruning.
A month of summer fruit.
Abijah.

It is not certain that the Gezer Calendar was written in Hebrew. The language could equally well be Canaanite, but it is clear evidence of literacy. The extent of Israelite literacy has been much debated. Certainly there were professional scribes and secretaries. Some served the court, others the Temple, still others may have served the ordinary people setting up a stall in the bazaar or marketplace, as is still the case in some parts of the Near East to this day. Informal inscriptions from the period of the Hebrew monarchy, some just names and brief notes, have turned up in at least twenty-five provincial sites in Palestine. These can hardly all be the work of professional scribes and suggest that the knowledge of writing was widespread in ancient Israel. Most of the surviving Hebrew inscriptions are to be dated after 750 BC, but this does not mean that they did not exist before then, merely that a commonly observable archaeological principle is in operation, whereby artefacts from the period immediately preceding a destruction greatly outnumber those of earlier periods. Furthermore, the variety of inscriptions from the period of the Hebrew monarchy – from monumental texts, letters and seals to names and lists scratched on pots – suggests the widespread use of writing.

THE ALPHABET SPREADS WIDER

Once the alphabet had been invented, it spread widely, but often in highly adapted forms. The Syrian port of Ugarit employed a twenty-nine character cuneiform alphabet in c. 1300 BC. Single texts in this alphabet have also been found in Taanach, Tabor and Beth Shemesh in Palestine. A different twenty-nine letter alphabet was used in south Arabia from the ninth century BC onwards. In the reign of Darius I (522–486 BC) the Persians invented a thirty-six character alphabet to record Old Persian. Much of the reason for the rapid spread of Aramaic in the Assyrian, Babylonian and Persian empires was that it used an alphabetic script, similar to that now used to record Hebrew. The twenty-eight letter Arabic script is ultimately derived from Nabataean which is a development of the Aramaic script.

Probably by the ninth, and certainly by the eighth, century BC the Greeks had adopted the Phoenician alphabet, but having consonants surplus to their requirements, they turned these into vowels. Thus Greek scribes could record all the sounds of their language. Before long the Greeks were to standardize the direction of their writing from left to right, thus reversing the Semitic practice of writing right to left. Later modifications were made to the Greek alphabet to record Coptic, the latest development of Egyptian, and some of the Slavic languages of eastern Europe, using the so-called Cyrillic alphabet.

From the Euboean Greeks a form of the alphabet was taken west to the Etruscans of Italy. With a few modifications this was used by the Romans to write Latin and ultimately by all the languages of western Europe, becoming the dominant script of the world.

The 'Gezer Calendar', c. 925 BC.

KEY
[1] Exodus 17:14; 34:27; Numbers 17:2
[2] Joshua 18:4
[3] Judges 8:14
[4] Deuteronomy 6:9; 11:20

The spread of writing
Writing is arguably one of humankind's greatest discoveries. The maps show many of the sites that were significant in the development and spread of writing thoughout the Near East and beyond.

ARCHIVES AND LIBRARIES OF THE ANCIENT WORLD

ARCHIVES AND LIBRARIES

Many ancient texts were not found in isolation. Throughout the ancient world there are numerous examples of texts being found in groups. The most common example of a collection of texts is that of an archive, where legal, economic or administrative documents are preserved.

Libraries preserve the learned tradition of any given people. These texts are literary, historical, religious or scientific and often exist in multiple copies. It is of course relatively easy to count texts in any given archive or library, but such a figure is often greatly exaggerated, since it represents all the extant fragments rather than complete texts. A good case in point is the Syrian site of Ebla, where an archive of 18,000 cuneiform texts dating to c. 2300 BC is sometimes claimed, although in reality this represents only some 3,000 tablets. Furthermore on some sites new texts are still being found. Thus at Kanesh (Kültepe) in central Turkey some 25,000 clay tablets dating to the nineteenth century BC have been found, but on average a thousand new tablets are discovered every year.

MESOPOTAMIA

The cuneiform archives of Mesopotamia are the largest in the ancient world. Many archives are huge: 22,000 texts or fragments at Mari (Tell Khariri) on the middle Euphrates, 12,000 from Nippur (Nuffar) in southern Mesopotamia and over 10,000 from Babylon. Even the provincial site of Nuzi (Yorghan Tepe), 16 km (10 miles) south-west of Kirkuk, yielded some 3,000 clay tablets, dating to c. 1500 BC. The largest archive of all was from the Shamash Temple at Sippar (Abu Habba) dating from the Neo-Babylonian and early Persian periods c. 625–486 BC. It contains some 60,000 to 70,000 fragments, representing some 30,000 texts.

Arguably the most famous Mesopotamian library was that of the Assyrian king Ashurbanipal (669–627 BC) from his palace at Nineveh. About 30,000 clay tablets are said to have come from the city, which represent some 11,000 texts. The library material of some 1,500 separate titles contained traditional Mesopotamian literature – epics, prayers, myths, historical and wisdom texts – as well as omens, incantations, medical texts and lexical lists.

EGYPT

One of the most significant archives of cuneiform tablets in fact comes from Egypt. The 382 so-called Amarna letters came from Tell el-Amarna, the abandoned capital of Amenophis IV, also known as Akhenaten (1353–1337 BC), in Middle Egypt. Many of the Amarna letters were written to the Egyptian pharaoh by various Egyptian vassals of Canaan. Although the language of the letters is Akkadian, the language of Mesopotamia and of diplomacy at the time, a strong Canaanite influence on the vocabulary and syntax is discernable.

A native Egyptian archive is that of Deir-el-Medina, a village for those who worked on the construction of tombs in the Valley of the Kings. The bulk of the texts are to be dated to the reigns of Ramesses III and IV (1194–1147 BC). They consist of over three thousand brief notes written in the hieratic script on *ostraca* and many papyri. Texts from the archive record that in the 29th year of Ramesses III (1155 BC) the workforce went on strike and rioting ensued.

PALESTINE

Archives have been discovered too in Palestine, although they are small in comparison with those of Mesopotamia and Egypt. 102 *ostraca* written in Hebrew were found in Samaria and are probably to be assigned to the reign of Jeroboam II (781–753 BC). They record the receipts of wine and olive oil, probably tax payments, from estates in the vicinity of Samaria. Scores of other *ostraca* were found at Arad.

Twenty-two letters written on *ostraca* were found at Lachish. They record the situation in the town as Nebuchadnezzar of Babylon was laying waste to Judah (588–586 BC). The so-called Dead Sea Scrolls, dating between c. 250 BC and AD 68, form a specialized library, composed of texts of the Old Testament and writings connected with the Essene sect.

UNDER THE PERSIAN EMPIRE

In the Persian capital of Persepolis two economic archives totalling over 30,000 tablets have been found. Both were written in Elamite cuneiform, and cover the period from 509–458 BC. An archive of some 730 texts, dating from 454–404 BC, was found at the southern Mesopotamian city of Nippur (Nuffar). These tablets record the dealings of a wealthy banker named Murashu, who charged up to 40 per cent interest. Among some 2,500 individuals mentioned in the texts about 70 (approximately 3 per cent) can be identified as Jews.

Another significant Persian archive was found on the island of Elephantine near Aswan at the first cataract of the Nile. Comprising 98 papyri and over 300 *ostraca* and dating between 495 and 398 BC, it is a collection of letters, legal deeds, accounts and a few books. Another archive from Egypt comprises thirteen letters written on leather sent by Arsames, the Persian satrap of Egypt. Dating from the late fifth century BC, it preserves Arsames' letters written in Babylon to his agents and was probably found at Memphis or the western Delta.

THE GREEK WORLD

The earliest Greek archives are those written in a syllabic script called Linear B. They are lists of commodities. Over 3,000 tablets were found at Knossos in Crete, which is thought to have been destroyed in c. 1375 BC. Later are the archives of Linear B tablets from the Greek mainland – Pylos (1,200 texts) and Mycenae (70 texts) – dating to c. 1200 BC.

A library was established at Pergamum in western Turkey under Eumenes II (197–158 BC). Located on the acropolis near the temple of Athena Polias, it consisted of a reading room, 16 m by 14 m (52 ft 6 in by 46 ft), and three other rooms about 13 m long (43 ft) and between 7 and 10 m in width (23 to 33 ft), identified as the book stacks. Shelves were not attached to the walls, a free space of some 50 cm (20 in) being left to protect the parchment scrolls from damp. Its contents were later added to the library at Alexandria.

Archives and libraries of the Ancient World
Archives and libraries, some of them almost overwhelmingly vast, have been found in many different places in the ancient world. The figures given are of the size of the archive or library.

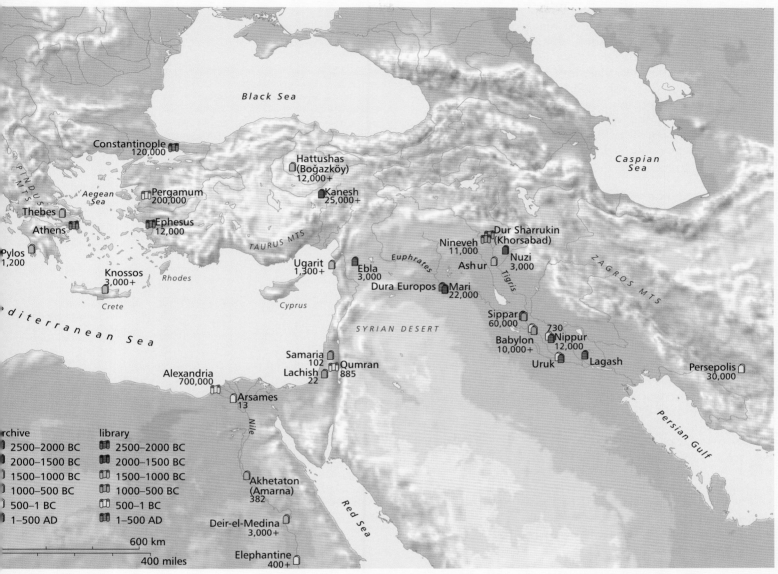

Black Sea

Constantinople
120,000

Hattushas
(Boğazköy)
12,000+

PINDUS MTS

Aegean
Sea

Pergamum
200,000

Kanesh
25,000+

Thebes

Ephesus
12,000

Athens

Dur Sharrukin
(Khorsabad)

Nineveh
11,000

TAURUS MTS

Pylos
1,200

Ugarit
1,300+

Ebla
3,000

Ashur

Nuzi
3,000

ZAGROS MTS

Knossos
3,000+

Rhodes

Euphrates

Crete

Cyprus

Dura Europos

Mari
22,000

Tigris

Mediterranean Sea

SYRIAN DESERT

Sippar
60,000

730

Babylon
10,000+

Nippur
12,000

Samaria
102

Qumran
885

Uruk

Lagash

Persepolis
30,000

Alexandria
700,000

Lachish
22

Arsames
13

Nile

archive		library	
	2500–2000 BC		2500–2000 BC
	2000–1500 BC		2000–1500 BC
	1500–1000 BC		1500–1000 BC
	1000–500 BC		1000–500 BC
	500–1 BC		500–1 BC
	1–500 AD		1–500 AD

Akhetaton
(Amarna)
382

600 km

400 miles

Deir-el-Medina
3,000+

Red Sea

Persian Gulf

Elephantine
400+

THE ROMAN WORLD

Rome was first introduced to libraries when the general Aemilius Paulus brought contents of a Greek library to Rome in the mid-second century BC. The library of Celsus at Ephesus was set up in AD 110 by Tiberius Julius Aquila Polemaeanus as a memorial to his father Tiberius Julius Celsus Polemaeanus. An estimated 12,000 rolls were housed in thirty niches. The library had a double wall to protect its scrolls from dampness.

Over 150 papyrus and leather documents from a Roman infantry unit known as a cohort were found at Dura Europos (as-Salihiya), sacked in AD 256, on the eastern frontier of the Roman empire in Syria. Right at the opposite end of the Roman empire at Vindolanda (Chesterholm), a fort close to Hadrian's Wall in northern England, some 1,900 wooden writing tablets with traces of tiny, spidery, ink writing were found. Thanks to infra-red photography a large collection of letters, reports and accounts can now be read.

A TINY PORTION OF ANCIENT LITERATURE

The survival of ancient archives and libraries is essentially a matter of chance. Where archives have survived it is generally the material from near the end of the archive's existence that is preserved. Documents no longer considered relevant were thrown away to create space. Only about one tenth of the works of the three great Greek tragedians – Aeschylus, Sophocles and Euripides – has come down to us. Menander, another Greek dramatist, is known to have written over a hundred plays, but only one complete play (discovered in 1955) and a number of fragments have come down to us. It is estimated that about 90 per cent of the literature of Classical Greece is irretrievably lost.

Although sources mentioned in the Bible – such as the book of the Wars of the Lord, the book of Jashar, the book of the Annals of Solomon and the book of the Annals of the Kings of Israel[1] are also irretrievably lost – the ancient library that we now know as the Bible has survived, doubtless because religious leaders, be they priests or church fathers, considered its message and contents were worthy of preservation.

SOLOMON

(970–930 BC)

SOLOMON BECOMES KING

Almost as soon as David's son Solomon (970–930 BC) succeeded to the throne of Israel, he moved ruthlessly to remove those who might challenge his authority. His half-brother Adonijah, who had previously tried to seize the throne, was executed. Abiathar was replaced as chief priest by Zadok. With Solomon's permission Benaiah killed Joab, David's army commander, and took over his position.

SOLOMON ASKS FOR WISDOM

Solomon went up to the 'high place' or shrine at Gibeon. It was here that the tabernacle,[1] having been salvaged from the Philistine attack on Shiloh, had been erected. After Solomon had offered a thousand burnt offerings, the Lord appeared to him in a dream and told him to ask for whatever he wanted.[2] Feeling his inexperience and the weight of his responsibilities, Solomon asked for a discerning heart to govern the people and to distinguish between right and wrong. Pleased with his answer, the Lord granted his request and also promised long life, wealth, honour and the death of his enemies.

A MAN OF PEACE

Solomon was a man of peace. Indeed his name means 'peaceful'. Under his rule Israel prospered and unprecedented wealth poured in. The book of Kings presents Israel as a numerous, happy and contented people, living in safety, each household under its own vine and fig tree.[3]

SOLOMON'S FOREIGN POLICY

Early in his reign Solomon made an alliance with Egypt, marrying Pharaoh's daughter. The

Wisdom Literature

SOLOMON AS A WRITER OF WISDOM LITERATURE

The writer of Kings records: 'God gave Solomon wisdom and very great insight and a breadth of understanding as measureless as the sand on the seashore. Solomon's wisdom was greater than the wisdom of all the men of the East [Mesopotamia] and greater than all the wisdom of Egypt'.[9] The story of Solomon's discerning the real mother in a dispute about a baby is a practical demonstration of his wisdom.[10] The writer of Kings also credits Solomon as being the author of three thousand proverbs and a thousand and five songs as well as recording his interest in plants, animals, birds, reptiles and fish. Several works of what is commonly called 'wisdom literature' are attributed to Solomon thus:

PROVERBS

The Hebrew book of Proverbs is full of pithy, wise sayings. Actually it contains a number of different collections of proverbs:

- Solomon's proverbs form the nucleus of the book (1:1–22:16).
- More proverbs of Solomon (25:1–29:27) copied by the men of Hezekiah, king of Judah (715–686 BC).
- 'The Words of the wise' (22:17–24:22)
- 'Additional sayings of the Wise' (24:23–34)
- 'The Words of Agur' (30:1–33)
- 'The Words of Lemuel' (31:1–9)
- 'In praise of a virtuous wife' (31:10–31).

Collections of proverbs can be traced in both Mesopotamia and Egypt to the third millennium BC. Of particular interest to the biblical book of Proverbs is the collection known as 'The Words of the Wise'. This is often compared with an Egyptian collection of proverbs called the 'Instruction of Amenemope', which was probably written about 1100 BC, and certainly no later than the end of the Twenty-first Dynasty, 945 BC. The 'Instruction of Amenemope' has thirty sections and it is sometimes suggested, probably misguidedly, that the text of Proverbs 22:20 be emended to reflect this, and that the 'Words of the Wise' be divided into thirty sections accordingly. Some have argued that the author of the 'Words of the Wise' borrowed from Amenemope, but it is equally possible that both works drew from a common ancient heritage of wise advice.

ECCLESIASTES

The Hebrew title for the book traditionally called Ecclesiastes is of uncertain meaning. It could mean 'speaker' (in the assembly) or a 'collector of sayings'. The author is simply identified in the opening verse as a 'son of David'. Certainly the author's great projects and his statement in 2:7 that he had more herds and flocks than anyone in Jerusalem before him fits well with Solomon, who sacrificed 22,000 cattle and 120,000 sheep and goats at the dedication of the temple.[11]

SONG OF SONGS

Solomon's interest in nature finds further expression in many images drawn from nature in the erotic book of 'Song of Songs': for example, 'I am a rose of Sharon, a lily of the valleys' (Song of Songs 2:1). The work is attributed to Solomon in the opening verse.

OTHER WISDOM LITERATURE

The book of Job is difficult to place in terms of both place and date. Certainly Job and his comforters are non-Israelite, and Job's lifestyle fits well with the patriarchal age. The book explores a timeless and important question: why do the innocent suffer?

KEY

[1] 1 Chronicles 21:29; 2 Chronicles 1:5
[2] 1 Kings 3:5
[3] 1 Kings 4:20, 24–25
[4] 1 Kings 9:16
[5] 1 Kings 4:22–23
[6] 1 Kings 9:20–22
[7] 1 Kings 11:28
[8] 1 Kings 5:13–14
[9] 1 Kings 4:29–30
[10] 1 Kings 3:16–28
[11] 1 Kings 8:63

Solomon's administrative districts
Under Solomon Israel underwent profound change. The old tribal structures were insufficient to meet the fiscal demands of his expanded state. Solomon created new administrative districts, often disregarding the old tribal allotments. The figures following the names of Solomon's governors refer to the verse numbers of 1 Kings 4.

LEFT: Shiloh was an important religious and administrative centre during the time of the Samuel, and was the location of the tabernacle before it was moved to Gibeon.

RIGHT: Like Solomon, other ancient Near Eastern rulers sought to exploit the timber resources of Lebanon. On this stone relief, workmen of the Assyrian king Sargon (722–705 BC) are shown transporting timber by sea. From Khorsabad, Iraq.

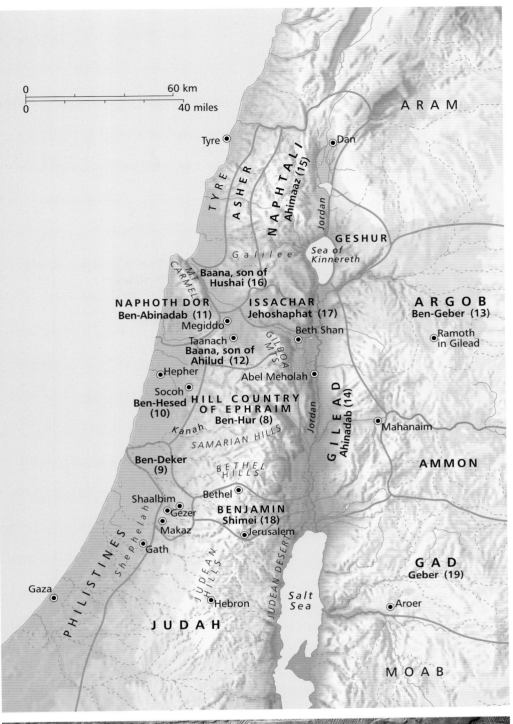

king in question was probably Siamun (979–960 BC) of the weak Twenty-first Dynasty. He attacked and burned the Canaanite town of Gezer, killed its inhabitants and then gave it as a wedding gift to his daughter, thus giving Solomon a modest addition to his territory.[4] Quite what provoked this Egyptian intervention is unknown. It may be that, with David dead, the Egyptians had hoped to re-establish themselves in Palestine, but, finding a force stronger than they had bargained for, thought it wiser to make peace.

Solomon found a valuable ally in Hiram, king of the Phoenician coastal city of Tyre in Lebanon. Hiram gave Solomon cedar and other wood for his building projects and Solomon gave him pressed olive oil in return. Solomon gave Hiram twenty towns in a predominantly non-Israelite border area of Galilee. Hiram was not impressed, calling them Cabul (meaning 'worthless'). Solomon recovered them at a later date.

SOLOMON'S ADMINISTRATION

The daily provisions for Solomon's court are listed as four tons of fine flour and eight tons of meal, thirty head of cattle, a hundred sheep and goats, as well as deer, gazelles, roebucks and choice fowl.[5] In contrast to David, Solomon did not mount campaigns of foreign conquest. With expenses mounting and revenue from tribute not increasing proportionately, Solomon imposed heavy taxation on his subjects, reorganizing the land into twelve administrative districts, each having its own governor. Each district was responsible for providing for the court for one month a year. Although in some cases these districts coincided with the old tribal areas, more often tribal boundaries were disregarded. The Canaanite territories were included, as Solomon sought to integrate the Canaanite population more thoroughly within his realm. Judah too may have had its own governor with responsibility for raising revenue.

FORCED LABOUR

Non-Israelites who remained in the territory Solomon controlled were 'conscripted for his slave labour force'[6] and 'Solomon had 70,000 carriers and 80,000 stonecutters in the hills' (1 Kings 5:15). Israelites had to work as labourers too.[7] For example, thirty thousand were sent to Lebanon to cut timber, spending one month there and two months at home.[8] It was this forced labour, so resented, that proved a major factor in the break-up of Solomon's kingdom immediately after his death.

SOLOMON'S TEMPLE

(967–960 BC)

SOLOMON BUILDS THE TEMPLE

Solomon's father, David, had been prohibited by the Lord from building a temple to the Lord at Jerusalem, 'because you are a warrior and have shed blood' (1 Chronicles 28:3). So it fell to Solomon to build the Temple, which he commenced in his fourth year (967 BC) and which took seven years.

The Temple is described in detail in 1 Kings 6:1–10, 14–38 and 2 Chronicles 3:3–17. It was sixty cubits long, twenty wide and thirty high (27 m by 9 m by 13.5 m or 89 ft by 30 ft by 44 ft), built of stone, shaped off-site, and composed of three main sections:

- the porch or portico

- the main hall or holy place

- the inner sanctuary, also known as the most holy place or 'holy of holies'. It was here that the ark of the covenant, which held the ten commandments, was placed.

Solomon also built three storeys of side rooms around the sides and rear. These in later times were to function as an arsenal, treasury and library. On each side of the porch Solomon placed bronze pillars, one named Jakin, the other Boaz. These were 18 cubits (about 8 m or 26 ft 3 in) high, with capitals 5 cubits (about 2 m or 6 ft 6 in) high. Solomon lined the interior walls with cedar from Lebanon. The cedars of the Lebanon mountains were a frequently exploited source of timber in the ancient world.

KING SOLOMON'S GOLD

Solomon covered the whole of the inside of the Temple, including the walls and floors, with gold. Certainly Solomon was not short of it. His annual revenue of gold, as reported in 1 Kings 10:14, was 666 talents (about 23 tons) and the visiting queen of Sheba (Yemen) gave him a present of 120 talents (about 4 tons).

One source of gold was Ophir, which is probably to be located in western Arabia, either in the gold-bearing areas north of Wadi Baysh or between Mecca and Medina. Incidentally, a Hebrew *ostracon* found at Tell Qasile, near modern Tel Aviv, and dated to the first half of the eighth century BC, reads 'Gold of Ophir for Beth Horon 30 shekels'.

The amount of Solomon's gold was immense, but it is not unique in the ancient world. Egyptian temples were sometimes lined with plates of gold, indeed the holes that held the securing joints still survive in places. The pharaohs Tuthmosis III (1479–1425 BC), Ramesses II (1279–1213 BC) and Ramesses III (1184–1153 BC) are all known to have plated temples with gold. A similar practice is known from Mesopotamia, witness Entemena of Lagash (c. 2400 BC) and the Assyrian kings Esarhaddon (681–669 BC) and Ashurbanipal (669–627 BC). Even larger amounts of gold are attested in antiquity. Pythius king of Lydia gave the Persian king Xerxes (486–465 BC) 3,993,000 gold darics, which amounts to 61.5 tons. The Roman emperor Trajan (AD 98–117) captured at least 4,394 tons of gold from the Dacians (modern Romania). The British gold reserves for 2005 were a mere 320 tons.

Interestingly, in Egypt it is a near contemporary of Solomon, the pharaoh Osorkon I (924–889 BC), who in the early years of his reign is credited with giving the largest recorded donation of gold to Egyptian temples, an estimated 18 tons. In total he gave about 383 tons of precious metals to Egyptian temples. Osorkon's father was Shoshenq (945–924 BC). He is commonly identified with Shishak, who attacked Judah in the fifth year of the reign of Solomon's son Rehoboam (926 BC) and carried off some of the treasures of the Temple of the Lord and of the royal palace, including the gold shields that Solomon had made.[1] Thus it may be that the last recorded mention of Solomon's gold is Osorkon's generous gifts to the Egyptian temples. And who knows what happened to the gold after that?

THE TEMPLE FURNISHINGS

In 1 Kings 7:23–26 we read of a huge, bronze, hemispherical water-tank for ceremonial purification called 'the Sea'. It rested on twelve bronze bulls, three facing to each point of the compass. It was 10 cubits (4.6 m or 15 ft) in diameter and had an estimated capacity of about 44 kilolitres (11,623 gallons).

At Amathus in Cyprus, 10 km (6 miles) east of Limassol, two huge stone vessels for ceremonial purification were found. One was taken to the Louvre Museum in Paris in 1865; the other, more fragmentary example is still *in situ*. The Louvre vessel has a diameter of 3.19 m (10 ft 6 in).

Among the furniture that Solomon had made were ten moveable wheeled bronze stands. These supported bronze basins holding some 880 litres (230 gallons) each. A 10-cm-high (4 in) bronze stand dated 1050–1000 BC has been found at Megiddo in northern Israel. Similar stands, some with wheels still in place, dating from twelfth century BC, have been found at several locations in Cyprus. In addition to the bronze items, furnishings of gold are listed, including a golden altar, table, lampstands and bowls.

Bronze wheeled stand for supporting a vessel, twelfth to thirteenth centuries BC. The openwork scene shows a harpist. From Cyprus.

However from the Bible's perspective the magnificence of the Temple was not its greatest feature, rather it was the visible presence of God. 'Then the temple of the Lord was filled with a cloud, and the priests could not perform their service because of the cloud, for the glory of the Lord filled the temple of God' (2 Chronicles 5:13b–14).

THE FATE OF SOLOMON'S TEMPLE

In 586 BC the commander of the Babylonian imperial guard, Nebuzaradan, set fire to the Temple of the Lord.[2] No trace of it has been found, although some would argue that an ivory pomegranate which mysteriously appeared on the antiquities market in 1979 inscribed '(property) of the house (of the Lord), sacred for the

priests' was possibly an ivory pommel that adorned the sceptre of a high-ranking priest in the Temple. We should note that the Israel Antiquities Authority has since pronounced the pomegranate a fake, although this is not accepted by all scholars. Pomegranates are mentioned a number of times in the description of the Temple as a decorative motif.[3] Later building work, especially by King Herod, probably obliterated all traces of Solomon's Temple.

The Babylonian army broke up the bronze pillars, the wheeled stands and the bronze 'Sea' and carried the bronze away to Babylon. The bronze and the gold and silver from the

Temple were doubtless reused, although the gold and silver goblets from the Temple feature in Belshazzar's feast, 539 BC.[4]

A possible reconstruction of Solomon's Temple and palace at Jerusalem. The partially cut-away Temple clearly shows its division into three sections of 1) the porch, 2) the main hall and 3) the inner sanctuary (the 'holy of holies'), where the ark of the covenant was kept. Outside in the courtyard the huge hemispherical water-tank known as 'the Sea' and the moveable wheeled bronze stands can be seen.

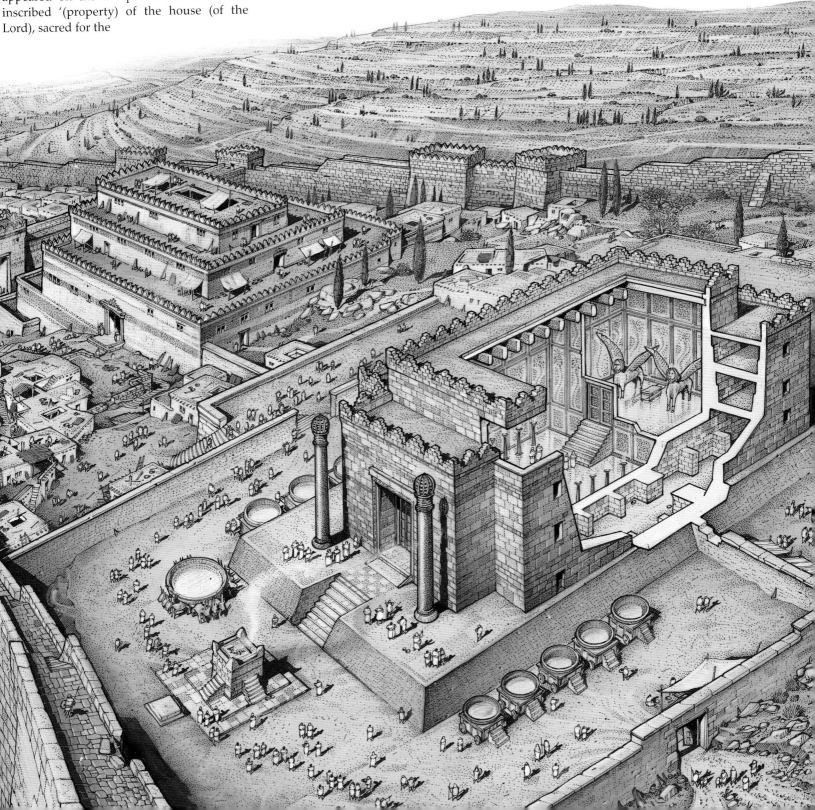

SOLOMON'S TRADE

(970–930 BC)

The books of Kings and Chronicles depict Solomon's reign as a kind of 'golden age' when trade flourished and wealth poured in. Some would dismiss these accounts as exaggerated or fictitious; but, seen in the broader context of international trading relations, evidence can be adduced.

RED SEA TRADE

Solomon had a fleet of trading ships, which acted in partnership with the ships of Hiram, king of Tyre. 'Once every three years it returned carrying gold, silver and ivory, and apes and baboons' (1 Kings 10:22b). This fleet was based at Ezion Geber, possibly Tell el-Kheleifeh at the northern end of the Gulf of Aqabah.[1] The last item in the list has been the subject of considerable debate. It was traditionally translated 'peacock', a native of south India. However, modern scholarship favours the identification 'baboon', which is based on an Egyptian word. The Egyptian queen Hatshepsut (1479–1457 BC) sent a trading expedition to Punt (eastern Sudan to the Red Sea and parts of Eritrea). Monkeys and baboons figure among the various creatures shown living in Punt on her reliefs at Deir el-Bahri, Egypt. So it is likely that Solomon, a number of centuries later, obtained the same creatures from the same source. Solomon also used this fleet to obtain gold from Ophir.

TRADE ELSEWHERE

Solomon's ships also went to Tarshish,[2] a word meaning 'refinery' and perhaps the Guadalquivir Valley in southern Spain or Sardinia. Solomon imported horses from Egypt and Keweh, classical Cilicia, the Çukurova plain of south-east Turkey, famed in antiquity as a source of good horses. The price of a horse at 150 shekels of silver[3] can be compared with 200 shekels at the Syrian port of Ugarit in the thirteenth century BC.

THE QUEEN OF SHEBA

Solomon's most famous visitor was the queen of Sheba from the kingdom of Saba (modern Yemen).[4] The state of Saba thrived on the irrigated land around the town of Marib and had grown rich on the export of frankincense and myrrh. The queen of Sheba was overwhelmed by what she saw: 'I did not believe these things until I came and saw with my own eyes. Indeed not even half was told me; in wisdom and wealth you have far exceeded the report I heard' (1 Kings 10:7).

The motive for the queen of Sheba's extraordinary visit may have been more than just to test Solomon with hard questions.[5] Economic issues could have come to the fore. Possibly the arrival of Solomon's fleet at the southern end of the Red Sea posed a threat to the Sabeans' caravan-based trade in frankincense and myrrh and the queen's mission was to charm Solomon into an agreement. Such a long royal journey is not without historical precedent. For example, the Hittite prince Hishmi-Sharruma visited Egypt in the thirteenth century BC.

The nett effect of Solomon's trade was a great increase in national wealth. As the writer of Kings remarks hyperbolically: 'The king made silver as common in

An expedition sent by the Egyptian queen Hatshepsut (1479–1457 BC) surveys a myrrh tree in the land of Punt, modern eastern Sudan or Eritrea. Mortuary temple of Hatshepsut, Deir-el-Bahri, Egypt.

Jerusalem as stones, and cedar as plentiful as the sycamore-fig trees in the foothills [the Shephelah]' (1 Kings 10:27).

THE ARCHAEOLOGICAL EVIDENCE

Until now the evidence we have adduced for Solomon has been from neighbouring states and from periods not strictly contemporary at that. There is one feature that can be offered as direct evidence of Solomon's rule, although it should be said that some would date it later. The book of Kings[6] records that Solomon used forced labour to build the Temple, his own palace, the supporting terraces, the wall of Jerusalem, Hazor, Megiddo and Gezer. Remains of city gates at Hazor, Megiddo and Gezer have survived. All share remarkably similar dimensions and the same three-part plan, suggesting a common outline was used, as the plans opposite clearly show.

SOLOMON THE FOOLISH

In the latter part of Solomon's forty-year reign Israel was weakened by Hadad the Edomite (with support from Egypt) and Rezon, who took control of Damascus.[7] Solomon is recorded as having no fewer than 700 wives and 300 concubines, many of them non-Israelites, and thus he defied the Lord's instructions to Moses in two ways.[8] Solomon's harem, although large even by ancient standards, was not without parallel. Ramesses II (1279–1213 BC) of Egypt had 100 sons and 100 daughters. The Persian king Darius III (336–330 BC) lost 329 concubines when he fled from Alexander the Great.

Solomon built high places, unauthorized shrines where his wives could worship their gods.[9] This, according to the biblical writers, aroused the Lord's wrath and set in motion a chain of events that would divide Solomon's kingdom in two. Never again would all the twelve tribes of Israel have a single ruler.

Solomon's trade
Under Solomon Israel's trade expanded extensively. Contacts were made with Cilicia (south-east Turkey), lands along the Red Sea and Tarshish (perhaps southern Spain). His most famous visitor, the queen of Sheba, came from Sheba (modern Yemen).

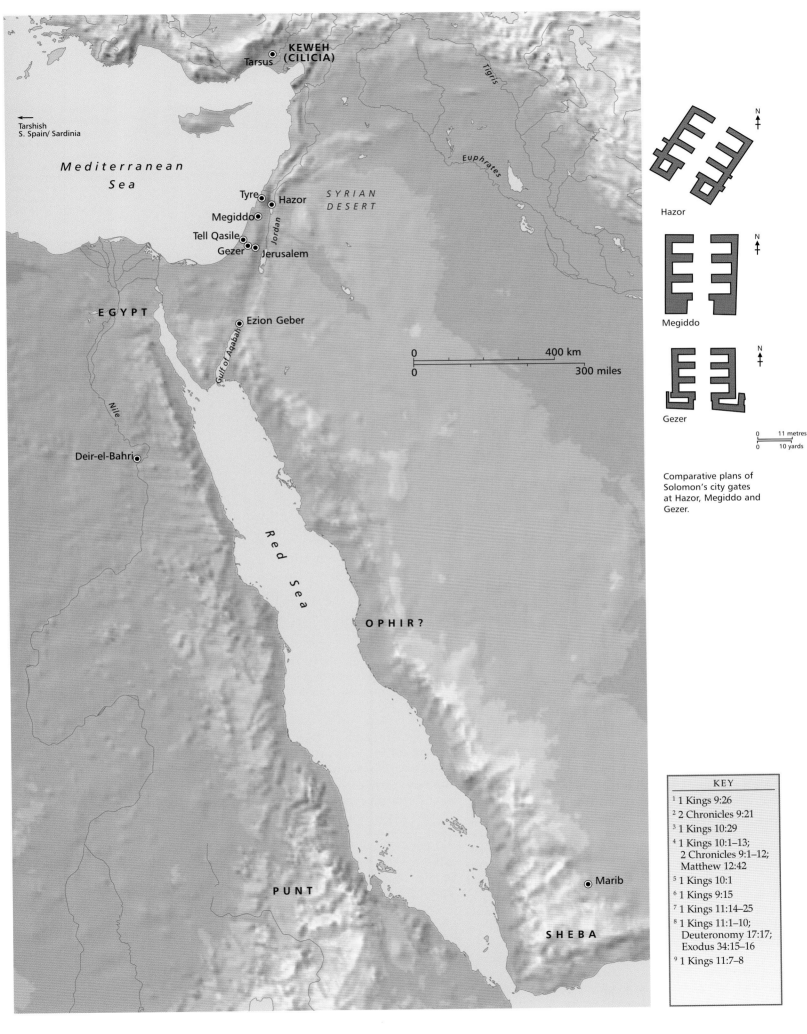

KEWEH
(CILICIA)

Tarsus

Tarshish
S. Spain/ Sardinia

*Mediterranean
Sea*

Tigris

Euphrates

Tyre
Hazor

*SYRIAN
DESERT*

Megiddo

Jordan

Tell Qasile
Gezer
Jerusalem

EGYPT

Ezion Geber

Gulf of Aqaba

Nile

0   400 km
0   300 miles

Deir-el-Bahri

Red Sea

OPHIR?

Marib

PUNT

SHEBA

Hazor

Megiddo

Gezer

0   11 metres
0   10 yards

Comparative plans of
Solomon's city gates
at Hazor, Megiddo and
Gezer.

KEY
[1] 1 Kings 9:26
[2] 2 Chronicles 9:21
[3] 1 Kings 10:29
[4] 1 Kings 10:1–13; 2 Chronicles 9:1–12; Matthew 12:42
[5] 1 Kings 10:1
[6] 1 Kings 9:15
[7] 1 Kings 11:14–25
[8] 1 Kings 11:1–10; Deuteronomy 17:17; Exodus 34:15–16
[9] 1 Kings 11:7–8

THE DIVISION OF THE KINGDOM

(930 BC)

Solomon's rule was not a 'golden age' for all his subjects.[1] Taxation to pay for his building projects and lavish court[2] and forced labour[3] fuelled resentment. Many found in a certain Jeroboam, son of Nebat, a former overseer of the forced labour force of the house of Joseph, a champion for their cause,[4] although the prophet Ahijah's premature prediction of Jeroboam's kingship forced Jeroboam to take sanctuary in Egypt until Solomon's death.

Solomon's successor, Rehoboam, insolently rejected the advice of his elders in favour of advice from a younger circle around him. His words: 'My father laid on you a heavy yoke; I will make it even heavier. My father scourged you with whips; I will scourge you with scorpions' (1 Kings 12:11) were hardly going to endear him to his subjects. When Rehoboam again rejected their demands, the ten northern tribes rallied around Jeroboam, turning their backs on Rehoboam and the house of David. 'What share do we have in David, what part in Jesse's son? To your tents, O Israel! Look after your own house, O David!' (1 Kings 12:16b).

The words of the ten northern tribes of Israel were to signal a significant event in Old Testament history: the division of the kingdom in 930 BC.

GEOGRAPHICAL CONSEQUENCES

With ten tribes seceding, only Judah and Benjamin were left to continue David's line in Jerusalem, although with Simeon's territory being surrounded by Judah they must have been included too. The Israelites had reverted to a division that had existed in the time of David, who had numbered 'Israel' and 'Judah' separately – a division perhaps forced on the country by the presence in its very centre of the Jebusite enclave of Jerusalem, until its capture by David.[5]

ISRAEL AND JUDAH GO SEPARATE WAYS

The Lord's prophet Shemiah averted civil war. The northern tribes under Jeroboam established their own kingdom, which took the name Israel, although somewhat confusingly the prophet Hosea called it 'Ephraim' (after the leading tribe) and the prophet Amos called it 'the house of Joseph' (Amos 5:6).

Jeroboam realized the power and influence the Temple in Jerusalem could have over his fledgling kingdom. If the people were to offer sacrifices there, they would again give their allegiance to Rehoboam king of Judah and would kill him. His solution was to create new religious centres. Golden calves were set up at Bethel and Dan, priests who were not Levites were appointed and a new religious calendar was instituted. These were the sins of Jeroboam, son of Nebat, as remembered by subsequent generations. Indeed, from the point of view of the biblical writers, the northern kingdom of Israel was under God's curse from the accession of Jeroboam. It would only be a matter of time before its people would be exiled.

Israel lacked the stability that on the whole characterized its southern neighbour, Judah. Whereas David's descendants ruled Judah in an unbroken line, this was not the case in the new Israel of ten tribes. Baasha, Zimri, Omri,

cult centre

0   40 km
0   30 miles

Dan (Tell el-Qadi)

Jordan

Galilee   Sea of Kinnereth

MT CARMEL

GILBOA MTS

ISRAEL

Samaria   Tirzah

Kanah   Shechem

Jordan

BETHEL HILLS

Bethel

Jerusalem

Shephelah

PHILISTIA

JUDEAN HILLS

JUDEAN DESERT

Salt Sea

JUDAH

Jehu, Shallum, Menahem, Pekah and Hoshea were all usurpers. Furthermore, the northern kingdom of Israel had a number of capitals: first Shechem, then Tirzah and finally Samaria.[6]

THE HIGH PLACE AT DAN

Remains of Jeroboam's cultic centre at Dan (Tell el-Qadi) have been found in Level IVA. Of a golden calf, unsurprisingly, there was no trace. However an 18-metre-long (59-ft) structure built of dressed stone may be the remains of the 'high place'. Three storerooms were found, one of which contained two storage jars of more than 300 litres (79 gallons) capacity, decorated with snakes in relief. A courtyard showed traces of an altar and a broken incense stand. A sunken basin was found, which was probably a place where water for libations was stored.

The divided kingdoms: Israel and Judah

On Solomon's death in 930 BC, the kingdom of Israel was divided. In the north, eventually centering on Samaria, a kingdom called Israel was established. It was ruled by a succession of short-lasting dynasties. To the south around Jerusalem was the kingdom of Judah, ruled by an unbroken line of kings descended from David.

The high place at Dan (Tell el-Qadi).

KEY
[1] 1 Kings 4:24–25
[2] 1 Kings 4:22–23
[3] 1 Kings 5:13–17
[4] 1 Kings 11:28
[5] 2 Samuel 5:6–8; 24:9
[6] 1 Kings 12:25; 15:33; 16:24
[7] 1 Kings 22:51; 2 Kings 3:1
[8] 1 Kings 15:23
[9] 2 Kings 15:5

The Chronology of the Kings of Israel and Judah

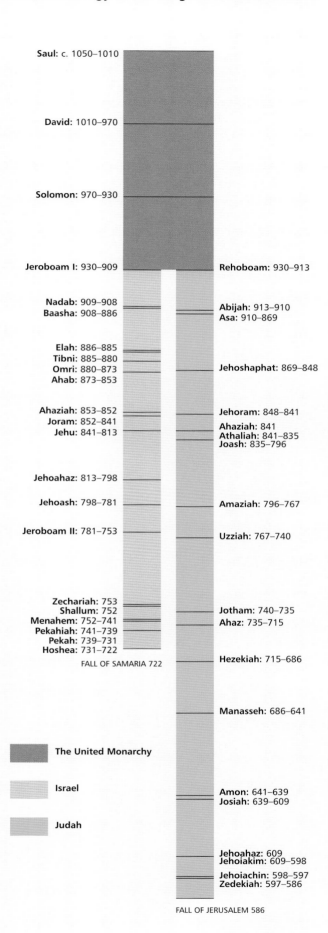

Saul: c. 1050–1010

David: 1010–970

Solomon: 970–930

Jeroboam I: 930–909   Rehoboam: 930–913

Nadab: 909–908   Abijah: 913–910
Baasha: 908–886   Asa: 910–869

Elah: 886–885
Tibni: 885–880
Omri: 880–873   Jehoshaphat: 869–848
Ahab: 873–853

Ahaziah: 853–852   Jehoram: 848–841
Joram: 852–841   Ahaziah: 841
Jehu: 841–813   Athaliah: 841–835
     Joash: 835–796

Jehoahaz: 813–798

Jehoash: 798–781   Amaziah: 796–767

Jeroboam II: 781–753   Uzziah: 767–740

Zechariah: 753
Shallum: 752   Jotham: 740–735
Menahem: 752–741   Ahaz: 735–715
Pekahiah: 741–739
Pekah: 739–731
Hoshea: 731–722
FALL OF SAMARIA 722   Hezekiah: 715–686

Manasseh: 686–641

The United Monarchy

Israel

Judah

Amon: 641–639
Josiah: 639–609

Jehoahaz: 609
Jehoiakim: 609–598

Jehoiachin: 598–597
Zedekiah: 597–586

FALL OF JERUSALEM 586

The Chronology of the Divided Kingdoms (930–586 BC)

TO REDUCE CONFUSION

The book of Kings details the history of the northern kingdom of Israel until its exile to Assyria in 722 BC and of the southern kingdom of Judah, centred on Jerusalem, until its exile to Babylon in 586 BC. As the focus shifts from Israel to Judah and back again in this period, we try to keep the histories of Israel and Judah as separate as possible to minimize confusion. Identical or very similar names, such as Jehoram of Judah and Joram of Israel or Joash of Judah and Jehoash of Israel, do not help. And sometimes different names are used for the same king: for example, Uzziah or Azariah of Judah. We can only be grateful that Ahaziah of Israel was not contemporary with Ahaziah of Judah!

SYNCHRONISMS

Even a cursory reading of the book of Kings shows that there is an abundance of data that should enable us to construct a detailed chronology. The kings of Israel are frequently tied into the chronological framework of the kings of Judah and vice versa. For example, 'in the fifteenth year of Amaziah, son of Joash, king of Judah, Jeroboam, son of Jehoash, king of Israel, became king in Samaria' (2 Kings 14:23). This is called a synchronism. Unfortunately these synchronisms, far from helping to tie the two chronologies together, seem to highlight differences and further complicate the picture.

AN EXTERNAL REFERENCE POINT

Clearly an external reference point would be of great value. This is provided by the chronology of Assyria. There, years were named after the king and then his important officials, called eponyms, usually in a standardized order. The fixed point in these lists is a solar eclipse during the eponymate of Bur-sagale in the reign of the Assyrian king Ashur-dan III, which can be pinpointed astronomically to 15 June 763 BC. This enables us to work out the dates for the kings of Assyria from 910 BC onwards.

COUNTING DIFFERENTLY

Between Ahab and Jehu the Bible places the two-year reign of Ahaziah and the twelve years of Joram,[7] which looks like a total of fourteen years. Yet if Ahab died in 853 BC, after contact with the Assyrian king Shalmaneser III in his sixth year (853 BC) and Jehu acceded and paid tribute in Shalmaneser's eighteenth year (841 BC) there is only space for twelve years. The explanation is that the ancients counted inclusively; parts of years were counted as wholes. Thus we have one full year plus eleven full years equalling the required twelve.

The complete picture is not quite so simple. Israel and Judah used different methods of computing regnal years. To begin with, following Egyptian practice, Israel counted the king's first year from his actual accession. Judah, following Assyrian practice, counted the king's first year only from the start of the New Year after his accession. The period between the king's accession and the end of that calendar year is sometimes called 'the accession year'. This continued until the early eighth century BC, when Judah adopted the other method.

If that is not enough, add the observation that two calendars appear to have been in operation, one beginning in the spring, the other in the autumn!

CO-REGENCIES

The last principle in operation is one we have a hint of in the book of Kings itself: 'In the fifth year of Joram son of Ahab king of Israel, when Jehoshaphat was king of Judah, Jehoram son of Jehoshaphat began his reign as king of Judah' (2 Kings 8:16). Here, Jehoram became king while his father was still alive, a phenomenon called 'co-regency'. The remaining conflicts in the data are virtually all solved by the postulation of a number of other co-regencies. Some make sound political sense, as in the case of Jehoshaphat, king of Judah, who became co-regent when his father Asa developed diseased feet,[8] and Jotham, king of Judah who became co-regent in 752 BC when his father Uzziah (Azariah) was smitten with a serious skin disease, traditionally but anachronistically translated as 'leprosy'.[9]

IN PERSPECTIVE

When all the above factors are taken into account a chronological scheme emerges that is about 99 per cent reliable. For the remaining problems there may be hitherto not understood, additional factors coming into play. Emendation of the text should not be ruled out (as in the case of 2 Kings 17:1 where for 'twelfth' perhaps we should read 'fourth'); but, given the extraordinarily good state of the data, it should only be considered as a last resort.

THE NEIGHBOURS OF ISRAEL AND JUDAH

THE LEGACY OF DAVID AND SOLOMON

Under David, Israel conquered many but not all of its neighbours. To the north, Hiram of Tyre and other Phoenician kings ruled an area along the Mediterranean coast approximating to modern Lebanon. Further south along the Mediterranean coast the Philistines maintained their independence. To the east across the Jordan River, and to the east and south of the Dead Sea, David conquered Ammon, Moab and Edom. After defeating Hadadezer of Zobah, David apparently gained control over a stretch of Syria up to the River Euphrates. But in the years that followed the death of Solomon these areas regained their independence.

AMMON

The kingdom of Ammon was centred on the great citadel of Rabbath-Ammon (now Amman, the capital of Jordan). The Ammonites were the descendants of Ben-ammi, the son of Abraham's nephew Lot and his younger daughter.[1] The area to the west, stretching to the Jordan Valley between the Jabbok and Arnon Rivers, was occupied by Amorites.

MOAB

The core of the kingdom of Moab was the plateau between the 500-metre-deep (1,640-ft) gorge of the Arnon River and the Zered Brook, to the east of the Dead Sea. Its chief town was Kir Hareseth, now the impressive stronghold of Kerak. The area north of the Arnon River was called the *Mishor* or Plateau of Moab. The Moabites were the descendants of Lot and his elder daughter. Ruth, the great-grandmother of David, was from Moab. Moab was a major sheep-rearing area, at one time obliged to deliver an annual tribute to Israel of 100,000 lambs and the wool of 100,000 rams.[2]

EDOM

The Edomites were the descendants of Jacob's older brother, Esau. They occupied land south of the Dead Sea and south-west of the Zered Brook. This rugged mountainous area was also known as Mount Seir, meaning 'hairy' because it was covered in thick shrub-forests. It included the Arabah, or Wilderness of Edom, the great depression connecting the Dead Sea to the Red Sea. Its capital Sela may be identified with Petra, which was later to become the spectacular 'rose-red', rock-cut capital of the Nabataean Arabs.

SOUTH TO THE RED SEA

South of a line from Gaza to Beersheba and extending eastwards to the south of the Dead Sea was the Wilderness of Zin. This vast area, which forms the northern extension of the Sinai Desert, receives less than 200 mm (8 in) annual rainfall and thus cannot support settled agriculture. Along with Edom it was an area over which Judah sought a measure of control. The ports of Ezion Geber (possibly Tell el-Kheleifeh) and Elath at the head of the Gulf of Aqabah gave Judah access to the Red Sea with its valuable trade.[3]

THE PHILISTINES

Four of the five Philistine cities – Ekron, Ashdod, Ashkelon and Gaza – remained independent of Israelite or Judean rule. Only Gath came under Judean control.

LEBANON

The hills of northern Galilee are divided from the Lebanon range to the north by the deep gorge of the Litani River, which flows into the Mediterranean a few kilometres south of Tyre. The mountains, which rise to 3,088 m (10,131 ft) and are snow-covered for some six months a year, explain the term 'Lebanon', which means 'white'. Lebanon's conifers and cedars provided the finest timber in the ancient Near East, being sought by the rulers of Mesopotamia and Egypt, as well as Solomon who obtained the wood for the Lord's Temple in Jerusalem from here.[4] East of the Lebanon range is the Biqa Valley, which, being in the rain shadow, has an annual rainfall of only 250 mm (10 in). Through this valley flow the rivers Litani and Orontes, south and north respectively, into the Mediterranean Sea. To the east of the

LEFT: Cedars growing in the mountains of Lebanon.

BELOW: The rock-cut city of Petra, Jordan, perhaps to be identified with Sela of the Old Testament. The Nabatean temple or tomb of el-Khazne is in view here.

Biqa is the Anti-Lebanon range, whose highest peak is Mount Hermon (also called Sirion or Senir) at 2,814 m (9,232 ft). The Mediterranean coast of Lebanon was blessed with harbours around which grew a number of port cities, inhabited by the Phoenicians, of which Tyre, Sidon and Byblos are arguably the most famous.

The neighbours of Israel and Judah
Many of the states that were neighbours of Israel and Judah at one time had come under David's rule.

ACROSS THE SEA

The Phoenicians of the Lebanese coast were competent seafarers. Solomon enlisted the help of the sailors of Hiram, king of Tyre for his trading ventures on the Red Sea. Essentially the Israelites were a land-loving people, who showed little enthusiasm for seafaring, as the psalmist makes clear: 'They mounted up to the heavens and went down to the depths; in their peril their courage melted away. They reeled and staggered like drunken men; they were at their wits' end. Then they cried out to the Lord in their trouble and he brought them out of their distress' (Psalm 107:26–28).

SYRIA

To the east of the Anti-Lebanon range lies the country now called Syria. This was the name the Romans gave to the area, including Palestine, when Pompey conquered it in 63 BC and made it a Roman province. In Old Testament times the region around Damascus and further north was called Aram. David made alliances with the Aramean kings of Geshur (to the east of Lake Galilee) and Hamath. He conquered Aram-Zobah (north of Damascus) thus extending his rule to the Euphrates River. Damascus asserted its independence in the reign of Solomon when a certain Rezon gained control there. Later kings of Damascus, such as Ben-Hadad II, Hazael and Ben-Hadad III, repeatedly clashed with the northern kingdom of Israel.

EAST OF THE JORDAN

Although Bashan and Gilead, east of the River Jordan, were part of the Promised Land and thus not Israel's neighbours, for the sake of completeness we shall take a brief look at these lands across the Jordan. Here the icy desert winds that buffet the eastern hills in winter prevent the cultivation of olives and in places vines.

● East of Lake Galilee and north of the gorge of the Yarmuk River lay the region of Bashan. A basaltic tableland with rich red soil resting on beds of ash, Bashan was a fertile region, renowned for its wheat and livestock, hence the expressions 'bulls of Bashan' and 'cows of Bashan'.[5] The region of Bashan was alloted to the tribe of Manasseh.

● The region of Gilead lay north of a line from Heshbon to the Dead Sea and extended to the Yarmuk River. It was alloted to the tribes of Manasseh and Gad. In antiquity Gilead was forested and was renowned for its medicinal balm.[6] The Ishmaelites to whom Joseph was sold as a slave were coming from Gilead, laden with two medicinal products, gum tragacanth and balsam, and ladanum,[7] a perfume derived from the cistus or rock rose. Gilead is bisected by the gorge of the Jabbok River, which flows into the Jordan. On the floor of the Jabbok Valley lay the town of Penuel, where Jacob wrestled with the angel.[8] In a wider sense 'Gilead' was sometimes used of all the Israelite lands east of the Jordan River, to include all the area from Bashan in the north as far as the Arnon River.

THE KINGS OF ISRAEL

(930–741 BC)

THE DYNASTY OF OMRI

As we have seen, the northern kingdom of Israel was characterized by instability, with usurpers seizing the throne. The usurper Omri established a dynasty that brought relative stability to Israel. Although the Bible gives only six verses to Omri's reign (880–873 BC),[1] it is clear from other sources that he was an important king. Omri's conquest of Moab is recorded on the famous Moabite Stone, now in the Louvre Museum in Paris (see below). It was Omri who established Samaria as the capital of Israel, which is why the Assyrians called Israel the 'house of Omri' long after Omri's dynasty had disappeared.

Omri was succeeded by his son Ahab (873–853 BC). The first book of Kings says: 'Ahab son of Omri did more evil in the eyes of the Lord than any of those before him' (1 Kings 16:30). It singles out Ahab's Phoenician wife Jezebel for leading Israel into idolatry. Excavations at Samaria have revealed many fragments of carved ivory. These were probably the inlays for the furniture of Ahab's 'Ivory House'[2] and show Phoenician and Egyptian influence.

In a famous incident Ahab and Jezebel were rebuked by the prophet Elijah for arranging the murder of Naboth the Jezreelite in order to acquire his vineyard: dogs would lick up Ahab's blood in the place where they had licked up Naboth's blood and they would devour Jezebel by the wall of Jezreel.[3] When Ahab was slain in battle and brought by chariot to Samaria, dogs did indeed lick the blood from his chariot.[4]

THE DYNASTY OF JEHU

The prophet Elisha, prompted by the Lord, anointed the army commander Jehu as king.[5]

Routes of armies
- → Israel
- → Israel and Judah
- → Israel, Judah and Edom
- → Moab
- ● garrison town captured by Mesha
- ● town built by Mesha

0 — 20 km
0 — 20 miles

The Moabite campaign

1 Mesha king of Moab revolts against Israelite hegemony and captures Israelite garrison towns (2 Kings 3:5)

2 Joram king of Israel, enlisting the help of Jehoshaphat king of Judah and the king of Edom, attacks Moab from the south through the desert of Edom (2 Kings 3:9)

3 Mesha moves south to challenge the allies

4 Following the advice of the prophet Elisha the army digs ditches in the desert. Flash floods fill these with water. Thinking that the water glinting in the morning sunlight is blood, the Moabites advance and are resoundingly beaten (2 Kings 3:17–24)

5 The allies lay siege to the Moabite capital of Kir Hareseth (Kerak) (2 Kings 3:25)

6 The king of Moab offers his firstborn son as a sacrifice on the city wall. This apparently causes the allies to break off the siege and return home (2 Kings 3:27).

The Moabite Stone (or Mesha stela)

In 1868 a German missionary based in Jerusalem, F.A. Klein, was shown a slab at Dhiban (biblical Dibon) in modern Jordan that was c.1.1 m (3 ft 7 in) high and inscribed with 34 lines of writing. During negotiations for the stone's purchase C. S. Clermont-Ganneau, working on behalf of the Louvre, had a 'squeeze' (cast) made of the whole inscription, which turned out to be a wise move, as the owners kindled a fire under the stone and poured water onto it to break it into fragments. Some of these were never recovered, but the cast more or less enables us to recover the text.

Written in c. 830 BC by Mesha, a king of Moab, the inscription is in the Moabite language (which has close similarities to Hebrew) and records: 'Omri was king of Israel and he oppressed Moab for many days' (lines 4–5).

Mesha continues: 'And Omri had taken possession of the land of Medeba and he lived in it his days and half the days of his son – forty years' (lines 7–8).

Mesha was eventually able to throw off Israelite rule.[9] He records that he captured some of the Lord's vessels: 'I took from there the vessels of the Lord' (lines 17–18).

This is the first mention outside the Hebrew Bible of the four consonants (YHWH in Hebrew) that constitute the name of the Lord.

KEY
[1] 1 Kings 16:23–28
[2] 1 Kings 22:39
[3] 1 Kings 21:19, 23
[4] 1 Kings 22:38
[5] 2 Kings 9:5–6
[6] 2 Kings 9:10, 35–36
[7] 2 Kings 14:25, 28
[8] 2 Kings 10:30
[9] 2 Kings 3:5

ABOVE: Ivory carving from Samaria, showing a winged sphinx wearing a wig and patterned kilt and standing in a lotus thicket.

BELOW: Jasper seal of Shema, servant of Jeroboam II (781–753 BC), Megiddo.

Pillared building at Hazor, once considered a stable, now identified as a storehouse.

Jehu brought Omri's dynasty to a violent end, not only killing Joram, king of Israel, but Ahaziah king of Judah too. Jehu also put to death the ministers of Baal, Ahab's surviving sons and Ahab's widow Jezebel. Of Jezebel, after she was slain by the usurper Jehu, only her skull, feet and hands remained: the rest of her was eaten by dogs.[6]

Right at the beginning of his reign Jehu (841–813 BC), or his ambassador, is shown giving tribute to the Assyrian king Shalmaneser III (859–824 BC) on his famous Black Obelisk from the Assyrian city of Nimrud. An inscription identifies Jehu as 'Jehu, son of Omri'. A long line of courtiers bring tribute: gold, silver and fruit. Israel thus had to acknowledge the growing power of Assyria.

Jehu's great-grandson Jeroboam II (781–753 BC), capitalizing on a weak Assyria, conquered much of Syria for Israel.[7] This had been predicted by the prophet Jonah. Jeroboam II's reign was characterized by increasing prosperity and with it idolatry. It is described vividly by the prophet Amos:

'You lie on beds inlaid with ivory and lounge on your couches.
You dine on choice lambs and fattened calves.
You strum away on your harps like David, and improvise on
* musical instruments.*
* You drink wine by the bowlful and use the finest lotions.'*
  AMOS 6:4–6

Splendid ivory carvings and large buildings found at the Israelite capital Samaria substantiate this prosperity archaeologically. In addition one hundred and two *ostraca* written in Hebrew were found in Samaria and are probably to be assigned to the reign of Jeroboam II. They record the receipts of wine and olive oil, probably tax payments, from estates in the vicinity of Samaria.

A splendid jasper seal with an inscription 'Belonging to Shema, servant of Jeroboam' was found at Megiddo. The Jeroboam is usually identified as Jeroboam II. However it was a prosperity that was not to last, as Amos himself goes on to predict:

'But you do not grieve over the ruin of Joseph. Therefore you will be among the first to go into exile, your feasting and lounging will end.'
AMOS 6:6b–7

The Lord had told Jehu that his dynasty would only last for four generations.[8] Zechariah, son of Jeroboam II, was assassinated by Shallum, who then took the throne, but for one month only, before he succumbed to another usurper, named Menahem (752–741 BC). Unfortunately for Israel, the fortunes of Assyria revived under their king Tiglath-pileser III (746–727 BC); within thirty years of Jeroboam II's death the Israelites were to be exiled to Assyria.

STABLES AT MEGIDDO?

Excavations at Megiddo have revealed an extensive series of buildings, sometimes identified as stables, capable of accommodating up to 450 horses. There was a central passage about 3 m (10 ft) wide, flanked by two rows of stone pillars which were considered both tie-posts and supports for the roof. Mangers, grain storage facilities and a mud brick water tank also formed part of the complex. When first discovered they were assigned to Solomon, partly because of the reference to 'chariot cities' in 1 Kings 10:26. This assignment is no longer tenable, as the south-east corner of the complex lies over a building of Solomon's time. The complex is now regarded as the work of Ahab, who is known to have put two thousand chariots into battle against the Assyrians at Qarqar on the River Orontes in Syria in 853 BC. The scholarly consensus is that they were not stables at all, but storehouses like the surrounding buildings. Similar buildings at Hazor are also now considered storehouses.

THE HEBREW PROPHETS

(Ninth and eighth centuries BC)

The English word 'prophet' is derived from a Greek word which means one who 'forthtells' (speaks out), not 'foretells' (predicts). Even in the eighteenth century BC at Mari in Syria there were individuals giving out the words of the gods. In the Old Testament the first term to be used was 'seer', but this was later replaced by 'prophet', a term incidentally used of Abraham, Moses and Samuel.[1]

ELIJAH AND ELISHA

The book of Kings describes the activities of two prophets of the ninth century BC, Elijah and his successor Elisha. During the reign of Ahab (873–853 BC) Elijah announces a drought as a sign of divine displeasure. Three and a half years into the drought[2] on Mount Carmel Elijah challenges four hundred and fifty prophets of the storm god Baal to send fire from heaven, and he demonstrates the Lord to be the true and living God when he sends fire to consume a water sodden sacrifice.[3] Pressing home his advantage, Elijah has the prophets of Baal put to death. Torrential rain ends the drought, but Elijah seemingly overwhelmed by depression flees into the desert and asks to die. Restored by the Lord, Elijah is not afraid to confront King Ahab over his confiscation of Naboth's vineyard.

When Elijah is taken up into heaven in a whirlwind,[4] his anointed successor Elisha inherits his cloak and with it a double portion of his spirit. Elisha is credited with several miracles, even of curing Naaman, an Aramean army commander, of a terrible skin disease[5] and anointing Jehu as king of Israel and Hazael as king of Damascus. Often, it seems, a company of adherent prophets is in attendance.[6]

THE WRITING PROPHETS

For all their activities Elijah and Elisha left no record of their spoken words except that which is preserved in the book of Kings. Yet some 22 per cent of the Old Testament is given over to the recorded words of a number of prophets. There are fifteen in the Hebrew Bible: Isaiah, Jeremiah, Ezekiel and the Book of the Twelve, (sometimes called the 'Minor Prophets'). In the Christian classification, the book of Daniel is also placed among the prophets.

HOSEA

According to the list of kings in Hosea 1:1, Hosea prophesied during the mid-eighth century BC. He laid much of the blame for Israel's moral decline on the Israelites' spiritual adultery with other gods. Israel's condition was likened to that of Hosea's adulterous wife, Gomer. The Israelites, or Ephraim as they are called, looked successively to Egypt and Assyria hoping for help.[7] Yet Hosea pleaded with the Israelites to turn back to God and avoid his coming judgment: 'Return, O Israel, to the Lord, your God. Your sins have been your downfall! Take words with you and return to the Lord. Say to him: "Forgive all our sins and receive us graciously, that we may offer the fruit of our lips"' (Hosea 14:1–2).

JOEL

The short book of Joel carries no reference to contemporary kings and is thus difficult to date. It describes devastations wrought by successive plagues of locusts. Such devastation can be observed in the modern world, where locusts are known to cover 370 square kilometres (150 square miles) at a time at a density of over 600,000 per hectare (250,000 per acre). Joel urges the people to repent.

'"Even now", declares the Lord,
"return to me with all your heart,
with fasting and weeping and mourning."
Rend your heart and not your garments.
Return to the Lord your God,
for he is gracious and compassionate,
slow to anger and abounding in love,
and he relents from sending calamity.'

JOEL 2:12–13

The Lord promises restoration: 'I will repay you for the years the locusts have eaten – the mature locust and the newly hatched locust, the young locust and the juvenile locust' (Joel 2:25, author's translation).

AMOS

Amos was a shepherd from Tekoa in Judah (Khirbet Tequ'a) and one who tended sycamore-fig trees.[8] Possessing an acute sense of social justice, he directed most of his prophecies at the prosperous but corrupt society of Israel under Jeroboam II (781–753 BC). He was thus a contemporary of Hosea. Israel, in Amos's view, was rotten to the core. It was only a matter of time until they would all be exiled. 'Gilgal will surely go into exile and Bethel will be reduced to nothing' (Amos 5:5b) and '"Therefore I will send you into exile beyond Damascus," says the Lord, whose name is God Almighty' (Amos 5:27). Yet he too concludes his prophecy with a promise of ultimate hope.[9]

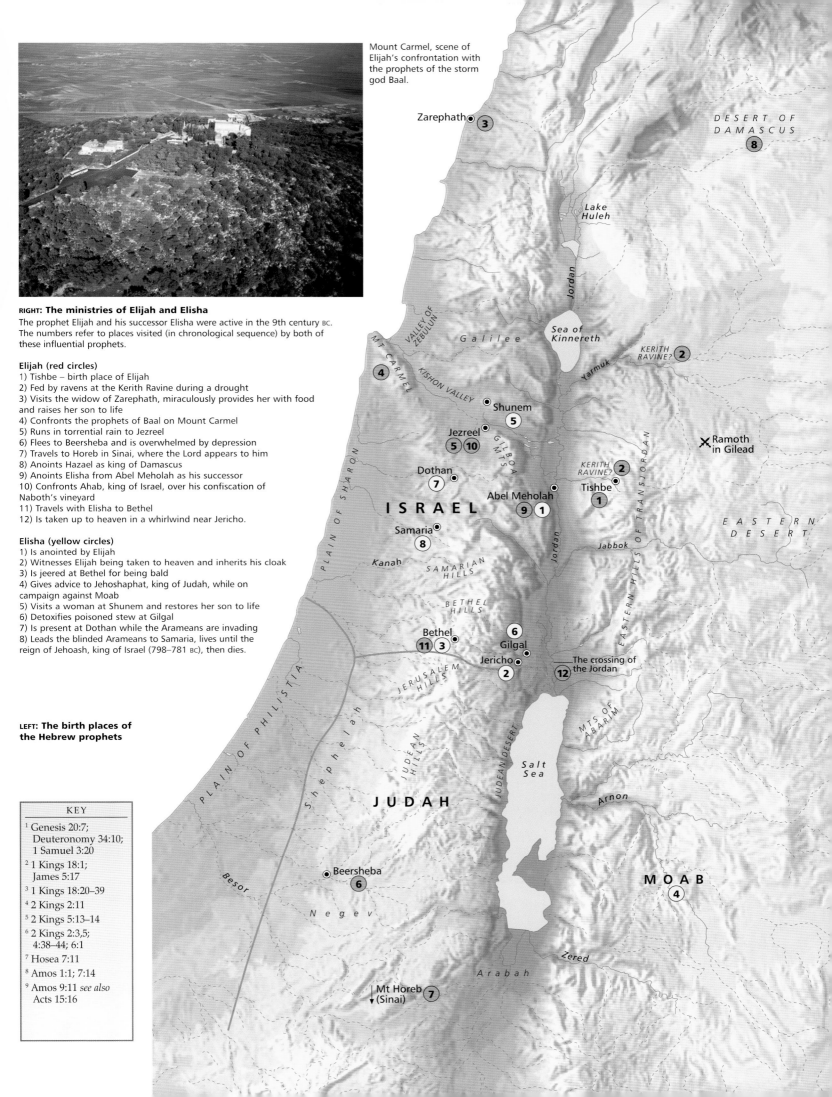

Mount Carmel, scene of Elijah's confrontation with the prophets of the storm god Baal.

RIGHT: **The ministries of Elijah and Elisha**
The prophet Elijah and his successor Elisha were active in the 9th century BC. The numbers refer to places visited (in chronological sequence) by both of these influential prophets.

Elijah (red circles)
1) Tishbe – birth place of Elijah
2) Fed by ravens at the Kerith Ravine during a drought
3) Visits the widow of Zarephath, miraculously provides her with food and raises her son to life
4) Confronts the prophets of Baal on Mount Carmel
5) Runs in torrential rain to Jezreel
6) Flees to Beersheba and is overwhelmed by depression
7) Travels to Horeb in Sinai, where the Lord appears to him
8) Anoints Hazael as king of Damascus
9) Anoints Elisha from Abel Meholah as his successor
10) Confronts Ahab, king of Israel, over his confiscation of Naboth's vineyard
11) Travels with Elisha to Bethel
12) Is taken up to heaven in a whirlwind near Jericho.

Elisha (yellow circles)
1) Is anointed by Elijah
2) Witnesses Elijah being taken to heaven and inherits his cloak
3) Is jeered at Bethel for being bald
4) Gives advice to Jehoshaphat, king of Judah, while on campaign against Moab
5) Visits a woman at Shunem and restores her son to life
6) Detoxifies poisoned stew at Gilgal
7) Is present at Dothan while the Arameans are invading
8) Leads the blinded Arameans to Samaria, lives until the reign of Jehoash, king of Israel (798–781 BC), then dies.

LEFT: **The birth places of the Hebrew prophets**

KEY
[1] Genesis 20:7; Deuteronomy 34:10; 1 Samuel 3:20
[2] 1 Kings 18:1; James 5:17
[3] 1 Kings 18:20–39
[4] 2 Kings 2:11
[5] 2 Kings 5:13–14
[6] 2 Kings 2:3,5; 4:38–44; 6:1
[7] Hosea 7:11
[8] Amos 1:1; 7:14
[9] Amos 9:11 *see also* Acts 15:16

Zarephath ③

DESERT OF DAMASCUS ⑧

Lake Huleh

KERITH RAVINE? ②

VALLEY OF ZEBULUN

Galilee

Sea of Kinnereth

MT CARMEL ④

KISHON VALLEY

Jordan

Yarmuk

Ramoth in Gilead ✕

Shunem ⊙
⑤

Jezreel ⊙
⑤ ⑩

GILBOA MTS

KERITH RAVINE? ②

Dothan ⊙
⑦

Abel Meholah ⊙
⑨ ①

Tishbe ⊙
①

EASTERN DESERT

ISRAEL

Jabbok

EASTERN HILLS OF TRANSJORDAN

PLAIN OF SHARON

Samaria ⊙
⑧

Kanah

SAMARIAN HILLS

Jordan

BETHEL HILLS

Bethel ⊙
⑪ ③

Gilgal ⊙
⑥

JERUSALEM HILLS

Jericho ⊙
②

The crossing of the Jordan ⑫

PLAIN OF PHILISTIA

Shephelah

JUDEAN HILLS

JUDEAN DESERT

Salt Sea

MTS OF ABARIM

Arnon

JUDAH

Besor

Beersheba ⊙
⑥

Negev

MOAB ④

Zered

Arabah

Mt Horeb (Sinai) ⑦

ASSYRIA: THE THREAT FROM THE NORTH

(Mid-ninth century to 722 BC)

ASSYRIA'S RISE

Some 900 km (560 miles) to the north-east of Israel lay the land of Assyria. Now situated in northern Iraq, it is a mountainous land watered by the River Tigris, which rises in the uplands of eastern Turkey. In the early ninth century BC the Assyrian army marched ever further afield to secure its frontiers and press home its demands for tribute from the surrounding states. The Assyrian king Ashurnasirpal II (884–859 BC) is known to have launched at least fourteen major expeditions during his twenty-five years on the throne. In his inscriptions he frequently gloried in his own cruelty (see page 87). To celebrate the construction of his new palace at Kalhu (Hebrew Calah, modern Nimrud) some 35 km (22 miles) south of Mosul, Ashurnasirpal hosted a sumptuous ten-day banquet for 69,574 people (see page 87).

In 853 BC Ashurnasirpal's successor, Shalmaneser III (859–824 BC), fought an alliance including the Israelite king Ahab at Qarqar on the Orontes in Syria. Assyrian records state that Ahab put 2,000 chariots into the battle. Later in his reign Shalmaneser met another Israelite king. In 841 BC Jehu, or his ambassador, is shown giving tribute to Shalmaneser on his famous Black Obelisk from Nimrud (now in the British Museum). A long line of courtiers bring tribute – gold, silver and fruit. Representatives of other states bring elephants, Bactrian camels and monkeys.

ASSYRIA IN DECLINE

Thirty-one years of Shalmaneser III's 35-year reign were devoted to war. After his death in 824 BC weaker Assyrian monarchs lost much of Syria to the Aramean kingdom of Damascus, which in turn also reduced Jehu's territory,[1] and in the first half of the eighth century BC provincial governors are known to have exercised great power over vast tracts of land to the detriment of the central Assyrian monarchy. It is in this period that the book of Kings places the Israelite prophet Jonah, who predicts the expansion of the northern kingdom of Israel under Jeroboam II (781–753 BC).[2]

JONAH

The book of Jonah narrates how, at first, Jonah resisted God's call to go to Nineveh, one of the main cities of Assyria, and proclaim the Lord's impending judgement against the city.[3] Doubtless he had heard of Assyria's cruelty and thought that such a people deserved God's punishment. He attempted to flee by ship in the opposite direction to Tarshish, perhaps the Guadalquivir Valley in southern Spain or Sardinia. Following a violent storm Jonah was thrown overboard, swallowed and disgorged by a 'great fish'. Perhaps surprisingly, the people of Nineveh responded favourably to Jonah's message. The book closes with Jonah sulking, being upset over the demise of a plant, commonly believed to be a castor-oil plant, rather than pleased at the deliverance of 120,000 people.

In Jonah 3:6 the king is called 'king of Nineveh', not the usual Old Testament and Assyrian title 'king of Assyria'. The decree recorded in Jonah 3:7 is that of the 'king and his nobles'. It may be that he was effectively king of Nineveh, but of little more besides; hence his title in the book of Jonah. It is possible that he had been obliged to surrender control over large parts of his kingdom to powerful provincial governors, whose power and influence he acknowledges when he issues his decree.

TIGLATH-PILESER III

Under its king Tiglath-pileser III (746–727 BC) Assyria became strong again. Menahem, king of Israel (752–741 BC), had to pay a heavy tribute of a thousand

KEY
[1] 2 Kings 10:32–33
[2] 2 Kings 14:25
[3] Jonah 1:2
[4] 2 Kings 15:19–20
[5] 2 Kings 16:5; Isaiah 7:1–6
[6] 2 Kings 16:10
[7] 2 Kings 15:29
[8] 2 Kings 15:30

LEFT: **Assyrian campaigns against Syria and Palestine**
The Assyrians from what is now northern Iraq mounted several campaigns against Syria and Palestine. The map shows their main campaigns for the period 853–732 BC.

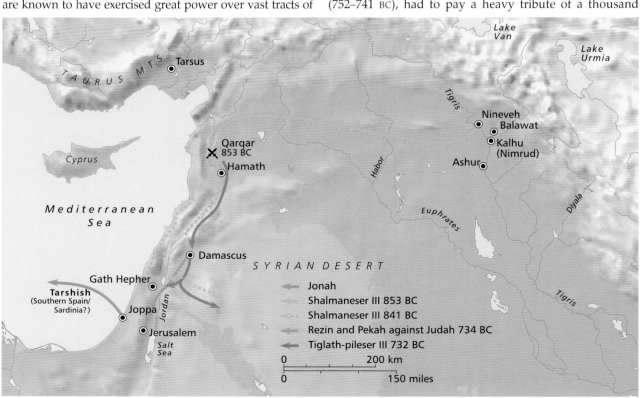

Assyria in the early eighth century BC
The early eighth century BC was the period when Assyrian provincial governors, Shamshi-ilu and Nergal-eresh, exercised their authority over large areas of land. This was also the period when the Hebrew prophet Jonah visited the Assyrian city of Nineveh.

talents of silver (c. 34 tons) to Tiglath-pileser. So fifty silver shekels (600 g or 21 oz) were levied on each wealthy man.[4]

By 734 BC an anti-Assyrian coalition was in place in Syria. Rezin, king of Damascus, and Pekah, king of Israel (739–731 BC) tried to force Ahaz, king of Judah, to join them in resisting Assyria. Rezin and Pekah invaded Judah with the intention of placing a certain Ben-Tabeel on the throne in Ahaz's place.[5] Isaiah prophesied the end for Damascus and Ephraim (Israel): 'It will not take place, it will not happen, for the head of Aram is Damascus, and the head of Damascus is only Rezin. Within 65 years Ephraim will be too shattered to be a people' (Isaiah 7:7–8).

Ahaz's solution was to pay Tiglath-pileser to attack Damascus, using the gold and silver found in the Temple and royal palace as his payment. Tiglath-pileser duly

obliged and attacked and captured Damascus. Ahaz then visited Tiglath-pileser in Damascus, where he saw an altar and sent Uriah the priest a sketch with detailed plans for its construction.[6] Ahaz's resulting displacement of the bronze altar in the Temple of Jerusalem was seen as a sign of his turning from the Lord.

Damascus fell in 732 BC and the Assyrian armies marched south to Israel, depriving it of most of its territory, including the whole of Gilead and Galilee and deporting its inhabitants to Assyria.[7] A layer of ash at Hazor one metre (39 inches) thick is taken as evidence of Tiglath-pileser's actions. In his own records Tiglath-pileser claims to have deposed Pekah and made Hoshea king. The book of Kings notes that Hoshea assassinated Pekah,[8] and it is possible that Tiglath-pileser connived with Hoshea in order to secure a more trustworthy ruler.

Hoshea (731–722 BC) was to be Israel's last king. Subsequent Assyrian kings Shalmaneser V and Sargon II conquered Samaria and exiled the remaining Israelites to far flung parts of the Assyrians' growing empire.

Ashurnasirpal's cruelty

'I captured many troops alive. I cut off the arms and hands of some; I cut off the noses, ears and extremities of others. I gouged out the eyes of many troops. I made one pile of the living and one of heads. I hung their heads on trees around the city. I burnt their adolescent boys and girls.'

The Assyrian army on campaign, from the reign of Shalmaneser III (859–824 BC). From the bronze gates of Balawat, Iraq.

THE ISRAELITES EXILED

(722 BC)

THE FALL OF SAMARIA

Israel's last king, Hoshea (731–722 BC), did not prove a reliable ally for the Assyrians. Seeking help from So, king of Egypt – probably the shadowy, last king of the Twenty-second (Libyan) Dynasty, Osorkon IV (730–715 BC) – he rebelled. The Assyrian king Shalmaneser V (727–722 BC) seized Hoshea and laid siege to Samaria.[1] After a three-year siege, in the late summer to early autumn of 722 BC, Samaria fell.[2] Shalmaneser V did not enjoy the victory long, as he died in the December. The new Assyrian king, the usurper Sargon II (722–705 BC), anxious to hide the internal strife that marked the beginning of his reign, also claimed the capture of the city in the first year of his reign. It would seem that it was the usurper Sargon II who is the 'king of Assyria' who according to 2 Kings 17:6 deported the Israelites to Assyria.

THE ISRAELITES DEPORTED

Thus the Israelites were deported to regions under Assyrian rule,

specifically to Halah, Gozan on the Habor River and the towns of the Medes. Halah was in Assyria to the northeast of Nineveh, Gozan on the Habor River was in modern Syria to the west of Assyria, the Medes lived around modern Hamadan in Iran to the east.

Sargon II records that 27,290 people were deported from Samaria. Exile was not a new punishment. Over a thousand years earlier exile had been specified as a curse for the disobedient.[3] Moses had viewed it similarly.[4] The Egyptian king Amenophis II (1427–1401 BC) is credited with transplanting over 100,000 assorted Syrians into Egypt in two campaigns. The Hittite king Mursilis II (1321–1295 BC) moved 66,000 in the fifth year of his reign. But it was the Assyrians, perhaps because we possess so many of their kings' own propagandistic inscriptions,

The Assyrian king Sargon II (722–705 BC).

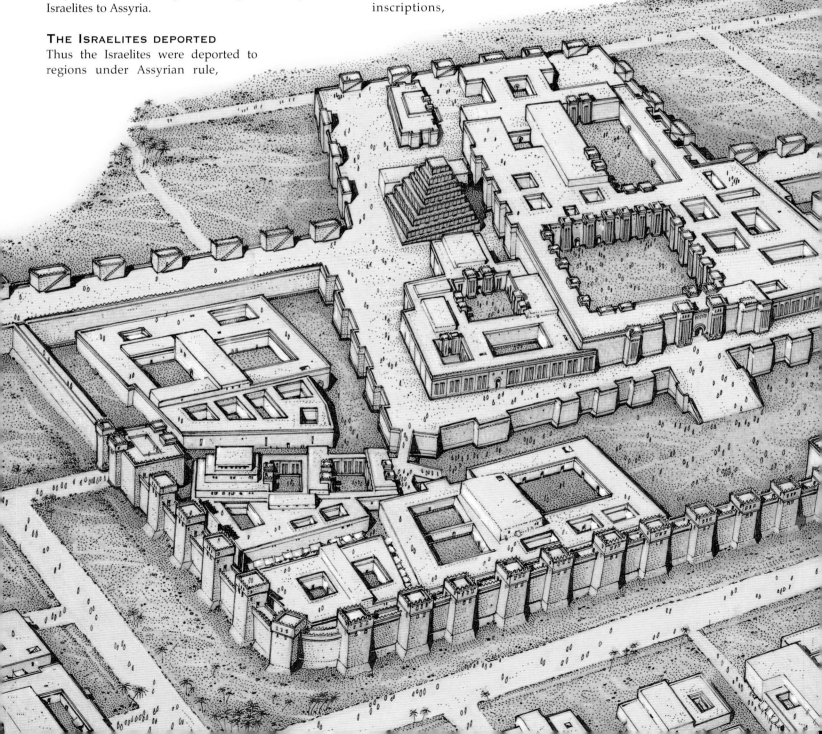

Prisoners working on building projects, guarded by Assyrian soldiers. Relief from Sennacherib's palace, Nineveh, c.700 BC.

KEY
[1] 2 Kings 17:4–5
[2] 2 Kings 17:5–6; *The Babylonian Chronicle* 28
[3] *Laws of Hammurabi* 49:73–75; 51:22–23
[4] Leviticus 26:33, 38–39; Deuteronomy 28:36–37, 63–65
[5] 2 Kings 17:24
[6] Luke 9:52–56; 10:30–37; John 4:9

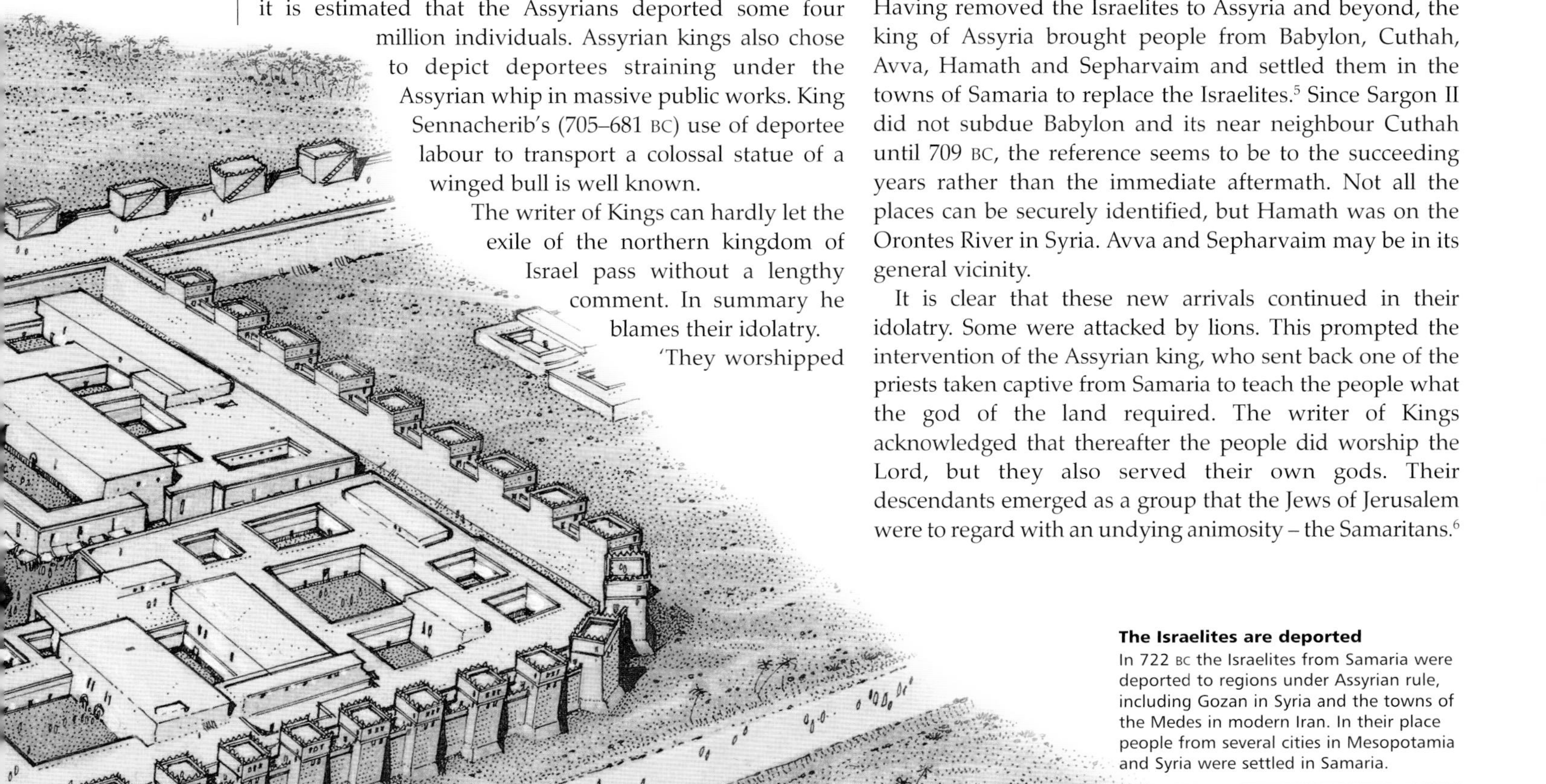

A reconstruction of Sargon's Palace

who seem to have been the greatest practitioners of mass deportation. Sargon II's own records list thirty-eight separate deportations and it is estimated that the Assyrians deported some four million individuals. Assyrian kings also chose to depict deportees straining under the Assyrian whip in massive public works. King Sennacherib's (705–681 BC) use of deportee labour to transport a colossal statue of a winged bull is well known.

The writer of Kings can hardly let the exile of the northern kingdom of Israel pass without a lengthy comment. In summary he blames their idolatry.

'They worshipped other gods and followed the practices of the nations the Lord had driven out before them, as well as the practices that the kings of Israel had introduced... They built themselves high places in all their towns. They set up sacred stones and Asherah poles on every high hill and under every spreading tree... They rejected the Lord's decrees and the covenant he had made with their fathers and the warnings he had given them. They followed worthless idols and themselves became worthless. They imitated the nations around them... So the Lord was very angry with Israel and removed them from his presence' (2 Kings 17:7b–8, 9b–10, 15, 18).

Amos's prophecy had come true: 'Therefore I will send you into exile beyond Damascus, says the Lord, whose name is God Almighty' (Amos 5:27).

SAMARIA REPOPULATED

Having removed the Israelites to Assyria and beyond, the king of Assyria brought people from Babylon, Cuthah, Avva, Hamath and Sepharvaim and settled them in the towns of Samaria to replace the Israelites.[5] Since Sargon II did not subdue Babylon and its near neighbour Cuthah until 709 BC, the reference seems to be to the succeeding years rather than the immediate aftermath. Not all the places can be securely identified, but Hamath was on the Orontes River in Syria. Avva and Sepharvaim may be in its general vicinity.

It is clear that these new arrivals continued in their idolatry. Some were attacked by lions. This prompted the intervention of the Assyrian king, who sent back one of the priests taken captive from Samaria to teach the people what the god of the land required. The writer of Kings acknowledged that thereafter the people did worship the Lord, but they also served their own gods. Their descendants emerged as a group that the Jews of Jerusalem were to regard with an undying animosity – the Samaritans.[6]

The Israelites are deported

In 722 BC the Israelites from Samaria were deported to regions under Assyrian rule, including Gozan in Syria and the towns of the Medes in modern Iran. In their place people from several cities in Mesopotamia and Syria were settled in Samaria.

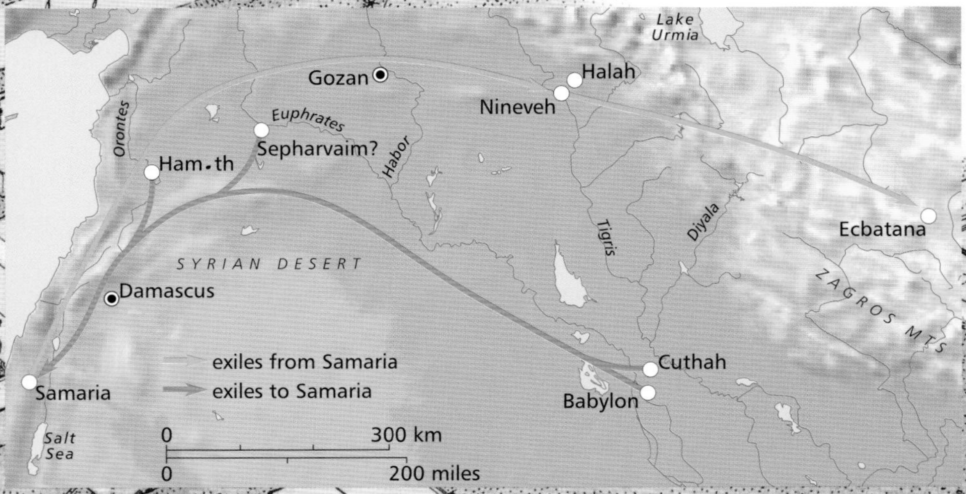

Lake Urmia

Gozan

Halah

Orontes

Euphrates

Nineveh

Sepharvaim?

Habor

Ham.th

SYRIAN DESERT

Tigris

Diyala

Ecbatana

ZAGROS MTS

Damascus

Cuthah

exiles from Samaria
exiles to Samaria

Samaria

Babylon

Salt Sea

0   300 km

0   200 miles

THE KINGS OF JUDAH

(930–701 BC)

We now turn to events in the southern kingdom of Judah, centred on Jerusalem. The kings who followed Rehoboam on David's throne constituted a dynasty much more stable and long lasting than their counterparts in the northern kingdom of Israel.

SHISHAK ATTACKS REHOBOAM

Rehoboam (930–913 BC) had only been on the throne for five years (926 BC) when he faced a major invasion from Shishak, king of Egypt.[1] Shishak carried off some of the treasures of the Temple and the royal palace, including the gold shields that Solomon had had made. Shishak is to be identified with the founder of the Twenty-second Dynasty, Shoshenq I (945–924 BC).

At the temple of Amun at Karnak, Shoshenq I left a triumphal relief scene which names many Palestinian towns and thus enables a detailed reconstruction of his campaign to be made. A broken stela bearing the distinctive cartouches of Shoshenq I has been found at Megiddo.

ZERAH ATTACKS ASA

Rehoboam's grandson Asa (910–869 BC) defeated an enormous invading force led by Zerah the Cushite at the Valley of Zephathah near Mareshah.[2] Cush denotes Egypt south of Aswan and Sudan as far south as Khartoum. The contemporary king of Egypt, Osorkon I (924–889 BC), is not to be identified with Zerah. The names cannot be equivalent. Furthermore, Osorkon I is known to have been of Libyan not Cushite origin. We should note that the book of Chronicles does not call Zerah 'king'. It may be that Zerah was a hitherto unidentified general of Osorkon, who by the time of the campaign was elderly and who preferred to send a general at the head of an expedition to Palestine.

DAVID'S LINE THREATENED BY ATHALIAH

The Lord had sworn to David that his line would be established for ever,[3] yet at one point that line was almost totally eradicated. Jehoram (848–841 BC), king of Judah, married a daughter of Israel's wicked king Ahab (873–853 BC), named Athaliah. When Israel's king, Jehu, killed Ahaziah, son of Jehoram, Athaliah seized the throne of Judah and held it for six years (841–835 BC).[4] She destroyed all the royal family except Ahaziah's baby son, Joash, who was hidden away in the Temple unknown to the queen for the six years of her rule. The high priest Jehoiada led a successful coup against Queen Athaliah, and young Joash was installed in her place.

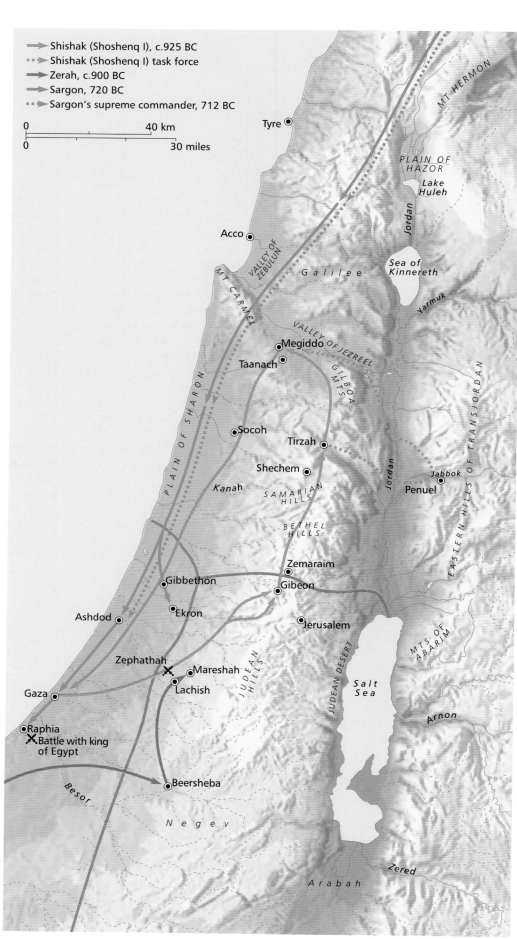

Shishak (Shoshenq I), c.925 BC
Shishak (Shoshenq I) task force
Zerah, c.900 BC
Sargon, 720 BC
Sargon's supreme commander, 712 BC

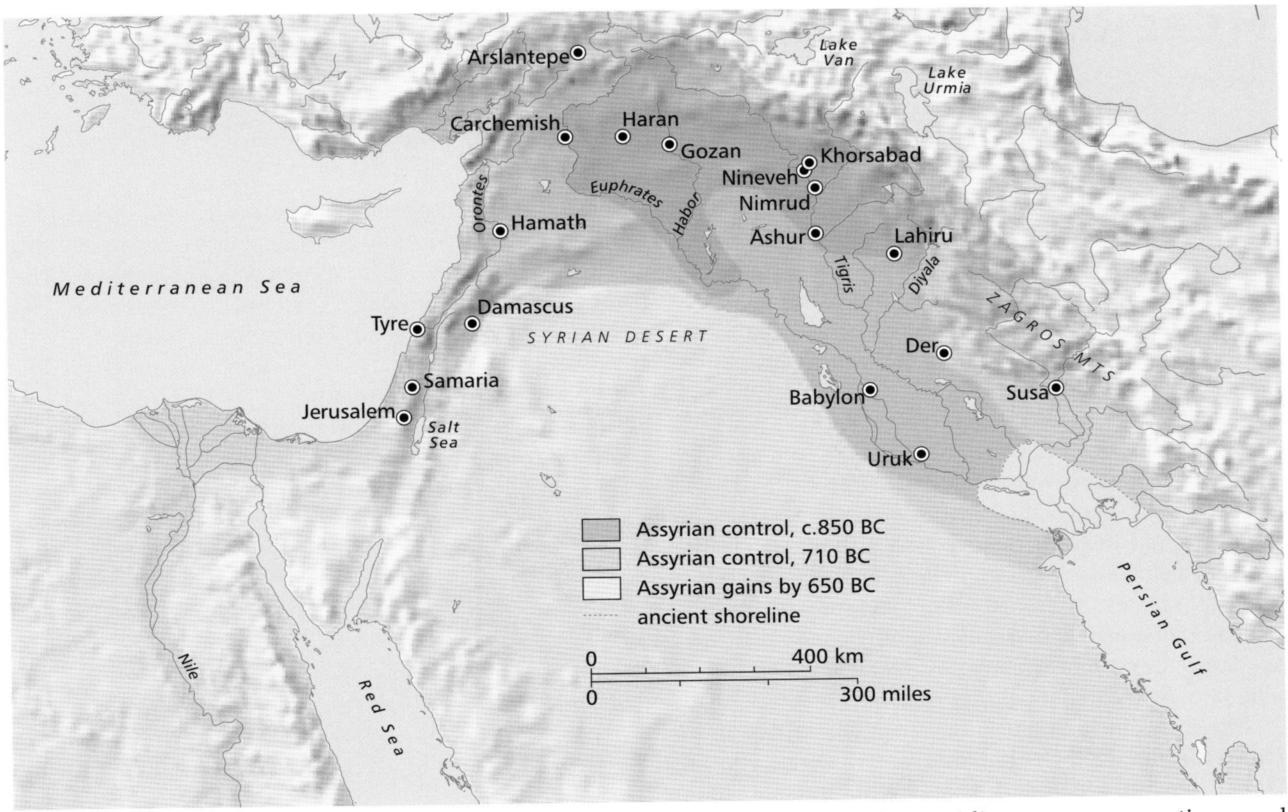
Arslantepe
Lake Van
Lake Urmia
Carchemish
Haran
Gozan
Khorsabad
Nineveh
Nimrud
Euphrates
Habor
Orontes
Hamath
Ashur
Lahiru
Tigris
Diyala
ZAGROS MTS
Mediterranean Sea
Tyre
Damascus
SYRIAN DESERT
Der
Samaria
Babylon
Susa
Jerusalem
Salt Sea
Uruk
Assyrian control, c.850 BC
Assyrian control, 710 BC
Assyrian gains by 650 BC
ancient shoreline
0
400 km
0
300 miles
Persian Gulf
Nile
Red Sea

RIGHT: The growth of the Assyrian empire from c. 850–650 BC
Assyria became the main power in the Near East, carving out an empire right across the fertile crescent and even briefly conquering Egypt.

KEY

[1] 1 Kings 14:25–27
[2] 2 Chronicles 14:9–15
[3] Psalms 89:28–37; 110:2; 132:11–18
[4] 2 Kings 11:1
[5] 2 Kings 15:2
[6] 2 Chronicles 26:15
[7] Diodorus Siculus, *Library of History*, 14.42.1
[8] 2 Kings 16:17–18
[9] Isaiah 2:6–8, 20; 8:19; Micah 5:12–14
[10] Isaiah 20:1

LEFT: The invasions of Judah from 926–712 BC
Judah was invaded several times from the south by Shishak, king of Egypt and Zerah the Cushite, and from the north by Sargon king of Assyria and his turtanu or supreme commander.

Uzziah

Uzziah (or Azariah as he is sometimes called) is credited with a 52-year reign over Judah.[5] There is good evidence that this included a co-regency with Amaziah, his father, from 792 BC until the latter's death in 767 BC. Similarly Uzziah's son Jotham was co-regent from 752 BC until Uzziah's death in 740 BC. Uzziah is credited with rebuilding Elath on the Gulf of Aqabah, defeating the Philistines and Arabians, building towers in the desert, digging cisterns, and increasing the agricultural potential of the land. He is also credited with developing devices for hurling arrows and large stones.[6] It remains uncertain whether these were catapults, invented in 399 BC according to the Greek writer Diodorus Siculus,[7] or special constructions on walls and towers that enabled the defenders to cast stones down onto the heads of attacking troops. The favourable portrait of Uzziah given in the books of Kings and Chronicles is tempered by the disclosure that, following his unauthorized offering of incense in the Temple of the Lord, he was smitten with a serious skin disease traditionally, but anachronistically, translated as 'leprosy'. Uzziah had to live in a separate house, excluded from the Temple until the day of his death, his son Jotham acting as regent.

Ahaz

The Judean king Ahaz (735–715 BC) is especially remembered for his wickedness. 'He walked in the ways of the kings of Israel and even sacrificed his son in the fire, following the detestable ways of the nations the Lord had driven out before the Israelites' (2 Kings 16:3). We have already considered how Ahaz met the threat from Pekah, king of Israel, by seeking help from Tiglath-pileser III (746–727 BC), king of Assyria. As well as installing a new altar in the Temple of the Lord, Ahaz removed the side panels and basins from the moveable, wheeled, bronze stands that Solomon had made for the Temple, removed the bronze 'Sea' from its bronze bulls, setting it on a stone base, and took away the sabbath canopy and the royal entrance to the Temple.[8] The contemporary prophets Isaiah and Micah describe invidious pagan practices and superstitions.[9]

The Assyrian threat under Sargon II

We have seen that the Israelite capital of Samaria fell to the Assyrians in 722 BC. The new Assyrian king, Sargon II (722–705 BC), having organized the deportation of the Israelites from Samaria, pressed south along the coastal plain in 720 BC, conquering Gaza and perhaps also Ekron and Gibbethon. In 712 BC Sargon sent his *turtanu* or supreme commander to put down a rebellion in the coastal town of Ashdod.[10] A fragmentary stela, set up by Sargon II's supreme commander, has been found at Ashdod. The prophet Isaiah used the occasion of the capture of Ashdod to warn against trusting in Egypt as an ally against the growing menace of Assyria. It was the Assyrians who were going to threaten the very existence of Judah in the dramatic events of the year 701 BC, which form the subject of our next two chapters.

HEZEKIAH AND SENNACHERIB

(701 BC)

In 701 BC the Assyrian king, Sennacherib (705–681 BC), led an army of at least 185,000 in an invasion of Judah under Hezekiah (715–686 BC). It was a major crisis, recorded in detail by 2 Kings 18–19, Isaiah 36–37 and 2 Chronicles 32. It is the clearest case in the Old Testament of an event that can, at least in part, be substantiated by other texts and by archaeological evidence.

HEZEKIAH

In contrast to his wicked father Ahaz, Hezekiah 'did what was right in the eyes of the Lord, just as his father David had done' (2 Kings 18:3). He removed the high places, smashed the sacred stones and cut down the Asherah poles. He even broke into pieces the bronze snake that Moses had made in the desert and which was being worshipped. He held fast to the Lord, keeping his commands. He rebelled against the king of Assyria and did not serve him.

Other cities, including the Phoenician coastal city of Tyre, joined the burgeoning revolt. An anti-Assyrian ally was the Babylonian king, Merodach-Baladan (Marduk-apla-iddina II), whose envoys visited Hezekiah in Jerusalem. Since Hezekiah showed Merodach-Baladan's men all the treasures of his storehouses, which were later taken away by the invading Sennacherib, it seems that the account of Merodach-Baladan's embassy to Hezekiah[1] should be placed before 701 BC, even though in the narrative it follows the account of Sennacherib's invasion. Hezekiah's action displeased the prophet Isaiah, who said that the treasures would one day be carried off to Babylon and the sons of the royal line would become eunuchs in the palace of the king of Babylon. Hezekiah did not seem unduly worried. He took comfort from Isaiah's words that there would be peace and security in his own lifetime.

SENNACHERIB ATTACKS

According to 2 Kings 18:13 Sennacherib attacked all the fortified cities of Judah and captured them. Part of the route of a subsidiary force may be preserved in Isaiah's prophecy.[2] A number of copies of Sennacherib's own account of the campaign have been preserved. Sennacherib tells of how he conquered forty-six of Hezekiah's strong walled towns by stamping down earth ramps, by bringing up battering rams, by the assault of foot soldiers, by breaches and by siege engines. He took 200,150 people and innumerable horses, mules, donkeys and camels as spoil and boasts of shutting up Hezekiah like a caged bird within Jerusalem his royal city.[3]

HEZEKIAH PAYS TRIBUTE

When Sennacherib reached the Judean provincial city of Lachish (modern Tell ed-Duweir), some 40 km (25 miles) south-west of Jerusalem, he pressed Hezekiah for tribute. Hezekiah sent a message to the Assyrian king saying he would pay.[4] The book of Kings and the so-called Taylor Prism agree on the amount of tribute: 300 talents (c. 10 tons) of silver, 30 talents (c. 1 ton) of gold. The Chicago Prism gives a figure of 800 talents of silver, which may be the figure exacted from the entire campaign. Hezekiah stripped off the gold from the Temple doors to meet this demand. The Chicago Prism also lists more of the tribute – precious stones, antimony, large blocks of stone, ivory couches, ivory arm chairs, elephant hides, elephant tusks, ebony wood and boxwood – most of which come into the category of valuable goods imported into Judah.

SENNACHERIB AT LACHISH

The Assyrian army's siege of one of the Judean cities is shown on low relief sculpture in a central room in Sennacherib's palace at Nineveh. The city chosen was Lachish, probably the

KEY

[1] 2 Kings 20:12–19; 2 Chronicles 32:31; Isaiah 39:1–8
[2] Isaiah 10:28–32
[3] Chicago Prism 3.19–29
[4] 2 Kings 18:14
[5] Chicago Prism 3.42–45
[6] 2 Kings 18:17; Isaiah 36:2

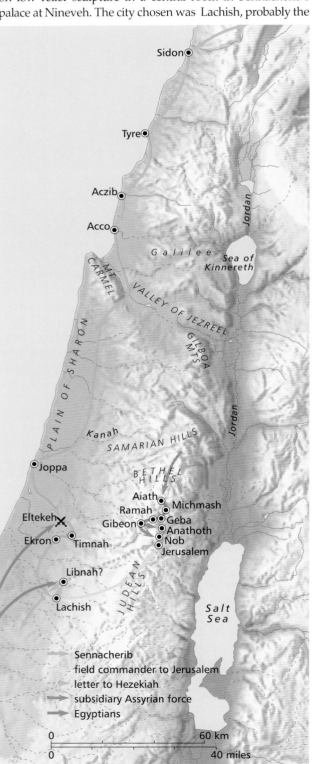

Sennacherib field commander to Jerusalem
— — letter to Hezekiah
→ subsidiary Assyrian force
→ Egyptians

0 ———— 60 km
0 ———— 40 miles

RIGHT: The Assyrian army besieges the city of Lachish, 701 BC. From Sennacherib's palace, Nineveh.

LEFT: **Sennacherib's invasion of Judah, 701 BC**
Sending a large force to attack Palestine, the Assyrian king Sennacherib boasts of conquering 46 strong-walled towns of Judah. An Egyptian force also joined the fray in support of Judah.

second city of the kingdom. Assyrian bowmen, slingers and spearmen advance up ramps towards the city. Siege engines and siege towers are employed against the walls. The desperate inhabitants of Lachish rain down stones and lighted torches from the city walls. The Assyrians have to pour water over their siege engines to prevent them from burning. But in time the city falls. A long line of prisoners with their belongings packed in carts is led away. Some of the Lachishites are flayed. Others bring tribute, including incense burners and ivory chairs, to Sennacherib, who is seated on an ivory throne surveying the scene. An inscription proudly proclaims: 'Sennacherib, king of Assyria, king of the universe, sitting on his ivory throne while the spoil of Lachish passes before him.' The head of Sennacherib has been defaced, maybe by a later Jew exacting revenge.

A siege-ramp from Lachish still survives. Assyrian arrows, armour and slingshots were also found at the site.

SENNACHERIB PRESSES HARDER

Sennacherib was not satisfied with Hezekiah's tribute from Lachish. He sent a task-force led by three officers – the supreme commander, the chief officer and the field commander – to Hezekiah in Jerusalem.[6]

The field commander (rab shakeh) is met by a deputation and makes a fast-moving speech in the Judean dialect urging the people not to rely on Egypt as an ally. Relying on the Lord was futile too, as Hezekiah had removed his high places. Clearly the field commander has heard of Hezekiah's reforms and, interestingly, he claims that the Lord himself had told him to march against the land and destroy it. At one point the field commander doubts that Judah could muster even two thousand men.

'Come now, make a bargain with my master, the king of Assyria: I will give you two thousand horses – if you can put riders on them! How can you repulse one officer of the least of my master's officials, even though you are depending on Egypt for chariots and horsemen?'
2 KINGS 18:23–24

He says Hezekiah won't deliver them and they shouldn't let him deceive them into thinking that the Lord would. Surrender is their best option.

'Do not listen to Hezekiah. This is what the king of Assyria says: Make peace with me and come out to me. Then every one of you will eat from his own vine and fig-tree and drink water from his own cistern, until I come and take you to a land like your own, a land of grain and new wine, a land of bread and vineyards, a land of olive trees and honey. Choose life and not death!'
2 KINGS 18:31–32b

He concludes his speech by listing other cities the Assyrians had conquered. If the gods of those cities had been powerless to deliver them from the hands of the Assyrians, how could the Lord deliver Jerusalem from Sennacherib's hand?

How the Assyrian field commander came to know the Judean dialect we do not know. Perhaps he used an interpreter. Clearly the people understood, as half way through the speech the Judean officials interrupt and ask the field commander to continue his speech in Aramaic, the language of international diplomacy, so that only the officials could understand, not the people listening from the wall.

We should note that a similar speech has been found on two letters from the Assyrian city of Nimrud, attempting to persuade a Babylonian rebel named Ukin-zer to surrender to the Assyrian king Tiglath-pileser III (731 BC). In both cases the Assyrians address themselves directly to the natives in the hope of leading them to withdraw support from the rulers of the city. In both cases the Assyrians promise favourable terms, yet the Assyrian officers fail to obtain a direct reply.

JERUSALEM DELIVERED

(701–681 BC)

SENNACHERIB DEMANDS SURRENDER

The task-force threatening Jerusalem at first withdrew, joining the main Assyrian army as Sennacherib moved closer from Lachish to Libnah, where, the writer of 2 Kings records, the Assyrian king heard that Tirhakah, 'King of Cush', was marching to fight him.[1] Cush was the area of Egypt south of Aswan and northern Sudan as far as Khartoum. Its kings ruled Egypt at the time. Hezekiah had been counting on help from the Egyptians, who had already sent an army that had been defeated at Eltekeh in the Philistine plain,[2] a fact alluded to by the field commander in his speech outside the walls of Jerusalem.[3] Sennacherib's response to the news was to send Hezekiah a letter again urging him to surrender. Hezekiah spread the letter out before the Lord.[4] Isaiah prophesied that Sennacherib would not attack Jerusalem:

'He will not enter this city,
or shoot an arrow here.
He will not come before it with shield
or build a siege ramp against it.
By the way that he came he will return;
he will not enter this city.'
2 KINGS 19:32

DELIVERANCE

The Lord's response is detailed in 2 Kings 19:35: 'That night the angel of the Lord went out and put to death 185,000 men in the Assyrian camp. When the people got up the next morning – there were all the dead bodies!'

The biblical writers – the writers of Kings, Isaiah and the Chronicles – all stress that Sennacherib himself escaped and returned to Nineveh. The Greek historian Herodotus has him going to Pelusium on the border of Egypt.[5] Perhaps he was pursuing the forces of Tirhakah. There field mice ate the Assyrians' quivers, bowstrings and shield handles. It is commonly proposed that the mice were carriers of a plague which ran wild through the Assyrian camp; but, if this were so, why were the Judeans not afflicted too?

Whatever the details, Sennacherib's obvious failure to capture Jerusalem cannot be dismissed. The fact that on his palace walls in Nineveh he chose to portray his capture of Lachish, a Judean provincial city, not Jerusalem, suggests something went seriously wrong with his action against Jerusalem. Furthermore, the strength of the beliefs of the people of Jeremiah's day, little over a century later, that Jerusalem would always be safe and would never fall,[6] can only really be explained if we assume the annihilation of Sennacherib's army and the miraculous protection of Jerusalem at that time.

THE SILOAM TUNNEL

Probably as part of his preparations for the expected invasion of Sennacherib and a possible siege of Jerusalem, Hezekiah had the Siloam tunnel dug.[7] Extending 553 m

ABOVE: Granite shabti (statuette buried with the dead) of Tirhakah (Taharqa), the Cushite king of Egypt 690–664 BC, from the pyramid of Tirhakah at Nuri. The writer of Kings (2 Kings 19:9), when referring to Tirhakah as 'king of Cush' in relation to the events of 701 BC, is simply using a title by which he was later well known.

LEFT: The camp of Sennacherib before Lachish, 701 BC. From Sennacherib's palace, Nineveh.

KEY
[1] 2 Kings 19:8–9
[2] Chicago Prism 3:3–5
[3] 2 Kings 18:21; Isaiah 36:6
[4] 2 Kings 19:14; Isaiah 37:14
[5] Herodotus, *Histories*, 2.141
[6] Jeremiah 7:4
[7] 2 Kings 20:20; 2 Chronicles 32:30
[8] Esarhaddon Prism B 1.44

(1,814 ft), it was intended to channel water from the Gihon spring outside the eastern walls of Jerusalem to the Siloam pool in the south-west of the city. It still survives. In the tunnel an inscription in the Old Hebrew script was found, now in the Istanbul Archaeological Museum, which tells how the tunnel was constructed, with teams digging from both ends at once and meeting in the middle (see below).

SENNACHERIB IS ASSASSINATED

The biblical writers are at pains to record that Sennacherib escaped the destruction of the Assyrian army and returned to Nineveh, meeting his death twenty years later in 681 BC. 'One day, while he was worshipping in the temple of his god Nisroch, his sons Adrammelech and Sharezer cut him down with the sword, and they escaped to the land of Ararat. And Esarhaddon, his son, succeeded him as king' (2 Kings 19:37).

It has been suggested that Adrammelech was Sennacherib's eldest surviving son Arad-Ninlil. *Arad* can be read 'Arda' and *Ninlil* 'Mulleshu'. The biblical scribe transposed *r* and *d* and, for the seemingly nonsensical '-melesh' substituted -*melech* (meaning 'king'). Sharezer corresponds to the Akkadian *shar-usur*, 'protect the king'; this would be preceded by the name of a god, which the biblical writer may have chosen not to include. No known sons of Sennacherib have this form of name, but there may have been sons whose names have not been preserved in the cuneiform record.

It may come as a surprise that the sons who assassinated Sennacherib did not occupy the vacant Assyrian throne. According to Esarhaddon's account, the two assassins fell out, 'butting each other like young goats trying to take the kingdom'.[8] The 'land of Ararat', to which 2 Kings 19:37 says they escaped, is a wide area comprising much of eastern Turkey that the Assyrians knew as Urartu.

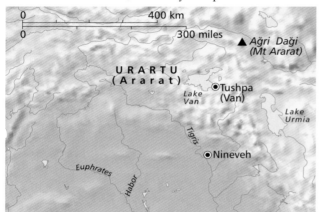

The location of the 'land of Ararat'
According to 2 Kings 19:37, Sennacherib's assassins escaped to the 'land of Ararat' – an area known by the Assyrians as Urartu, comprising much of eastern Turkey.

The Siloam tunnel inscription

'[*The completing*] of the tunnelling. And this was the story of the tunnelling. While [*the stone cutters were swinging*] the pick each to his mate, and while there were three cubits yet to be dug, the voice of a man calling to his mate [*was heard*]. For there was a crack in the rock from south to north. On the day of the tunnelling the stone cutters struck each to meet his mate, axe against axe. The waters flowed from the source to the pool for 1,200 cubits. And 100 cubits was the height of the rock above the head of the stone cutters.'

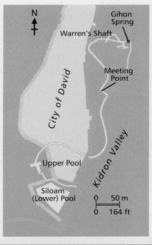

LEFT: The course of Hezekiah's water tunnel in Jerusalem (the Siloam tunnel).

RIGHT: Interior of the Siloam tunnel, Jerusalem.

BELOW: The Siloam tunnel inscription.

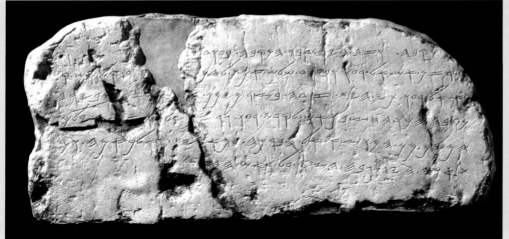

WARFARE AND FORTIFICATIONS

WARFARE IN THE OLD TESTAMENT

Hostile activity is recorded right at the beginning of the Bible: 'Cain attacked his brother Abel and killed him' (Genesis 4:8). Indeed the violence of the antediluvian inhabitants of earth is cited as one of the main reasons for the Lord sending the flood.[1] Palestine's geographical position between Egypt and the Near East ensured that it was frequently a theatre for war. But, more than that, the biblical writers frequently saw war as a sign of divine displeasure, a punishment for the Israelites' disobedience: 'The Lord will cause you to be defeated before your enemies. You will come at them from one direction but flee from them in seven... Your carcasses will be food for all the birds of the air, and the beasts of the earth, and there will be no-one to frighten them away' (Deuteronomy 28:25a, 26).

Limitations were placed on the Israelites concerning the conduct of war: for example, a besieging army was not to cut down fruit trees.[2] Yet there is another view of war found in the Old Testament. The Israelites' destruction of the Canaanites was ordered by the Lord, their wickedness being cited as the reason,[3] and failure to carry out God's 'holy war' to the letter met with the direst of consequences.[4]

THE ISRAELITE ARMY

Military service was a religious obligation for male adults over twenty, but there were a number of exemptions, including newly-weds, the fearful and fainthearted.[5] Saul collected valiant men for his bodyguard. David had his 'thirty' mighty men (who actually numbered thirty-seven) and an army made up of two separate parts: a regular force of career soldiers and a people's militia of reservists. He also employed foreign mercenaries: Kerethites (perhaps Cretans) and Pelethites and Gittites (Philistines).

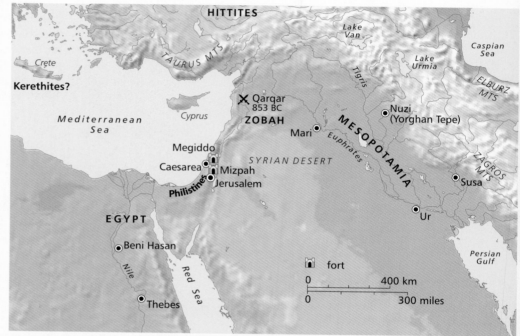

Warfare and fortifications in the Old Testament
The map shows the places of origin of some of the most important mercenaries – the Kerethites, Pelethites and Gittites (Philistines).

The Egyptian king Tutankhamun (1336–1327 BC) in his war chariot. From a chest found in Tutankhamun's tomb.

TECHNOLOGICAL ADVANCE

In the history of ancient warfare new weapons of war were developed. This in turn led to new defensive measures being adopted to counteract them. Three examples illustrate this point.

1 THE COMPOSITE BOW AND SCALE ARMOUR

Bows are depicted on many monuments from both Egypt and Mesopotamia dating to the end of the fourth millennium BC. But the composite or reinforced bow made of four different materials – wood, animal horn, animal sinews and tendons, and glue – had a greatly increased range, (some 300 to 400 m or 1,000 to 1,300 ft), and an increased power of penetration. The composite bow is first depicted on the *stela* of the Akkadian king Naram-Sin (2291–2255 BC) found at Susa in south-west Iran, yet it was not until the middle of the second millennium BC that the composite bow became common. The response to it was the development of scale armour, the earliest example of which is from Nuzi in Mesopotamia, dating to c. 1500 BC. Another example of scale armour is depicted on a wall painting from the tomb of Kenamun at Thebes in Egypt, dating to the reign of Amenophis II (1427–1401 BC); and actual scales were found at Thebes in the palace of Amenophis III (1391–1353 BC).

2 CHARIOTS AND CITY GATES

Two-wheeled and four-wheeled carts pulled by onagers (wild donkeys) are attested in Mesopotamia as early as 2800 BC. They can be seen on the Standard of Ur (c. 2500 BC). Their wheels were solid and the carts slow and difficult to manoeuvre. In the eighteenth century BC horse-drawn chariots are first mentioned in texts from Mari in Syria. Essentially mobile firing-platforms, from which limited firepower could quickly be directed on decisive spots in a battle, chariots were complex vehicles, fashioned only by nations commanding rich resources and advanced techniques, their use limited to level and unbroken terrain. The major powers of the mid-second millennium BC, the Egyptians and Hittites, were quick to adopt them for use in battle. The celebrated chariot from the tomb of Tutankhamun (1336–1327 BC) gives us a clear understanding of what they looked like.

Until the mid-second millennium BC attackers could make their way obliquely along the side of the slopes on which towers stood and approach the gate parallel to the walls. This gave the defenders an advantage. With the advent of chariots, direct access to city gates was a prerequisite, so the earlier L-shaped gates were abandoned. Gates were lengthened to contain a number of chambers, into which extra doors could be placed. The central double-doors had to be wide enough to allow chariots in, but were reinforced on the inside with huge bolts. Towers were added to enable the defenders to molest the attackers, and sloping ramparts built up against the walls.

Although the Canaanites had used chariots and introduced them to Egypt, the Israelites were slow to adopt them. Doubtless being confined to the hill country was a factor. When David defeated Hadadezer king of the Aramean state of Zobah, he captured a thousand of his chariots. Seeming not to realize their military potential, and perhaps not wanting the expense of fodder and stabling, he hamstrung all but a hundred of the chariot horses.[6] It fell to Solomon to develop Israel's chariot force.

Ahab, king of Israel (873–853 BC), contributed two thousand chariots to the combined forces of Syria and Palestine against Assyria at the battle of Qarqar on the Orontes River in Syria in 853 BC.

3 BATTERING RAMS AND CITY WALLS

The earliest depiction of a battering ram is probably on wall paintings from Beni Hasan, Egypt, dating from c. 1900 BC, but it was not until the ninth century BC that the Assyrians began to use the battering ram with devastating effect. The iron head of the battering ram would be thrust with force against the wall so that it became lodged deeply between the stones. It would then be levered right and left to dislodge the stones. The battering ram was protected from the defenders by a long, wooden, box-like structure. Later the ram was suspended from the roof of this structure so it could be swung back and forth.

In the early part of the Hebrew monarchy towns were defended with 'casemate' walls. Two parallel walls about 1.5 m (5 ft) thick were built about 2 m (6 ft 6 in) apart, the space between joined by cross-walls at regular intervals. The long, narrow rooms could be used for storage or filled in for extra strength. As the Assyrians began to employ battering rams, some towns were surrounded by solid walls 3 to 4 m (10 to 13 ft) thick. At Mizpah (Tell en-Nasbeh) the city wall was 600 m (1,970 ft) long with ten towers. It probably stood about 12 m (40 ft) high, on top of a steep sloping rampart, no doubt an extra protection against battering rams.[7]

WARFARE IN THE NEW TESTAMENT

In the New Testament, in contrast to the Old Testament, warfare is not seen in political terms. The Christian's struggle is not against flesh and blood. A Christian's warfare is a spiritual one, against the spiritual forces of evil in the heavenly realms. Christians are to put on the full armour of God so that when the evil day comes they may be able to stand their ground.[8]

The Roman army once held sway over an empire from Hadrian's Wall in northern England to the Euphrates. The Roman army at different times had from twenty-five to thirty-five legions each of which comprised a maximum of six thousand heavy infantrymen. A legion was divided into ten cohorts of approximately six hundred men. The cohort was divided into six centuries each commanded by a centurion. Legions were supported by cavalry units of five hundred men. Some soldiers had special roles – clerks, standard bearers, messengers, doctors, executioners and grooms. In the first half of first century AD three thousand troops were stationed at Caesarea on the Mediterranean coast of Palestine. A cohort (600 men) was stationed at Jerusalem, in the Antonia fortress and at the governor's palace, supplemented at times of unrest and during festivals by additional troops from Caesarea.

JUDAH FROM MANASSEH TO THE FALL OF NINEVEH

(686–612 BC)

MANASSEH

Hezekiah's son Manasseh (686–641 BC) succeeded him as king and there could hardly be a greater contrast between father and son. The writer of the book of Kings describes how Manasseh did evil in the eyes of the Lord, following the detestable practices of the nations the Lord had driven out before the Israelites.[1] Specifically he rebuilt the high places, erected altars to Baal, made an Asherah pole and bowed down to the starry hosts, even before their altars in the Temple of the Lord. He practised sorcery and divination, consulted mediums and spiritists and even sacrificed his own son in the fire. He filled Jerusalem from end to end with innocent blood.

The Lord spoke to the people of Judah through an unknown prophet, promising to bring about such a disaster on Jerusalem and Judah that the ears of all who heard of it would tingle. He would stretch out over Jerusalem the measuring line used against Samaria and the plumb-line used against the house of Ahab and wipe out Jerusalem as one wipes out a dish.[2] When the people paid no heed, 'The Lord brought against them the army commanders of the king of Assyria, who took Manasseh prisoner, put a hook in his nose, bound him with bronze shackles and took him to Babylon' (2 Chronicles 33:11).

The Assyrian kings Esarhaddon, in 676 BC, and Ashurbanipal, in c. 666 BC, mention Manasseh as a payer of tribute. That Manasseh was taken to Babylon is worthy of comment. Between 650 BC and 648 BC Ashurbanipal laid siege to Babylon, which was ruled by his elder brother, Shamash-shum-ukin. Esarhaddon put hooks through the noses of two other client kings, as is clearly

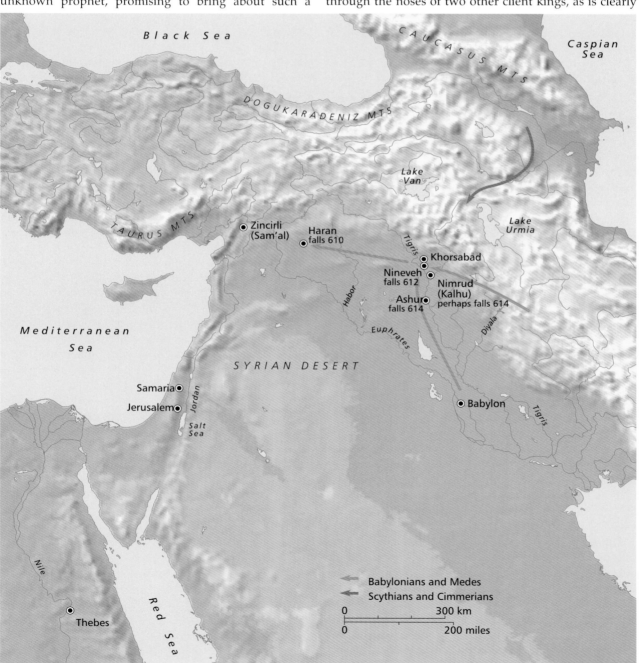

The Fall of Assyria
In the early seventh century BC the Scythians and Cimmerians from southern Russia put Assyria under pressure. In 612 BC the Assyrian capital of Nineveh fell to the Babylonians from southern Iraq and the Medes from Iran. An Assyrian general held out for a further two years in Haran.

KEY
[1] 2 Kings 21:2
[2] 2 Kings 21:13
[3] 2 Kings 21:21
[4] Nahum 3:8
[5] Xenophon, *Anabasis*, 3.4.12
[6] Diodorus Siculus, *Library of History*, 2.27.1
[7] Nahum 2:9
[8] Nahum 3:7b

shown on his stela from Sam'al (modern Zincirli, near Islahiye, in south-east Turkey).

In Babylon Manasseh sought the favour of the Lord, humbled himself and was allowed to return to his native land. He removed the images of foreign gods, including an image from the Temple of the Lord, restored the altar of the Lord and reinstituted offerings to him. He told the people to serve the Lord – but old habits die hard, it seems, for the people continued to sacrifice at the high places, albeit to the Lord.

AMON

Manasseh was succeeded by his son Amon (641–639 BC), who worshipped all the idols Manasseh had made,[3] but did not humble himself. After only two years on the throne his officials assassinated him in his palace and 'the people of the land' (perhaps a term for 'landed gentry') set his eight-year-old son Josiah on the throne.

NAHUM

The prophet Nahum's brief prophecy is difficult to date exactly, but he knew of the Assyrian capture of the Upper Egyptian city of Thebes, which happened under Ashurbanipal in 663 BC.[4] In vivid language Nahum predicts the seemingly impossible – the fall of Assyria's capital, Nineveh, a huge city 749 hectares (1,850 acres) in area and surrounded by over 12 km (8 miles) of walls. 'The river gates are thrown open and the palace collapses [or more literally 'melts']. It is decreed that the city be exiled and carried away. Its slave girls moan like doves and beat upon their breasts. Nineveh is like a pool, and its water is draining away. "Stop!

Stop!" they cry, but no one turns back' (Nahum 2:6–8).

ZEPHANIAH

The prophet Zephaniah, writing in the reign of Josiah (639–609 BC), also looked ahead to the coming destruction of Assyria's capital Nineveh:

'He will stretch out his hand against the north
and destroy Assyria,
leaving Nineveh utterly desolate
and dry as the desert.
Flocks and herds will lie down there,
creatures of every kind.
The desert owl and the screech owl
will roost on her columns.'
ZEPHANIAH 2:13–14

THE FALL OF NINEVEH

Assyria was not as invincible as the Assyrian kings themselves portrayed in their inscriptions. The Indo-European Scythians and Cimmerians from the steppes of southern Russia are known to have caused serious problems for Assyria in the reign of Esarhaddon (681–669 BC). On Ashurbanipal's death in 627 BC a revolt broke out against his son Ashur-etil-ilani. His brother Sin-shar-ishkun (627–612 BC) also met with opposition. Meanwhile, in the south, a Chaldean tribal leader from southern Babylonia called Nabopolassar (the father of Nebuchadnezzar) seized the throne of Babylon in 626 BC. In 616 BC, according to the Babylonian *Fall of Nineveh Chronicle*, Nabopolassar with help from the Medes under Cyaxares began to attack Assyria.

In 614 BC the important city of Ashur fell and perhaps also Calah (Nimrud). In 612 BC Nineveh itself was besieged. The *Fall of Nineveh Chronicle* records: 'The king of Akkad [Nabopolassar] and Cyaxares marched along the bank of the Tigris and encamped against Nineveh. From the month of Sivan [May/June] until the month of Ab [July/August] – for three months – they subjected the city to a heavy siege' (*Fall of Nineveh Chronicle* 40–43a).

The Greek historians Xenophon[5] and Diodorus Siculus[6] allude to a storm that inundated a portion of the city and broke down a section of the walls. The palace was set on fire, perhaps connected with Sin-shar-ishkun's committing suicide. Nahum's prophecy of the melting of the palace had been fulfilled.

Nahum's other predictions, the plunder of the treasures of Nineveh[7] and the ruin of the city[8] are fulfilled in the laconic statement of the *Fall of Nineveh Chronicle*: 'They carried off the vast booty of the city and the temple and turned the city into a ruin heap' (*Fall of Nineveh Chronicle* 45).

An Assyrian general, Ashur-uballit, held out for two more years in Haran, in what is now south-east Turkey. But Assyria had come to an end, as Nahum had predicted at the conclusion of his prophecy: 'Everyone who hears the news about you claps his hands at your fall, for who has not felt your endless cruelty?' (Nahum 3:19b).

Stela showing the Assyrian king Esarhaddon (681–69 BC) holding two diminutive client kings on leashes secured to hooks through their noses. Height 3.2 m (10ft 6in). From Zincirli, south-east Turkey.

Plan of Nineveh
With an area of 749 hectares (1,850 acres), Nineveh was the largest of the Assyrians' cities. Excavations have centered on the two main mounds of Kuyunjik and Nebi Yunus.

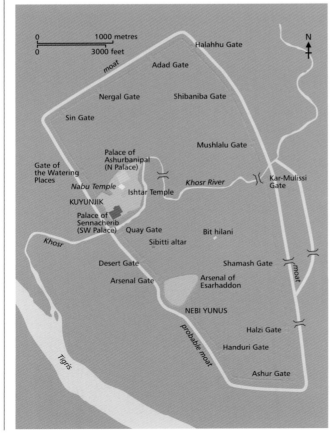

JOSIAH AND THE RISE OF BABYLON

(639–605 BC)

JOSIAH

Josiah (639–609 BC) succeeded to the throne of Judah at the age of eight. The writer of Chronicles notes that in the eighth year of his reign (632 BC) Josiah 'began to seek the God of his father David' (2 Chronicles 34:3). Between his twelfth and eighteenth years (628–622 BC) Josiah embarked on a radical programme of reform. He smashed or burned pagan articles, altars and idols, eradicated pagan priests and shrine prostitutes, desecrated the high places and removed pagan features that had been installed in the Temple of the Lord. It was a programme that he carried far beyond Jerusalem to the towns of Manasseh, Ephraim and Simeon, as far as Naphtali, territories that had once belonged to the northern kingdom of Israel but over which, with the weakening power of Assyria, he was able to exert his influence. He was able to desecrate the high place at Bethel made by Jeroboam, son of Nebat, burning the bones of the pagan priests on the pagan altars.[1]

In Josiah's eighteenth year the high priest, Hilkiah, found in the Temple of the Lord a copy of the book of the Law.[2] What this book was remains speculative, but on hearing its words the king tore his robes exclaiming, 'Great is the Lord's anger that burns against us because our fathers have not obeyed the words of this book' (2 Kings 22:13). To fulfil the requirements of the book of the Law, Josiah got rid of the mediums and spiritists, the household gods, the idols and all the other detestable things seen in Judah and Jerusalem.

The writer of Kings narrates that even Josiah's far-reaching reform was not enough to avert the Lord's impending judgment. He cites the prophetess Huldah: 'This is what the Lord, the God of Israel, says: "I am going to bring disaster on this place and its people, according to everything written in the book the king of Judah has read. Because they have forsaken me… my anger will burn against this place and will not be quenched"' (2 Kings 22:16–17). The consolation for Josiah was that his eyes would not witness the impending disaster.

JOSIAH'S DEATH

The fall of Assyria in 612 BC had upset the balance of power in the Near East. The Egyptian pharaoh Neco (610–595 BC), alarmed at the growth of Babylonian power, sent an army to Syria to help the remnant of Assyria and restrain the rising power of the Babylonians. Neco claimed to have received a command from God.[3] Not believing this, Josiah opposed him at Megiddo in northern Israel in 609 BC and was killed. His untimely death shocked the nation. Jeremiah composed laments[4] and even some one hundred and thirty years later the prophet Zechariah recalled Josiah's death as a time of great weeping.[5]

HABAKKUK

Josiah's death brought an abrupt end to his reform programme. It seemed that the Lord had abandoned his people. Subsequent rulers had no desire to follow the Lord. Neco was not satisfied with Josiah's son, Jehoahaz, and so at Riblah in Syria he placed his brother Jehoiakim (Eliakim) on the throne.[6] The prophet Habakkuk was baffled by the destruction and violence he saw around him. The Lord's answer was hardly what he was expecting:

'Look at the nations and watch – and be utterly amazed. For I am going to do something in your days that you would not believe, even if you were told. I am raising up the Babylonians, that ruthless and impetuous people, who sweep across the whole earth to seize dwelling-places not their own. They are a feared and dreaded people; they are a law to themselves and promote their own honour. Their horses are swifter than leopards, fiercer than wolves at dusk. Their cavalry gallops headlong; their

The Plain of Esdraelon from the mound of Megiddo.

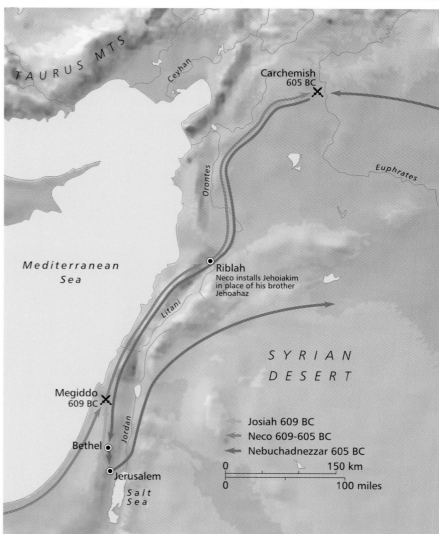

horsemen come from afar. They fly like a vulture swooping to devour; they all come bent on violence.'

HABAKKUK 1:5–9a

NEBUCHADNEZZAR TAKES CHARGE

Nabopolassar, king of Babylon, grew elderly and so placed his son, crown prince Nebuchadnezzar, in charge of the army. In 605 BC Nebuchadnezzar routed the Egyptian army at Carchemish on the Euphrates (by the modern Turkish–Syrian border).[7] Marching south, Nebuchadnezzar invaded Judah, anxious to secure the loyalty of Neco's former vassal and ally, Jehoiakim of Judah. Just as Jehoiakim was capitulating, news reached Nebuchadnezzar that his father Nabopolassar was dead. Nebuchadnezzar took the desert road back to Babylon to secure his throne and took with him some items from the Temple of Lord and several young men from the royal family and the nobility, four of whom were to prove of great value to the new king: Daniel, Hananiah, Mishael and Azariah.[8] This was the first and smallest of four deportations that were ultimately to lead to the exile of the Jews to Babylon.

A reconstruction of the Ishtar Gate at Babylon. This represents the final form of the gate when it was overlaid with blue glazed bricks showing bulls and mushhushshu dragons.

LEFT: Neco fights Josiah and Nebuchadnezzar
Between 609 and 605 BC Judah faced threats from two fronts. In 609 BC Neco, king of Egypt, killed Judah's king Josiah at Megiddo. Nebuchadnezzar, crown prince of Babylon, was to defeat Neco at Carchemish in 605 BC. As he pressed on towards Judah news came of his father's death, forcing him to set out across the desert to claim the vacant throne.

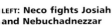

KEY
[1] 2 Kings 23:15–20
[2] 2 Kings 22:8
[3] 2 Chronicles 35:21
[4] 2 Chronicles 35:25
[5] Zechariah 12:11–14
[6] 2 Kings 23:34
[7] Jeremiah 46:2
[8] Daniel 1:1–2, 6

JUDAH EXILED

(604–582 BC)

JEHOIAKIM

The death of King Josiah in 609 BC struck a mortal blow to continuing religious reform in Judah. Under Josiah's son, Jehoiakim, pagan practices crept back. The prophet Jeremiah rebuked Jehoiakim for exploiting the people and for building a luxurious palace with the fruits of his exploitation.[1] This may possibly be the palace found at Ramat Rahel, just south of Jerusalem. As well as having the prophet Uriah murdered for prophesying against the city and the land, Jehoiakim personally opposed the prophet Jeremiah, burning a scroll from which Jehudi read Jeremiah's words to him.[2]

Jehoiakim submitted to Nebuchadnezzar in 604 BC (a year after the latter's victory at Carchemish), but with the encouragement of Egypt he rebelled three years later. It was not until 598 BC that Nebuchadnezzar responded, having Jehoiakim bound in bronze shackles and taken to Babylon. At that point the 36-year-old king died, but whether from natural causes or intrigue is not known. Jeremiah prophesied that Jehoiakim would not have a proper burial, he would have the burial of a donkey – dragged away and thrown outside the gates of Jerusalem.[3]

THE SECOND DEPORTATION

Jehoiakim was succeeded by his 18-year-old son, Jehoiachin, who reigned for only three months and ten days.[4] In 597 BC Nebuchadnezzar laid siege to Jerusalem and Jehoiachin surrendered. 'Nebuchadnezzar encamped against the city of Judah and on the second day of the month of Adar [15/16 March] he captured the city and seized its king. A king of his own choice he appointed in the city and taking a vast tribute he brought it to Babylon' (*The Nebuchadnezzar Chronicle*, Rev. 12–13).

Nebuchadnezzar deported Jehoiachin to Babylon, together with his mother, wives, officials and leading men of the land, the entire force of seven thousand fighting men and a thousand craftsmen and artisans – a total of ten thousand,[5] including a young trainee priest named Ezekiel.[6] He also took the treasures of the royal palace and the gold articles that Solomon had had made for the Temple of the Lord. This can be termed the 'second deportation'.

In Babylon Jehoiachin received rations at the court. His name (Ya'u-kinu) occurs on Babylonian tablets dated between 595 BC and 570 BC, recording his rations and those of his sons: 'Half a *panu* (c. 14 litres or 3 gallons) for Ya'u-kinu, king of the land of Judah. Two and a half *sila* (c. 2 litres or half a gallon) for the five sons of the king of the land of Judah.' Years later, following the death of Nebuchadnezzar in 562 BC, his son and successor, Amel-Marduk (Evil-Merodach), released Jehoiachin from prison and allowed him to eat regularly at his table as long as he lived.[7]

THE SIEGE OF JERUSALEM (588–586 BC)

The prophet Jeremiah cursed Jehoiachin, saying none of his offspring would sit on the throne of David.[8] Nebuchadnezzar took Jehoiachin's uncle, Mattaniah, and made him king, changing his name to Zedekiah and

summoning him to Babylon in 593 BC to affirm his loyalty. Eventually Zedekiah rebelled, again with encouragement from Egypt, but this brought the whole Babylonian army against him. Nebuchadnezzar encamped outside Jerusalem and built siege works all around it, commencing the siege, according to 2 Kings 25:1, on the tenth day of the tenth month (15 January) 588 BC. The siege was lifted temporarily to meet the threat posed by an invading Egyptian army under its pharaoh Hophra (589–570 BC). However, as Jeremiah predicted, the Babylonians returned. Jeremiah advocated surrender and was thrown into a cistern, but was later taken out and kept under guard.

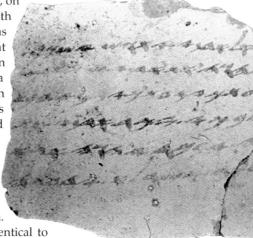

Lachish Letter 2. An ostracon or letter written on a potsherd to Yaosh, the military governor of the Judean city of Lachish, 588 BC.

The tense situation is depicted on twenty-two letters on *ostraca* found in the Judean city of Lachish. They are in language virtually identical to that of Jeremiah. In one of them the commander of an outpost reports that signals, probably fire signals from the town of Azekah, cannot be seen: 'My lord will know that we are watching for the signals of Lachish, according to all the signals which my lord has given me we cannot see Azekah' (*Lachish Letter*, 4.10–12). This could mean that Azekah had already been captured by the Babylonians or, more likely, that climatic conditions were unfavourable, so the signal could not be seen. In another letter an unnamed prophet is mentioned as the bearer of a letter. His identity remains uncertain.

By the ninth day of the fourth month (18 July 586 BC) the famine in Jerusalem had become so severe there was no food for the people to eat. The city walls were breached. Zedekiah and his whole army fled at night, only to be captured on the plains of Jericho. He was taken to Riblah in Syria. His sons were killed before his eyes, which were then put out, and he was taken to Babylon bound in bronze shackles.

THE THIRD DEPORTATION

A month after the wall had been breached on the seventh day of the fifth month (14 August 586 BC) Nebuzaradan, commander of the imperial guard, set fire to the Temple of the Lord, the royal palace and all the houses of Jerusalem. The walls were then broken down. Nebuzaradan carried into exile the people who remained in the city, along with the rest of the populace and those who had gone over to the king of Babylon. He left behind some of the poorest

KEY
[1] Jeremiah 22:13–17
[2] Jeremiah 26:20–23; 36:20–23
[3] Jeremiah 22:19
[4] 2 Chronicles 36:9
[5] 2 Kings 24:14–16
[6] Ezekiel 1:1–3
[7] 2 Kings 25:27–30; Jeremiah 52:31–34
[8] Jeremiah 22:30
[9] 2 Kings 25:26; Jeremiah 42:19; 43:7
[10] Jeremiah 52:30
[11] Ezekiel 3:15; Ezra 2:59; 8:17; Jeremiah 29:5

Balustrade from a window in the palace of Ramat Rahel near Jerusalem. This may possibly be the work of Jehoiakim, king of Judah (609–598 BC).

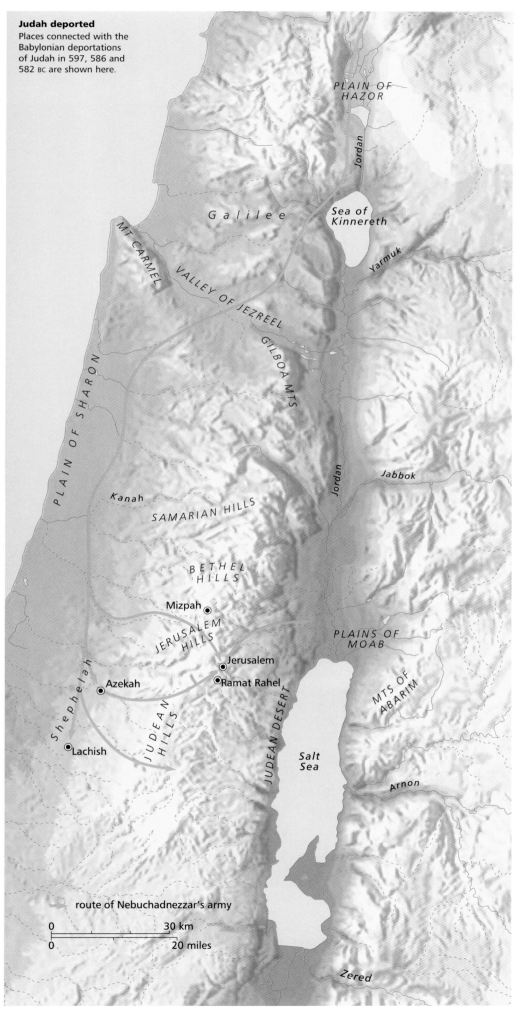

Judah deported
Places connected with the
Babylonian deportations
of Judah in 597, 586 and
582 BC are shown here.

PLAIN OF
HAZOR

Jordan

Galilee

Sea of
Kinnereth

MT CARMEL

Yarmuk

VALLEY OF JEZREEL

GILBOA MTS

PLAIN OF SHARON

Jordan

Jabbok

Kanah

SAMARIAN HILLS

BETHEL
HILLS

Mizpah

JERUSALEM
HILLS

PLAINS OF
MOAB

Shephelah

Azekah

Jerusalem

Ramat Rahel

MTS OF
ABARIM

JUDEAN HILLS

Lachish

JUDEAN DESERT

Salt
Sea

Arnon

route of Nebuchadnezzar's army

0   30 km

0   20 miles

Zered

people of the land, to work the vineyards and
fields, but the vast majority of the people were
deported to Babylon. This can be termed the
'third deportation'. However, Judah's woes
were not ended.

THE FOURTH DEPORTATION

The Babylonians appointed as governor a Jew
from a noble family named Gedaliah, the
imprint of whose seal inscribed 'belonging to
Gedaliah, who is over the house' has been
found at Lachish. Before long Gedaliah was
assassinated by a certain Ishmael, who was of
royal blood. Many of the remaining Jews,
including the prophet Jeremiah, who had been
released from confinement at the capture of
the city, fled to Egypt – despite Jeremiah's
prophetic warning that they should not go.[9] A
further contingent of Jews was exiled to
Babylon in 582 BC.[10] This can be termed the
'fourth deportation'.

THE TRAUMA OF EXILE

Those Jews who survived the long trek to
Babylonia were apparently placed in
settlements of their own, free to engage in
agriculture and to earn their living,[11] but the
traumatic nature of their exile is expressed
clearly by the psalmist:

*'By the rivers of Babylon we sat and wept
when we remembered Zion.
There on the poplars we hung our harps,
for there our captors asked us for songs,
our tormentors demanded songs of joy;
they said, "Sing us one of the songs of Zion!"
How can we sing the songs of the Lord
while in a foreign land?'*
PSALM 137:1–4

THE LATER HEBREW PROPHETS

(740–571 BC)

ISAIAH

The prophet Isaiah began his ministry in the year Judah's King Uzziah died, 740 BC. He lived at least until the assassination of Sennacherib, king of Assyria, in 681 BC.[1] Later Jewish tradition records that Isaiah was sawn in half during the reign of Manasseh (686–641 BC), an event perhaps alluded to in Hebrews 11:37.

Isaiah's great work has a historical interlude (chapters 36–39) that divides it into two. In the earlier chapters (1–35) Isaiah addresses Judah and many of its neighbours. The latter chapters (40–66) constitute a message to a Judah in exile. The fact that Isaiah did not live to see Judah's exile to Babylon in 586 BC and his specific prediction of Cyrus,[2] who authorized the Jews to return from exile in 538 BC, have prompted many to suggest that the latter chapters were written by a second, later Isaiah. However, many striking verbal parallels between the earlier and latter sections – most notably the expression 'the Holy One of Israel', occuring twelve times in the earlier chapters, fourteen in the latter chapters, but only six times in the rest of the Old Testament – are seen as evidence that the work is by a single author.

Isaiah looks ahead to a new, messianic age. A king descended from David will reign in righteousness. The Lord's righteous servant will be smitten by God and afflicted,[3] but 'After the suffering of his soul, he will see the light [of life] and be satisfied; by his knowledge my righteous servant will justify many, and he will bear their iniquities' (Isaiah 53:11).

JEREMIAH

The prophet Jeremiah began his ministry in the thirteenth year of Judah's King Josiah, 626 BC, continuing until after the exile of Judah to Babylon in 586 BC. The book that bears Jeremiah's name is the longest in the Bible. It follows a thematic rather than chronological order. From a priestly family from Anathoth near Jerusalem, Jeremiah gives greater details of his personal life and struggles than any other Old Testament prophet. He was convinced that, since Judah had failed in its obligations to the Lord, Judah would know nothing of his promises. Judah was under the Lord's judgment. In short, it was doomed. Yet there was hope: 'The time is coming,' declares the Lord, 'when I will make a new covenant with the house of Israel and with the house of Judah... I will put my law in their minds and write it on their hearts. I will be their God, and they will be my people... They will all know me, from the least of them to the greatest,' declares the Lord. 'For I will forgive their wickedness and will remember their sins no more' (Jeremiah 31:31, 33b, 34b).

EZEKIEL

Like Jeremiah, Ezekiel was from a priestly family, but in 597 BC he was among the ten thousand Jews exiled to Babylon. Thirteen dates given in the book enable a precise reconstruction of Ezekiel's ministry to be made. On 31 July 593 BC, apparently aged thirty, Ezekiel was called to be a prophet through an awe-inspiring vision of the Lord's glory by the Kebar canal, near Nippur, south of Babylon. Ezekiel

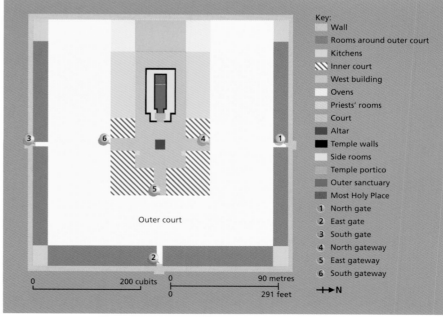

Key:
- Wall
- Rooms around outer court
- Kitchens
- Inner court
- West building
- Ovens
- Priests' rooms
- Court
- Altar
- Temple walls
- Side rooms
- Temple portico
- Outer sanctuary
- Most Holy Place
- 1 North gate
- 2 East gate
- 3 South gate
- 4 North gateway
- 5 East gateway
- 6 South gateway

Outer court

0   200 cubits

0   90 metres

0   291 feet

N

LEFT: An aerial view of the ruins of Babylon. After its rebuilding by Nebuchadnezzar (606–562 BC), Babylon had an area of 1,012 hectares (2,500 acres).

Prophecies against the nations
Many of the Hebrew prophets delivered prophecies against the neighbouring nations. The biblical references show where these prophecies are to be found.

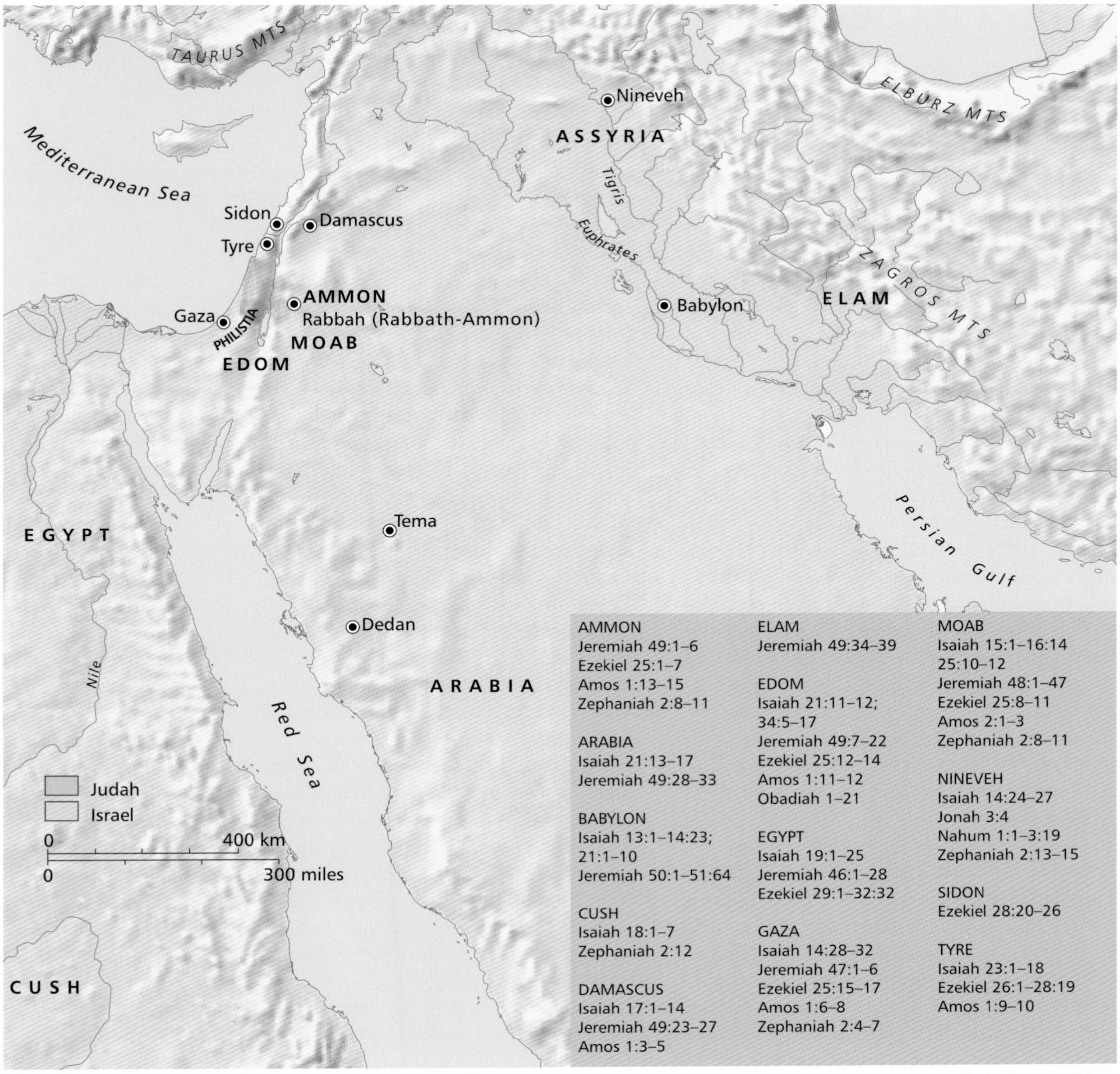

KEY
[1] Isaiah 37:38
[2] Isaiah 44:28; 45:1
[3] Isaiah 9:6–7; 32:1; 53:4
[4] Ezekiel 10:18–22
[5] Ezekiel 24:18, 27
[6] Jeremiah 51:59–64

Plan of Ezekiel's Temple
On 28 April 573 BC the prophet Ezekiel saw a vision of a huge restored Temple, the floor plan of which he describes in intricate detail in chapters 40–43 of his prophecy.

Map labels: TAURUS MTS · ELBURZ MTS · Nineveh · ASSYRIA · Mediterranean Sea · Sidon · Damascus · Tyre · Tigris · Euphrates · ZAGROS MTS · ELAM · Babylon · Gaza · AMMON · Rabbah (Rabbath-Ammon) · PHILISTIA · MOAB · EDOM · EGYPT · Tema · Nile · ARABIA · Red Sea · Persian Gulf · Dedan · CUSH

Judah / Israel

0 — 400 km
0 — 300 miles

AMMON Jeremiah 49:1–6 Ezekiel 25:1–7 Amos 1:13–15 Zephaniah 2:8–11	**ELAM** Jeremiah 49:34–39 **EDOM** Isaiah 21:11–12; 34:5–17 Jeremiah 49:7–22 Ezekiel 25:12–14 Amos 1:11–12 Obadiah 1–21	**MOAB** Isaiah 15:1–16:14 25:10–12 Jeremiah 48:1–47 Ezekiel 25:8–11 Amos 2:1–3 Zephaniah 2:8–11
ARABIA Isaiah 21:13–17 Jeremiah 49:28–33		**NINEVEH** Isaiah 14:24–27 Jonah 3:4 Nahum 1:1–3:19 Zephaniah 2:13–15
BABYLON Isaiah 13:1–14:23; 21:1–10 Jeremiah 50:1–51:64	**EGYPT** Isaiah 19:1–25 Jeremiah 46:1–28 Ezekiel 29:1–32:32	**SIDON** Ezekiel 28:20–26
CUSH Isaiah 18:1–7 Zephaniah 2:12	**GAZA** Isaiah 14:28–32 Jeremiah 47:1–6 Ezekiel 25:15–17 Amos 1:6–8 Zephaniah 2:4–7	**TYRE** Isaiah 23:1–18 Ezekiel 26:1–28:19 Amos 1:9–10
DAMASCUS Isaiah 17:1–14 Jeremiah 49:23–27 Amos 1:3–5		

saw the Lord's glory leave the Temple in Jerusalem and go to be with the exiles in Babylonia.[4] While Ezekiel was in exile, Jerusalem fell to the Babylonians. Ezekiel relates how his wife died on the same day the Temple was burned, 14 August 586 BC.[5] Ezekiel heard the news nearly five months later on 8 January 585 BC. He continued prophesying until at least 26 April 571 BC. He too saw hope beyond the tragedy of the exile. The Lord would breathe his spirit upon the bones of the defunct nation causing it to rise again as a vast army. He would bring his people back to their land, make an eternal covenant of peace with them and place his sanctuary in their midst for ever. The last nine chapters of his prophecy detail a restored Temple in a restored land.

PROPHECIES AGAINST THE NATIONS

The Old Testament prophets did not deliver prophecies only against Israel and Judah. Jonah was commanded to go to Nineveh, the capital of Assyria. His prophecy is the shortest in the entire Old Testament – 'Forty more days and Nineveh will be overturned' (Jonah 3:4) – and arguably the one that produced the greatest response, since the entire city put on sackcloth and called urgently on God, thus averting God's judgment, much to Jonah's disappointment.

Amos delivered prophecies against six neighbouring nations (Amos 1:3–2:3). His hearers would doubtless have applauded his forthright condemnation of their atrocities; but, when the spotlight turned inward, there was no room for complacency. Judah was condemned for rejecting the Law of the Lord, and Israel for oppression of the poor.

In general there is no record of the nations addressed ever hearing the prophet's words, let alone understanding them, but Jeremiah's long prophecy against Babylon was taken there in written form by one of the exiles. After a scroll containing the words had been read, presumably in Hebrew not in Babylonian, a stone was to be tied to it and the scroll cast into the River Euphrates.[6] Of the foreign nations the prophets addressed, the object of the most prophecies were the Philistines, Edom and Moab, each receiving five.

THE TRADE OF TYRE

(586 BC)

TYRE

The city of Tyre was built on an island just off the coast of modern Lebanon. Growing rich on trade with Egypt, Tyre dominated most of the other Phoenician coastal cities and the hinterland of Lebanon. Hiram (969–936 BC), king of Tyre, sent Solomon (970–930 BC) cedar and conifer wood for the construction of the Temple of the Lord in Jerusalem.[1] Tyre founded colonies in various parts of the Mediterranean: Kition on Cyprus (the Kittim of Genesis 10:4 and Ezekiel 27:6), Karatepe in Turkey, as well as in Sicily and Sardinia. Its settlement of Tarshish, destination of the fugitive prophet Jonah, may be located in the Guadalquivir Valley in southern Spain. Arguably its most famous colony was Carthage, in Tunisia, founded according to tradition in 814 BC. Tyre later came under Assyrian rule, but with the decline of Assyria at the end of the reign of Ashurbanipal (c. 636–627 BC) Tyre regained its autonomy and much of its former sea-trade. According to the later Jewish historian Flavius Josephus, the Babylonian king Nebuchadnezzar II besieged Tyre for thirteen years between c. 587 and 574 BC.[2]

EZEKIEL PROPHESIES AGAINST TYRE

The prophet Ezekiel addressed a number of his prophecies to the nations around. In the eleventh year, from the exile of 597 BC, that is, in 586 BC, Ezekiel prophesied against Tyre.[3] Jerusalem was to fall to the Babylonians under Nebuchadnezzar later in that year on 18 July. In a prophecy most likely dating from 13 February or 15 March 586 BC Ezekiel envisages Tyre rejoicing at the fall of Jerusalem: 'Aha! The gate to the nations is broken, and its doors have swung open to me; now that she lies in ruins I will prosper' (Ezekiel 26:2).

The Lord's perspective, as revealed to Ezekiel, was rather different. Nebuchadnezzar would lay siege to Tyre. The walls of Tyre would be destroyed, her towers pulled down, her rubble scraped away, and she would be made a bare rock, a place for spreading fishing nets, never to be rebuilt.[4] Lack of contemporary evidence prevents verification of how the details of this prophecy were fulfilled in the siege of Nebuchadnezzar, but certainly they were fulfilled in 332 BC, when Alexander the Great built a causeway to the island and after a seven-month siege captured the city.

THE LAMENT FOR TYRE

Ezekiel gives a lament for Tyre (Ezekiel 27:1–36). After a lengthy description of its trade Ezekiel prophesies the ruin of Tyre, which he likens to a shipwreck. The description of Tyre's trade is the most detailed description of trade in the Old Testament. Not only can we see the geographical range of Tyre's trading contacts, but we can also see the variety of the products traded.

● That Tyre controlled the timber and boat-building trade of Lebanon is no great surprise. Conifers are listed from Senir (Mount Hermon) or the whole Anti-Lebanon range. Cedar from Lebanon was used for a mast and oaks from Bashan in Transjordan for oars. Cypress wood from Kittim was to be used for a deck, which was inlaid with ivory. The source of the ivory is uncertain, but we need not suppose an African origin, the Syrian elephant, a sub-species of the Indian elephant inhabited the Euphrates Valley in Syria until c. 800 BC. Egypt supplied embroidered, fine, white linen for the sail; awnings were dyed blue and purple using dye extracted from shellfish from Elishah in Cyprus.

● Men from the coastal cities of Sidon and Arvad were oarsmen. Those from Tyre itself, a seemingly higher class of sailor, were helmsmen. Men from Byblos were commissioned to keep the ship watertight. Men from Persia, Lydia (western Turkey) and Put (Libya) served as mercenaries. Men from up the coast in Arvad, Helech (Cilicia in Turkey) and Gammad (possibly in northern Turkey) were charged with defending the city.

● The location of Tarshish, arguably Tyre's most distant trading partner, is uncertain. Perhaps it is Tyre's colony in the Guadalquivir Valley in southern Spain or its colonies in Sardinia or Sicily or, much closer to home, Tarsus in southern Turkey. Wherever it was, Tarshish had access to a variety of metals – silver, iron, tin and lead – to trade with Tyre. Areas in modern Turkey – Javan, Tubal and Meshech – traded in slaves and bronze articles. Another area now in Turkey is Beth Togarmah, probably the modern town of Gürün, which in antiquity was famous for its horse-rearing.

● Men of Rhodes engaged in trade with Tyre, paying in ivory tusks and a wood translated as 'ebony', but which was a reddish black wood from the drier parts of tropical Africa, not true ebony, which was at that time unknown.

● The products listed from Aram (turquoise, purple fabric, embroidered work, fine linen, coral and rubies) better fit Edom, the area south of the Dead Sea with access to the Red Sea (for coral) and the Sinai Peninsula (for turquoise). Edom is only one letter different from Aram in Hebrew, so it seems plausible to emend the text here.

● Judah and Israel exchanged wheat from Minnith in Ammon, honey, olive oil and balm, a product for which Gilead was famous.[5]

● Damascus, in Syria, traded products from its vicinity: wine from Helbon and wool from Zahar. If a slight emendation to the Hebrew text is made, the merchants of Damascus also dealt in vats of wine from Uzal, the Tur Abdin region of south-east Turkey from where Nebuchadnezzar (605–562 BC) obtained his wine. Furthermore they dealt in two spices called cassia (cinnamon blossom) and calamus (a type of cane). In this period it is unlikely, though not impossible, that the spices were regularly obtained from India or farther east, from where they were obtained in Roman times. Southern Arabia, however, is a more likely source.

● The list concludes with Tyre's remaining trading partners. The locations of Haran, Eden, Sheba and Asshur are known. Haran is in south-east Turkey, Eden further south in modern Syria. Sheba is modern Yemen and Asshur is Assyria in northern Iraq. Canneh may be close to Haran, but this is only a guess. Kilmad may be a reference to the Medes of Iran. The trading partners' products are rich and various – beautiful garments, blue fabric, embroidered work

and multicoloured rugs with cords twisted and tightly knotted, the latter being a distinctive product of the whole region to this day.

THE END OF TYRE

Tyre's trade, so graphically described by Ezekiel, was to come to an end. 'The east wind will break you to pieces in the heart of the sea. Your wealth, merchandise and wares, your mariners, seamen and shipwrights, your merchants and all your soldiers and everyone else on board will sink into the heart of the sea on the day of your shipwreck' (Ezekiel 27:26b–27). Tyre, the great sea power, had itself been shipwrecked.

Tyre submits to the Assyrian king Shalmaneser III (859–824 BC). From the bronze gates of Balawat, Iraq.

Tyre's trading partners
Tyre's extensive trade is described in detail in Ezekiel 27. Numbers on both maps refer to verses of this chapter.

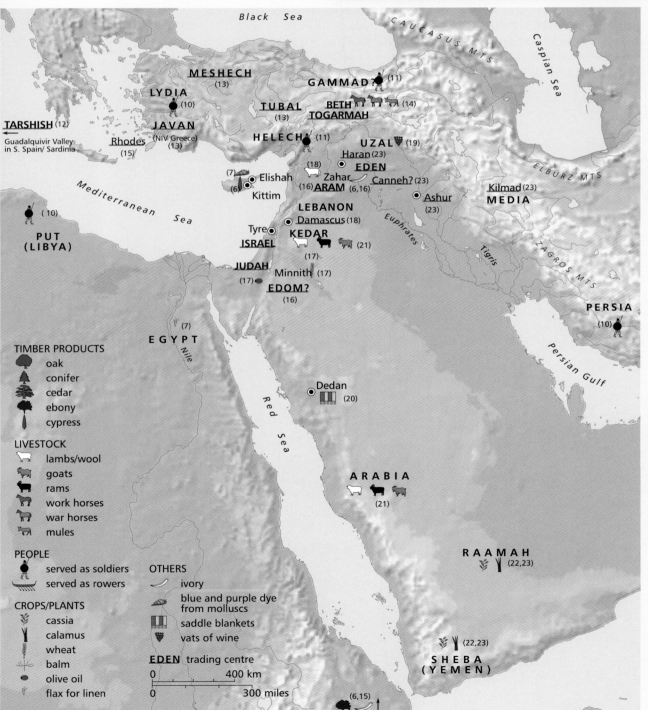

MESHECH (13)

LYDIA (10)

TARSHISH (12)
Guadalquivir Valley in S. Spain/ Sardinia

JAVAN (NIV Greece) (13)

Rhodes (15)

GAMMAD? (11)

TUBAL (13)

BETH TOGARMAH (14)

HELECH (11)

UZAL (19)

Haran (23)

EDEN

Canneh? (23)

Kilmad (23)

MEDIA

(18)

Elishah (7)

(6)

Kittim

Zahar (16) ARAM (6,16)

Ashur (23)

LEBANON

Damascus (18)

Tyre

KEDAR

ISRAEL

(21)

(17)

JUDAH

Minnith (17)

(17)

EDOM? (16)

PUT (LIBYA) (10)

PERSIA (10)

Black Sea

CAUCASUS MTS

Caspian Sea

ELBURZ MTS

Euphrates

Tigris

ZAGROS MTS

Mediterranean Sea

EGYPT (7)

Nile

Red Sea

Dedan (20)

ARABIA (21)

Persian Gulf

RAAMAH (22,23)

SHEBA (YEMEN) (22,23)

(6,15)

TIMBER PRODUCTS
- oak
- conifer
- cedar
- ebony
- cypress

LIVESTOCK
- lambs/wool
- goats
- rams
- work horses
- war horses
- mules

PEOPLE
- served as soldiers
- served as rowers

OTHERS
- ivory
- blue and purple dye from molluscs
- saddle blankets
- vats of wine

CROPS/PLANTS
- cassia
- calamus
- wheat
- balm
- olive oil
- flax for linen

EDEN trading centre

0   400 km
0   300 miles

KEY
[1] 1 Kings 5:1–12; 2 Chronicles 2:3–16
[2] Josephus, *Antiquities*, 10.228
[3] Ezekiel 26:1
[4] Ezekiel 26:4–14
[5] Jeremiah 8:22; 46:11

DANIEL AND NEBUCHADNEZZAR

(605–562 BC)

DANIEL AND HIS FRIENDS

Daniel and his three friends, Hananiah, Mishael and Azariah, had been deported to Babylon in 605 BC. They quickly had to resolve not to defile themselves with the royal food and wine, almost certainly because it had first been offered to idols.[1] Nebuchadnezzar was impressed with his four new courtiers. In every matter of wisdom and understanding about which he questioned them he found them to be ten times better than all the magicians and enchanters in his kingdom. In the second year of his reign (604 BC) Nebuchadnezzar had a dream.[2] Perhaps to secure a divinely inspired interpretation, the troubled king said that his advisers would first have to tell him the dream and then give the interpretation. With the help of his God Daniel was able to tell Nebuchadnezzar his dream, in which he saw a great statue in four parts, and he gave an interpretation concerning five kingdoms,

the first of which was Nebuchadnezzar's Babylon.

According to the book of Daniel 3:1 Nebuchadnezzar commissioned the construction of a gilded statue in the Plain of Dura, possibly Duru-sha-karrabi, a suburb of Babylon. With a height of sixty cubits (27 m or 89 ft) the statue could well have included a plinth or column. Nebuchadnezzar ordered everyone to fall down and worship it. But Daniel's three friends, who by that time had received the Babylonian names of Shadrach, Meshach and Abednego, refused and were thrown into a brick kiln. The Lord miraculously preserved them. A fourth man – according to Nebuchadnezzar's astonished exclamation 'one like a son of the gods'[3] – was there with them.

ANOTHER DREAM

Daniel served faithfully in Nebuchadnezzar's court. The king had another dream, in which he saw a great tree cut

KEY
[1] Daniel 1:8
[2] Daniel 2:1
[3] Daniel 3:25b
[4] Daniel 4:1–17
[5] Daniel 4:33

A reconstruction of the northernmost part of Babylon, as rebuilt by Nebuchadnezzar. The Processional Way leading to the Ishtar Gate, the great ziggurat (Entemenanki), the North Palace, the city wall and moat and a possible reconstruction of the Hanging Gardens can all be clearly seen.

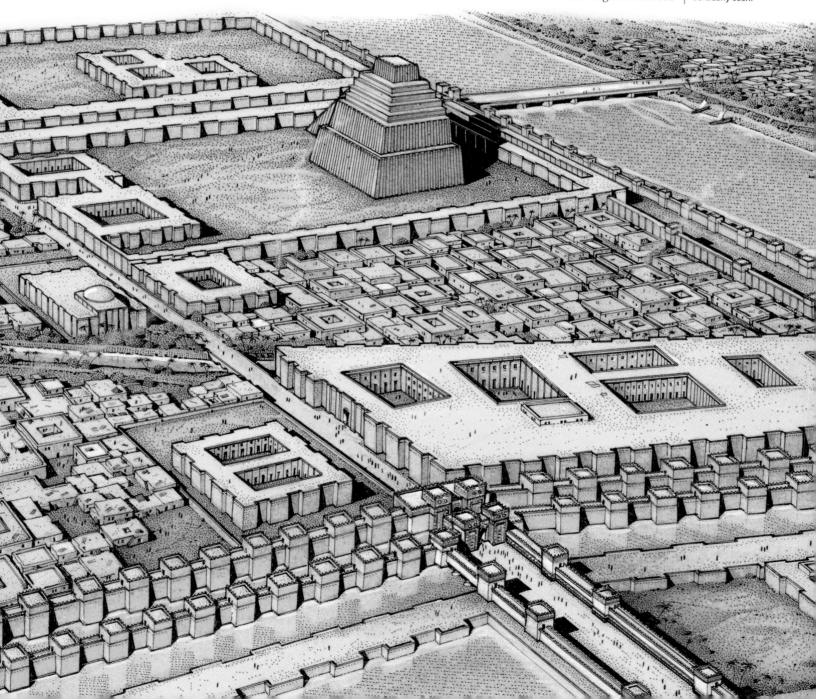

down, leaving just a stump and roots.[4] Daniel interpreted this as referring to the king himself and urged him to renounce his wickedness, so that from his roots a fresh, new life could grow. But Nebuchadnezzar would have none of it. Twelve months later, while walking on the roof of his royal palace, he boasted: 'Is not this the great Babylon I have built as the royal residence, by my mighty power and for the glory of my majesty?' (Daniel 4:30).

Plan of Babylon
Babylon – as rebuilt by Nebuchadnezzar – was vast, with an area of 1,012 hectares (2,500 acres).

1 Etemenanki Temple
2 Esagila Temple
3 North Palace of Nebuchadnezzar

4 Nebuchadnezzar's Palace
5 Hanging Gardens (?)
6 Ishtar Gate
7 Processional Way
8 New Quarter
9 River Tigris
10 Bridge

NEBUCHADNEZZAR'S BABYLON

At 1,012 hectares (2,500 acres) Nebuchadnezzar's Babylon was indeed great – larger than ancient Alexandria, Antioch and Constantinople, though smaller than Rome. It was surrounded by an outer wall 27 km (17 miles) long and wide enough for chariots to pass by on the top. A bridge was built over the Euphrates and a new quarter developed on the west bank. The bridge had wooden platforms which could be withdrawn if an enemy attacked. Of all the hundred or so gates the greatest was the great north gate, dedicated to the goddess Ishtar. It was originally built in plain-glazed brick with reliefs depicting lions, dragons and bulls. Later Nebuchadnezzar overlaid the whole structure with blue-glazed, enamelled bricks bearing the same designs. Away from the gate led a 920-metre-long (3,018 ft) processional way, along which the king passed out of the city every year to celebrate the *akitu* or New Year Festival.

Great temples were built: the massive Etemenanki ziggurat (temple-tower), the Esagila (temple of Babylon's national god, Marduk) crowned with three massive gold statues with a total weight of nearly a hundred and fifty tons, and at least fifty-three other temples, many of them capped with gold or silver tops shining like the sun. Nebuchadnezzar's own palace was a vast complex of rooms in the northern part of the city. The largest room was the great throne room, 52 m by 17 m (170 ft by 56 ft). A huge panel of glazed bricks from here is now in the Staatliche Museum in Berlin. It is now generally accepted that the 'hanging gardens', one of the Seven Wonders of the Ancient World, were to the north of Nebuchadnezzar's north palace. Here there is plenty of room for a series of vaulted terraces planted with all kinds of trees, shrubs and flowering plants to remind Nebuchadnezzar's wife, Amytis, of the mountains of her native Media (in what is now Iran).

NEBUCHADNEZZAR'S PRIDE

It is estimated that 164 million bricks were made for the northern, outer defence wall of Babylon alone. On many of the bricks in his great city Nebuchadnezzar had the following stamped: 'Nebuchadnezzar, king of Babylon, who provides for Esagila and Ezida [two temples] the eldest son of Nabopolassar, king of Babylon, am I.'

However, according to the book of Daniel the Lord had had enough of the king's arrogance. Nebuchadnezzar was driven away from people and ate grass like an ox. His hair grew like the feathers of an eagle and his nails like the claws of a bird.[5] Only after he acknowledged that the Lord's dominion was eternal, and that his kingdom endured from generation to generation, was he restored to sanity and to his kingdom. Significantly, since we have very few inscriptions from the latter years of Nebuchadnezzar's reign, we know virtually nothing about it. The 'madness' could fit into those last few years. Its duration, specified in Daniel 4:32 as 'seven times', could be seven years, but a less specific period is also possible, perhaps to be preferred.

THE FALL OF BABYLON AND CYRUS'S DECREE

(562–537 BC)

AFTER NEBUCHADNEZZAR

Nebuchadnezzar died in 562 BC and was succeeded by his son, Evil-Merodach (Amel-Marduk), who released Judah's former king Jehoiachin from prison. Evil-Merodach reigned for only two years (562–560 BC) before he was murdered by a former general, his brother-in-law, Neriglissar (560–556 BC). After a four-year reign Neriglissar died and was succeeded by his son, Labashi-Marduk (556 BC). He was quickly murdered and Nabonidus (556–539 BC), who had possibly married a daughter of Nebuchadnezzar, seized the throne.

NABONIDUS IN ARABIA

Nabonidus appointed his son Bel-shar-usur (King Belshazzar of Daniel 5:1) as regent and took off to Tema, an oasis in the western Arabian desert. He captured Tema, massacred the king and most of its inhabitants, established his authority and then stayed for ten years, from 553 to 543 BC. Ostensibly he was restoring the temple of the moon-god Sin at Tema. But why did he stay away from Babylon for so long?

Perhaps he was securing the incense route that ran up western Arabia from Yemen, keeping it from falling into the hands of the king of Egypt, Amasis II (570–526 BC). Perhaps his devotion to the moon-god Sin had alienated him from the priests of Marduk in Babylon and he felt he could not return. Perhaps Nabonidus himself was ill. The so-called 'Prayer of Nabonidus' from the 'Dead Sea Scrolls' found at Qumran says that Nabonidus was smitten with malignant boils for seven years in the city of Teman.

THE FALL OF BABYLON

Those Jews who took Jeremiah's prophetic word seriously realized that the seventy years of exile he predicted (if measured from the first deportation of 605 BC) were coming to an end.[1]

During Nabonidus's absence in Arabia a new world power was emerging. The Medes and Persians under Cyrus II moved north to outflank the Babylonians. In 547 BC Cyrus defeated Croesus of Lydia in western Turkey and captured his capital Sardis. Nabonidus, recognizing the growing Persian threat, returned to Babylon. In the late summer of 539 BC the Persians struck. Cyrus defeated the Babylonian armies at Opis on the Tigris. On the fourteenth of Tishri (10 October) Sippar was captured without a battle and Nabonidus fled.

In the security of Babylon Belshazzar was not afraid. Babylon's mighty walls could withstand many years of siege. In an act of bravado Belshazzar called for the gold and

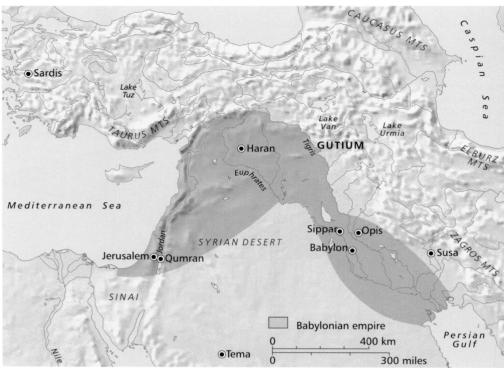

silver goblets from the Temple of the Lord in Jerusalem. Then mysterious writing appeared on the wall: 'MENE, MENE, TEKEL, PARSIN'. Daniel, now aged eighty or so, was summoned, perhaps out of retirement, to give an interpretation. The words concerned three weights – the mina, shekel and half mina – containing hidden puns, including in PARSIN (singular PERES) a reference to the Persians. Daniel's interpretation – 'God has numbered the days of your reign and brought it to an end. You have been weighed on the scales and found wanting. Your kingdom is divided and given to the Medes and Persians' (Daniel 5:26–28) – found immediate fulfilment. 'That very night Belshazzar, king of the Babylonians, was slain and Darius the Mede took over the kingdom, at the age of sixty-two' (Daniel 5:30–31).

The *Nabonidus Chronicle* records that on the sixteenth of Tishri (12 October) Ugbaru, the rebel governor of Gutium (Assyria), and the troops of Cyrus entered Babylon without a battle.[2]

DARIUS THE MEDE

The book of Daniel ascribes the capture of Babylon to a certain 'Darius the Mede'. Some have equated Darius with Ugbaru, but the *Nabonidus Chronicle* records his death on 6 November that year. Others have equated Darius with another official named Gubaru, who may or may not be the same as Ugbaru. However, there is no specific evidence that either Ugbaru or Gubaru was a Mede, called

king, named Darius, a son of Xerxes[3] and aged sixty-two. The Persian king, Cyrus, however, is known to have been about sixty-two when he became king of Babylon. He also styled himself 'King of the Medes'. Darius the Mede may simply be another name for Cyrus the Persian, with Daniel 6:28 being translated 'in the reign of Darius, that is, in the reign of Cyrus the Persian'. Cyrus was not a son of Xerxes either, his father being Cambyses, but he was half-Mede through his mother, Mandane.

THE PERSIANS CAPTURE BABYLON

The Greek historians Herodotus[4] and Xenophon[5] say that the Persians diverted the waters of the River Euphrates into the nearby

A Babylonian account, known as the Cyrus Cylinder, of the accession of the Persian king Cyrus to the throne of Babylon, 539 BC. It describes the favourable reception Cyrus received from the Babylonians.

LEFT: The Babylonian empire after Nebuchadnezzar
After the death of Nebuchadnezzar in 562 BC the Babylonian empire went into gradual decline. In 539 BC the Persians under Cyrus captured Babylon.

KEY

[1] Jeremiah 25:11–12; Daniel 9:2

[2] *Nabonidus Chronicle,* 3.15–16

[3] Daniel 9:1

[4] Herodotus, *Histories,* 1.191

[5] Xenophon, *Cyropaedia,* 7.5.10–16

[6] Daniel 5:7, 29

[7] Daniel 9:2, 18b–19

[8] Daniel 6:1–27

RIGHT: A stone relief showing the Assyrian king hunting lions. From the palace of King Ashurbanipal (669–627 BC), Nineveh.

LEFT: Stela, from Babylon, of the Babylonian king Nabonidus (556–539 BC) standing before emblems of the deities Sin, Shamash and Ishtar.

Aqarquf depression and waded up to the thighs along the riverbed into the city. Herodotus speaks of the inhabitants of Babylon dancing and making merry at a festival. Xenophon says that the Persians struck during a festival, 'when all Babylon was accustomed to drink and revel all night long'. Belshazzar's feast was thus his last act before meeting his fate at the hand of the Persian armies. The kingship of Nabonidus and regency of Belshazzar explain why Daniel can only be offered the post of third-highest ruler in the kingdom.[6]

Nabonidus appears to have been captured and brought back to Babylon. On the third of Marcheswan (29 October) Cyrus himself entered Babylon.

CYRUS ISSUES HIS DECREE

Many in Babylon were pleased to see the end of Nabonidus's rule and we can believe Cyrus's words recorded in his own 'Cyrus Cylinder': 'All the inhabitants of Babylon, as well as the entire country of Sumer and Akkad, princes and governors, bowed to him and kissed his feet, jubilant that he had received the kingship, and with shining faces they happily greeted him as master through whose help they had come to life from death and had been spared damage and disaster.'

Cyrus treated the Babylonians well. Indeed he sought to treat all his loyal subject peoples well, including the Jews. Daniel, aware of the prophecy of Jeremiah that the desolation of Jerusalem would last seventy years, petitioned his God to act.[7]

Daniel's prayers were quickly answered. In 538 BC Cyrus made his great proclamation, recorded at the end of 2 Chronicles, the last book of the Hebrew Bible:

'This is what Cyrus, king of Persia, says:

"The Lord, the God of heaven, has given me all the kingdoms of the earth and he has appointed me to build a temple for him at Jerusalem in Judah. Anyone of his people among you – may the Lord his God be with him, and let him go up."'

2 CHRONICLES 36:23; EZRA 1:2–3a

He thus fulfilled the prediction made by the prophet Isaiah some 160 years earlier concerning Cyrus, the Lord's anointed:

'Who says of Cyrus, "He is my shepherd
and will accomplish all that I please";
he will say of Jerusalem, "Let it be rebuilt,"
and of the temple, "Let its foundations be laid."

ISAIAH 44:28

DANIEL IN THE LIONS' DEN

Daniel would have been at least eighty years old by the third year of Cyrus as king of Babylon (537 BC), when the first group of exiles returned to Jerusalem. Daniel did not go with them, perhaps he was content to rest on what God had said at the end of his prophecy: 'As for you, go your way till the end. You will rest, and then at the end of the days you will rise to receive your allotted inheritance' (Daniel 12:13).

Darius the Mede fell for a plot hatched by his advisers and so was obliged to consign the aged Daniel to a den of lions.[8] However, after having spent a night in the den, Daniel told the anguished king: 'My God sent his angel, and he shut the mouths of the lions.' From the perspective of the biblical writers, God had just as clearly delivered his righteous servant Daniel as he had set in motion events that would lead his exiled people back from Babylon.

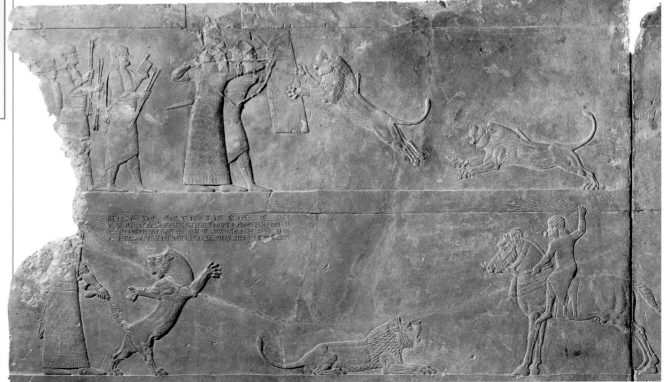

REBUILDING THE TEMPLE

(537–520 BC)

SHESHBAZZAR

According to the book of Ezra 2:64, a total of 42,360 Jews responded to the challenge to return to Jerusalem. What proportion of the Jews living in exile in Babylon this represents is uncertain. The historian Josephus says that many were not willing to leave their possessions.[1] The returning Jews were led by a certain Sheshbazzar, the prince of Judah.[2] They took with them the articles belonging to the Temple of the Lord which Nebuchadnezzar had carried away from Jerusalem.[3] Their journey back to Jerusalem probably took place in 537 BC.

THE TEMPLE FOUNDATIONS ARE LAID

Thereafter, Sheshbazzar fades out of the action. His place as leader of Judah is taken by Zerubbabel, son of Shealtiel and a grandson of Jehoiachin. Immediately the returnees rebuilt the altar and recommenced sacrifices. The following year they laid the foundations for the new Temple. The book of Ezra records mixed emotions:

'And all the people gave a great shout of praise to the Lord, because the foundation of the house of the Lord was laid. But many of the older priests and Levites and family heads who had seen the former temple wept aloud… while many others shouted for joy.'

EZRA 3:11b–12

The rejoicing was short lived. When their offers to help were refused, the descendants of those resettled in Samaria and others hired counsellors to work against them to frustrate their plans.[4] So work on the Temple ceased for the rest of the reign of Cyrus and his son Cambyses II (530–522 BC), sixteen years in all. In c. 400 BC the Samaritans were to obtain Persian authorization for the construction of their own temple to the Lord on Mount Gerizim, near Shechem.

A NEW BEGINNING – DARIUS, HAGGAI AND ZECHARIAH

In 522 BC, following the death of Cambyses, a power struggle ensued for the Persian throne. The victor was Darius, the son of the satrap Hystaspes and a member of the Royal family by a collateral line. He describes his accession to the Persian throne on his famous rock-cut inscription at Behistun, or Bisitun, some 30 km (18½ miles) east of Kermanshah in Iran. (Incidentally, this inscription which carries Babylonian, Elamite and Old Persian versions was used to decipher the cuneiform writing system of Mesopotamia.)

By 520 BC Darius's position was secure. It was in that very year that the Lord raised up two prophets, Haggai and Zechariah, to urge his people to complete the Temple.[5]

Haggai's style was direct and to the point: 'Is it a time for you yourselves to be living in your panelled houses, while this house remains a ruin?' (Haggai 1:4).

The Lord spoke to Zechariah through a series of visions: 'This is the word of the Lord to Zerubbabel: "Not by might, nor by power, but by my Spirit," says the Lord Almighty. "What are you, O mighty mountain? Before Zerubbabel you will become level ground. Then he will bring out the capstone to shouts of 'God bless it! God bless it!' "' (Zechariah 4:6–7).

Matters were delayed further when the governor of the Trans-Euphrates province Tattenai asked who authorized the Jews to rebuild the Temple. Fortunately for the Jews a copy of the original decree of Cyrus was eventually found in the citadel of Ecbatana (the modern Iranian city of Hamadan) in the province of Media.

The prophets' words had the desired effect. Work on the Temple was begun on the twenty-fourth day of the sixth month (21 September 520 BC) and completed three and a half years later on the third of Adar (12 March 516 BC).[6] Zerubbabel's Temple certainly was not as large and ornate as Solomon's. It was eventually replaced by Herod's magnificent Temple. It is possible that part of the masonry of Zerubbabel's Temple has survived.

DARIUS

Darius (522–486 BC) was a successful warrior king. His exploits were recorded by the celebrated Greek historian Herodotus of Halicarnassus (modern Bodrum in southwest Turkey). Throwing a bridge of boats across the Bosphorus to the north of modern Istanbul, Darius conquered the Scythians of southern Russia and the whole of the Balkans south of the Danube. He also cut a canal linking the Nile and the Red Sea, recording his actions on four red granite *stelae*.

His only failure was his expedition against Greece. A storm off Mount Athos in northern Greece destroyed much of his fleet. In 490 BC the surviving Persian fleet anchored in the bay at Marathon on the east coast of the peninsula of Attica just 40 km (26 miles) from Athens. In the absence of help from Sparta it was left to the Athenians and their allies, the Plataeans, to take on the Persians alone. The Athenians were able to drive the Persians back to the sea, capturing seven Persian ships. The Persians then turned round and sailed back to Asia. But it was a defeat that galled the Persians and provoked a much larger invasion under Darius's son Xerxes (486–465 BC) ten years later.

LEFT: The 'seam' located in the eastern wall of the Temple enclosure, where the very neat Herodian masonry (on the left) meets parts of a wall built earlier. This is often thought to be that of Zerubbabel's Temple.

RIGHT: The Persian Empire The Persians ruled over an empire stretching from the Aegean Sea to the Indus River. The Persian king Cambyses conquered Egypt in 525 BC and the Persian kings Darius and Xerxes mounted unsuccessful campaigns against Greece in 490 and 480 BC.

KEY
[1] Josephus, *Antiquities*, 11.8
[2] Ezra 1:8
[3] Ezra 1:7
[4] Ezra 4:5
[5] Ezra 5:1; Haggai 1:1; Zechariah 1:1
[6] Ezra 6:15

RIGHT: Persepolis. The apadana or great audience hall of Darius I (522–486 BC).

INSET: Silver plaque in three languages – Old Persian, Elamite and Babylonian – placed in the foundation of the apadana of Darius I.

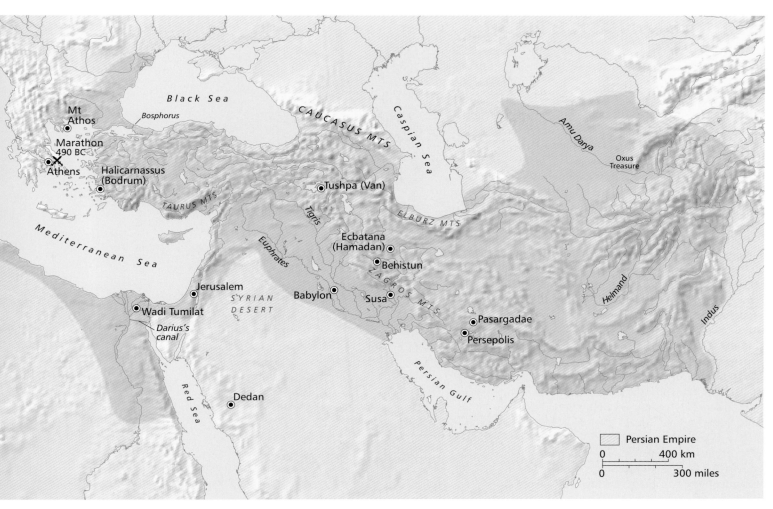

Xerxes and Esther

(486–465 BC)

Xerxes plans revenge

Darius was succeeded by his son, Xerxes (486–465 BC). The prophet Daniel speaks of Xerxes in the form of a prophecy: 'Three more kings will appear in Persia, and then a fourth, who will be far richer than all the others. When he has gained power by his wealth, he will stir up everyone against the kingdom of Greece' (Daniel 11:2). Xerxes could not forget the stinging defeat his father, Darius, had suffered at the hands of the Athenians. He had his servant remind him every day – 'Master, remember the Athenians' – and made preparations to invade Greece on a massive scale.

In 483 BC Xerxes had a canal dug through the narrow stretch of land to the north of Mount Athos, where Darius's fleet had been wrecked. In 480 BC to transport the Persian army across the Dardanelles, the narrow straits separating Asia from Europe, Xerxes had two bridges made. Warships were lashed together to support the bridges: 360 ships for the northern bridge, 314 for the southern one. Brushwood was put on top and spread evenly, with a layer of soil trodden down hard. A fence was put along each side to prevent horses and mules from seeing and taking fright at the water. It took seven days and seven nights for the Persian troops to cross the bridges.

Xerxes invades Greece

The Persian army advanced into Greece. Herodotus describes in detail the various nationalities in the army, their clothes and weapons, and he gives his own estimate of the total number of troops and helpers as 5,283,220 – a figure which modern scholars reduce considerably. He describes the Persian army drinking rivers dry: 'I am not surprised that, with so many people and so many beasts, the rivers sometimes failed to provide enough water' (Herodotus, *Histories*, 7.187).

The vast army's progress was impeded by a force of three hundred Spartans holding the pass of Thermopylae in central Greece. Eventually a traitor showed the Persians a secret path over the mountains, the Spartans were removed and the army turned its attention to Athens. Most of the Athenians deserted the city and took refuge on the islands of Aegina and Salamis. A few, believing an oracle from Delphi that a wooden wall would stand intact, erected a temporary wooden wall on the Acropolis and took refuge behind it. Persian soldiers attached lighted tow to arrows and burnt the wooden wall. Still the Athenians there resisted, rolling huge boulders down on top of the advancing Persian army.

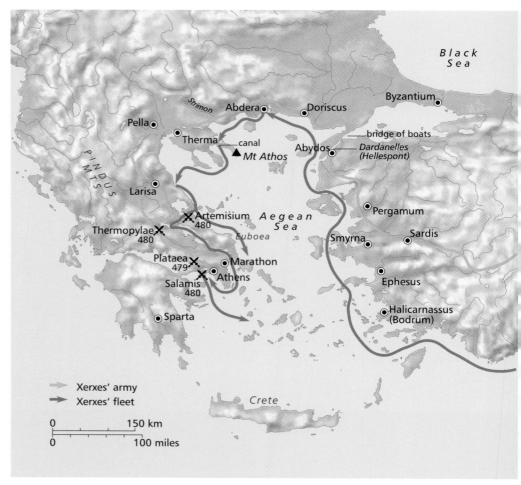

Eventually however Persian soldiers climbed up the side of the Acropolis and burned all the temples to the ground.

It seemed that Xerxes had fulfilled his ambition of capturing Athens and avenging his father's defeat at Marathon ten years earlier. The Greek fleet still remained, however, and many Athenians believed that the wooden

Limestone relief showing a Median officer paying homage to the Persian king Darius I (522–486 BC), from the Treasury, Persepolis, Iran.

TOP LEFT: **Xerxes' invasion of Greece** Xerxes mounted an ultimately unsuccessful campaign against Greece in 480 BC. His assault was on both land and sea using massive resources.

KEY

[1] Herodotus, *Histories*, 7.61
[2] Esther 2:16–17
[3] Esther 3:8–11
[4] Esther 5:2–3
[5] Esther 7:6
[6] Esther 8:2; 10:2
[7] Esther 9:18–32

LEFT: Persian gold model chariot, c. 500 BC. Length 18.8 cm (7½ in). From the Oxus Treasure, Tajikistan.

wall referred to by the Delphic oracle was their fleet of some three hundred and ten ships.

DEFEATS AT SALAMIS AND PLATAEA

The Greeks lured the Persian fleet into a narrow stretch of water between the island of Salamis and the Greek mainland, near Athens. Xerxes watched the ensuing battle from his throne on the Greek mainland. In the narrow waters the action was intense. Once again the Persians came off worse. They are said to have lost two hundred ships, the Greeks forty. The surviving Persian ships sailed away across the Aegean sea to protect the bridges on the Dardanelles. Most of the soldiers in the vast Persian army made their way back to Asia with Xerxes. A force of the best troops, perhaps consisting of seventy-five thousand men, was left behind under the command of a general named Mardonius. This was defeated by the Greeks at Plataea in central Greece in the following year (479 BC).

QUEEN VASHTI

The book of Esther begins with Xerxes (called Ahasuerus in the Authorized Version) giving a seven-day banquet for all his nobles and officials in the third year of his reign (483 BC). We are told that the military leaders and the nobles of the provinces were present, so this could have been the meeting that launched the disastrous campaign against Greece. On the seventh day, when Xerxes was in high spirits from wine, he sent for his queen to join the banquet. Queen Vashti, who is sometimes equated with Xerxes' queen Amestris,[1] declined. For disobeying the king's order and setting a bad example to wives throughout his kingdom, she was stripped of her queenship.

ESTHER

The next date in the book of Esther is the tenth month of the seventh year (479 BC), the time gap between the third and seventh years no doubt accounted for by Xerxes' débâcle in Greece. A beautiful Jewish girl called Hadassah,

or Esther, was urged by her cousin and guardian, Mordecai, to present herself in the palace harem but to keep her background and nationality secret. She was selected as Xerxes' new queen.[2]

Set in Susa, the winter residence of the Persian kings in what is now south-western Iran, the story of Esther is one of great pathos and drama. The court of the Persian king, described in the first chapter of the book of Esther, fits well with the inscriptional and archaeological evidence from Susa. 'The garden had hangings of white and blue linen, fastened with cords of white linen and purple material to silver rings on marble pillars. There were couches of gold and silver on a mosaic pavement of porphyry, marble, mother-of-pearl and other costly stones' (Esther 1:6)

Mordecai uncovers a conspiracy to assassinate Xerxes, but his actions, though recorded in the royal annals, are forgotten when the wicked Haman gets Xerxes to agree to the extinction of the Jews.[3] Mordecai urges Esther to take action to save her people: 'And who knows but that you have come to royal position for such a time as this?' (Esther 4:14b).

Risking her life, Esther seeks a private audience with her husband. The king holds out his gold sceptre as a sign of his approval and offers to grant her request.[4] Esther invites Xerxes and Haman to a banquet, but defers presenting her request until another banquet the following day. That night Haman prepares a gallows to hang 'that Jew Mordecai', and the sleepless king reads in the royal annals of Mordecai's earlier deeds. When Haman enters the court to ask Xerxes for permission to hang Mordecai, he is asked what should be done for the man the king delights to honour? Thinking he is being asked to honour himself, Haman proposes a number of ostentatious actions. He is then told to do them for Mordecai the Jew.

Haman's wife sees this as a presage of worse to come: 'Since Mordecai, before whom your downfall has started, is of Jewish origin, you cannot stand against him – you will surely come to ruin!' (Esther 6:13). At the second banquet Esther unmasks Haman's plot[5] and saves the Jews from universal extinction. Haman is hanged on the gallows he had prepared for Mordecai, together with his sons, and Mordecai is promoted to be Xerxes' chief minister.[6]

LATER DEVELOPMENTS

In 465 BC Xerxes was assassinated in a palace plot and was succeeded by his son, Artaxerxes (Hebrew: Artahshasta). He was a son of Amestris (proposed above to be Vashti), who acted as queen mother until her death in c. 424 BC. If this proposal is true, Vashti clearly made a comeback (whether at the expense of Esther we know not), but at least this is consistent with the book of Esther, which nowhere mentions Vashti's being killed or formally divorced.

The Jews instituted the festival of Purim to commemorate Mordecai, their deliverance under Esther and the rescinding of the lot (*pur*) that the vile Haman had cast for them.[7]

EZRA AND NEHEMIAH

(458–433 BC)

EZRA

In Artaxerxes' seventh year (458 BC) a teacher well-versed in the Law of Moses, named Ezra, left Babylon for Jerusalem.[1] With him came a large group of families carrying silver and gold that the king, his advisers, his officials and the Jews had donated for the Temple in Jerusalem. It was a journey that took four months. Ezra was concerned that God might punish his people again because many men had defied the Law and married into neighbouring peoples.[2] Such men would have to divorce their foreign wives and abandon their children.[3] Ezra attained a great reputation among the Jews in later times, being seen as a 'second Moses' giving the Law again to his people.

NEHEMIAH

Nehemiah was Artaxerxes' cupbearer, serving wine to the king in the citadel of Susa, in what is now south-west Iran. In Artaxerxes' twentieth year (445 BC) Nehemiah had heard from his relative Hanani that Jerusalem's walls had been broken down. What walls these were is the subject of debate. Were they the walls destroyed 141 years earlier by Nebuchadnezzar? Or had there been some kind of rebellion or trouble, (perhaps alluded to in Ezra 4:23), during which the wall mentioned in Ezra 4:12 had been broken down? We do not know, but Hanani's words provoked Nehemiah into action. He returned to Jerusalem with letters from the king authorizing him to requisition materials, especially timber for the gates, to build a new wall for Jerusalem.

Nehemiah went out at night to examine the walls, then mobilized the people for action: 'Come, let us rebuild the wall of Jerusalem, and we will no longer be in disgrace' (Nehemiah 2:17).

Chapter 3 of Nehemiah details how the inhabitants of Jerusalem set about building the wall, divided into forty-five or so sections. It is arguably the most important chapter in the Old Testament for determining the geography of Jerusalem. A total of ten gates are mentioned.

NEHEMIAH'S OPPONENTS

Nehemiah was opposed by Sanballat the Horonite, Tobiah the Ammonite and Geshem the Arab.[4] Two of them are directly attested in the archaeological record.

- Sanballat is attested as the governor of Samaria in the papyri from Elephantine, near Aswan on the first cataract of the Nile, in Year 17 of Darius II (407 BC).
- The name of Geshem has also turned up in Egypt. A silver bowl from an Arabian shrine at Wadi Tumilat in the eastern Delta carries an inscription: 'What Qaynu son of Geshem, king of Kedar, brought as an offering to the goddess Hanilat.' Like his successor, his son Qaynu, Geshem was the king or paramount chief of the northern Arabian tribe of Kedar. A memorial from ancient Dedan (Khuraybah), near al-Ula in north-west Arabia, is inscribed: 'in the days of Geshem, son of Shahr and (of) Abdi, governor of Dedan'.

Persian gold rhyton (drinking horn) terminating in the foreparts of a winged lion. Said to be from Hamadan, Iran.

RIGHT: Tomb of a Persian king, possibly Artaxerxes I (465–424 BC), Naqsh-e Rustam, Iran.

KEY
[1] Ezra 7:8
[2] Deuteronomy 7:3; Ezra 10:12–14
[3] Ezra 10:3a, 18–44
[4] Nehemiah 2:19
[5] Nehemiah 6:15
[6] Josephus, *Antiquities*, 11.179
[7] Nehemiah 8:1–18
[8] Nehemiah 13:6
[9] Nehemiah 12:22

Nehemiah's wall

Present wall of old city

Tower of the Hundred

Tower of Hananel

Sheep Gate

Fish Gate

Inspection Gate

Jeshanah (Old) Gate

East Gate

Broad Wall

Horse Gate

Ophel

Tower of the Ovens

Great Projecting Tower

Valley Gate

Older Wall

Projecting Tower

Water Gate

Projecting Tower

Fountain Gate

N

Dung Gate

Stairs descending from City of David

Plan of Jerusalem in the time of Nehemiah

With the authorization of the Persian king Artaxerxes I, Nehemiah rebuilt Jerusalem's walls in 445 BC. On this plan the line of his walls is superimposed on the line of the present walls of the old city.

FAR RIGHT: An Aramaic inscription on a silver bowl from Wadi Tumilat, Egypt, mentioning Qaynu, son of Geshem (one of Nehemiah's opponents).

THE WALL IS COMPLETED

Despite strong opposition the wall was completed in fifty-two days.[5] The exact course of the wall is subject to differing interpretations, but part of it still survives in Jerusalem today. Josephus states that the rebuilding of the wall took two years and four months,[6] this doubtless included further strengthening and finer details. Its dedication when two large choirs joyfully walked around it in opposite directions is described in Nehemiah 12:27–47.

Ezra read from the Law[7] and the people responded by confessing their sin and describing their plight: 'We are slaves today, slaves in the land you gave our forefathers... Because of our sins, its abundant harvest goes to the kings you have placed over us. They rule over our bodies and our cattle as they please. We are in great distress' (Nehemiah 9:36a–37).

Nehemiah served as governor until Artaxerxes' thirty-second year (433 BC).[8] During this time, to avoid being a burden to his people, he did not eat the food allotted to him as governor. He was recalled to the court, but returned for a second term of unspecified duration. Certainly he was no longer in office in 407 BC when the Elephantine papyri attest another governor of Judah.

MALACHI CONCLUDES THE OLD TESTAMENT

The last of the Persian kings mentioned in the Old Testament is 'Darius the Persian',[9] who is either Darius II (424–404 BC) or Darius III (336–330 BC). It is in this general period that the prophet Malachi, the last of the Old Testament prophets is to be placed. At the conclusion of his prophecy Malachi states: 'See, I will send you the prophet Elijah before that great and dreadful day of the Lord comes. He will turn the hearts of the fathers to their children, and the hearts of the children to their fathers; or else I will come and strike the land with a curse' (Malachi 4:5–6).

So ends the Old Testament (at least according to the Christian order), with the promise of a curse on those who do not recognize the prophet Elijah who is to come. Until John the Baptist appeared in the spirit and power of Elijah, for some four hundred years no new prophets appeared. It was as if God himself was silent, as if the land was under a curse.

ALEXANDER THE GREAT AND THE SPREAD OF HELLENISM

(336–323 BC)

GREECE

The land now known as Greece was home to a number of different groups of 'Greeks', all of Indo-European origin. Tablets in a syllabic script known as Linear B and dating from between 1450 and 1375 BC have been found at Knossos in Crete. This has been shown to be an early form of Greek. Later Linear B tablets have also been found in the so-called Mycenaean cities of mainland Greece – Mycenae, Pylos, Tiryns and Thebes – the latest dating to c. 1200 BC.

With the collapse of the Mycenaean civilization at the hands of the Dorian Greeks in c. 1200 BC written evidence for Greek disappears until the introduction of the alphabet sometime between 825 and 750 BC. The Greek historian Herodotus records that the Greeks learned to write from the Phoenicians.[1] This is certainly true; there are marked similarities between the names, order and forms of individual Greek letters and those of contemporary Phoenicia.

Greece was peripheral to the Old Testament. 'Javan' of the Table of the Nations may represent the Ionian Greeks who lived on the west coast of modern Turkey. 'Tiras' may represent Thrace in northern Greece.[2] Limited trade contacts with Greece are mentioned in the Old Testament.[3]

High mountain ranges, numerous gulfs and islands dictated that Greece remained divided into numerous city states, at one time numbering 158. At the time of the Persian invasion some, such as Thessaly and Boeotia, sided with the invader, but it was Athens that in the fifth century BC took the lead in the intellectual and cultural flowering that

followed the defeat of the Persians. The temples on the Acropolis in Athens are eloquent memorials to this golden age. At the end of the fifth century BC Athens locked horns with Sparta in a bitter conflict known as the Peloponnesian War (431–404 BC), but the ultimate beneficiaries were the Macedonians from northern Greece.

PHILIP II OF MACEDON

The victory over Athens, Thebes and their allies at Chaeronea in central Greece in 338 BC gave Philip of Macedon (359–336 BC) mastery over Greece. Two years later Philip was assassinated. Excavations of the royal tombs of the Macedonian kings at Vergina in northern Greece revealed a gold casket possibly containing his cremated remains, now in the museum at Vergina. His skull has been reconstructed, complete with its right eye socket damaged by an arrow, shot from above.

ALEXANDER THE GREAT

In 336 BC Philip II was succeeded by his twenty-year-old son, Alexander. The Old Testament book of Daniel has several references to Alexander. They are presented as predictions: 'Then a mighty king will appear who will rule with great power and do as he pleases' (Daniel 11:3). He is also the 'goat' of Daniel's vision: 'Suddenly a goat with a prominent horn between his eyes came from the west, crossing the whole earth without touching the ground' (Daniel 8:5).

Gold casket from the tomb of Philip II of Macedon (died 336 BC), Vergina, Greece. It is decorated with the sixteen-point star emblem of the Macedonian dynasty.

KEY
[1] Herodotus, *Histories*, 5.58–59
[2] Genesis 10:2
[3] Joel 3:6; Ezekiel 27:13, 15
[4] Arrian, *The Life of Alexander*, 7.4.8

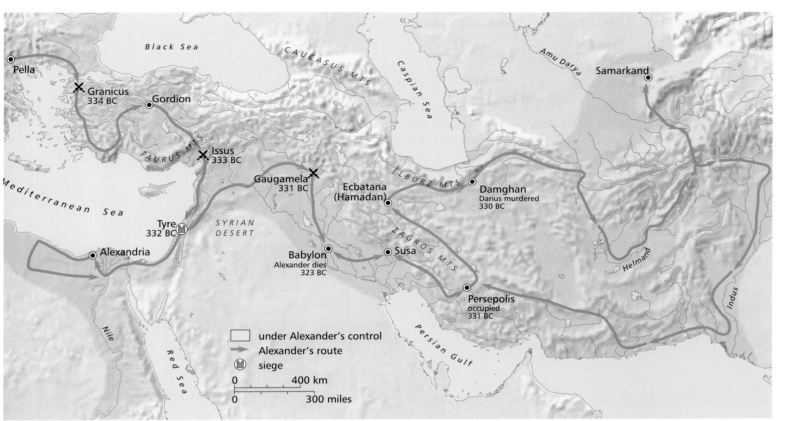

The Campaign of Alexander the Great 334–323 BC

Crossing over into Asia from Europe in 334 BC, Alexander the Great's army numbering less than 40,000 conquered the Persian empire. They went as far as Samarkand in modern Uzbekistan and the Indus River in Pakistan. On his return in 323 BC Alexander died in Babylon aged only 32.

LEFT: Mosaic showing Alexander the Great fighting Darius III at the battle of Issus, 333 BC, after a Greek painting by the fourth century BC artist Philoxenos. From the House of the Fawn, Pompeii, Italy.

Greek colonies in Palestine

Following the death of Alexander the Great, the Greeks established colonies in Palestine. The different culture that the Greeks brought posed a challenge to Jewish values.

In 334 BC at the age of twenty-two Alexander crossed the Dardanelles with a highly trained, disciplined army numbering less than 40,000. Almost immediately afterwards he faced a Persian force at the River Granicus (Kocabaş). He routed the Persian army and his audacious victory gave him and his men great confidence. He marched through what is now Turkey, liberating Greek cities from Persian rule. The following year, 333 BC, at Issus (Dörtyol, near Iskenderun) he cut to pieces the armies of the Persian king, Darius III. Daniel says: 'I saw him [i.e. the goat] attack the ram furiously, striking the ram and shattering his two horns. The ram was powerless to stand against him; the goat knocked him to the ground and trampled on him, and none could rescue the ram from his power' (Daniel 8:7).

In 332 BC Alexander took the Lebanese port city of Tyre after a seven-month siege. Passing through Palestine, he annexed Egypt without resistance, founding the major city at the mouth of the Nile that was to bear his name: Alexandria. On 1 October 331 BC Darius made his last stand at Gaugamela, near Arbela in northern Iraq. The Persian king managed to escape but lost all his treasure, family and army. Alexander then entered Babylon, Susa and Persepolis, the latter being burned to the ground. In July 330 BC, after a hot pursuit, Darius was murdered by one of his own men at Damghan in eastern Iran. Alexander then moved eastward through Parthia to Samarkand (in modern Uzbekistan). He crossed the Indus (in modern Pakistan) and was hoping to reach the Ganges when his homesick soldiers refused to go any further. As legend has it, he wept because there were no more realms for him to conquer.

Alexander adopted the customs of the sovereigns he had displaced and attempted a fusion of all races. He himself married the Persian princess Roxane and had more than ten thousand soldiers married off to local women on a single day[4].

His return was partly on land, partly by sea. The army suffered great hardship. In early June 323 BC he entered Babylon. Here he fell ill; and after a short illness, perhaps malaria, he died on 13 June, not yet 33 years old, precisely what Daniel had seen in his vision of the goat: 'at the height of his power his large horn was broken off' (Daniel 8:8a).

ALEXANDER THE GREAT'S SUCCESSORS

Daniel goes on to say: 'And in its place four prominent horns grew up towards the four winds of heaven' (Daniel 8:8b). In similar vein Daniel predicts: 'His empire will be broken up and parcelled out towards the four winds of heaven. It will not go to his descendants, nor will it have the power he exercised, because his empire will be uprooted and given to others' (Daniel 11:4).

Alexander's twelve-year-old son, also called Alexander, was a victim of widespread violence that followed his father's death. Rival generals fought to establish kingdoms of their own.

HELLENIZATION

Alexander's conquests opened the Near East to Greek culture and thought. Alexander sought to establish Greek cities right across his vast realm. Greek was established as the language of learning and trade. Greek colonies such as Samaria, Ptolemais (Acco/Acre), Scythopolis (Beth Shan) and Philoteria (south of the Sea of Galilee) were established in Palestine. Some Jews adopted Greek culture, others firmly resisted. It was an issue that was to polarize Jewish society as events unfolded, and was even to be carried over into the early church: 'The Hellenistic Jews among them complained against the Hebraic Jews because their widows were being overlooked in the daily distribution of food' (Acts 6:1).

THE PTOLEMIES AND SELEUCIDS

(323–175 BC)

AFTER ALEXANDER

After the death of Alexander the Great, Egypt was seized by Ptolemy I (323–285 BC) nicknamed 'Lagi' (hare) – apparently because of his large ears – and 'Soter' (saviour). He chose as his capital Alexandria, the city Alexander had founded on the Mediterranean coast. All the subsequent kings of Egypt until the Roman conquest in 30 BC were called Ptolemy.

In Syria the eventual victor was Seleucus I Nicator (311–280 BC), who was to establish a line of kings in Syria named after himself – the Seleucids.

PTOLEMY I

The Jews in Palestine found themselves sandwiched between these two rival powers, Egypt and Syria, which Daniel 11 refers to as 'the king of the South' and 'the king of the North' respectively. Daniel 11 describes in great detail the constant warfare between the two powers. They are written in the form of predictions. Daniel 11:5 tells of Ptolemy I and Seleucus I: 'The king of the South [Ptolemy I] will become strong, but one of his commanders [Seleucus Nicator] will become even stronger than he and will rule his own kingdom with great power.'

PTOLEMY II

The kings of Egypt and Syria became allies, specifically Ptolemy II (285–246 BC) and Antiochus II (261–246 BC), with Antiochus II cementing the alliance by taking the Egyptian king's daughter in marriage.[1] Since Antiochus II was already married to Laodice, he had to divorce her. Laodice exacted revenge by having Antiochus II and his new wife, Berenice, put to death.

Ptolemy II has a special place in Bible history as being responsible for the first translation of the Hebrew Scriptures, a version translated into Greek and known as the Septuagint (see opposite).

PTOLEMY III

Berenice's death was avenged by her brother, who became Ptolemy III (246–221 BC)[2] and succeeded in putting Laodice to death. Syria took action in c. 240 BC under Seleucus II (246–226 BC), but was not successful.

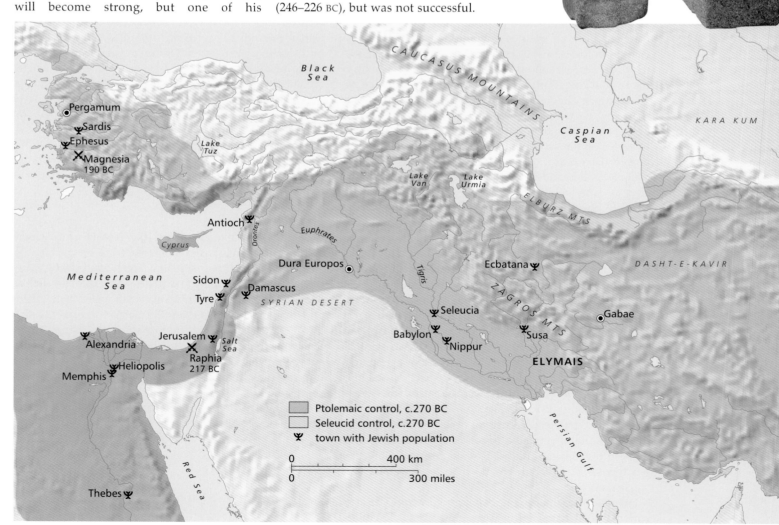

Ptolemaic control, c.270 BC
Seleucid control, c.270 BC
☥ town with Jewish population

0   400 km
0   300 miles

KEY
[1] Daniel 11:6
[2] Daniel 11:7
[3] Daniel 11:11b–12
[4] Polybius, *Histories*, 5.86.5
[5] Daniel 11:17
[6] Daniel 11:19; 1 Maccabees 6:16
[7] Philo, *On the Life of Moses* 2.37
[8] *Massekhet Sopherim* (Tractate for Scribes 35a, Rule 1.7)

PTOLEMY IV

In 217 BC Egypt and Syria were at war again. The two sides, both using elephants, faced each other at Raphia in southern Palestine. The army of Antiochus III was defeated, even humiliated.[3] The Greek historian Polybius records that Antiochus lost nearly ten thousand infantrymen.[4]

THE SYRIANS MOVE IN

From 323 BC Palestine had been under the control of the Ptolemies of Egypt. In 198 BC the tables were turned. Antiochus III (223–187 BC) of Syria gained control of Israel, called the 'Beautiful Land' in Daniel 11:16.

In 194 BC Antiochus III gave his daughter Cleopatra in marriage to Ptolemy V.[5] In 190 BC Antiochus III was defeated by the Roman general Lucius Cornelius Scipio Asiaticus at Magnesia, in what is now western Turkey, and he met his death in 187 BC while attempting to plunder a temple in Elymais in south-west Iran.[6] His successor,

Seleucus IV (187–175 BC), fell victim to a plot hatched by his finance minister, Heliodorus, and was succeeded by his younger brother, Antiochus IV (175–164 BC), 'a contemptible person who has not been given the honour of royalty' (Daniel 11:21). He was to arouse the ire of the Jews as none of his predecessors had done.

The Septuagint

The traditional story of the Greek translation of the Old Testament is told in the so-called *Letter of Aristeas* to his brother Philocrates. Ptolemy II of Egypt (285–246 BC) wanted every piece of world literature in Greek. The letter tells how the king commissioned the royal librarian, Demetrius of Phaleron, to collect by purchase or by copying all the books in the world. He wrote a letter to Eleazar, the high priest at Jerusalem, requesting six elders of each tribe, in total seventy-two men, of exemplary life and learned in the Law, to translate it into Greek. On arrival at Alexandria the translators were greeted by the king and given a sumptuous banquet. They were then closeted in a secluded house on the island of Pharos, close to the seashore.

The translation, made under the direction of Demetrius, was completed in seventy-two days. When the Alexandrian Jewish community assembled to hear a reading of the new version, the translators and Demetrius received lavish praise and a curse was pronounced on anyone who should alter the text by addition, transposition or omission. The work was read to the king who, according to the *Letter of Aristeas*, marvelled at the mind of the lawgiver. The translators were then sent back to Jerusalem, endowed with gifts for themselves and the high priest Eleazar.

Later generations embellished the story. Philo of Alexandria, writing in the first century AD, says that the translators' texts were all said to agree exactly with one another, thus proving that their version was directly inspired by God.[7] Their resulting translation was called the 'Septuagint' from the Latin for 'seventy'.

Ptolemy II's patronage may be evidenced in the Septuagint itself. In listing the unclean animals the translators are wary of the normal Greek word for 'hare' (*lagos*) – the nickname of Ptolemy II's father – and substitute 'young pig' in Leviticus 11:6 and 'rough foot' in Deuteronomy 14:7. The later Greek version of Aquila knew no such restraint in using 'hare'.

The truth surrounding the origins of the Septuagint was probably rather different to the account given in the *Letter of Aristeas*. After several centuries in Egypt many of the Jews were beginning to forget Hebrew. At first impromptu oral translations of the Law into Greek were made, and these were eventually written down. The Septuagint was probably a translation made by a number of different people during the third to first centuries BC, but it is quite possible that Ptolemy II commissioned a translation of at least the Pentateuch (the first five books).

The Septuagint did not receive a universally favourable reception among the Jews: 'That day was as ominous for Israel as the day on which the golden calf was made, since the Torah could not be accurately translated.'[8]

The significance of the Septuagint translation can hardly be overstated. Following the conquests of Alexander the Great (336–323 BC), Greek became the official language of Egypt, Syria and and other lands at the eastern end of the Mediterranean. The Septuagint became the Bible of the Jews outside Palestine who, like the Alexandrians, no longer spoke Hebrew. The scriptures were available both to the Jews who no longer spoke their ancestral language and to the entire Greek-speaking world. The Septuagint later became the Bible of the Greek-speaking early Christian church and is frequently quoted in the New Testament.

Fragment of the Septuagint from second century BC, Manchester Papyrus 458, containing part of the text of Deuteronomy, extracted from the wrappings of a mummy.

ANTIOCHUS EPIPHANES AND THE MACCABEAN WARS

(175–164 BC)

ANTIOCHUS SEIZES THE THRONE

In 175 BC Seleucus IV was succeeded by his younger brother, Antiochus IV (175–164 BC), who seized the throne while Demetrius, the son of Seleucus and rightful heir, was held hostage in Rome. Antiochus IV, entitled 'Epiphanes' (God manifest, illustrious) but nicknamed 'Epimanes' (mad) by his enemies, is the focus of Daniel 11:21–35.

THE BEGINNINGS OF HELLENIZATION

In 169 BC, on his return from a successful campaign against Ptolemy VI (181–146 BC) of Egypt, Antiochus IV 'set his heart against the holy covenant' (Daniel 11:28). He entered the Temple in Jerusalem, carrying off the gold altar and the lampstand with all its fittings. He stripped the gold plating from the front of the Temple and seized the silver, gold and the precious vessels.[1] He may have used in-fighting between two rival high priests, Jason and Menelaus, as an excuse to intervene in Jerusalem, but there is no doubt he was happy to get his hands on the Temple treasures to ease a chronic shortage of funds. The high priest Jason, with Antiochus's full blessing, had embarked on a policy of aggressive Hellenization, building a gymnasium in the gentile style in Jerusalem, which caused particular offence to the Jews since participants were naked. Furthermore, participation in Greek sports was inseparable from the cult of the Greek gods.

FURTHER HELLENIZATION

Antiochus IV mounted a new campaign on Egypt in 168 BC. Marching to within 6 km (4 miles) of Alexandria, he received an ultimatum from the Roman Senate, delivered by the legate Popilius Laenas, ordering him to leave Egypt. Antiochus knew well what Rome could do and dared not disobey.[2]

His temper was not improved by reports of resistance to Hellenization in Jerusalem. In the words of Daniel 11:30b, 'vent[ing] his fury against the holy covenant', Antiochus dispatched his commander Apollonius to Jerusalem. He launched a sudden and savage attack. Many of the Israelites were killed, and their city was sacked and set ablaze. On every side the houses and city walls were demolished; the women and children were captured and the livestock seized.

The more the Jews resisted, the more steps Antiochus IV took to eradicate Judaism. Regular sacrifices were suspended, together with observance of the sabbath and traditional feasts. Pagan altars were erected throughout the land and unclean animals were offered on

them. Circumcision was forbidden. On the 15th of Kislev, in December 168 BC, the cult of Olympian Zeus was introduced into the Temple at Jerusalem. An altar of Zeus was set up and pig's flesh was offered on it. This was 'the abomination that causes desolation' spoken of in Daniel 11:31.

Copies of the Law were ordered to be destroyed. Jews were forced to eat pork on pain of death. Hellenized Jews welcomed the royal edicts and gladly complied, while others

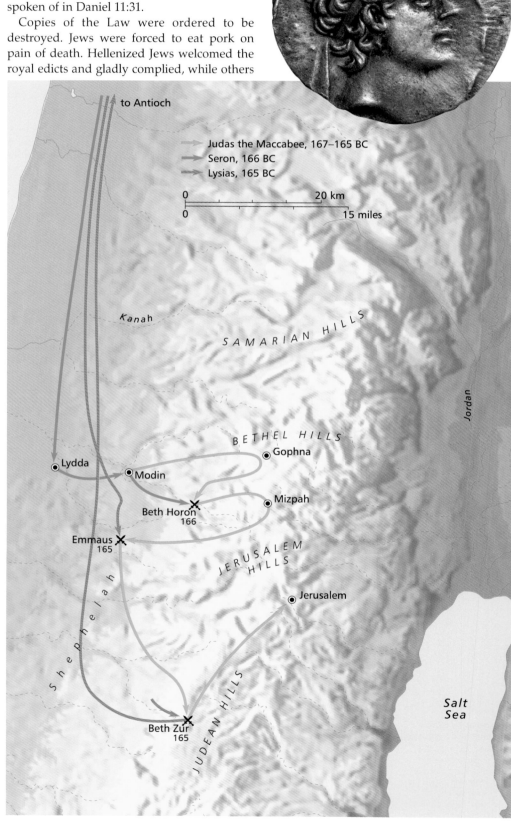

to Antioch

Judas the Maccabee, 167–165 BC
Seron, 166 BC
Lysias, 165 BC

0   20 km
0   15 miles

Kanah

SAMARIAN HILLS

BETHEL HILLS
Gophna

Lydda
Modin
Mizpah
Beth Horon
166

Emmaus
165

JERUSALEM
HILLS

Shephelah

Jerusalem

JUDEAN HILLS

Beth Zur
165

Salt
Sea

Jordan

LEFT: Silver coin bearing the image of Antiochus IV 'Epiphanes', the Seleucid king whose efforts to Hellenize the Jews caused the Maccabean revolt.

RIGHT: The village of Modin in the foothills east of Lydda, where Jewish resistance to the rule of Antiochus IV began.

LEFT: **The wars waged by Judas the Maccabee against Antiochus IV of Syria 167–165** BC Jewish resistance to Antiochus IV was led by Judas the Maccabee (hammer).

Terracotta figurine of an Indian war elephant attacking a Galatian soldier. From Myrina (Aliağa), Turkey.

either willingly or through fear forsook the religion of their fathers.[3]

THE RESISTANCE

'But the people who know their God will firmly resist him', stated Daniel (Daniel 11:32b). A similar sentiment is expressed by 1 Maccabees 1:62–63: 'But many in Israel stood firm and were resolved in their hearts not to eat unclean food. They chose to die rather than be defiled by food or to profane the holy covenant.'

Resistance exploded not long after Antiochus IV had issued his infamous decree. A godly priest, Mattathias, was asked by one of Antiochus's officers to sacrifice to a pagan god at the village of Modin, in the foothills east of Lydda.[4] Incensed at the sight of a Jew offering sacrifice on a pagan altar, Mattathias rushed forward and cut him down on the altar. At the same time he killed the officer sent by the king to enforce the sacrifice and demolished the pagan altar.

Shouting 'Let every one who is zealous for the Law and supports the covenant come out with me!' (1 Maccabees 2:27) Mattathias fled with his sons into the hills. He then launched a guerilla war against Antiochus IV and his allies. Within a few months old Mattathias died, but leadership of the resistance passed to his son, Judas, nicknamed Maccabee 'the hammer'.

THE TIDE TURNS

Judas was successful. An army under Apollonius was defeated at an unspecified location.[5] The army of Seron, commander of the army in Syria, was defeated at Beth Horon in 166 BC. Antiochus IV issued orders for the mobilization of all the forces of his empire and took himself off to Persia to collect tribute there, placing his relative Lysias in charge of the effort against Judas. Further victories for Judas followed at Emmaus (Ma'aleh Hahamisha) and Beth Zur (Khirbet el-Tubeiqa) in 165 BC.

THE TEMPLE IS REDEDICATED

Lysias withdrew to Antioch, leaving the way open for Judas to march into Jerusalem and to cleanse the desecrated temple.[6] On 25th of Kislev, that is, in December 165 BC, three years and ten days after the desecration, the Temple was rededicated with feasting and great joy. The Jews have celebrated the Feast of Hanukkah (dedication) ever since in commemoration of this great event. It is mentioned in the New Testament in John 10:22.

ANTIOCHUS MEETS HIS END

Antiochus IV's campaign in Persia was to be his last. He suffered from some form of madness and died at Gabae, near Isfahan in modern Iran, in late 164 BC.

THE JEWS IN EGYPT

(Sixth to second centuries BC)

A WIDENING DIASPORA

Not all the exiled Jews settled in Babylon, many scattered further afield. Jews had reached Morocco by 200 BC, and Mumbai (Bombay) in India by 175 BC.

ELEPHANTINE

Apart from Babylonia the largest concentration of Jews was in Egypt. Jews had first settled there after the fall of Jerusalem in 586 BC. Despite the prophetic warnings of Jeremiah a group of Jews, including Jeremiah himself, had settled at Tahpanhes (Daphnae) just inside Egypt.[1] By the time the Persians under Cambyses had conquered Egypt in 525 BC, a group of Jews had settled at Elephantine, an island at the first cataract of the Nile in the far south of the country. Aramaic texts from the settlement show that the Jews there had their own temple with an altar on which burnt offerings and sacrifices were offered. However, deities other than the Lord were also worshipped there. The Jews there, if not overt polytheists, were certainly highly syncretistic.

ALEXANDRIA

In 332 BC Alexander the Great founded a new city at the mouth of the Nile, between the Mediterranean coast of Egypt and the inland Lake Mareotis. Not surprisingly the city, 640 hectares (1,580 acres) in area, was named Alexandria. It was the capital of Egypt under the Ptolemaic dynasty. The streets of Alexandria were laid out in a grid plan. Many of its inhabitants were crammed into tenement blocks. In 60 BC Alexandria had more than 300,000 free men.[2] Alexandria was famous for its great library (see opposite).

The island of Pharos was joined to the mainland by a causeway. On the island was the 110-metre-high (360-ft) lighthouse, one of the Seven Wonders of the Ancient World. The lighthouse, built by Sostratus of Cnidus in the early third century BC, had a huge lantern with a bronze reflector. Its light could be seen 55 km (34 miles) out to

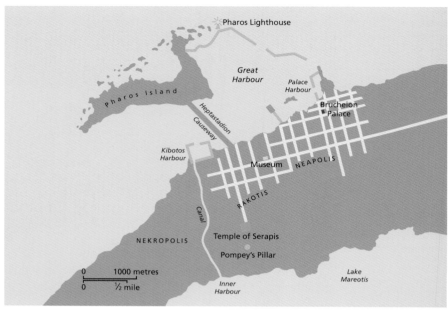

Plan of Alexandria
Alexander the Great founded the city that was to bear his name between the Mediterranean Sea and Lake Mareotis. The city was the capital of Ptolemaic Egypt. Boasting the Pharos lighthouse and the ancient world's greatest library, Alexandria was also the home of a large Jewish community.

KEY

[1] Jeremiah 42:17 – 43:7

[2] Diodorus Siculus, *Library of History*, 17.52.6

[3] Josephus, *The Jewish War*, 4.613

[4] Tosephta Sukkah, *Tractate on Booth*, 51b

[5] Josephus, *The Jewish War*, 7.427–430

[6] Plutarch, *Life of Antony*, 58.5

[7] Aulus Gellius, *Attic Nights*, 7.17.3; Ammianus Marcellinus, *Histories*, 22.16.13

A colossal statue, believed to be one of the Ptolemies, is removed from Alexandria's Great Harbour. Including the pedestal and crown, the statue was 13 metres (42 ft 6 in) high and weighed 20 tons.

sea.[3] It was crowned with a colossal, bronze statue of the Egyptian goddess Isis.

Many Jews settled in Alexandria. Two out of the city's five quarters were predominately settled by Jews. Jewish sources claim that in the first century AD one of Alexandria's synagogues was so vast that its leader had to raise a scarf to the worshippers at the back so they would know when to say 'Amen'.[4]

Major Jewish settlements in Egypt
As well as Alexandria, Jews settled in different parts of Egypt. The settlements at Elephantine and Leontopolis were of particular note.

LEONTOPOLIS

Onias IV was the rightful high priest of the Temple in Jerusalem, but his claims were ignored in favour of Alcimus, so in 162 BC Onias obtained permission from Ptolemy VI of Egypt to build a Jewish temple at Leontopolis in the vicinity of Heliopolis in Lower Egypt. Ptolemy VI, anxious to court Jewish support against Syria, agreed. The temple's altar and inner furniture were

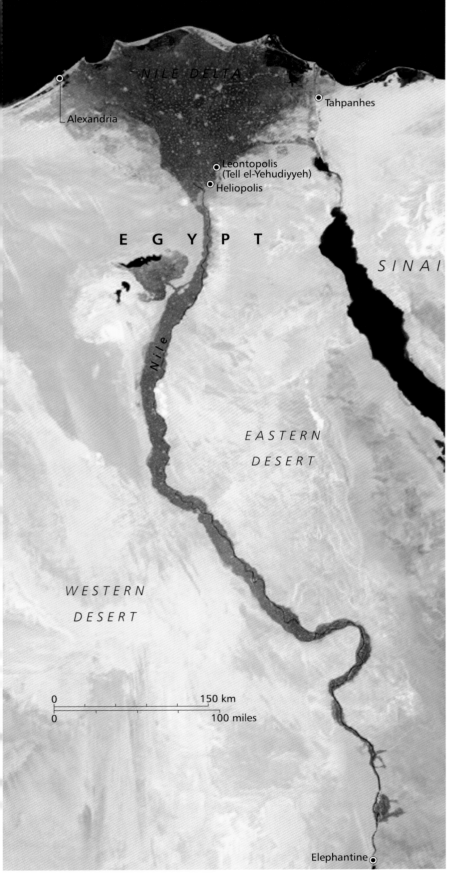

Major Jewish settlements in Egypt
As well as Alexandria, Jews settled in different parts of Egypt. The settlements at Elephantine and Leontopolis were of particular note.

The library at Alexandria

Established in the reign of Ptolemy II (285–246 BC), the library at Alexandria is arguably the most famous in the ancient world. A succession of celebrated scholars who served as librarians strove to make it the depository of everything ever written. Books on board ships anchored in the harbour were confiscated. When the librarian borrowed from Athens official copies of the works of the three great Greek tragedians – Aeschylus, Sophocles and Euripides – he returned a copy, not the originals, and forfeited a huge deposit.

The library was housed in two separate locations: within the royal palace of Brucheion and in the temple of Serapis. After the former was destroyed in 47 BC, during Julius Caesar's campaign, the latter became the library. By way of compensation Calvisius, who was an associate of Caesar, is reported to have offered the Egyptian queen Cleopatra the contents of the Pergamum library: 200,000 scrolls.[6] Roman historians credit the library at Alexandria with 700,000 scrolls,[7] although this should not be taken as the number of works. Many texts had multiple copies and often several scrolls were used for a single work.

The story that the library was destroyed by Arabs in AD 641, its volumes used to heat the public baths for six months, first appears in the writings of the Arab historian Abu'l Faraj in the thirteenth century and is certainly apocryphal. The reality is slightly less sensational. The Brucheion was torn down by the Roman emperor Aurelian in AD 272 while suppressing an insurgency. The temple of Serapis was closed by Theophilus, patriarch of Alexandria in AD 391.

modelled after those in the Jerusalem Temple, except Onias substituted a lamp hanging from a golden chain for the lampstand. The temple itself was not like that in Jerusalem, being a tower-like stone structure some 30 m (98 ft) high, and surrounded by a wall of baked brick with stone gateways.[5] Tell el-Yehudiyyeh is believed to be the site of this temple, the significance of which is not to be underestimated. The Jerusalem ritual was duplicated and the legitimate Zadokite priesthood was perpetuated by Onias IV and his successors for 233 years until the Romans destroyed the temple in AD 73. It is seen by some as the fulfilment of Isaiah's prophecy, 'In that day there will be an altar to the Lord in the heart of Egypt, and a monument to the Lord at its border' (Isaiah 19:19).

THE JEWS IN THE SECOND AND FIRST CENTURIES BC

(164–63 BC)

The Babylonian exile had purged the Jews from their tendency to idolatry. In exile Judaism emerged as a fiercely monotheistic and 'separate' faith. Israel was no longer a national entity but became a community built on the Law (the Pentateuch, the first five books of the Old Testament). Non-Jews could join if they submitted to the requirements of the Law, most notably circumcision, ritual purity and the avoidance of ceremonially unclean food. Within Judaism several 'sects' emerged, although the lines between them were not always rigid. Some of the historical factors in the development of Judaism are outlined below.

SYNAGOGUES

As the Jews spread and were deprived of access to the Temple in Jerusalem, they evolved meeting places of their own called 'synagogues' (from the Greek word for 'bringing together'). In the synagogue there was no altar. Prayer and reading the Law took the place of sacrifices.

The ancient Jewish town of Gamala is on the east side of Lake Galilee. The Roman general Vespasian is known to have captured the town in AD 67. A pillared hall some 20 m (66 ft) long, surrounded by four rows of stone steps each about 50 cm (3 in) high, is believed to be a synagogue. At Herod's fortress at Masada beside the Dead Sea, destroyed in AD 73, a room was found with four tiers of plastered benches around the sides. Nearby, in the corner of a small room, two leather scrolls were found containing parts of the books of Deuteronomy and Ezekiel. It is suggested that this too was a synagogue.

JOHN HYRCANUS I

In 134 BC Judah's ruler, the high priest Simon (140–134 BC), the last of the Maccabee brothers, was assassinated at a feast by his son-in-law, Ptolemy. Ptolemy intended to seize power but was thwarted by Simon's son, John Hyrcanus I (134–104 BC).

Antiochus VII, the Seleucid ruler of Syria, pressed Judah hard, even besieging Jerusalem for more than a year. But in 129 BC Antiochus was killed in battle in Iran by the Parthians and, as rival claimants fought each other for the Seleucid throne, Hyrcanus I was quick to exploit the situation to expand his own territory. In 128 BC he destroyed a temple to the Lord that the Samaritans had built on Mount Gerizim near Shechem, which doubtless exacerbated tensions with the Jews. He conquered the Idumeans, the descendants of the Old Testament Edomites, to the south of Judah, forcing them to embrace Judaism and undergo circumcision. He also made extensive conquests east of the Jordan and conquered Samaria.

The high priestly rulers of Judah were called Hasmoneans after Hasmon, the father of Mattathias the Maccabee. Initially the dynasty had received much support from a sect who under Judas the Maccabee had been called the *hasidim* ('pious ones') and who were later known as the Pharisees ('separated ones'). John Hyrcanus I, however, transferred his allegiance to another sect, the Sadducees.

ALEXANDER JANNAEUS

John Hyrcanus's first son, Judah Aristobulus (104–103 BC), further expanded the Jewish state by conquering Galilee.

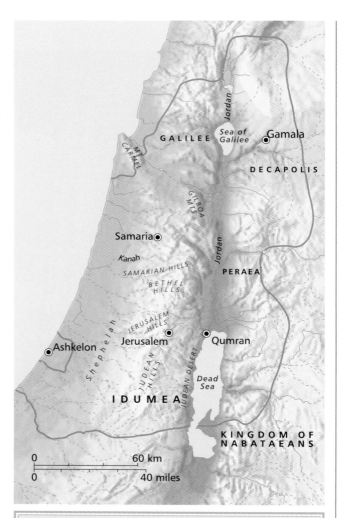

LEFT: **The Jewish state under Alexander Jannaeus**
The borders of the Jewish state of the Hasmoneans roughly coincide with those of David's kingdom.

FAR RIGHT: The Hasmonean family tree.

RIGHT: **Pompey's campaign in Palestine**
In 63 BC the Roman general Pompey invaded Palestine and entered Jerusalem.

The Pharisees

The Pharisees ('separated ones') had a wide, popular following. They believed Israel's exile to Babylon was caused by failure to keep the Law and that its keeping was both an individual and a national duty. They summarized the Law in 613 commandments, 248 positive and 365 negative. This was a 'hedge' around the Law so that no one could break any of the commandments by accident or ignorance. They were the party of the synagogue and were the only party to survive the destruction of the Jerusalem Temple in AD 70, becoming the spiritual fathers of modern Judaism.

The Sadducees

The name Sadducee is perhaps derived from Zadok, David's high priest, but was popularly derived from the Hebrew word for 'righteous'. The Sadducees were relatively few in number. Drawing their support from the ruling classes, they controlled the high priesthood and the Temple. Seeking to maintain the status quo, they readily cooperated with secular rulers, whether Hasmonean priest-kings or Roman governors. The Sadducees accepted only the Law. They thus rejected the doctrines of the soul and afterlife, resurrection, angels and demons found in the later books of the Old Testament.

KEY
[1] Josephus, *The Jewish War*, 2.118; Acts 5:37
[2] Luke 6:15; Acts 1:13
[3] Josephus, *The Jewish War*, 1.97

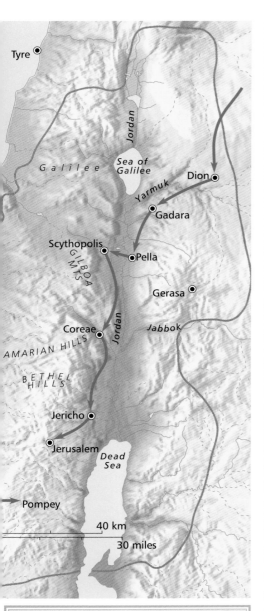

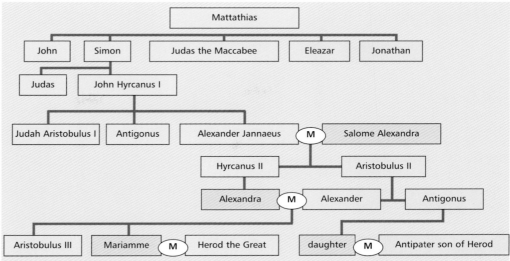

The Zealots

The Zealots were founded by Judas the Galilean in AD 6.[1] They opposed the payment of taxes to the Romans and the use of the Greek language. One of Jesus' disciples was known as Simon the Zealot.[2] It was the Zealots who were the prime movers in the revolts against the Romans in AD 66–70 and 132–135.

Like the Idumaeans, the Galileans were compelled to accept circumcision and become Jews. Aristobulus was soon succeeded by his brother, Alexander Jannaeus (103–76 BC), who added the title of king to that of high priest. This action further alienated the Pharisees. Under Alexander Jannaeus the Hasmonean state reached its zenith. Conquering all the coastal plain except for Ashkelon, and large tracts east of the Jordan, he extended the borders of his kingdom until it roughly coincided with the kingdom David had ruled. However, his campaign against the Arab Nabataeans to the south and east of his realm was a disaster. The people of Jerusalem rose in rebellion, with the insurgent Jews even enlisting the help of a Seleucid prince from Damascus, Demetrius III. Alexander Jannaeus wreaked a cruel revenge on the Pharisees, crucifying eight hundred of them while he caroused with the women of his harem.[3] When he succumbed to an illness brought on by drunkenness in 76 BC he was succeeded by his wife, Salome Alexandra.

PHARISEES VERSUS SADDUCEES

Since women were disbarred from being high priest, Salome Alexandra (76–67 BC) was compelled to hand over the high priesthood to her older son, Hyrcanus II. The queen and Hyrcanus II threw in their lot with the Pharisees, who now sought to exact revenge upon the Sadducees. On Salome's death her younger son, Aristobulus II, who had strong sympathies with the Sadducees, successfully fought Hyrcanus II

for the throne. However, there was much popular support for Hyrcanus II and the Pharisee party. An Idumaean named Antipater sought to exploit Hyrcanus II for his personal advantage. He induced the Nabataeans to intervene on Hyrcanus's behalf. Aristobulus II and his followers, who were largely priests, were besieged on the Temple mount.

POMPEY AT JERUSALEM

In 63 BC the Roman general Gnaeus Magnus Pompeius, more commonly known as Pompey, came to Damascus. He received appeals not only from the two warring brothers, but also from representatives of the Jews who begged him to abolish the Hasmonean kingship and make the head of state a high priest like those of old. When Pompey arrived at Jerusalem, Aristobulus II surrendered, but the priests held out for three months on the Temple mount before they were massacred. Pompey left the Temple treasure untouched, but insisted on entering the Most Holy Place to satisfy his curiosity and was amazed to find it empty. It was an inauspicious start to Roman rule, an action the Jews could neither forgive not forget.

Aristobulus II was taken to Rome to take part in Pompey's triumphal procession. Hyrcanus II was reinstated not as king, nor as high priest, but as a nominal ruler called an ethnarch. Judah's territory was much reduced, the area around Samaria and the Greek-speaking cities of the Decapolis, largely to the east of the River Jordan, were taken away, leaving Galilee, the Transjordanian area of Peraea, Idumaea and Judah itself. The real power in Judah however lay in the hands of Antipater, whose chief claim to fame is that he was the father of Herod the Great.

THE ROMANS

EARLY HISTORY

The long mountainous peninsula now known as Italy is somewhat peripheral to the biblical world, but as the centre of an empire it had a vital role in the New Testament. Between the seventh and fourth centuries BC much of central Italy was ruled by a people called the Etruscans, who may be identified as the Tiras of Genesis 10:2. The origins of the Etruscans are shrouded in mystery. Their language was not from the Indo-European family; in fact, the only clear parallels are with another non-Indo-European language spoken on the Greek island of Lemnos. The Greek historian Herodotus suggests (in his *Histories*, 1.94) that a group of Lydians (from western Turkey) were forced by a severe famine to sail away to Ombriki (perhaps Umbria in Italy). Whether there is any truth in this story is not known, but certainly there are a number of features, particularly in religious practice, that point to an eastern Mediterranean origin for the Etruscans.

The city of Rome was established, according to tradition, by the legendary Romulus on 21 April 753 BC. It grew up around the first crossing point of the River Tiber, some 20 km (13 miles) from the sea. Three of the first seven kings of Rome were Etruscans, but in 509 BC the Romans threw off Etruscan rule and established the Roman republic.

ROME DOMINATES ITALY

By 499 BC Rome was the dominant town in the region of Latium. It destroyed the neighbouring Etruscan city of Veii in 396 BC and continued to expand its influence further into Italy. In 290 BC, after a long struggle, Rome crushed the Samnites of central Italy, extending Roman rule from the Tyrrhenian Sea to the Adriatic. By 272 BC all of southern Italy was under Roman control.

THE WARS WITH CARTHAGE

Between 264 and 241 BC Rome fought the first of three wars with the north African city of Carthage which, according to tradition, was founded by Phoenician colonists from Tyre in 814 BC. Ownership of Sicily was the point of contention.

By 218 BC Rome ruled almost all of Italy south of the River Po and also the islands of Sardinia and Corsica. Hostilities with Carthage were renewed when a Carthaginian general named Hannibal took an army supported by elephants over the Alps into Italy and inflicted severe defeats on the Romans at Lake Trasimine in 217 BC and Cannae in 216 BC. Eventually Rome recovered enough to take the war to north Africa. In 202 BC Publius Cornelius Scipio Africanus defeated the Carthaginians at Zama in central Tunisia.

ROME EXPANDS FURTHER

In the following years Rome took over Carthaginian territory and expanded its influence over much of the Mediterranean lands. In 168 BC Rome ordered Antiochus IV of Syria to call off his advance on Alexandria and leave Egypt (an event referred to in Daniel 11:29–30, where the Romans are called 'Kittim', a name probably derived from the town of Kition, modern Larnaca in Cyprus). In 146 BC the Romans completely destroyed Carthage and established their province of Africa. In the same year Rome conquered Greece, razing Corinth to the ground. Of all Rome's conquests this was probably the most significant, as it opened the Romans to the greater cultural sophistication of Greece. Greek statues, architectural features and educational methods made their way to Italy. As the Roman poet Horace observed: 'Captive Greece made captive her ferocious conqueror and brought the arts to rustic Latium' (Horace, *Epistles*, 2.1.156–157a).

When King Attalus III of Pergamum died in 133 BC, he bequeathed his kingdom to Rome. This became their province of Asia. Further provinces were constituted in Cilicia in 102 BC, Bithynia–Pontus and Cyrenaica in 74 BC, Crete in 67 BC and Cyprus in 58 BC.

ROME CONQUERS PALESTINE

In 63 BC Syria became a Roman province. The Roman general Pompey took Jerusalem after a three-month siege of the Temple area, massacring priests in the performance of their duties and entering the Most Holy Place. This sacrilege began Roman rule in a way that Jews could neither forgive nor forget.

CIVIL WAR

All this territorial expansion placed severe pressure on the Roman republic. For much of the first century BC there was bitter rivalry between leading generals, which in turn resulted in further territorial expansion. Gaius Julius Caesar conquered Gaul (most of modern France) between 58 and 51 BC and paid two brief visits to Britain (55 and 54 BC), but Marcus Licinius Crassus met his death while fighting the Parthians at Carrhae (Haran) on the eastern flanks of Rome's domains in 53 BC. In 49 BC Caesar took his army from Gaul across the Rubicon river into Italy. It was a clear

Bust of Augustus (27 BC to AD 14), emperor at the time of the birth of Jesus.

The expansion of the Roman empire
After gaining dominance over Italy, Rome was to create for itself an empire that eventually completely enclosed the Mediterranean Sea.

A scene from Trajan's column, Rome, AD 113, showing the Roman army attacking a Dacian fort.

challenge to Pompey, who fled to Greece, where Caesar defeated him at Pharsalus in central Greece the following year. Caesar's triumph was short lived. On 15 March 44 BC he was assassinated in the Senate of Rome, ironically at the foot of a statue of Pompey.

Caesar's death merely opened a new chapter of civil war, this time between his former ally, Mark Antony, and his great-nephew Octavian. It was Octavian who finally ended the civil war with his naval victory over Antony and his ally Cleopatra, the queen of Egypt, at Actium in western Greece on 2 September 31 BC.

Egypt itself became a Roman province in 30 BC. Octavian returned to Rome. On 11 January 29 BC he closed the temple of Janus in Rome, a sign that the world was at peace, and in 27 BC he was given the title Augustus ('majestic, worthy of honour') by the Roman Senate, becoming the first Roman emperor. By the time Jesus was born, in c. 5 BC, not only was almost the entire Mediterranean coast under Roman rule, but it was also enjoying unprecedented prosperity and peace – the so-called *Pax Romana* (the Roman peace).

A KINGDOM THAT WILL NEVER BE DESTROYED

It should not be forgotten that this Roman peace had been established by centuries of fighting. The fourth kingdom, strong as iron that smashes everything, breaks things to pieces, and that crushes and breaks all the other kingdoms, described in Nebuchadnezzar's dream in Daniel 2:40, is an apt description of the military might of Rome. For over four centuries the Roman empire ruled the Mediterranean basin, but it was to suffer increasing pressure from the 'barbarians' outside. The emperor Diocletian (AD 284–305) divided the empire into two and this ultimately led to the inauguration of the second Rome, Constantinople (modern Istanbul), by Constantine the Great on 11 May 330.

Rome fell to Alaric the Goth in AD 410. Constantinople, capital of the Byzantine empire, was to live on for over a thousand years until its conquest by the Turks on 29 May 1453. Following the fall of Rome, Christians took comfort from more of Daniel's words: 'In the time of those kings [that is in the days of the Roman empire], the God of Heaven will set up a kingdom that will never be destroyed, nor will it be left to another people. It will crush all previous kingdoms and bring them to an end, but it will itself endure for ever' (Daniel 2:44).

HEROD THE GREAT

(40–4 BC)

HEROD GAINS THE THRONE

Of the later rulers of Judea the greatest, without a doubt, was Herod the Great. He was not a Jew by race. His father, Antipater, was an Idumean, the descendants of the Edomites of the Old Testament. His mother, Cyprus, was a Nabataean Arab. The Romans appointed Antipater governor in 47 BC. He in turn appointed his son, Herod, as prefect of Galilee. In 40 BC the Roman Senate gave Herod the title 'King of the Jews', but to claim his prize he had to fight a three-year war against the Hasmonean ruler Antigonus and lay siege to Jerusalem. Throughout his rule Herod remained a loyal friend and ally of Rome.

MASTER OF INTRIGUE

Herod chose as one of his ten wives Mariamme, granddaughter of the exiled high priest Hyrcanus II, and thus tried to legitimize his rule in the eyes of the Jews. In 29 BC he had Mariamme murdered and set about the systematic eradication of the Hasmonean family. In 7 BC he even had his two sons by Mariamme, Alexander and Aristobulus, put to death. A few days before his death in 4 BC Herod had another son, Antipater, put to death. Alluding to the Jewish prohibition on eating pork the Roman emperor Augustus is reported to have quipped that it was safer to be Herod's pig than his son![1] Herod's other victims included the high priest Aristobulus III, drowned on his orders at the swimming pool at Jericho in 36 BC, and the reinstated Hyrcanus II in 30 BC.

THE MASTER BUILDER

Herod's rebuilding of the Temple in Jerusalem is by far his most famous building project. This is covered in depth elsewhere. Of the Temple only the so-called Wailing Wall (or Western Wall) survives, but consideration of a number of Herod's other building projects shows the grand scale on which he built.

● At Strato's Tower on the Mediterranean coast Herod built a harbour, 36 m (118 ft) deep, protected by a seawall 60 m (197 ft) wide. The largest artificial harbour in the Mediterranean was named Caesarea after the Roman emperor. Concrete blocks, some as long as 13.5 m (44 ft) were used to make the breakwaters, and a sluice was specially devised to flush sand out of the harbour. The 66-hectare (163-acre) site, now known as Qisariya, boasts immense warehouses, aqueducts, a hippodrome, a

KEY

[1] Macrobius, *Saturnalia*, 2.4.11

[2] Josephus, *Antiquities*, 18.116–119; Matthew 14:3–12; Mark 6:17–29

[3] Matthew 2:22; Luke 3:1

TOP LEFT: Herod's work at Caesarea in constructing the largest artificial harbour in the Mediterranean can still be partly seen today.

FAR LEFT: Coin of Herod the Great.

BOTTOM LEFT: Territories ruled by Herod the Great

On Herod's death his realm was divided among his sons, with two small territories also being given to his sister Salome.

The Herodium (Jebel Fureidis), burial place of Herod the Great.

theatre and an amphitheatre, the latter still unexcavated at the time of writing.

- Herod built extensively at Samaria, the former capital of the northern kingdom of Israel. His city was named Sebaste (Augusta) in honour of the Roman emperor. The 64-hectare (158-acre) site, now known as Sebastiya, has a colonnaded street, hippodrome and theatre.
- At Hebron he built a massive monument to the patriarchs (Haram el-Khalil), surrounded by a towering wall, simply but effectively decorated with alternating pilasters and recesses. Its largest stone is 7.5 m by 1.4 m (24 ft 6 in by 4 ft 6 in).
- At Masada, a precipitous hilltop overlooking the Dead Sea, he built a huge, fortified palace. It was surrounded by a 6-metre-high (20 ft) wall, 3.5m (11 ft 6 in) wide, with thirty-eight towers each 21 m (69 ft) high or more. On the northern point, the only place on the site shaded from the sun for most of day, Herod had a three-tiered palace built hanging over the abyss.
- At Jericho he built a winter palace with ornamental gardens and two castles in its vicinity, at Tell el-Akabe on a mountain edge overlooking the Wadi Qelt, and a castle overlooking the town, named Cyprus after his mother.
- Other castles built by Herod include Hyrcania (Khirbet Mird), 13 km (8 miles) south-east of Jerusalem, close to the Dead Sea, and the spectacular site of Machaerus (el-Mekawer) across the Dead Sea in modern Jordan and according to Josephus, the site of the later beheading of John the Baptist.[2]
- Finally we should mention the Herodium, modern Jebel Fureidis, an artificial, circular hill fortress 11 km (7 miles) south of Jerusalem that marks the site of a battle Herod fought in 40 BC, repelling a ferocious attack from hostile Jews. The fortress was approached by two hundred steps and surrounded by two concentric walls. It was here that Herod was buried, although the precise whereabouts of his body remain a mystery.

HEROD, THE PAGAN

Herod, always anxious to curry Roman favour, built temples to Rome and Augustus at Caesarea and Sebaste. He restored the temple of Pythian Apollo in Rhodes, dedicated two statues on the Acropolis in Athens and accepted the honorific presidency of the Olympic Games at Olympia in Greece. Pagan sympathies such as these, his eradication of the Hasmonean family and his Edomite origins ensured that Herod never found acceptance with a large body of Jewish opinion.

HEROD'S DEATH

After a long and painful illness, perhaps syphilis, Herod died at Jericho at the end of March 4 BC. His body was carried in procession 40 km (25 miles) to the Herodium, the place he had had prepared for his burial. His realm was divided between his three surviving sons: Judea and Samaria went to Archelaus, Galilee and the region across the Jordan known as Peraea to Herod Antipas (also known as Herod the Tetrarch) and his north-eastern territories to Philip.[3] His sister Salome also received two small tracts of land.

HEROD THE GREAT REBUILDS THE TEMPLE

(19–4 BC)

HEROD'S MOTIVES

Hoping to win Jewish favour, Herod announced that he would rebuild the Temple of the Lord in Jerusalem, that had been built by Zerubbabel between 520 and 516 BC. If his reign is reckoned from his capture of Jerusalem in 37 BC, this announcement, made in his eighteenth year,[1] is to be dated to 19 BC. Not everyone received his declaration favourably, because it was feared that he would pull down the old building and never construct a new one. To reassure such suspicions, he published all his plans for the reconstruction before starting on the demolition. He would use the same soft white stone that Solomon had used for the first temple. It was transported to the site in a thousand wagons.

The work was made difficult by the need to carry on the services and sacrifices and by the rule that only priests could enter the Temple building itself. Herod hired ten thousand skilled workmen and had a thousand priests trained in stonemasonry, so that they could erect the sacred building. The priestly masons managed to construct the inner part of the new temple within eighteen months, but work continued until the time of Jesus – hence the Jews' comment, 'It has taken forty-six years to build this temple' (John 2:20). The courtyards were not finally finished until AD 63. Seven years later the Temple was destroyed by the Romans.

THE TEMPLE COMPLEX

The entire complex, was an irregular rectangle. Its east wall was 470 m (1,542 ft), the west wall 485 m (1,592 ft). The north wall was 315 m (1,033 ft), the south 280 m (918 ft). This huge enclosure, five times the area of the Acropolis in Athens, is represented today by the great rectangular platform of the Haram esh-Sharif. It was surrounded by a massive external wall. The lowest fourteen courses of the western side, the so-called Wailing Wall, are still visible. Its blocks are from 1.25 m (4 ft) to 3 m (10 ft) long and weigh from 2 tons upwards. Underground tunnels have revealed stones as long as 12 m (39 ft), 3 m (10 ft) high and 4 m (13 ft) thick, weighing an estimated 400 tons. No wonder one of Jesus' disciples is reported to have exclaimed to him: 'Look, Teacher! What massive stones!' (Mark 13:1b).

On the western side are the remains of two viaducts, the so-called Wilson's and Robinson's arches. On the south-east corner was the 'highest point of the Temple'. The Gospels record that Jesus was tempted to jump off from here into the Kidron Valley some 130 m (426 ft) below.[2] It was here too that the early church historian Eusebius records that Jesus' brother James was thrown to his death.[3] Below the Temple complex were sewers to carry the blood from the sacrifices into the Kidron Valley. Part of a sewer can still be seen in the south wall.

GATES AND COLONNADES

Nine gates all overlaid with gold led inside. On the eastern side was the Golden Gate or Shushan Gate, by which Jesus is believed to have made his triumphal entry into Jerusalem. Inside the courtyard was a colonnade of Corinthian columns each 11.5 m (38 ft) high and cut from single blocks of white marble. It ran the length of all four sides, some 1,200 m (3,937 ft). The colonnade on the east side bore the name 'Solomon's Portico'. The triple colonnade on the south,

comprising one hundred and sixty-two columns, was called the Royal Porch. It was here that sellers of sacrificial animals and money-changers operated. They were to be forcibly evicted by Jesus twice during his ministry. These colonnades flanked the Court of the Gentiles, which, covering about 14 hectares (35 acres), was almost twice the size of the court of Zerubbabel's Temple.

TEMPLE INSCRIPTIONS

A brief Hebrew inscription 'To the house of trumpeting' from the south-west corner indicates that it was here that trumpets were sounded to announce the beginning and end of the sabbath.

A 1.3-metre-high (4 ft 3 in) stone balustrade marked the edge of the Court of Gentiles. Beyond this only Jews could enter. In 1871 a Greek inscription was found prohibiting non-Jews from entering the inner courts. It is now in the Istanbul Archaeological Museum and reads: 'Let no foreigner enter within the balustrade and enclosure surrounding the holy place; whoever is caught shall be responsible to himself, because death follows.' Part of a duplicate inscription was found in 1936. Its letters were painted red to make them stand out.

A Greek inscription prohibiting non-Jews from entering the inner courts of the Temple at Jerusalem.

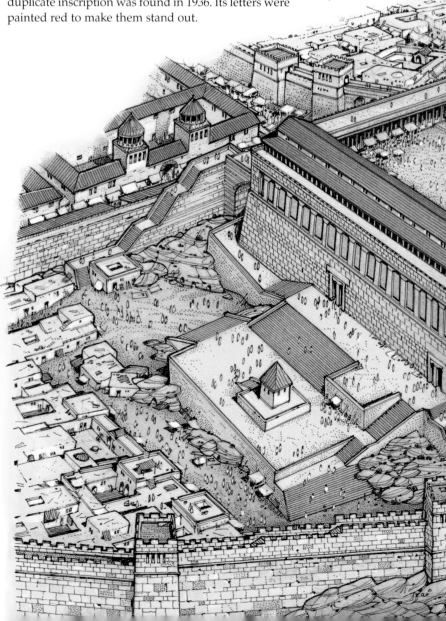

THE INNER COURTS

The first of the inner courts was the Court of Women. This was entered through a bronze gate, probably the Beautiful Gate of Acts 3:2. Jesus, aged eight days, was presented at the Court of Women.[4] In one of the courtyards surrounding the Court of Women were thirteen trumpet-shaped containers for the receipt of financial gifts.[5]

Only male Jews could enter the next court, the Court of Israel, which led into the Court of Priests. Here, in front of the sanctuary, stood the altar of burnt offering, approached by a ramp. Its site was believed to be the place where Abraham was commanded to sacrifice his son Isaac and where David was commanded to build an altar to the Lord on the threshing floor of Araunah the Jebusite.[6] Its site is now within the Dome of the Rock mosque.

THE SANCTUARY

Twelve steps led up to the sanctuary itself, a 45-metre-high (148 ft) structure with thick, white walls. These were covered with gold plates. The roof too was covered with gold and had gold spikes to keep birds away. The first room, as in Solomon's Temple, was a porch. Gigantic doors encrusted with precious metals led to the Holy Place. Above the doors was the sculpture of a giant golden vine, symbolizing triumphant Israel, with each of its clusters as large as a human being. The sanctuary was flanked by three storeys of store-rooms. The Holy Place housed the table for the shewbread, the *menorah* (seven-branched lampstand) and the altar of incense. A thick curtain, which on Jesus' death was torn in two,[7] separated the Holy Place from the Most Holy Place (the Holy of Holies), which the high priest entered only once a year on the Day of Atonement. But the ark of the covenant, which seems to have been destroyed when Nebuchadnezzar's armies sacked Jerusalem in 586 BC, was no longer kept here; the Most Holy Place, as the Roman general Pompey found out, was empty.

A reconstruction of Herod's Temple

1 Sanctuary (the Holy of Holies and the Holy Place)
2 Priests' Court
3 Laver
4 Altar
5 Place of slaughtering
6 Court of Israel
7 Nicanor Gate
8 Oil store
9 Women's Court
10 Beautiful Gate

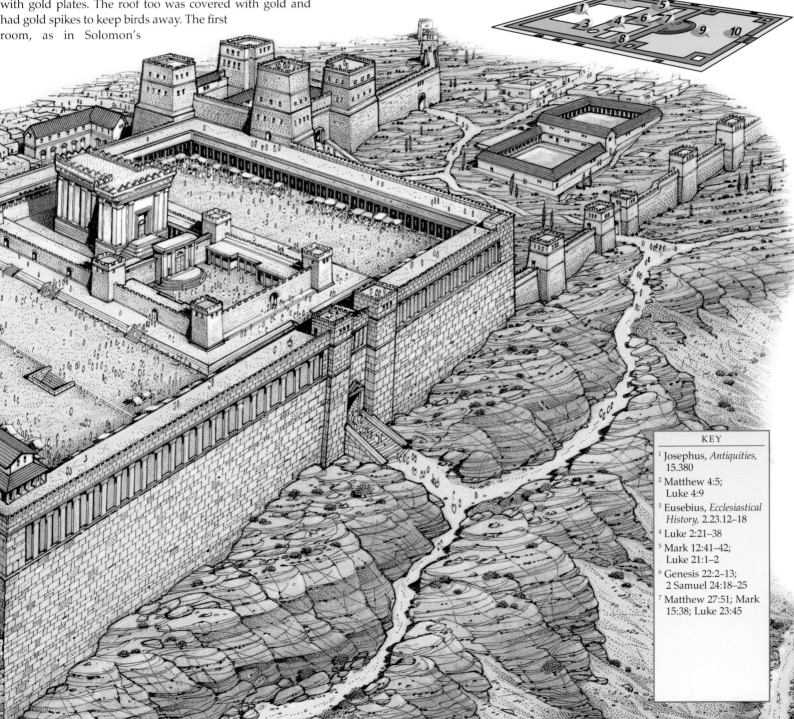

KEY

[1] Josephus, *Antiquities*, 15.380
[2] Matthew 4:5; Luke 4:9
[3] Eusebius, *Ecclesiastical History*, 2.23.12–18
[4] Luke 2:21–38
[5] Mark 12:41–42; Luke 21:1–2
[6] Genesis 22:2–13; 2 Samuel 24:18–25
[7] Matthew 27:51; Mark 15:38; Luke 23:45

Amulets and Scrolls

The Ketef Hinnom amulets

In 1979 archaeologists were excavating a tomb on the western edge of Jerusalem. It was a site partly occupied by the Scottish church of St Andrew, known to Arabs as Ras ed-Dabbous and to Jews as Ketef Hinnom. A small shiny object, 2.7 cm (12 in) long to be exact, caught the eye of one of the excavators. The object was 99 per cent silver, but there was something about it more significant than that. It was a rolled-up sheet of thin silver, 9.7 by 2.7 cm (3¾ by 12 in), with writing scratched in the Old Hebrew script. The writing suggested a date in the seventh or sixth century BC.

It was soon clear that this tiny sheet of silver contained most of the words of the priestly blessing from the Old Testament book of Numbers 6:24–26. A second, shorter, text was also found. They were not just quotations from the Bible; the silver sheets contained other words too, suggesting they were amulets, worn to give protection and to ward off evil. Strictly speaking, the amulets are not a biblical text, since the texts do not exclusively contain passages from the Old Testament, but they are the oldest citation – by several hundred years – of any part of the Old Testament.

The scrolls from Qumran

In the spring of 1947, while looking for lost goats, a Bedouin shepherd boy named Muhammed ed-Dhib ('the wolf') threw a stone into a desert cave near Qumran, some 1½ km (c. 1 mile) inland from the western shore of the Dead Sea. The stone broke some clay jars. The boy went in to investigate and found inside the jars some old, leather scrolls, which he thought he could use to patch his shoes. However, he noticed that the scrolls had writing on them, so he sold them to a dealer. Soon archaeologists and Bedouin were competing with each other to find more scrolls. The Bedouin, who knew the area better, found more.

Eventually it became clear that a very important archaeological find had been made. A total of eleven caves in the vicinity of Qumran have produced some 25,000 manuscript fragments, some no bigger than a postage stamp. Over the years these have been painstakingly pieced together to reveal approximately 670 extra-biblical religious texts and a total of 215 manuscripts of every Old Testament book except Esther and Nehemiah. Most of the Old Testament texts were very fragmentary, but there was a complete scroll of Isaiah, 7.3 m (24 ft) in length.

Near the caves at Qumran were the ruins of buildings belonging to the Jewish Essene sect. The complex contained a communal dining room, baptismal cisterns and a scriptorium (or writing room) complete with ink-wells. It is believed that the Essenes hid the scrolls in the surrounding caves on the approach of the Roman general Vespasian in the early summer of AD 68.

The scrolls date from c. 250 BC up to the destruction of AD 68 and have survived because of the extreme aridity of the environment. Changes in handwriting style have enabled scholars to place the scrolls in a relative order, accurate to within one generation of scribes. The extra-biblical texts can be grouped into five types:

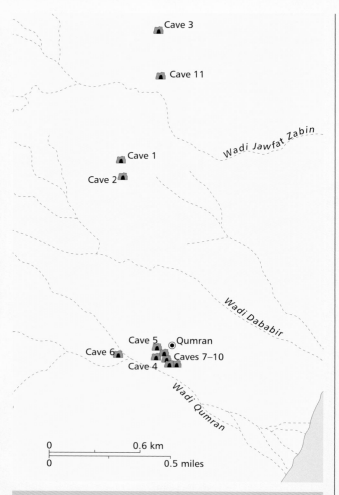

Findspots of the Dead Sea Scrolls

Four locations near the western shore of the Dead Sea have produced 227 texts of the Hebrew Old Testament. These are often called the 'Dead Sea Scrolls'. By far the largest collection was from the caves around Qumran. It dates from c. 250 BC until the destruction of Qumran by the Romans in AD 68.

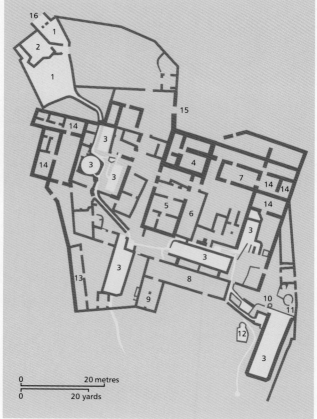

Plan of Qumran

The complex of buildings that once belonged to the Jewish Essene sect at Qumran near the western shore of the Dead Sea.

1. decantation pool
2. probable baptistry
3. cistern
4. tower
5. council chamber
6. scriptorium
7. kitchen
8. assembly hall and refectory
9. pantry
10. potter's wheel
11. kiln
12. clay preparation area
13. cattle pen
14. store rooms
15. main entrance
16. entrance of aqueduct

thus be shown that there was a Masoretic-type text as early as the second century BC. The texts from Wadi Murabba'at, dating at the latest from the early second century AD, are all of the Masoretic type.

In all the commentaries found at Qumran a text virtually identical to the Masoretic text is used. This suggests that even as early as the second century BC the Masoretic-type text was recognized as the standard text of the Hebrew Bible.

THE NASH PAPYRUS

There is only one other Hebrew text of any part of the Old Testament from outside of Palestine dating before the Christian era. The so-called Nash papyrus from Egypt is a somewhat damaged copy of a liturgical text of the Ten Commandments (Exodus 20 and Deuteronomy 5). It is dated to the second or first century BC.

THE MASORETIC SCRIBES

The Jewish scribes responsible for the Masoretic text counted the words, even the letters in a given book. They marked the mid-point of a book, of the Pentateuch and of the whole Bible, counting backwards and forwards from that point to ensure nothing had dropped out. Their care and respect for the text fell nothing short of reverence: old scrolls were buried, which explains why no Masoretic texts from before the ninth century survive. Their meticulous copying of the Hebrew text is the prime reason why the Masoretic text is still the base text for translations of the Old Testament.

1. rules and regulations of the Essene community

2. poetic and wisdom texts, including some texts from the collection of writings known as the Apocrypha

3. reworked or rewritten scripture

4. commentaries on the Old Testament text

5. miscellaneous writings, including the 'copper scroll' which contained descriptions of the hiding places of gold and silver treasures.

OTHER 'DEAD SEA SCROLLS'

Searches of sites in the wider vicinity – the ruins of Masada and the caves at Wadi Murabba'at, 18 km (11 miles) south of Qumran, and at Nahal Hever 17 km (10½ miles) further south – have revealed a further twelve Old Testament texts. Masada was the scene of the Jewish resistance to Roman rule in AD 73. The caves at Wadi Murabba'at and Nahal Hever contain material left behind by Jews resisting Rome in the Bar-Kokhba revolt of AD 132–135. Once again these revolts provide upper limits to dating these texts.

THE DEAD SEA SCROLLS IN RETROSPECT

In total Dead Sea Scrolls cover some 34 per cent of the Old Testament. They are evidence of the Hebrew text at least eight centuries before its traditionally known form, the so-called Masoretic text, the earliest example of which dates from AD 896. Many, but by no means all, of the Dead Sea Scrolls do not differ substantially from the Masoretic text. It can

---

The Habakkuk commentary, 1QpHab.

The Habakkuk commentary consists of two pieces of parchment sewn together about 1.5 m (5 ft) in length and an average of 17 cm (7 in) wide. Its text is virtually identical to the Masoretic text of Habakkuk 1:8–9a:

'Their [the Chaldeans'] horses are swifter than leopards, fiercer than wolves at dusk. Their cavalry gallops headlong; their horsemen come from afar. They fly like a vulture swooping to devour; they all come bent on violence. Their hordes advance like a desert wind.'

There then follows the commentary under the text. It identifies the Chaldeans with the Kittim (Romans) thus:

'Interpreted, this concerns the Kittim [Romans], who trample the earth with their horses and beasts. They come from afar from the islands of the sea, to devour all the peoples like a vulture which cannot be satisfied and they address all the peoples with anger, wrath, fury and indignation. For it is, as he said, their hordes advance like a desert wind.'

JESUS IS BORN

(c. 5 BC)

JESUS IS BORN IN BETHLEHEM

In the small Judean town of Bethlehem an event took place that, even though wrongly computed by the sixth century monk Dionysus Exiguus, has been used to divide history into two – BC (Before Christ) and AD (anno Domini – in the year of the Lord). Bethlehem, 9 km (5½ miles) south of Jerusalem, had been the home of King David's family and, according to the prophet Micah, the birthplace of the one 'whose origins are from of old, from ancient times'.[1]

Luke's Gospel tells how Jesus' mother, Mary, and her husband Joseph responded to a decree from Caesar Augustus (31 BC – AD 14) by making a journey of 120 km (75 miles) from Nazareth to Bethlehem to be registered; and Luke notes this was the first census that took place while Quirinius was governor of Syria.[2] Publius Sulpicius Quirinius is known to have served two terms as governor of Syria: 6–4 BC and AD 6–9. Thus, the census could not have been held in the period 3 BC – AD 5 and Jesus could not have been born in the year notionally termed AD 1. That he was actually born a few years prior to that date is corroborated by the death of the other main character in the story, Herod the Great, in late March 4 BC.

NO ROOM IN THE INN

The story of Jesus' birth in Bethlehem occurs only in the Gospels of Matthew and Luke. Mark and John do not mention it. Luke simply records: 'While they were there, the time came for the baby to be born, and she gave birth to her firstborn, a son. She wrapped him in cloths and placed him in a manger, because there was no room for them in the inn' (Luke 2:6–7). The Greek word for 'inn' is used by Luke later in his gospel to mean the 'guest room' which Jesus requests as the venue for the Passover meal shortly before his crucifixion.[3] So Mary and Joseph, because of the influx of people being registered, were unable to use any guest room.

Exactly where the birth took place we know not. Justin Martyr, writing in the mid-second century, states that Jesus was born in a cave.[4] The gospel writers are not that specific, but someone gave Mary and Joseph a manger (an animal's feeding trough) to put the baby Jesus in. The traditional site of Jesus' birth, the so-called 'Church of the Nativity', was built over a cave by Constantine the Great in AD 325 and enlarged by Justinian (AD 527–565).

SHEPHERDS IN THE FIELDS

Luke records that an angel appeared at night to some shepherds who were in the fields guarding their flocks against thieves and predatory animals. Flocks so close to Jerusalem could have been those reserved for sacrifice in the Temple. The angel announced: 'Today in the town of David a Saviour has been born to you; he is Christ the Lord. This will be a sign to you: You will find a baby wrapped in cloths and lying in a manger' (Luke 2:11–12). The shepherds hurried off and found that the angel's word was true, the baby was lying in a manger.

This perhaps gives a clue as to the time of year. Sheep were normally put out to grass between March and November. The winter months were cold and wet and sheep were not normally kept in the fields then. Thus December, when Jesus' birth is now celebrated, would seem not to have been the time. We celebrate Christmas in December because the early Christians chose to remember their Lord's coming into the world during the Roman festival of the 'invincible sun' that took place at the winter solstice, observed on 25 December.

Luke records the circumcision and naming of Jesus in the Temple 'on the eighth day' and describes how the devout Simeon and the prophetess Anna recognize the baby at once as the Jews' promised redeemer.[5]

THE WISE MEN

Matthew's Gospel records that Mary and the baby Jesus were visited by some mysterious visitors from the east, whom the Greek text calls 'magoi'. This has been Latinized to 'magi' and traditionally rendered 'wise men'. This event seems to have been sometime after Jesus' birth, as the family are recorded as living in a house. Perhaps their initial, emergency accommodation, whatever it was, proved unsuitable for a young child. Herod's response of ordering the death of all boys in Bethlehem two years old or under could mean that Jesus was nearly three when the visitors arrived.

Where could such wise men have come from? Babylon, the centre of ancient astronomy, is often advanced. Astrologers there had from a very early period busied themselves with astronomical observations which portended good or evil for the 'west land', that is, Syria–Palestine. However, Persia is a more likely possibility. Magos is derived from a Persian term 'magush', which denoted a class of astrologers.

The number three is traditionally associated with the number of wise men because they brought three gifts. The appellation 'kings' has no New Testament evidence, but rests on a desire to portray the eastern visitors as the fulfilment of three Old Testament prophecies in which kings pay homage to the Lord.[6]

FOLLOWING THE STAR

Matthew's Gospel explains that the wise men had become aware of Jesus' birth by looking at the stars. One star in particular grabbed their attention and they recognized that it heralded the birth of the 'king of the Jews'. Matthew notes that the star, which led the wise men to Bethlehem, had appeared in the east at an exact time and went ahead of them until it

KEY
[1] 1 Samuel 16:1; Micah 5:2
[2] Luke 2:2
[3] Luke 22:11
[4] Justin Martyr, *Dialogue with Trypho the Jew*, 78
[5] Luke 2:21–38
[6] Psalm 72:10; Isaiah 49:7; 60:3
[7] Matthew 2:2, 7, 9
[8] Exodus 30:34, 23
[9] John 19:39
[10] Matthew 1:23

The interior of the Church of the Nativity, Bethlehem.

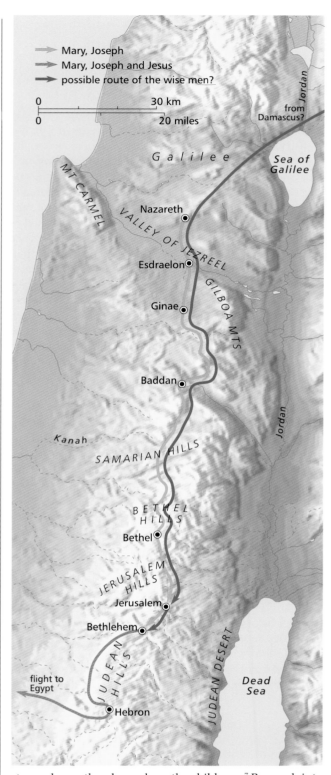

3. Chinese records refer to three comets. One in August 12 BC is the famous Halley's comet. This is also mentioned in Roman records, but is clearly too early. One in April 4 BC is too late, since Herod died at the end of March that year. This leaves a comet visible for some seventy days in March to April 5 BC. In Chinese this is called a *sui-hsing* (broom star), meaning a comet with a tail. A comet, as it rounded the sun, would have temporarily disappeared from view – and the wise men's star disappears from view while they travel from Jerusalem to Bethlehem.

GOLD, FRANKINCENSE AND MYRRH

Matthew records that the wise men presented the baby Jesus with three gifts: gold, frankincense and myrrh. Frankincense and myrrh were ultimately of south Arabian origin, the Sheba of the Old Testament. This need not mean that the wise men came from there. Well-worn caravan routes took these valuable substances north to Syria and Palestine, a branch went across to Babylon, so the wise men could have bought their frankincense and myrrh in Babylon. Equally well, they could have bought these gifts en route, maybe in the bazaar at Damascus or even in the market in Jerusalem.

Gold spoke of kingly splendour. Frankincense was a component of the sacred incense used in the tabernacle. It was burnt both in worship and as a fumigant. Myrrh was one of the ingredients of the anointing oil.[8] It was used in cosmetics, embalming and together with aloes was applied to Jesus' body after his crucifixion.[9]

ESCAPE TO EGYPT

Matthew's Gospel explains how the wise men's assumption that 'the king of the Jews' was bound to be born in Jerusalem led to their informing Herod the Great (37–4 BC) of the birth of 'the king of the Jews' whom they were trying to visit. Warned by an angel in a dream, Joseph took his family to Egypt.

RETURN TO NAZARETH

After the death of Herod, Jesus' family settled once again in Nazareth – a small, somewhat insignificant town in the hills of Galilee. Apart from the record of a trip to Jerusalem when Jesus was twelve, we know nothing more about his life until he commenced his public ministry when he was about thirty. His mother, Mary, must have wondered how his virgin birth,[10] and the series of special events that had surrounded it was going to prepare Jesus to fulfil the divine mission encapsulated in the name that the angel had told Joseph: 'You are to give him the name Jesus [the Lord Saves] because he will save his people from their sins' (Matthew 1:21).

stopped over the place where the child was.[7] Research into such a star, which must have appeared before the death of Herod the Great in late March 4 BC, has suggested the following possibilities:

1. A conjunction of Jupiter and Saturn in the constellation of Pisces is known to have taken place three times during 7 BC (in May, October and December). But its duration would have been brief and it would not be referred to as a single star.

2. Some have postulated a supernova, a star that 'explodes'. It has been suggested that a supernova visible near the star Alpha Aquilae is mentioned in Chinese records for 4 BC, but supernovae are very rare astronomical events and do not move through the sky – and the term in question is actually a comet.

THE MINISTRY OF CHRIST: FIRST YEAR

(AD 30 to March AD 31)

The hull of the so-called 'Jesus boat', a first-century fishing boat found in Lake Galilee in 1985.

JOHN THE BAPTIST

In the desert of Judea, the arid region virtually devoid of vegetation between Jerusalem and the Dead Sea, a somewhat unusual character, clad in clothes of camel-hair and eating locusts and wild honey, began to preach: 'Repent, for the kingdom of heaven is near' (Matthew 3:2). Because of his mass baptisms in the River Jordan he was called John the Baptist. He was a relative of Jesus, since their mothers were related.

Luke dates the start of John's ministry to the fifteenth year of Tiberius Caesar.[1] Tiberius's predecessor, Augustus, is known to have died on 19 August AD 14, so this yields AD 29 as the date for the start of John's ministry. Jesus himself came from Galilee to Bethany on the east side of the River Jordan to be baptized by John. Luke records that at his baptism the Holy Spirit descended on Jesus and he began his ministry, being about thirty years old.[2]

THE FOUR GOSPELS

For a detailed record of the life and ministry of Jesus we are entirely dependent on the four Gospels. The Gospels of Matthew, Mark and Luke are noticeably similar. 91 per cent of Mark's Gospel is contained in Matthew and 53 per cent of Mark is found in Luke; the use of common sources, both written and oral, is often postulated as a reason. The Gospel of John presents Jesus' life from a markedly different angle, emphasizing Jesus' teaching.

The Gospels record that Matthew and John were two of Jesus' apostles, who spent three years with Jesus. (John) Mark is believed to have been a close associate of the apostle Peter. Luke, a doctor and travelling companion of the apostle Paul,[3] though not an eye-witness himself, compiled his account from the testimony of eye-witnesses.[4]

FURTHER CHRONOLOGICAL CONSIDERATIONS

Although the four Gospels cover the ministry of Jesus in considerable detail, they group the material thematically rather than follow a strict chronological sequence. We have attempted in this *Atlas* to put the events of Christ's ministry into some kind of sequence. If others looking at the same evidence have reached differing conclusions, they should be equally respected, although there are a few chronological signposts that should not be missed. John's Gospel records three Passovers including the one at Jesus' death.[5] The ministry of Christ thus spanned a minimum of two years, although the scholarly consensus favours three. At the first Passover the Jews remark that Herod's temple had been 46 years in the building. Since Herod is known to have 'undertaken to build' the Temple in Jerusalem in 19 BC,[6] the resultant date of AD 25 is taken by some as the start of Jesus' ministry. This is four years earlier than the date obtained from Luke's Gospel mentioned above, so it is argued that the 46-year figure does not include the time spent on assembling the materials before building commenced.

JESUS IS TEMPTED BY SATAN

The Gospels relate how, after his baptism, Jesus was led by the Spirit into the desert and tempted by the devil. One temptation involved a visit to Jerusalem, since Jesus was tempted to throw himself off the highest point of the Temple.[7] The reference may be to the south-east corner of the temple, from which there was a drop of some 130 m (426 ft) to the Kidron Valley below. Another temptation involved a visit to a high mountain where the devil showed Jesus all the kingdoms of the world and their splendour.

JESUS' FIRST MIRACLE

Jesus and his mother, Mary, were invited to a wedding at Cana in Galilee. When the wine ran out, Mary turned to Jesus for help. Here he performed his first miracle, turning the water in six large, stone jars used for ceremonial washing into wine, some 600 litres (160 gallons) in total. The master of the banquet was suitably impressed by the

KEY
[1] Luke 3:1
[2] Luke 3:23
[3] Colossians 4:14
[4] Luke 1:2
[5] John 2:13; 6:4; 13:1
[6] Josephus, *Antiquities*, 15.380
[7] Matthew 4:5; Luke 4:9
[8] Matthew 27:56; Mark 15:40
[9] Mark 1:21–27; Luke 4:31–36
[10] Luke 7:4–5
[11] Mark 3:14; Luke 6:13

LEFT: The desert region of the lower Jordan Valley, where Jesus was tempted by the devil.

RIGHT: The synagogue at Capernaum. The present visible ruins date from the fourth century. Underneath, partially preserved walls of black basalt may be from the earlier first century synagogue.

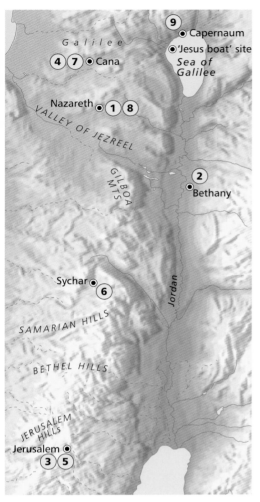

The first year of Jesus' ministry

The numbers refer to the events of the first year of Jesus' ministry in chronological sequence.

1) Jesus leaves his childhood home at Nazareth

2) Jesus is baptized by John the Baptist at Bethany on the East Side of the River Jordan

3) Jesus is tested by the devil in the desert, and tempted to throw himself off the highest point of the Temple at Jerusalem

4) Jesus changes water into wine at a wedding at Cana in Galilee

5) Jesus visits Jerusalem and cleanses the Temple

6) Jesus talks with a Samaritan woman at Sychar

7) Jesus meets a royal official at Cana and heals his son, who was sick, at Capernaum

8) Jesus is thrown out of the synagogue at his home town of Nazareth

9) Jesus moves to Capernaum, calls his disciples and teaches in the vicinity of Capernaum, performing many miracles

quality of the wine. In total the four Gospels record some thirty-five of Jesus' miracles.

JESUS CLEANSES THE TEMPLE

Jesus went to Jerusalem at Passover time. If a date of AD 30 is adopted, the Passover itself would have occurred on 7 April. Angered by those selling cattle, sheep and doves and those changing money in the Temple courts, Jesus made a whip out of cords and drove them from the Temple area. 'How dare you turn my Father's house into a market!' he declared (John 2:16).

NICODEMUS AND THE SAMARITAN WOMAN

Not surprisingly, Jesus' action at the Temple aroused the indignation of the Jewish religious authorities. But Nicodemus, a member of the Jewish ruling council, sought Jesus out at night. Jesus' reply to him is a succinct summary of God's plan to save humankind: 'For God so loved the world that he gave his one and only Son, that whoever believes in him shall not perish but have eternal life' (John 3:16).

Travelling back to Galilee, Jesus stopped at a town in Samaria called Sychar (modern Aksar). The Samaritans were the inveterate enemies of the Jews. Their temple to the Lord at Gerizim near Shechem had been destroyed by the Jewish ruler, John Hyrcanus in 128 BC. At midday by Jacob's well he had a long conversation with a local woman about living water and true worship. Privately he revealed to the woman that he was the messiah, called Christ.

JESUS RETURNS TO GALILEE

Returning to Galilee, Jesus met a royal official at Cana whose son lay sick at Capernaum. The Gospel of John 4:43–54 relates how a word from Jesus was all that was required to restore the son to health. On his return to Nazareth, his boyhood home, Jesus read from the prophet Isaiah in the town's synagogue:

'The Spirit of the Lord is on me, because he has anointed me to preach good news to the poor. He has sent me to proclaim freedom for the prisoners and recovery of sight for the blind, to release the oppressed, to proclaim the year of the Lord's favour.'
LUKE 4:18–19

Jesus' proclamation that this scripture was being fulfilled in their hearing, today, riled the people in the synagogue, who drove him from the town.

JESUS CALLS HIS FIRST DISCIPLES

Jesus moved to Capernaum beside Lake Galilee, a lake which now contains eighteen species of fish, ten of which are commercially important. He called two sets of brothers: Simon, called Peter, and his brother Andrew; and James, son of Zebedee, and his brother, John. All four were fishermen, but Jesus called them to leave their nets and follow him. This meeting might not have been the chance encounter that the Gospel writers make out. Probably John, certainly Andrew, had been a disciple of John the Baptist and met Jesus just after his baptism, when Andrew introduced his brother, Peter, to him. Furthermore, James and John might have been Jesus' cousins, if, as is sometimes proposed, their mother, Salome, was a sister of Jesus' mother, Mary.[8]

JESUS IN GALILEE

Mark and Luke describe how Jesus confronted a man with an unclean spirit in the synagogue at Capernaum.[9] The ruins of the synagogue at Capernaum date from the fourth century AD, but underneath them partially preserved walls of black basalt can be seen, probably constructed in the first century. This may have been the synagogue given to the town by a centurion and visited by Jesus.[10]

Jesus then embarked on a tour of Galilee, teaching in synagogues, preaching the good news of the kingdom of God and healing the sick and diseased. Many more sick were brought to him and large crowds followed him. Some of these were from regions further afield than Galilee, from Jerusalem and beyond the Jordan. On one occasion, with the people crowding around the lakeside, Jesus taught the people from a boat. Later the disciples put out into the lake. At Jesus' command they put down their nets and caught such a large number of fish that their nets began to break.

In 1985 there was a drought in Israel. An unusually low water level in Lake Galilee revealed the hull of ancient boat 8.2 m (26 ft 11 in) long and 2.35 m (7 ft 9 in) wide near Magdala. A cooking pot and lamp found with the boat suggested a first century date, which was confirmed by a Carbon 14 test on a sample of the boat's wood. There is no way of proving a connection between the boat and any of the figures in the Gospels, but almost certainly the boat belongs to the period of the Gospels or very close to it. Not surprisingly, journalists were quick to name it 'the Jesus boat'.

JESUS DESIGNATES THE APOSTLES

At Capernaum Jesus called Matthew, also known as Levi, to be his disciple. He collected taxes for the Roman government. Since tax collectors were considered collaborators with the pagan conquerors and frequently abused their position to defraud, theirs was a profession despised by many Jews. On one occasion Jesus went up a mountainside and called to him twelve of his closest disciples. These men he designated 'apostles' (a term meaning 'those sent out').[11] Over the next two years Jesus sought to train and mentor his apostles. Many were to become significant leaders of the early church.

THE MINISTRY OF CHRIST: SECOND YEAR

(March AD 31 to April AD 32)

JESUS RETURNS TO JERUSALEM

John 5:1 records that Jesus went up to Jerusalem for a feast of the Jews. The identity of this feast is unknown, though many suggest the Feast of the Passover, which in AD 31 would have fallen on 27 March. This is thus seen as the start of the second year of Jesus' ministry. On this trip to Jerusalem Jesus healed an invalid by the pool of Bethesda.

JESUS THE TEACHER

All four Gospels – Matthew, Mark, Luke and John – contain large sections of teaching purporting to be the words of Jesus. Some scholars regard these passages at best as the fabrication of the Gospel writers, at worst as the fabrications of unknown writers as late as the second century. Recent discoveries make such claims virtually untenable. Wooden writing-boards or wax-covered writing tablets, such as the archive of some 1,900 discovered at Vindolanda (Chesterholm) near Hadrian's Wall in the north of England, were used to record all kinds of information. Some listeners may have had sufficient skills to take down Jesus' words verbatim. The words could then have been transferred to more durable writing materials such as papyrus or parchment, which were in turn used by the Gospel writers to compile their gospels.

In Jesus' longest discourse, the so-called 'Sermon on the Mount', he gives much ethical teaching. He emphasizes the importance of thoughts and motives and contrasts this with Jewish tradition. At the end Jesus urges his listeners to put his words into practice and be like a wise man who built his house on a rock. The site of the sermon is difficult to identify, but must meet the twin criteria of being on a mountainside and being a level place.[1]

JESUS' MIRACLES IN GALILEE

With four separate accounts a precise order of events is difficult to ascertain, but it can reasonably be deduced that, once he had returned from Jerusalem, Jesus stayed in the vicinity of Lake Galilee for the rest of his second year of ministry. This year is sometimes termed 'the Year of Popularity' in which Jesus was pressed by crowds wherever he went. Certainly his miracles increased his popularity.

It was at this time that Jesus' relative, John the Baptist, was imprisoned. He had rebuked Herod the Great's son, Herod Antipas, 'the tetrarch' (4 BC – AD 39) for marrying Herodias, his brother Philip's wife.[2] When John asked some disciples to check on reports he had been hearing about Jesus, Jesus sent John a report which could serve as a summary of his ministry:

'Go back and report to John what you hear and see: The blind receive sight, the lame walk, those who have leprosy are cured, the deaf hear, the dead are raised, and the good news is preached to the poor.'

MATTHEW 11:4–5; LUKE 7:22

The Gospel writers record a wide variety of miracles:
- At Capernaum Jesus healed the sick servant of a centurion. The centurion had faith that all Jesus needed to do was to say the word and his servant would be healed. His faith caused Jesus to exclaim:

'I tell you the truth, I have not found anyone in Israel with such great faith' (Matthew 8:10b).
- Also in Capernaum Jesus raised from the dead the twelve-year-old daughter of Jairus, the synagogue ruler, and that same day he healed a woman who had been subject to bleeding, and thus ritually unclean, for twelve years.
- At Nain, south of Nazareth, Jesus raised from the dead the only son of a widow.
- On Lake Galilee Jesus calmed a storm that had blown up, frightening the disciples who were with him in the boat.[3]
- On the eastern side of the lake Jesus delivered two demon-possessed men of their unclean spirits.[4] The demons entered a herd of some two thousand pigs who rushed down a steep bank into the lake and were drowned. The presence of the pigs suggests that the area in question had been settled by Gentiles. The location of this incident at Kursi, the only site on the eastern shore of the lake where there is a steep slope down to the lake, would seem certain; but a textual problem – in which the people are variously referred to as Gergesenes, Gadarenes or Gerasenes among different manuscripts of three Gospels – makes it unclear where the demon-possessed men hailed from. Gergesa, the ancient name for Kursi, would seem the most probable, with Gadara (Umm Qeis) being some 10 km (6 miles) south-east of the lake and Gerasa (modern Jerash) some 46 km (29 miles) further south-east.
- On one occasion Jesus returned to his home town of Nazareth, but the people there took offence. The Gospel writers note that he did not do many miracles there because of their lack of faith.[5]

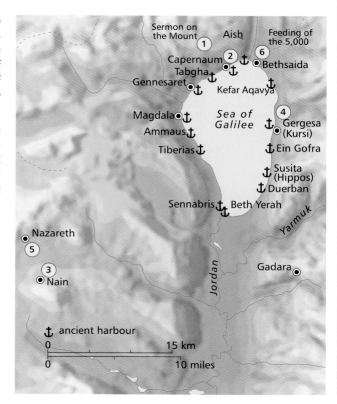

Reconstruction of Capernaum, which Jesus used as his base in Galilee.

KEY
[1] Matthew 5:1; Luke 6:17
[2] Matthew 14:3–4; Mark 6:17–18
[3] Matthew 8:23–27; Mark 4:35–41; Luke 8:22–25
[4] Matthew 8:28–34
[5] Matthew 13:58; Mark 6:5–6
[6] Matthew 13:18–23; Mark 4:13–20; Luke 8:11–15
[7] Matthew 14:3–12; Mark 6:14–29
[8] John 6:4
[9] Mark 6:39; Luke 9:10; John 6:10

The second year of Jesus' ministry
The numbers refer to the events that took place in the vicinity of Lake Galilee during the second year of Jesus' ministry.

1) Jesus preaches the 'Sermon on the Mount'

2) Jesus performs several miracles at Capernaum

3) Jesus raises to life the dead son of a widow at Nain

4) Jesus delivers two demon-possessed men from unclean spirits

5) Jesus pays a return visit to Nazareth

6) Jesus feeds a large crowd well in excess of five-thousand near Bethsaida, and leaves Galilee for Tyre and Sidon

JESUS' PARABLES

The Gospel writers record forty or so of Jesus' parables. These were short stories, drawn from everyday life, designed to teach spiritual truth. Some – such as the Lost Sheep, the Lost (Prodigal) Son and the Good Samaritan – are well known. However, the meaning of a number of parables was not always evident. On several occasions, as with the Parable of the Sower, Jesus had to explain the meaning to his disciples.[6]

JOHN THE BAPTIST IS BEHEADED

John the Baptist languished in prison at the hilltop fortified palace of Machaerus on the far side of the Dead Sea until Herod Antipas's birthday. The daughter of his new wife, Herodias, was called upon to perform a dance. Impressed, Herod promised to give her whatever she wanted. Prompted by her mother, the young woman demanded the head of John the Baptist on a tray.[7]

JESUS FEEDS THE FIVE THOUSAND

When he heard of John's death, Jesus sought solitude. The crowds had other ideas, but Jesus had compassion on them and healed their sick. The Passover was near,[8] which in AD 32 fell on April 13. Jesus had just one year to live.

The crowd were getting hungry and in such a remote region there was no possibility of feeding them. Miraculously multiplying five small barley loaves and two small fish, Jesus fed the crowd of five thousand men, besides women and children. The miracle took place near Bethsaida, at the northern end of Lake Galilee, at a site where there was plenty of green grass.[9]

It is significant that after this miracle Jesus sought to avoid the crowds, since he knew that they intended to make him king by force.

JESUS LEAVES GALILEE

Realizing that he could not find solitude in Galilee, Jesus travelled north out of Herod Antipas's realm to Tyre and Sidon on the Mediterranean coast (of modern Lebanon). When he eventually returned, he encountered much greater opposition. Indeed the last year of Jesus' life is sometimes called 'the Year of Opposition'. Jesus' impending suffering and death in Jerusalem increasingly become the focus of the Gospel writers.

JERUSALEM IN NEW TESTAMENT TIMES

JERUSALEM AND ITS ENVIRONS

Jerusalem is situated on the ridge that forms the backbone of Judea, some 750 m (2,460 ft) above the Mediterranean and some 1,150 m (3,773 ft) above the Dead Sea. It is easily defended, being flanked by the Kidron Valley to the east and the Hinnom Valley to the south and east. For the Jews Jerusalem, set in the centre of the nations, with countries all around her, was the navel of the earth.[1] The city was completely ringed with high hills, so any journey to Jerusalem involved an ascent.[2] Although the city was near a route going north from Hebron through the middle of Palestine to Samaria, this was only used for inland trade. A route went west to east from Emmaus, through Jerusalem and down into Jericho. As Jesus' parable of the Good Samaritan makes clear, bandits posed an extra danger.[3]

The natural resources of the area around Jerusalem were limited. There was stone in abundance, but metals were entirely lacking and clay was of inferior quality. Wool and hides were produced from the rearing of sheep and cattle, but most of Jerusalem's grain had to be imported. Jerusalem possessed only one spring of any importance, that of Siloam in the south. Water had to be collected in cisterns or brought in from a distance by aqueducts. One such aqueduct, some 80 km (50 miles) long, was the work of Pontius Pilate, the Roman governor of Judea, whose use of Temple funds provoked a public uproar.[4] Since agricultural products were largely imported, the cost of living in Jerusalem was high. Cattle and wine fetched a higher price in the city than in the country. The price of fruit was three to six times more expensive than in the countryside.

A RELIGIOUS CENTRE

The main feature of first-century Jerusalem was the Temple of the Lord, which had been rebuilt by Herod the Great from 19 BC onwards. This great structure is described in detail on page 132 of this *Atlas*. Vast sums of money flowed into the city, especially at the great feasts of Passover, Weeks (Pentecost) and Tabernacles, when Jerusalem was packed with pilgrims. The pilgrims not only provided the Temple with offerings and sustained a souvenir industry, they crowded into numerous inns, or slept outside the city in tents or in the surrounding villages. Many Jews settled in Jerusalem to be near the Temple and to be buried outside the holy city. In addition, a two-drachma Temple tax was levied annually on all Jews.[5] When work on the Temple finally came to an end in c. AD 63 more than eighteen thousand workers faced unemployment. The Temple authorities used their labour to pave Jerusalem with white stone[6].

Jerusalem also, reputedly, had some four hundred synagogues, with schools attached to them for the study of the Law. A displaced inscription of a synagogue ruler named Theodotus was discovered in 1913 at the southern end of the Ophel hill. As well as building a synagogue, Theodotus built an inn for overseas visitors.

PALACES

The Hasmonean rulers had built a palace to the west of the Temple. It was called the Acra or citadel. Herod the Great, however, built a new palace in the Upper City on the western extremity of the city, in the area of the present Jaffa Gate. It contained huge banqueting halls and guestrooms. Its exterior wall was 14 m (46 ft) high, and had three towers named Hippicus, Phasael and Mariamme respectively, after Herod's friend, brother and his one-time favourite wife. The towers were 39, 31 and 22 m (128, 102 and 72 ft) high respectively. Part of the tower of Phasael still remains, incorporated into the present 'Tower of David'.

THE ANTONIA FORTRESS

On the north-west corner Herod built a fortress, named Antonia after the Roman general Mark Antony. Three 23-metre-high (75 ft 6 in) towers rose precipitously into the sky, a fourth was over 30 m (98 ft) high. A cohort, a Roman infantry unit of six hundred men, kept a close watch on the Temple and could intervene quickly if rioting broke out (as in Acts 21:30–32). The Romans kept the high priest's vestments here, only releasing them to Jewish keeping on feast days. It may be that the stone pavement known as Gabbatha, on which Pilate sat to judge Jesus,[7] was the 2,500-square-metre (2,990-square-yards) courtyard of the Antonia fortress.

OTHER BUILDINGS IN JERUSALEM

In the Lower City Herod had a theatre and hippodrome built. At the foot of the ridge on which the City of David was situated was the pool of Siloam, where Jesus healed the man born blind.[8]

Another pool mentioned in the Gospels is the Pool of Bethesda, which was originally surrounded by five covered colonnades. Believing that from time to time an angel would disturb the waters and perform a healing, many sick people congregated here waiting for a cure. Jesus healed a man who had been an invalid for thirty-eight years.[9] The twin pools discovered in the grounds of the Church of St Anne, to the north of the Temple area, seem to be the most plausible site.

North of the second wall, and hence originally outside the city, is the Church of the Holy Sepulchre. This could well be the site of Jesus' empty tomb.

Herod Agrippa I (AD 41–44) started building a

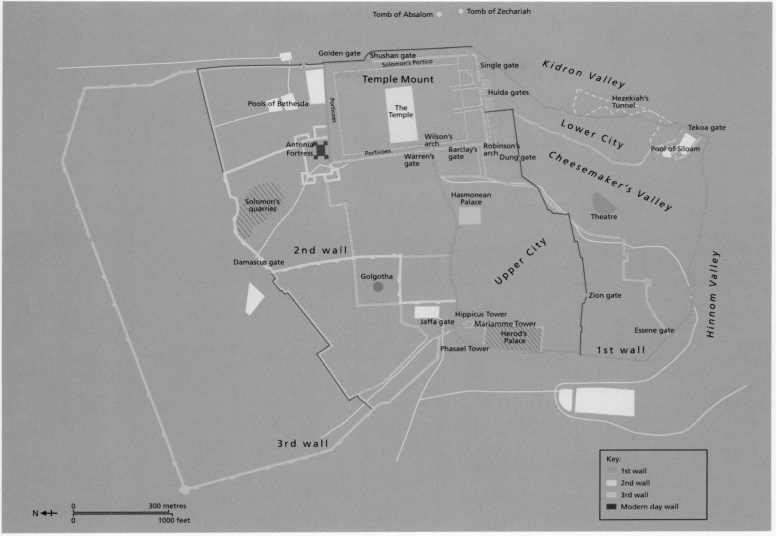

Tomb of Absalom   Tomb of Zechariah

Golden gate Shushan gate
Solomon's Portico
Single gate
Temple Mount
Kidron Valley

Pools of Bethesda
Hulda gates
Hezekiah's Tunnel

The Temple
Lower City
Tekoa gate

Antonia Fortress
Wilson's arch
Porticoes
Warren's gate
Barclay's gate
Robinson's arch
Dung gate
Cheesemaker's Valley
Pool of Siloam

Solomon's quarries

Hasmonean Palace

Theatre

2nd wall
Upper City

Damascus gate
Hinnom Valley

Golgotha
Zion gate

Hippicus Tower
Jaffa gate Mariamme Tower
Essene gate
Herod's Palace
1st wall
Phasael Tower

3rd wall

Key:
1st wall
2nd wall
3rd wall
Modern day wall

N
0   300 metres
0   1000 feet

Jerusalem in New Testament Times
In the early first century AD there was much building in Jerusalem. Herod Agrippa I (AD 41–44) built a third wall to the north of the city.

KEY

[1] Ezekiel 5:5; 38:12
[2] Psalms 122:4; 125:2
[3] Luke 10:30
[4] Josephus, *The Jewish War*, 2.175
[5] Matthew 17:24
[6] Josephus, *Antiquities*, 20.219
[7] John 19:13
[8] John 9:7
[9] John 5:2–9
[10] Matthew 23:29
[11] Mark 11:11; Matthew 21:17; Luke 24:50

Modern Jerusalem from the Mount of Olives
The massive enclosure wall of the Haram esh-Sherif follows the line of the outer wall of Herod's Temple.

third wall in the north of the city, which enclosed that area. Over 3 km (2 miles) long and 5.25 m (17 ft 3 in) thick and graced with ninety massive towers, it was finished in AD 66.

TOMBS

In the Kidron Valley several tombs have been preserved, dating from the period prior to the destruction of Jerusalem by the Romans in AD 70. The so-called 'Tomb of Absalom', graced with Ionic and Doric columns, had a conical top. A monument associated with the so-called 'Tomb of Zechariah' had a rock-cut square tower with a pyramid on top.

Between AD 46 and AD 55 Queen Helena of the Adiabene, a convert to Judaism from Assyria (northern Iraq), erected a family tomb some 600 m (1,970 ft) north of Jerusalem. With a ceremonial staircase and three conical towers it was the most elaborate of all known tombs in Jerusalem. It is now commonly called the 'Tombs of the Kings'. It may have been monuments such as these which Jesus had in mind when he uttered his condemnation of the teachers of the Law and Pharisees for building tombs of the prophets and decorating the graves of the righteous.[10] Less elaborate tombs were carved in the hillsides around the city and many have been uncovered in modern times.

OUTSIDE THE CITY

To the east of the city was the Mount of Olives. This very name implies that its olives were abundant in comparison with the surrounding land. On its lower slopes, just across the Kidron Valley from Jerusalem, was the Garden of Gethsemane, scene of Jesus' arrest. Its name means 'olive oil press'. Imported olives, especially those from Peraea across the River Jordan, may have been pressed here too. Large quantities of olive oil were needed as fuel for the lamps in the Temple. On the eastern slopes of the Mount of Olives was the village of Bethany, home of Mary, Martha and Lazarus, where Jesus stayed during the week before his death. According to the Gospels it was from near here that he ascended to heaven.[11]

THE LATER HISTORY OF JERUSALEM

Jerusalem was destroyed by the Romans in AD 70. It lay in ruins until the revolt of Bar-Kokhba in AD 132. In AD 135 it was destroyed again, when the revolt was crushed, and rebuilt as a Roman city called Aelia Capitolina, from which Jews were excluded. After the Roman emperor Constantine issued his edict tolerating Christianity in AD 313, Christians began to make pilgrimages to the city, to visit the sites of their Lord's passion, resurrection and ascension. Constantine's mother, Helena, began construction of the Church of the Holy Sepulchre in AD 326. Jerusalem fell to the Arabs in AD 637, and came under the rule of the Crusaders from 1099 to 1244. The present walls of the Old City are the work of the Turkish sultan Suleiman the Magnificent in 1542.

THE MINISTRY OF CHRIST: FINAL YEAR

(April AD 32 to April AD 33)

JESUS AMONG THE GENTILES

Jesus' journey to Tyre and Sidon took him to a predominately Gentile and pagan area. Here he responded to the faith in him shown by a local woman and delivered her daughter from demon-possession. On his return Jesus went through the Decapolis, a league of ten Greek cities which, with the exception of Beth Shan, were situated east of Lake Galilee and the River Jordan. In the Decapolis region Jesus healed a man who was deaf and could hardly talk.

PETER DECLARES JESUS TO BE THE CHRIST

Near Lake Galilee Jesus fed another large crowd of four thousand, besides women and children. He landed on the western shore of the lake at Magadan (Magdala) and made his way north to Caesarea Philippi (modern Banias), near the slopes of Mount Hermon. A shrine of the Greek shepherd god Pan was located there, where a river emerges from a cavern in the cliff.

It was at Caesarea Philippi that Jesus asked his disciples a question: 'Who do you say I am?' Simon Peter answered, 'You are the Christ, the Son of the living God' (Matthew 16:16). Jesus then told Peter that he would build his church on the rock. What exactly Jesus meant by 'rock' is the subject of much debate. Peter himself or Peter's declaration that Jesus was the Christ are the most common interpretations.

Jesus then explained to his disciples that he had to go to Jerusalem and suffer many things at the hands of the elders, chief priests and teachers of the Law. He would have to be killed, but on the third day would be raised to life. When Peter tried to rebuke him, Jesus told Peter: 'Get behind me, Satan. You are a stumbling-block to me; you do not have in mind the things of God, but the things of men' (Matthew 16:23).

THE TRANSFIGURATION

Six days later Jesus took Peter, James and John up a mountain by themselves. The Gospels record that here the three disciples saw Jesus in his glorified state. His face shone like the sun and his clothes became as white as the light. Moses, representing the Old Testament Law, and Elijah, representing the Old Testament prophets, appeared in glorious splendour too.[1] Since the fourth century, tradition has identified the site as Mount Tabor (588 m or 1,930 ft) to the south east of Lake Galilee, although the far higher Mount Hermon (2,814 m or 9,232 ft), the closest mountain to Caesarea Philippi, is much more likely.

MOUNTING OPPOSITION

Jesus and his disciples made their way to Capernaum, where Jesus paid his Temple tax and that of Peter from a four-drachma coin found in a fish's mouth. Passing through Samaritan territory, where Jesus and his disciples were not welcome, Jesus made his way to Jerusalem for the Feast of Tabernacles. This was early autumn AD 32. On the last day of the feast Jesus stood and said in a loud voice: 'If anyone is thirsty, let him come to me and drink. Whoever believes in me, as the Scripture has said, streams of living water will flow from within him' (John 7:37–38).

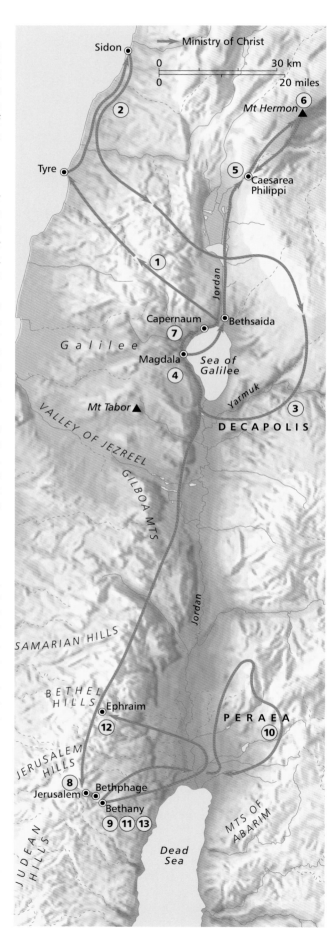

RIGHT: Shrine of Pan, the Greek shepherd god, at Caesarea Philippi.

The final year of Jesus' ministry

The numbers refer to the events of the final year of Jesus' ministry in chronological sequence.

1) Jesus travels from Galilee to Tyre and Sidon, where he delivers the daughter of a local woman from demon-possession

2) Jesus heads back to Galilee

3) Passing through the Decapolis, Jesus heals a deaf man who can barely talk

4) Jesus feeds a large crowd well in excess of four thousand and travels by boat to Magadan (Magdala)

5) Jesus makes his way to Caesarea Philippi. Peter declares that Jesus is the Christ

6) Peter, James and John see Jesus transfigured, probably on Mount Hermon

7) Jesus returns to Capernaum, where he pays his Temple tax

8) Jesus visits Jerusalem for the Feast of Tabernacles

9) Mary, Martha and Lazarus welcome Jesus at Bethany

10) Jesus ministers in Peraea

11) Jesus returns to Bethany, and raises Lazarus from the dead

12) Jesus withdraws to Ephraim

13) Jesus returns to Bethany. Mary pours expensive perfume over his feet at the house of Simon the Leper

KEY
[1] Matthew 17:1–8; Mark 9:2–8; Luke 9:28–36
[2] John 10:22-39
[3] Matthew 19:1–2; Mark 10:1; John 10:40–42
[4] Luke 19:43
[5] Mark 11:11; Matthew 21:17
[6] Matthew 26:14–16; Mark 14:10–11; Luke 22:1–6
[7] Mark 14:12; Luke 22:15
[8] John 13:1

From then on Jesus faced mounting opposition from the Jewish leaders, but a family living at Bethany, (modern el-Azariyeh) just 3 km (1¾ miles) south-east of Jerusalem on the southern shoulder of the Mount of Olives, opened their home to him. Mary and Martha and their brother Lazarus were to become some of Jesus' closest friends.

Jesus healed a man born blind, but incurred the displeasure of the Pharisees because he had healed on the sabbath. In December at the Feast of Dedication (commemorating the rededication of the Temple by Judas the Maccabee in 165 BC) Jesus debated with the Jews who accused him of blasphemy for claiming to be God's Son.[2]

JESUS RAISES LAZARUS FROM THE DEAD

As opposition mounted in Jerusalem Jesus went across the River Jordan to the Jewish region of Peraea, where many believed in him.[3] He returned to Bethany when he heard of the death of his friend Lazarus and raised him from the dead, although by then Lazarus had been dead for four days. The chief priests and Pharisees were greatly alarmed at what Jesus had done and called a meeting of the supreme Jewish council, the Sanhedrin. Jesus was no longer able to move about publicly among the Jews, so he withdrew to a village called Ephraim near the desert and stayed with his disciples.

JESUS GETS CLOSER TO JERUSALEM

Jesus' mind was now increasingly focused on his impending passion in Jerusalem. At Jericho he healed two blind men and saw the tax collector Zacchaeus renounce his cheating and ill-gotten gains. Jesus travelled the 23 km (14 miles) of desert road up to Bethany to be entertained by Simon the Leper. Here Martha's sister, Mary, poured an expensive perfume on Jesus' feet and wiped his feet with her hair. The apparent wastefulness of such an act angered one of Jesus' disciples, Judas Iscariot, who was later to betray him.

JESUS ENTERS JERUSALEM IN TRIUMPH

On the Sunday before his death the crowd heard that Jesus was on his way to Jerusalem. They cut palm branches and spread their cloaks in front of Jesus as he rode on a young donkey from Bethphage on the Mount of Olives down into the Kidron Valley and into Jerusalem. They shouted at the tops of their voices: 'Hosanna to the son of David! Blessed is he who comes in the name of the Lord!' (Matthew 21:9; Mark 11:9; Luke 19:38; John 12:13). But when Jesus saw the city he wept over it. He foresaw the siege less than forty years later in AD 70, when the Roman armies would build an embankment against the city, encircle it and hem it in on every side.[4] That night, and apparently every night until his arrest on the Thursday, Jesus walked to Bethany to spend the night with his friends Mary, Martha and Lazarus.[5]

JESUS CLEANSES THE TEMPLE

On the Monday Jesus entered the Temple area and drove out those buying, selling and changing money in the Temple courts. He also healed the blind and lame there. This raised the hackles of the chief priests and teachers of the Law, who began to look for a way to kill him.

DEBATES WITH THE JEWS

For the next two days Jesus was locked in debate with the leaders of the Jews in the Temple. Several of the questions posed by the Jews were designed to trap him, but he steered a careful course through them all. He also directed three parables at the Jews, challenging their rejection of him. He pronounced seven devastating woes against the Pharisees and once again lamented over Jerusalem. On leaving the city for the Mount of Olives he spoke about the end of the age, the coming judgment and his coming again in glory.

JUDAS BETRAYS JESUS

It was probably on the Wednesday that one of Jesus' twelve disciples, Judas Iscariot, went to the chief priests and arranged with them to betray Jesus for thirty pieces of silver, the equivalent of some four months' wages. The Jews wanted to know Jesus' exact whereabouts, so they could arrest him quickly when no crowd was present.[6]

THE LAST SUPPER

On the Thursday evening Jesus and his disciples gathered in a large upper room in Jerusalem. Jesus washed his disciples' feet and shared with them a loaf of bread and a cup of wine. These he interpreted as his body and his blood, clear symbols of the life he would soon lay down. It was during this meal that Judas slipped out to betray Jesus. Since the chronological schemes adopted by John and by the three other Gospel writers are at seeming variance there is much debate as to whether this was a proper Passover meal[7] or a Passover-like meal being held a day before the true Passover.[8]

GETHSEMANE

After singing a hymn they went into the night to the Mount of Olives. Jesus took Peter, James and John with him to the Garden of Gethsemane. With his three companions falling asleep, Jesus was left alone to pray: 'My Father, if it is possible, may this cup be taken from me. Yet not as I will, but as you will' (Matthew 26:39). In the end, realizing that the cup of suffering would not be taken away, Jesus submitted to his Father's will and went to meet his betrayer.

The Garden of Gethsemane, where Jesus was arrested.

JESUS' DEATH AND THE EMPTY TOMB

(AD 33)

JESUS IS ARRESTED

All four Gospel writers describe the events leading up to the death of Jesus in considerable detail. On the Thursday night Jesus and his disciples went outside the city Jerusalem, across the Kidron Valley to the olive grove known as the Garden of Gethsemane. It was here that a large crowd armed with swords and clubs, sent from the chief priests, arrested Jesus after Judas had identified him.[1]

JESUS IS TRIED

Jesus was taken to Annas, the father-in-law of Caiaphas, the high priest, then to Caiaphas himself and to the Sanhedrin, the highest Jewish court. The decision was reached to put Jesus to death, but the Jewish leaders had no authority to pass the death sentence in such a case, so they sent Jesus to Pontius Pilate, the Roman governor of Judea from AD 26 to AD 36. Pilate, hearing that Jesus was from Galilee, realized that Jesus was under the jurisdiction of Herod Antipas, and so he sent Jesus to Herod Antipas, who was also in Jerusalem at that time.

In 1961 Italian archaeologists excavating a theatre built by Herod the Great at Caesarea, north of modern Tel Aviv, found a re-used limestone block measuring 82 by 68 by 20 cm (32 by 27 by 8 in). It had a Latin inscription on it, the second line of which read '...TIVSPILATVS', followed by his title on the next line, Prefect of Judea. It was immediately obvious that most of Pontius Pilate's Latin name had been fortuitously preserved.

JESUS IS CRUCIFIED

It was Pilate who, in response to the Jewish leaders' demands, gave Jesus up to be crucified. The site chosen was Golgotha (an Aramaic word meaning 'skull').[2] For the Gospel writers the simple statement, 'they crucified him,' is sufficient.[3] They make no attempt to describe in detail the searing pain of a victim of crucifixion. Doubtless their readers would have been all too familiar with the sight of victims nailed by their wrists and ankles to two planks of wood. Crucifixion, which may have a Phoenician origin, was used commonly by the Romans from 200 BC onwards. In 71 BC the Roman general Marcus Lucinius Crassus is known to have crucified 6,000 rebellious slaves along the Appian Way from Capua to Rome.[4]

Jesus' cross carried a notice in Aramaic, Latin and Greek saying that he was the 'King of the Jews'. According to Matthew 27:37 this was placed above his head, suggesting that the traditional cross shape is in fact correct.

In 1968 excavation of an ancient cemetery at Giv'at ha-Mivtar, just north of Jerusalem, revealed some limestone chests or 'ossuaries' containing the remains of thirty-five individuals. In one ossuary, inscribed with the name Yehohanan, are the skeletal remains of a victim of crucifixion, probably in his mid-twenties, from the first century AD. Yehohanan's heel bones were still transfixed by a single nail 18 cm (7 in) long. It was easier for those who took Yehohanan's body down from the cross to cut off the feet with the nail than to remove it from the feet. It would also seem that Yehohanan was nailed to the cross by his forearm, not his hand. So it is suggested that the word

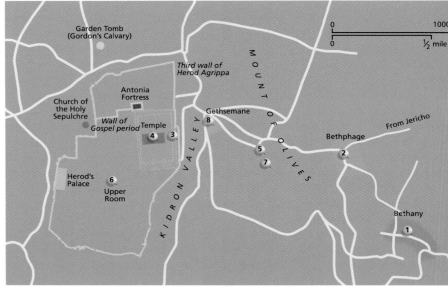

usually translated 'hands' in Luke 24:39–40 and John 20:20, 25, 27 should be probably be translated 'arms'.

'Later, knowing that all was now completed, and so that the Scripture would be fulfilled, Jesus said, "I am thirsty." A jar of wine vinegar [cheap wine drunk by the common people] was there, so they soaked a sponge in it, put the sponge on a stalk of a hyssop plant and lifted it to Jesus' lips. When he had received the drink, Jesus said, "It is finished." With that he bowed his head and gave up his spirit.'
JOHN 19:28–30

And so it was that on that first Good Friday – probably 14 Nisan, that is, Friday 3 April AD 33 – at about 3 pm, the precise time that Jewish Passover lambs were being slain, Jesus died.

In the case of Yehohanan, his right shin bone was fractured into slivers by a blow which was administered to hasten death. Concerning Jesus, John records:

'Because the Jews did not want the bodies left on the crosses during the sabbath, they asked Pilate to have the legs broken and the bodies taken down. But when they came to Jesus and found that he was already dead, they did not break his legs. Instead one of the soldiers pierced Jesus' side with a spear.'
JOHN 19:31b, 33–34a

THE SIGNIFICANCE OF JESUS' DEATH

The Gospel writers record a darkness for the last three hours Jesus spent on the cross and detail a number of phenomena that immediately followed his death. The curtain of the Temple was torn in two from top to bottom, the earth shook and the rocks split, the tombs broke open and the bodies of many holy people who had died were raised to life.[5] The writers of the New Testament letters are more concerned with the theology of Jesus' death, how it was all part of God's foreordained plan to deal with the sin of humankind and to give them the possibility of restoring them to God: 'For Christ died for sins once for all, the righteous for the unrighteous, to bring you to God' (1 Peter 3:18).

The last week of Jesus' life

The numbers refer to events in Jesus' final week in chronological sequence

1) Jesus travels from Bethany to Bethpage

2) Riding a young donkey, Jesus is acclaimed by the crowds

3) Jesus enters Jerusalem in triumph

4) Jesus cleanses the Temple

5) On the Mount of Olives he speaks of the coming destruction of Jerusalem and the end of the age

6) Jesus and his disciples eat the last supper

7) Jesus and his disciples return to the Mount of Olives

8) Jesus is arrested in the Garden of Gethsemane

Gordon's Calvary (Golgotha), Jerusalem.

The interior of the garden tomb, Jerusalem.

Limestone block, 82 cm x 68 cm x 20 cm (32 x 27 x 8 in), mentioning Pontius Pilate, Prefect of Judea. From the theatre in Caesarea.

The interior of the Church of the Holy Sepulchre, Jerusalem.

KEY

[1] Matthew 26:47–50; Mark 14:43–46; Luke 22:47–54; John 18:2–12

[2] Matthew 27:33; Mark 15:22; John 19:17

[3] Mark 15:24; Luke 23:33; John 19:18

[4] Appian, *The Civil Wars*, 1.120

[5] Matthew 27:51–52

[6] Matthew 28:13

[7] John 19:17; Hebrews 13:12

JESUS IS BURIED

Matthew 27:57–66 relates how, late on the Friday afternoon, Joseph of Arimathea, one of Jesus' wealthy disciples, obtained Jesus' body from Pilate and placed it in his own tomb. Jesus' body was wrapped in a clean linen cloth. A stone was rolled across the entrance to the tomb. Matthew emphasizes that the Romans, taking seriously Jesus' claims to rise from the dead, placed a guard at the entrance to the tomb and sealed it.

JESUS RISES FROM THE DEAD

On the Sunday reports began circulating that the tomb was empty and that Jesus was alive. The Jewish authorities paid the guards a large sum of money to say that the disciples had come during the night and stolen the body.[6] But the rumours persisted and the Jewish authorities were unable to quash them by producing Jesus' body. The demoralized disciples were transformed. Within seven weeks of Jesus' resurrection Peter was boldly proclaiming on the day of Pentecost: 'But God raised him from the dead, freeing him from the agony of death, because it was impossible for death to keep its hold on him' (Acts 2:24).

These reports have formed the pivotal point of faith of countless millions of Christians for nearly two millennia. They have never been satisfactorily refuted or explained away.

It is sometimes claimed that an inscription purporting to be from Nazareth, where Jesus spent his boyhood years, may be the response of an unnamed Roman emperor to the aftermath of Jesus' crucifixion and reported resurrection. The stone is 60 cm by 37.5 cm (24 in by 15 in). It is itself a translation from Latin into Greek and the forms of the letters point to a date in the first century. 'Decree of Caesar. It is my will that graves and tombs… lie undisturbed for ever… Respect for those who are buried is most important; no one should disturb them in any way at all. If anyone

does, I require that he be executed for tomb-robbery' (lines 1–2, 5–6, 17–22).

The text does not seem to be an imperial decree so much as an official reply to a local governor who had reported to the emperor a specific case of tomb-robbery. Either tomb-robbery on a such large scale had taken place that it was considered worthy of drawing the emperor's attention to it or the event of which the emperor was informed was most unusual. The threat of the death penalty, unprecedented for such a crime in the first century, shows the gravity of the emperor's response.

Even if the inscription from Nazareth makes no allusion to the death and reported resurrection of Jesus, it makes the charge that the disciples had removed the body far less likely. Disheartened as they were after Jesus' death, why should they run the risk of being executed for tomb-robbery? And if the disciples had stolen the body, why did the Roman authorities not use the death penalty against them?

THE EMPTY TOMB OF JESUS

We know from the New Testament[7] that both the hill where Jesus was crucified and the tomb, were outside the city walls. Jewish law did not allow burials inside the city. Both sites that are commonly proposed for the empty tomb of Jesus lie to the north of the first century city of Jerusalem.

The so-called 'garden tomb' was only identified in the late nineteenth century by the English general Charles Gordon. Taking his cue from 'the place of the skull' and noticing that two caves on a neighbouring hill looked like the eye sockets of a skull, he proposed a new site for the crucifixion of Jesus: the so-called 'Gordon's Calvary'. The garden tomb is close to Gordon's Calvary and outside the walls of modern Jerusalem. Its popularity derives largely from its peaceful simplicity. But the garden tomb cannot be the tomb of Jesus Christ, since it is not a first-century tomb. In fact it is as old as the eighth or seventh centuries BC.

Since AD 326 the site of Jesus' tomb has been marked by the Church of the Holy Sepulchre. Of the original tomb there is virtually no trace, as it was destroyed by the mad Caliph Hakim in AD 1009. But a description of the French pilgrim Arculf in about AD 680 that there was a single shelf stretching from head to foot without division, which would take one person lying on his back, fits very well with first-century tombs of a richer type.

There has been considerable debate as to whether in the first century the site was outside Jerusalem's second wall at the north of the city. No traces of the second wall have been discovered in this part of the city. But a quarry found 40 m (131 ft) south of the Church of the Holy Sepulchre and a number of first-century burials in the vicinity of the church seem to make it certain that the site was to the north of Jerusalem's second wall and thus outside the city. The site may well be authentic.

THE BIRTH OF THE CHURCH

(AD 33–49)

THE BOOK OF THE ACTS OF THE APOSTLES

The New Testament book known as 'The Acts of the Apostles' is traditionally accepted as the work of Luke, writer of the Gospel bearing his name and the doctor mentioned in one of Paul's letters.[1] Luke traces the growth of the early church from the Day of Pentecost AD 33 to the house-arrest of the apostle Paul in Rome AD 60–62. He thus traces the fulfilment of the last words of Jesus to his disciples before his ascension to heaven: 'You will be my witnesses in Jerusalem, and in all Judea and Samaria, and to the ends of the earth' (Acts 1:8b).

JERUSALEM

Luke records that the initial group of some 120 believers in Jesus were together on the Day of Pentecost, the Feast of Weeks, fifty days after Jesus had risen from the dead. A violent wind filled the whole house where they were sitting. What seemed to be tongues of fire came to rest on each of them. All the believers were filled with the Holy Spirit and began to speak in other tongues as the Spirit enabled them. God-fearing Jews from many nations who were attending the festival at Jerusalem heard them speaking in their own languages and were amazed. The visitors came from as far away as Rome in the west and Parthia (modern Iran and Afghanistan) in the east. Visitors also included those from Pontus (north-west Turkey) in the north and Arabs in the south. Capitalizing on their amazement, Peter declared that these events were a fulfilment of Joel's prophecy: 'Everyone who calls on the name of the Lord will be saved' (Acts 2:21). That day three thousand accepted his message and were baptized.

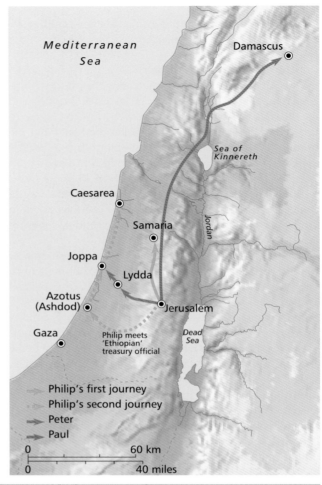

Philip's first journey
Philip's second journey
Peter
Paul

Philip meets 'Ethiopian' treasury official

0   60 km
0   40 miles

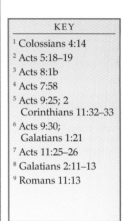

Journeys of the leaders of the early church
This map shows the early journeys of Philip, Peter and Paul.

KEY
[1] Colossians 4:14
[2] Acts 5:18–19
[3] Acts 8:1b
[4] Acts 7:58
[5] Acts 9:25; 2 Corinthians 11:32–33
[6] Acts 9:30; Galatians 1:21
[7] Acts 11:25–26
[8] Galatians 2:11–13
[9] Romans 11:13

Visitors to Jerusalem at the Feast of Pentecost
The book of Acts (2:5–11) records that when the Holy Spirit was poured out on believers in Jesus on the Day of Pentecost, visitors to Jerusalem from as far away as Parthia (modern Iran and Afghanistan), and many other peoples including Cretans and Arabs, heard them declaring the wonders of God in their own languages.

As the church grew, so did the opposition. The high priest and his associates, who were members of the party of the Sadducees, arrested the apostles and put them in prison, but during the night an angel opened the doors and brought them out.[2] The apostles returned to the Temple courts to resume teaching the people and despite warnings from the highest Jewish court, the Sanhedrin, they never stopped teaching and proclaiming that Jesus was the Christ, both in the Temple courts and from house to house. Opposition came to a head with the stoning of Stephen, the first Christian martyr. The result of this persecution was that all except the apostles were scattered throughout Judea and Samaria.[3] The church was thus no longer confined to Jerusalem.

SAMARIA

To the north of Jerusalem was an area known as Samaria. The Jews of Jerusalem regarded the Samaritans with deep animosity. The book of Acts records that, scattered by the persecution, Philip preached about Christ in a city in Samaria, where the people responded with great joy. When the apostles in Jerusalem heard that Samaria had accepted the word of God, they sent Peter and John, who prayed that the Samaritans too might receive the Holy Spirit. Their prayers were granted, and Peter and John preached the gospel in many Samaritan villages.

CONTACT WITH AFRICA

On the desert road from Jerusalem to Gaza, the book of Acts records, Philip met an important official in charge of the treasury of Candace, queen of the Upper Nile region, known then as Ethiopia, but which more accurately corresponds to the north of modern Sudan. Returning home from worshipping God in Jerusalem, the official was reading of the suffering servant in Isaiah 53. Philip explained how this chapter had been fulfilled in Christ's death and baptized his new convert there and then. Philip was taken away by the Spirit of the Lord, re-appearing near the coast at Azotus (Ashdod) and preaching in all the towns until he reached Caesarea.

THE DAMASCUS ROAD

The chief opponent of the early church at this time was a Jew called Saul.

Luke first mentions him in connection with the stoning of the first Christian martyr, Stephen.[4] It was at Saul's feet that those hurling stones laid their clothes and he approved the death.

Saul was born at Tarsus, a city on the Cilician Plain in what is now southern Turkey, and studied in Jerusalem under Gamaliel, the most renowned rabbi of the first century. He obtained letters from the high priest at Jerusalem authorizing him to arrest those in Damascus who believed in Jesus and bring them to Jerusalem. As Saul, later called Paul, was to admit: 'You have heard of my previous way of life in Judaism, how intensely I persecuted the church of God and tried to destroy it' (Galatians 1:13).

While on the road to Damascus Saul had a life-changing encounter with the risen Lord Jesus. At once he began to preach in the synagogues of Damascus that Jesus was the Son of God. The Jews there conspired to kill Saul, but he escaped the city by night, being lowered in a basket from a window in the city wall.[5] He made his way to Jerusalem and tried to join the disciples. Not surprisingly, they were afraid of him. However, Barnabas, a Levite from Cyprus, vouched for him. Saul then returned to his native Cilicia.[6]

The James Ossuary

On 21 October 2002 at a news conference in Washington, DC, claims were made that a limestone burial box (or ossuary) bore an inscription giving the oldest archaeological reference to Jesus. Since the box was obtained from the antiquities market, not from archaeological excavation, questions were immediately raised over its authenticity. The inscription is in Aramaic and says:

James, son of Joseph, brother of Jesus.'

It was claimed that this box once held the bones of James, the brother of Jesus of Nazareth, the same James who became leader of the Jerusalem church, who convened the council of Jerusalem and was also probably the author of the New Testament letter that bears his name. Although the names James and Jesus were common in the first century, the use of the term 'brother' is highly unusual on ossuaries. It was argued that the term 'brother of Jesus' must mean the occupant of the ossuary was none other than Jesus' brother.

Others argued that if an ossuary bearing James' bones had survived it would have identified him as 'brother of the Lord', just as in Galatians 1:19. Many thought that some or all of the words on the ossuary showed signs of being added recently, so on 18 June 2003 the Israel Antiquities Authority pronounced the inscription a fake.

Not all scholars share this conclusion, however, so it is perhaps wiser, pending further investigation, to keep open the question of the inscription's authenticity.

THE DISCIPLES ARE FIRST CALLED CHRISTIANS

Those who had been scattered by the persecution that had resulted in Stephen's death travelled as far as Phoenicia (modern Lebanon), Cyprus and Antioch on the Orontes (in south-east Turkey) telling the message of Jesus to their fellow Jews. Some men from Cyprus and the north African city of Cyrene went to Antioch and began to speak to Gentile Greeks too. A great number believed and turned to the Lord. When news of this reached the church at Jerusalem, they sent Barnabas to Antioch to investigate. He then went to Tarsus to look for Saul. Together Barnabas and Saul spent a whole year in Antioch teaching great numbers of people. It was here that the disciples were first called Christians,[7] perhaps originally by their enemies as a term of reproach, but with a meaning 'belonging to Christ' it was a term they readily embraced. Saul and Barnabas were commissioned to take a financial gift to the brothers living in Judea, which they duly accomplished.

DISPUTES ABOUT JEWISH RITUALS

Peter too moved out of Jerusalem. At Lydda he healed a paralyzed man named Aeneas and at Joppa he raised a woman named Dorcas from the dead. In Joppa Peter stayed for some time with a tanner named Simon. Since tanners handled the skins of dead animals, they were regarded as ritually unclean by the Jews. Whilst in Joppa, Peter's attachment to the rituals of the Law was further challenged by a divinely given vision in which he was commanded to eat ritually unclean animals: 'Do not call anything impure that God has made clean' (Acts 10:15). Peter's change of mind on this issue, with the encouragement of a Roman centurion named Cornelius, is of great significance. But later even Peter was to be confronted by Paul (Saul) over his refusal to eat with Gentiles.[8]

A related question that was hotly debated was 'should male Gentile Christians be circumcised?' Eventually, in AD 49, a council of apostles and elders was convened at Jerusalem to thrash out the issue. It was agreed that, since faith in Christ brought salvation, Gentile Christians were not required to keep the rituals of Mosaic Law. It was this principle, more than anything else, that clearly differentiated Christianity from its origins in Judaism. It was this that enabled Christianity to take root in Gentile communities. The ministry of Saul of Tarsus who became Paul, 'the apostle to the Gentiles', exemplifies this most clearly.[9]

TRAVEL IN THE ROMAN WORLD

THE ROMAN PEACE

When Augustus defeated Mark Antony and his ally Cleopatra, the queen of Egypt, at the naval battle of Actium in 31 BC, he brought peace to a war-weary world. By the time Christ was born in c. 5 BC, not only was almost the entire Mediterranean coast under Roman rule, but it was enjoying unprecedented prosperity and peace: the so-called *Pax Romana*, the Roman peace. Trade flourished. Travel became much easier.

ROMAN ROADS

The Roman empire boasted some 85,000 km (52,800 miles) of roads. Major roads were paved in stone over a width of 6 to 8 m (20 to 26 ft), and were laid on a foundation of concrete, crushed stone and mortar. They ran on as straight a course as possible and formed the basis of the road network of much of Europe until the twentieth century. Milestones set up every thousand paces (1.48 km or almost 1 mile) recorded the distance to the nearest city. The Roman road system was not extended to Palestine until after the Romans had quashed the Jewish revolt of AD 70.

Apart from by the army, the road system was used by the imperial post, but private persons wishing to send letters had to make their own arrangements, as in the case of Paul. For example, he entrusted his letter to the Romans to Phoebe and his letter to the Philippians to Epaphroditus.[1] Horse-drawn waggons carried couriers and officials 40 km (25 miles) a day, after which they spent the night at official resting places. There were additional posts for changing horses about every 13 km (8 miles). Ordinary travellers could stay at inns run by private owners. Some provided food and lodging, others lodging only. Many were little different from brothels; hence the New Testament command to practise hospitality.[2] Most land travel was on foot, but some wealthy people used light chariots.[3] Horses were ridden primarily by messengers and troops.[4]

Land travel was, by modern standards, slow. In 37 BC the Roman poet Horace took fifteen days to travel the 500 km (311 miles) from Rome to Brindisi. In AD 333 a Christian pilgrim from Bordeaux went to Jerusalem via northern Italy, the Balkans and Constantinople. His journey of nearly 5,000 km (3,108 miles) took 170 days.

SEA TRAVEL

The Romans preferred to sail between 26 May and 15 of September. Thereafter storm clouds could obscure the sky, making navigation by the sun and stars impossible. Certainly Paul was alarmed at the prospect of setting sail from Fair Havens in Crete after the Fast, the Day of Atonement, which fell in the latter part of September or early October.[5] Most merchant ships were sailing ships, but would carry oars for emergencies. Two large oars at the stern served as rudders, which could be lashed in position in bad weather. Ships were generally between 70 and 300 tons, exceptionally as large as 1,300 tons. Most of Paul's sea voyages were probably undertaken

Geographical knowledge in the time of the New Testament

It is difficult to ascertain the geographical knowledge of the writers of the New Testament, as we do not know their knowledge and acceptance of the findings of Greek science. These can be summarized briefly thus:

The sphericity of the earth seems to have first been suggested by Pythagoras, of 'square on the hypotenuse' fame, who was a native of the Greek island of Samos and moved to Croton in southern Italy around 530 BC.

Eratosthenes (c. 275–194 BC) from Cyrene in north Africa, and once director of the library at Alexandria, calculated the circumference of the earth by comparing the angle between the sun and the vertical at midday on the summer solstice at Alexandria and Syene (Aswan). Eratosthenes' estimated circumference of 252,000 stadia[8] computes to 39,690 km (24,636 miles) and falls only just short of the actual 40,120 km (24,930 miles), but then Eratosthenes did not know the world was flattened at the poles. It was thus clear that the earth was much bigger than had previously been realized.

Crates of Mallos in c. 150 BC postulated three other, hitherto unknown, inhabited worlds on the surface of the globe – North and South America and Australia would fit his bill! Jesus' commission to his disciples to 'go and make disciples of all nations, baptizing them in the name of the Father and of the Son and of the Holy Spirit' (Matthew 28:19) was greater than they may have realized.

Arguably the most famous writer on ancient geography, Claudius Ptolemy (c. AD 90–168), lived after the New Testament had been written. However, contacts with China, indirect through central Asia if not direct, had certainly been established by then, witness the silk mentioned in Revelation 18:12. Chinese records for AD 166 report that the Romans established sea trade with China. The Romans brought back ivory, rhinoceros horn and tortoise shell.

KEY
[1] Romans 16:1; Philippians 2:25
[2] Romans 12:13; 1 Peter 4:9
[3] Acts 8:28
[4] Acts 23:23
[5] Acts 27:9
[6] Acts 27:37
[7] 2 Corinthians 11:25
[8] Strabo, *Geography*, 2.5.34

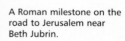

A Roman milestone on the road to Jerusalem near Beth Jubrin.

HISPAN

Gades

MAURETA

RIGHT: As demonstrated by this street in Ephesus, Roman roads frequently carried a great deal of traffic and were susceptible to wear and tear.

FAR RIGHT: Model of a Roman merchant ship c. first century BC.

Travel and trade routes of the Roman Empire
By AD 74 all the lands surrounding the Mediterranean Sea had come under Roman rule. The so-called Roman peace brought unparalleled prosperity. An extensive network of paved roads and regular sailings of cargo ships caused trade to flourish.

in small coastal vessels, but on his journey to Rome he sailed on two great grain ships plying between Egypt and Italy. His ship that was wrecked at Malta carried 276 passengers.[6] Shipwrecks were relatively common, Paul had already been shipwrecked three times before his journey to Rome.[7]

Normally grain ships from Alexandria to Ostia, the port of Rome, took three weeks, although faster ships could make the voyage in nine days. In favourable conditions sea travel was relatively fast. It took five days to travel the c. 950 km (590 miles) from Corinth to Puteoli in Italy, five days to travel the c. 900 km (560 miles) from Tarraco in Spain to Ostia, and three days to travel the c. 500 km (311 miles) from Carthage in north Africa to Ostia. Documents sent from Thessalonica in northern Greece routinely reached Ascalon on the coast of Palestine, c. 1,100 km (685 miles) away, within twelve days.

GAUL

Tanais

Olbia

Aquileia

Genoa

Arelate

Narbo

Forum Julii

Ancona

Salonae

ILLYRICUM

Constanta

corn

corn, hides

Black Sea

Byzantium (Constantinople)

ITALY

Adriatic Sea

Rome

Ostia

Puteoli

Brindisi

Dyrrhachium

via Egnatia

Thessalonica

ASIA

arraco

textiles

Balearic Islands

fish sauce

ivory, negroes

Palermo

Messina

Rhegium

marble, honey

Corn

Sicily

Corinth

Ephesus

Carthage

Crete

Fair Havens

Antioch

SYRIA

Euphrates

Mediterranean Sea

drugs, papyrus, animals, corn

Cyrene

Jerusalem

CYRENAICA

Alexandria

EGYPT

Nile

— main Roman road
— shipping route
☐ Roman empire, AD 117

0   600 km
0   400 miles

Paul's first journey: Cyprus and Asia Minor

(AD 47–48)

Antioch on the Orontes

Antioch on the River Orontes, the modern city of Antakya in south-east Turkey, was a large cosmopolitan city that had been founded by Seleucus I in c. 300 BC in honour of his father, Antiochus. It was here that the disciples were first called Christians[1] and from here, as the the the writer of the Acts of the Apostles, Luke records, that Saul and Barnabas launched their first mission to the non-Jewish world. Most of ancient Antioch was destroyed in an earthquake in AD 526, but the aqueduct of Trajan (AD 98–117) and mosaics from the many fine houses in the city survive. The museum in Antakya has the second largest collection of Roman mosaics in the world.

In AD 47 Saul and Barnabas, commissioned by the ethnically diverse leaders of the Antioch church, made their way to the port of Antioch, Seleucia (ad Pieria), the modern village of Çevlik, from where they sailed to Cyprus. The most interesting feature of this town, the water tunnel of the Roman emperors Titus and Vespasian, was made several decades after Saul and Barnabas's visit.

Cyprus

Cyprus, known as Elishah in the Old Testament, was Barnabas's homeland.[2] Saul and Barnabas arrived at Salamis, on the eastern side of the island, where they preached in the Jewish synagogues.[3] A first-century Roman theatre and gymnasium survive.

They travelled through the island until they came to Paphos, on the east coast, the administrative capital of Sergius Paulus, the Roman proconsul. It was here that Saul – now, significantly, renamed with the Roman name Paul – confronted a sorcerer named Bar-Jesus, or Elymas, and used God's power to blind him temporarily. The proconsul, amazed at the teaching about the Lord, was led to faith in

him. The remains of ancient Paphos include an impressive *odeon* (open air concert hall).

Perga and Pisidian Antioch

From Cyprus Paul and his companions journeyed to the coast of southern Turkey. They came to Perga, 8 km (5 miles) inland, which now boasts an ancient theatre and a stadium seating 14,000 and 12,000 respectively. It was here that John Mark left Paul to return to Jerusalem.[4] Travelling some 175 km (109 miles) into the mountainous interior, Paul came to Pisidian Antioch. Now situated near the modern Turkish town of Yalvaç, like its more famous namesake it had been founded by Seleucus I in honour of his father, Antiochus. In Paul's day it was a Roman colony (Caesarea Antiocheia), which meant that a contingent of retired soldiers had

Mosaic showing Oceanus, son of Uranus, second century AD. From Antakya, Turkey.

The *odeon* (open air concert hall), Paphos, Cyprus.

KEY

[1] Acts 11:26
[2] Acts 4:36
[3] Acts 13:5
[4] Acts 13:13
[5] Acts 14:5–6

Paul's first journey

The map traces the route
of Paul's first journey
(with Barnabas), from
Antioch on the Orontes
via Cyprus to Derbe in
southern Turkey, AD 47–48.

Lake
Tuz

Pisidian Antioch
(Yalvaç)

Lake
Egridir

Lake
Beysehir

Iconium
(Konya)

Lystra
(Hatunsaray)

PISIDIA

Derbe
(Devri Sehri)

TAURUS MOUNTAINS

Euphrates

Attalia
(Antalya)

Perga

Seleucia ad Pieria
(Çevlik)

Antioch
(Antakya)

SYRIA

Orontes

Paul's first journey

0   100 km
0   80 miles

Cyprus

Salamis

Paphos

Aqueduct at Pisidian
Antioch (Yalvaç).

settled there. They were given free land and made Roman
citizens. On the sabbath Paul, focusing primarily on the
Jews in the city, addressed those gathered in the synagogue.
The following sabbath almost the whole city gathered to
hear the word of the Lord. So great was the response that
the Jews stirred up persecution against Paul and Barnabas
and expelled them. Symbolically shaking the dust off their
feet, to show that they had absolved themselves of
responsibility, Paul and Barnabas went some 120 km
(75 miles) across the Sultan mountains to Iconium.

ICONIUM, LYSTRA AND DERBE

Iconium is now the modern Turkish city of Konya, situated
on the edge of a fertile plain, but little survives of its Roman
past. Once again there was opposition, but Paul and
Barnabas, getting wind of a plot against them, fled to the
Lycaonian cities of Lystra and Derbe.[5]

Lystra (near modern Hatunsaray) was a Roman colony
some 30 km (19 miles) back across the mountains from
Konya. Here Paul healed a man who had been lame from
birth. Fêted as the gods Hermes and Zeus, Paul and
Barnabas had great difficulty in restraining the crowd from
worshipping them. Once again there was opposition. Some
Jews came from Antioch and Iconium and won the crowd
over. They stoned Paul and dragged him outside the city,
thinking he was dead. But after the disciples had gathered
round him he got up and went back into the city. The next
day he and Barnabas left for Derbe – identified by an
inscription as Kerti Höyük, some 100 km (62 miles) from
Lystra. Paul preached in Derbe and won a large number of
disciples. They then returned to the cities that had proved
so hostile – Lystra, Iconium and Antioch – strengthening
the disciples and encouraging them to remain true to the
faith.

They were later to return to Perga and from there to the
coast at Attalia, the modern Turkish city of Antalya. From
Attalia they sailed, presumably via Seleucia, back to
Antioch on the Orontes. Luke records: 'On arriving there,
they gathered the church together and reported all that
God had done through them and how he had opened the
door of faith to the Gentiles' (Acts 14:27).

Paul's second journey: Philippi and Thessalonica

(AD 49)

Silas replaces Barnabas

Luke, the writer of the Acts of the Apostles, records that Paul and Barnabas disagreed over the suitability of John Mark as a companion because he had deserted them at Perga in Pamphylia.[1] So in AD 49 Paul took Silas with him in the place of Barnabas and travelled through Syria and Cilicia, strengthening the churches.[2] They were joined at Lystra by Timothy, whose mother was a Jewish believer in Jesus and whose father was a Greek. They then travelled throughout the regions of Phrygia and Galatia.

Alexandria Troas

Being prevented by the Holy Spirit from preaching in the provinces of Asia and Bithynia,[3] they came to Troas. This was some 20 km (13 miles) south of the site of Troy, scene of Homer's epic poem, the *Iliad*, and was known as Alexandria Troas. The town boasted an artificial harbour. It was at Troas that Paul had a vision of a man of Macedonia begging him to come over to Macedonia and help. The province of Macedonia comprised much of what is now northern Greece. It might have been at Troas that Luke joined Paul's party, since it is here that the narrative begins to employ the 'we' form.[4]

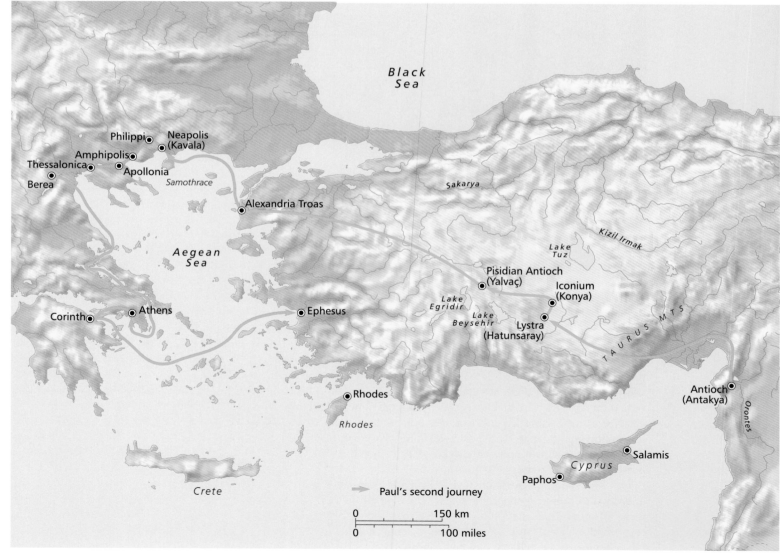

Paul's second journey

0 — 150 km
0 — 100 miles

LEFT: Paul and Silas passed the Greek island of Samothrace on their way from Alexandria Troas to Neapolis.

RIGHT: Philippi. The Roman forum looking towards the ruins of a sixth-century Byzantine church.

Part of an inscription from Thessalonica mentioning the local rulers known as politarchs. Second century AD.

Paul's second journey
The map traces the route of Paul's journey (partly with Silas) in AD 49–52, from Antioch on the Orontes, through Turkey and northern Greece, to Athens and Corinth and onto Ephesus.

KEY
[1] Acts 13:13; 15:38
[2] Acts 15:39–41
[3] Acts 16:6–7
[4] Acts 16:10
[5] Acts 16:12

PHILIPPI

Paul and Silas responded to the vision and sailed for the island of Samothrace, whose 1,600-metre (5,250-foot) peak, highest in all the Aegean islands, is an extinct volcano. The next day they arrived in Europe at Neapolis, the modern Greek port of Kavala.

From Neapolis Paul and Silas went some 16 km (10 miles) inland to Philippi, a town named after Philip, the father of Alexander the Great, and which was a Roman colony (Colonia Augusta Julia Philippensis).[5] Its Roman forum and theatre, rebuilt in the second century, are partially preserved. Here Paul led to faith in Christ a woman named Lydia, a dealer in purple cloth from the city of Thyatira, in the district of Lydia in the province of Asia. 'Lydia' was thus probably a nickname.

Delivering a slave girl from a spirit which let her predict the future and arousing the wrath of her owners, Paul and Silas were dragged to the market place and brought before the authorities. Flogged and thrown into prison, they were freed following a night-time earthquake, after which Paul led the jailer to faith in Christ.

THESSALONICA

Passing through Amphipolis and Apollonia, Paul and Silas continued through Macedonia to the port city of Thessalonica, where they stayed with a believer named Jason. The response to Paul's message incited the Jews to riot. Jason and several other believers were dragged before the city officials. The words of the mob, 'These men who have caused trouble all over the world have now come here,' (Acts 17:6), show how Paul and his friends were viewed in popular thinking. The term *politarch* (city ruler) is used in Acts 17:8 and also on a Greek inscription discovered in 1835 on an arch spanning the Egnatian Way on the west side of the city. The inscription dates from the second century AD and is now in the British Museum. The term *politarch* has since been found in sixteen other inscriptions from Thrace and Macedonia, but is not used of city officials in other parts of the Roman empire. Its use by Luke, the author of the Acts of the Apostles, to describe the officials of Thessalonica points to his reliablity as a historian. Thessalonica's Roman forum is partially preserved.

BEREA

Paul and Silas escaped from Thessalonica by night and were sent some 80 km (50 miles) further south to Berea. Luke comments: 'Now the Bereans were of more noble character than the Thessalonians, for they received the message with great eagerness and examined the Scriptures every day to see if what Paul said was true' (Acts 17:11). The response to Paul's message in Berea was encouraging with a number of prominent Greek women and many Greek men believing, as well as many Jews. Eventually, however, the Jews of Thessalonica came to Berea and incited the crowds against Paul. While Silas and Timothy stayed at Berea, Paul travelled alone to Athens.

PAUL'S SECOND JOURNEY: ATHENS AND CORINTH

(AD 49–52)

ATHENS

In the Acts of the Apostles Luke records how Paul, continuing his travels in Greece alone, came to Athens in AD 49. It was a city with an illustrious past.

Athens had led the Greek resistance to the Persian armies invading Greece in 490–479 BC. The famous temples on the Acropolis which the Persians had destroyed were all rebuilt and already nearly five centuries old by the time he arrived, pride of place going to the Parthenon, 69 m by 31 m (226 ft by 102 ft), the temple of the goddess Athena. The vertical lines of this celebrated Doric temple are actually slightly curved. This effect, known as entasis, avoids the appearance of sagging. Athens had been the home of the great dramatists Aeschylus, Sophocles, Euripides and Aristophanes and celebrated philosophers Plato and Aristotle. It was renowned as a university town.

Paul was greatly distressed by the city's idolatry.[1] A group of Epicurean and Stoic philosophers began to dispute with him. He was brought before the celebrated council of the Areopagus, which in earlier times had governed the city. In Paul's day it no longer met on the hill of the Areopagus, just west of the Acropolis and south of the *agora* (market place), but in the Royal Portico at the north-west corner of the agora and its authority was now confined to matters of religion and morals.

Paul had observed an altar with an inscription 'TO AN UNKNOWN GOD' and he used it as the theme of his address to the court of the Areopagus.[2] His choice of this phrase in addressing the Athenians seems to have been deliberate. The third-century Greek writer Diogenes Laertius records a plague which began to decimate the city during the forty-sixth Olympiad, that is, 595–592 BC.[3] Thinking that some unknown god must be angry, the Cretan poet Epimenides (whose words 'in him we live and move and have our being' Paul quotes in Acts 17:28) took sheep, some black and some white, and brought them to the Areopagus, letting them go wherever they pleased. He instructed those who followed to mark the spot where each sheep lay and offer a sacrifice to the local divinity. Altars without a name inscribed on them were erected, sacrifices

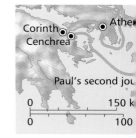

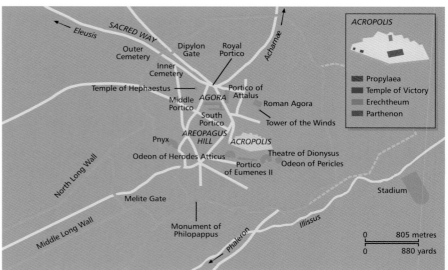

were offered, the plague was lifted immediately and the city spared.

Two other writers refer to 'unknown gods'. Pausanias, a travel writer of the late second century AD, says Athens had 'altars of gods, named unknown',[4] and Flavius Philostratus, writing in the early third century AD, says that at Athens 'altars were set up in honour of unknown deities'.[5] In both cases the word for 'unknown' is the same as that used by Luke in Acts 17:23.

Paul, doubtless with the Acropolis in mind if not in view, proclaimed that 'The God who made the world… does not live in temples built by hands' (Acts 17:24). In Acts 17:34 Luke notes that 'a few men became followers of Paul and

Plan of Athens
Athens, visited by Paul in AD 49, was a renowned centre of learning and culture. Its walls enclosed an area of 223 hectares (550 acres).

The Acropolis from the Areopagus. The Acropolis was the religious centre of ancient Athens, crowned with temples. The Parthenon, dedicated to the goddess Athene, was built between 447 and 438 BC.

LEFT: **Paul's journey to Athens and Corinth**
The map traces part of the route of Paul's second journey to Athens and Corinth.

KEY
[1] Acts 17:16
[2] Acts 17:22–23
[3] Diogenes Laertius, *Lives and Opinions of Eminent Philosophers*, 1.110
[4] Pausanias, *Description of Greece*, 1.1.4
[5] Flavius Philostratus, *Life of Apollonius of Tyana*, 6.3
[6] Acts 18:11
[7] Acts 18:4, 7
[8] Acts 18:19

RIGHT: **Plan of Corinth**
In Paul's day Corinth was a cosmopolitan port city and capital of the Roman province of Achaea.

Part of an inscription from Delphi in Greece, mentioning Gallio, the proconsul (governor) of Achaea.

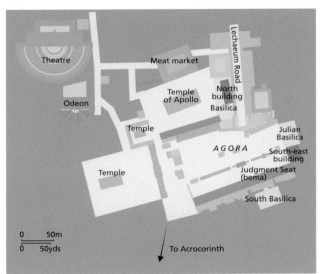

believed.' These included Dionysius, a member of the Areopagus, but clearly the impact of Paul's visit was modest, not spectacular.

CORINTH

Paul moved on to Corinth, where he was joined by 'a Jew named Aquila and his wife Priscilla' (Acts 18:1–2).

The city of Corinth occupied a strategic position on the Corinthian isthmus of the Peloponnese. It had two harbours, Cenchrea on the Saronic Gulf, 14 km (8½ miles) to the east, and Lechaeum on the Corinthian Gulf, 2.5 km (1½ miles) to the west. A stone causeway called the Diolkos was used to haul boats across the isthmus. Corinth was the capital of the Roman province of Achaea (the southern part of Greece), a Roman colony and a cosmopolitan port city, infamous for immorality. It had an estimated population of 250,000 free persons and as many as 400,000 slaves. The town is dominated by Acrocorinth a steep, 556-metre-high (1,824-foot), flat-topped rock, which formed the acropolis.

Luke records how, plying his trade as a tent-maker and teaching the word of God, Paul spent a year and a half in Corinth.[6] He encountered virulent opposition from the Jews, which brought him into contact with Gallio, the Roman proconsul of Achaea. This allows Paul's time in Corinth to be dated exactly by an inscription found at Delphi in central Greece mentioning Gallio, proconsul of Achaea.

Lucius Junius Annaeus Gallio was born in Cordoba, Spain, and was a brother of the philosopher Seneca. The inscription found at Delphi survives in four main fragments, but much can be restored by analogy with similar inscriptions, which follow a conventional style. It contains the transcript of a letter, in the sixth line of which the emperor Claudius describes Junius Gallio as 'my friend and proconsul (of Achaea)'. Gallio held the proconsulship of Achaea in the twenty-sixth acclamation of Claudius as emperor. The twenty-seventh acclamation is known from an inscription on the Porta Maggiore in Rome to have begun on 1 August AD 52, so the twenty-sixth acclamation corresponds to the first seven months of AD 52. Since proconsuls are known to have taken up office on 1 July, Gallio's term began on 1 July AD 51. This information helps us to fix Paul's second journey within the chronology of the Acts of the Apostles, and also the writing of Paul's two letters to the church at Thessalonica, since Paul wrote 1 and 2 Thessalonians during his stay in Corinth, AD 51–52.

In the *agora* the proconsul's judgment seat, before which Paul doubtless appeared, is still visible with a second-century inscription. It is the court referred to in Acts 18:12. Also preserved are the *odeon* (open-air concert hall) and many ancient shops. A stone lintel inscribed in Greek found on the Lechaeum Road at Corinth reads: 'Synagogue of the Hebrews'. Its lettering points to a date later than Paul's time, but perhaps it stood on the site of the synagogue that Paul visited.[7]

After staying in Corinth for a year and a half, Paul sailed for Ephesus, in what is now Turkey.[8]

PAUL'S THIRD JOURNEY: EPHESUS

(AD 52–55)

PAUL ARRIVES IN EPHESUS

From Corinth Paul crossed the Aegean Sea to Ephesus. It was at best a fleeting visit, for as Luke, the writer of the Acts of the Apostles, explains, he was on his way via Caesarea to report back to the church at Antioch.[1]

Making good his promise, Paul travelled overland and returned to Ephesus. For three months he argued persuasively about the kingdom of God in the synagogue. Eventually Paul moved out of the synagogue and, taking his disciples with him, for the next two years held daily discussions in the lecture hall of Tyrannus. One manuscript of Acts 19:9 states that Paul used the lecture hall between 11 a.m. and 4 p.m. When many of the townspeople were free to enjoy a siesta, Paul used the vacant lecture hall to further God's kingdom.

EPHESUS

Ephesus has a venerable history. It may be the town known in Hittite texts of the second millennium BC as Apasa. In Paul's day it was a major port with population of about a third of a million. Today the ruins of Ephesus are some 10 km (6¼ miles) inland, but even in Paul's day ships faced a difficult voyage through shallow waters to enter the harbour that was gradually silting up.

Ephesus was renowned for the temple of the goddess Artemis, one of the Seven Wonders of the Ancient World. The original temple of 560 BC was rebuilt after a fire (in 356 BC) between 334 BC and 250 BC. It was 104 m by 50 m (341 ft by 164 ft) and had 127 Ionic marble columns, each 17.4 m (57 ft) high and 1.5 m (5 ft) in diameter. Its site was covered by alluvial mud and lost from view until 1874. The English excavator J.T. Wood used directions given in an ancient inscription to help him find the site. Today the site is on marshy ground which often floods. A single column has been restored, but not to its full height.

PAUL AT EPHESUS

Paul's time at Ephesus, Luke writes, was particularly

KEY
[1] Acts 18:18–22
[2] Acts 19:12–19
[3] Acts 19:35

Statue of the many-breasted goddess Artemis, first century AD.

Reconstruction of Ephesus, showing the temple of the goddess Artemis and the Arcadian Way, stretching from the theatre to the harbour.

fruitful. Even handkerchiefs and aprons that Paul had touched were used to heal the sick. Those who had practised sorcery brought their scrolls to a public burning. The total value of the scrolls came to 50,000 drachmas – a drachma being a silver coin worth about a day's wages.[2]

The devotees of Artemis, led by a silversmith named Demetrius, alarmed at the drop in sales of silver Artemis shrines, orchestrated a riot against Paul in the theatre. This had been built during the reign of Claudius (AD 41–54), although in Paul's day it was somewhat smaller than its present form with a capacity of 24,000. It now has sixty-six rows of seats and a stage 25 m by 40 m (82 ft by 131 ft). The riot in the theatre is one of the few events in the biblical narrative that can be pinpointed to a specific location visible today. For two hours it resounded to cries of 'Great is Artemis of the Ephesians!' (Acts 19:34).

An inscription from the Scholastika Baths (c. AD 100) mentions an official called the *Asiarch* (Ruler of Asia), the term used by Luke in Acts 19:31 of a local council comprising men of wealth and influence. The city clerk reminded the Ephesians that their city was the 'guardian' of the temple of the great goddess Artemis.[3] Another inscription describing Ephesus as the 'guardian' of Artemis shows that Luke used the correct local term.

THE RUINS OF EPHESUS

The remains of Ephesus are truly impressive. We can see several houses of wealthy Ephesians, dating from the first century but with many subsequent additions. The line of the famous Arcadian Way, named after the Roman Emperor Arcadius (AD 395–408) and extending 600 m (1,968 ft) from the theatre to the harbour, is known from Hellenistic times onwards, although the four-columned monument about half-way down belongs to the reign of Justinian (AD 527–565). Arcadius installed a hundred street-lights on the 11-metre-wide (36-ft) street. Other buildings are also later than Paul's time, such as the late first-century Harbour Gymnasium and Baths.

The library of Tiberius Julius Celsus Polemaenus, Roman governor of Asia, the first Greek to be appointed to the Roman senate, dates from AD 110. The library façade 11 m by 16.7 m (36 ft by 55 ft) has been heavily restored. The central Corinthian columns and capitals are larger than those at the ends. Celsus himself is buried in a marble sarcophagus in a tomb under the west side of the library.

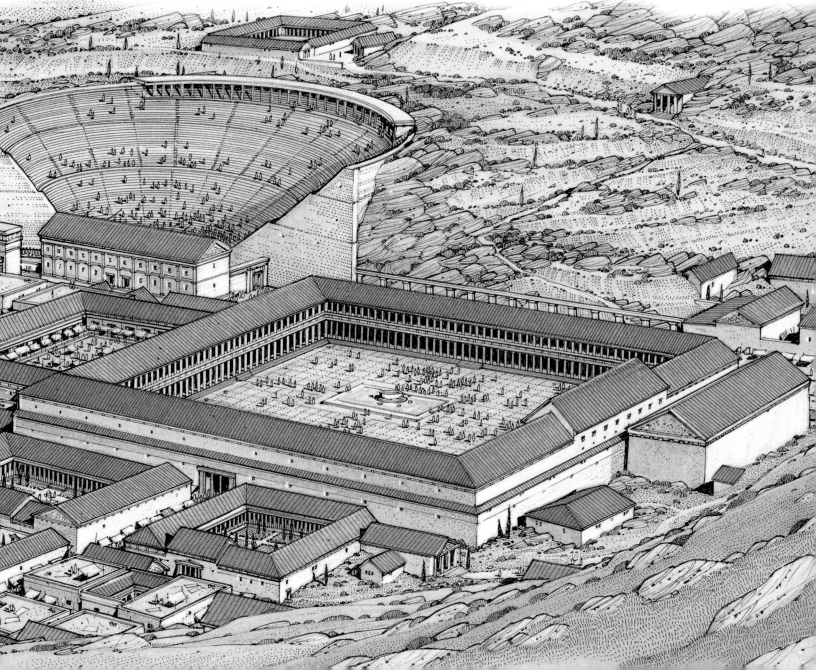

Paul's third journey: from Ephesus to Jerusalem

(AD 55)

Alexandria Troas

Luke records that Paul left Ephesus for three months in Greece.[1] On his way back he met those in Alexandria Troas who believed in Jesus. As Paul talked on and on deep into the night in a room lit by olive oil lamps, a young man named Eutychus (which, very aptly, means 'lucky') was overcome by a deep sleep and fell out of a third-storey window. He was picked up as dead, but Paul went down, threw himself on the young man and, putting his arms around him, said: 'Don't be alarmed. He's alive!'

Miletus

Sailing from Assos, Paul and his company made their way past the Aegean islands of Mitylene (Lesbos), Chios and Samos. Since Paul was in a hurry to reach Jerusalem by the day of Pentecost, he decided to sail past Ephesus and land at Miletus. From here he summoned the elders from the church of Ephesus.[2]

Some suggest it was the difficulty of a ship reaching the harbour at Ephesus that led to Paul's request for the elders of Ephesus to visit him some 50 km (31 miles) south at Miletus. However, it might have been Paul's desire to avoid time-wasting trouble like the riot of the previous year.

Like Ephesus, Miletus has a venerable history. It is probably the Millawanda mentioned in Hittite texts and, like Ephesus, is an ancient port now far removed from the sea. Today Miletus is some 10 km (6¼ miles) from the coast. Two big stone lions stand either side of the harbour, now completely dry. The theatre at Miletus, first built in the fourth century BC, seats some 15,000. Unusually, this theatre was not cut into a hillside but stands free on an almost level site. The façade is 140 m (460 ft) long.

Paul's words to the Ephesian elders on the beach at Miletus give us insight into his concerns and struggles.[3]

LEFT: Remains of the temple of Artemis, Ephesus, rebuilt between 334 and 250 BC. The site was covered by alluvial mud and was lost from view until 1874. Today it is on marshy ground that often floods. A single column has been restored.

RIGHT: Paul's third journey
The map traces the route of Paul's third journey (with Luke), from Antioch on the Orontes, through Turkey and Greece and back via Alexandria Troas and Miletus to Jerusalem.

KEY
[1] Acts 20:2
[2] Acts 20:14–17
[3] Acts 20:22–35

LEFT: The theatre at Miletus, the town where Paul met with the Ephesian elders.

RIGHT: A corbita or slow moving cargo ship. Carthage, second century AD.

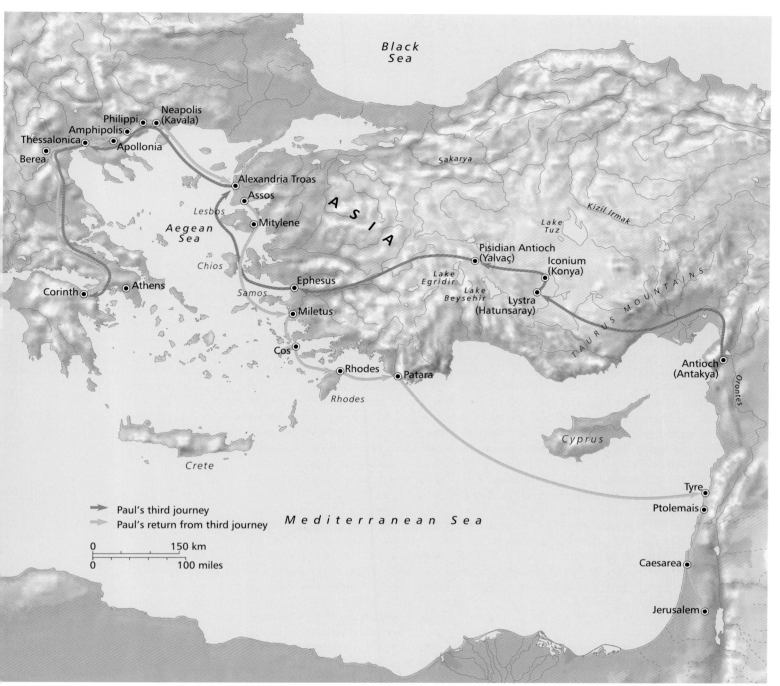

Paul's third journey

Paul's return from third journey

0   150 km

0   100 miles

And now, compelled by the Spirit, I am going to Jerusalem, not knowing what will happen to me there. I only know that in every city the Holy Spirit warns me that prison and hardships are facing me. However, I consider my life worth nothing to me, if only I may finish the race and complete the task the Lord Jesus has given me ... Now I know that none of you among whom I have gone about preaching the kingdom will ever see me again... I have not coveted anyone's silver or gold or clothing... In everything I did, I showed you that by this kind of hard work we must help the weak, remembering the words the Lord Jesus himself said: "It is more blessed to give than to receive".'

ACTS 20:22–24a, 25, 33, 35

As Luke graphically records, 'When he had said this, he knelt down with all of them and prayed. They all wept as they embraced him and kissed him. What grieved them most was his statement that they would never see his face again. Then they accompanied him to the ship' (Acts 20:36–38).

AND SO TO JERUSALEM

From Miletus Paul and his companions sailed via Cos and Rhodes to Patara (on the south-east coast of modern Turkey), where they changed ships. Passing to the south of Cyprus, they landed at Tyre, where they stayed with disciples for seven days. These urged Paul not to go on to Jerusalem and another painful good-bye on the beach followed.

Paul and his companions continued via Ptolemais to Caesarea where they stayed with Philip the evangelist. Once again Paul was urged not to go to Jerusalem. Luke vividly describes the prophet Agabus's reaction. 'Coming over to us, he took Paul's belt, tied his own hands and feet with it' (Acts 21:11a). Agabus then warned: 'The Holy Spirit says, "In this way the Jews of Jerusalem will bind the owner of this belt and will hand him over to the Gentiles"' (Acts 21:11b).

Paul, however, was not dissuaded and went up to Jerusalem.

PAUL'S JOURNEY TO ROME

(AD 57–60)

PAUL AT JERUSALEM

On arrival at Jerusalem Paul and his companions went to see Jesus' brother James, who was leader of the church in Jerusalem.[1] James rejoiced at Paul's account of his work among the Gentiles, but urged him to pay the expenses of four men who had made a Jewish vow. This, argued James, would show the Jews that there was no truth in the rumours that Paul was inciting Jews to abandon the Law.

Paul was obliged to give notice to the priests in the Temple of when the offering would be made for the four men. Luke relates that some Jews from the province of Asia saw Paul in the Temple and, stirring up the crowd, seized him shouting: 'Men of Israel, help us! This is the man who teaches all men everywhere against our people and our Law and this place. And besides, he has brought Greeks into the Temple area and defiled this holy place' (Acts 21:28).

The noise of the angry mob trying to kill Paul provoked Claudius Lysias, the commander of the Roman troops in the Antonia fortress, to move in and arrest Paul. The commander agreed to Paul's request to address the crowd. Paul carefully outlined his experience on the road to Damascus when he had come to faith in Christ. When the crowd demanded that Paul be flogged, the commander found out that Paul was a Roman citizen.[2] Roman citizens were exempt from all degrading forms of punishment and, besides, Paul had not yet been found guilty. Wanting to know exactly why Paul was being accused by the Jews, the commander sent Paul to the Sanhedrin, the supreme Jewish court. Paul, playing upon his upbringing as a Pharisee and his hope of the resurrection of the dead, opened up a bitter dispute in the court between the Pharisees and Sadducees. The commander intervened and escorted Paul to the barracks.

TO CAESAREA

When the commander learned of a plot to kill Paul, he arranged for armed guards to escort Paul nearly 100 km (62 miles) to the Roman governor Antonius Felix at Caesarea on the Mediterranean Sea.[3] Felix kept Paul in prison for two years hoping that he would offer him a bribe. Paul then fell under the jurisdiction of Felix's successor, Porcius Festus.

When asked if he would go up to Jerusalem to stand trial there, Paul replied: 'If the charges brought against me by these Jews are not true, no one has the right to hand me over to them. I appeal to Caesar!' (Acts 25:11b). Festus conferred with his council and agreed to Paul's request. It was the right of every Roman citizen to have his case heard before the emperor himself. This was the highest court of appeal and winning the case would have resulted in official recognition of Christianity. Later, King Herod Agrippa II was also to hear Paul's case. He remarked to Festus that Paul could have been set free if he had not appealed to Caesar (Acts 26:32).

EN ROUTE FOR ROME

The resumption of the pronoun 'we' in Acts 27:1 suggests that Luke had rejoined Paul for his journey to Rome. Paul was among a group of prisoners under the jurisdiction of a centurion named Julius. Paul and his party boarded a ship from Adramyttium (the modern Turkish port of Edremit). They landed at Sidon before sailing north of Cyprus for the Turkish coast. At Myra (modern Demre) in Lycia they changed to an Alexandrian grain ship bound for Italy.

It was now September and the weather turned against them. Passing Cnidus at the very tip of the Datça peninsula, they made their way to Crete, to a harbour known as 'Fair Havens' (modern Kali Limenes) on the south coast of the island. The centurion wanted to move on to the harbour of Phoenix (modern Loutron), further to the west. It was a more convenient harbour to winter in and, not heeding Paul's warnings, the ship set sail again.

THE STORM

Before long a hurricane-force, north-easterly wind swept down from Mount Ida on Crete.[4] It blew the ship past the small island of Cauda (modern Gavdos) and out into the wilds of the open sea. A small boat which was being towed along behind, and now in danger of being crushed against the ship, was hoisted aboard. Ropes were passed under the ship to hold it together. The crew feared that the ship would be driven onto the sandbars of Syrtis, off the Libyan coast, so they lowered the sea-anchor and threw the ship's cargo and tackle overboard.

On the fourteenth night of being driven across the Adriatic Sea soundings revealed that land was close. (Incidentally, in antiquity the term 'Adriatic' was used of the sea well south of Italy, not just of the sea to the east as today.)[5] The sailors' attempt to use the lifeboat to escape from the ship was thwarted by Paul. Knowing from God that all 276 passengers on board would be safe, he urged the crew to eat. Then they lightened the ship still further by throwing the remaining grain into the sea.

Paul's journey to Rome
The map traces Paul's journey (with Luke), from Jerusalem via Crete, Malta and Italy to Rome.

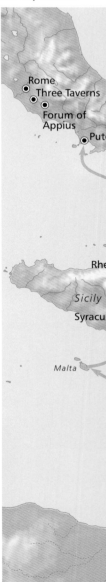

Rome
Three Taverns
Forum of Appius
Putec
Rheg
Sicily
Syracuse
Malta

Statue of Paul in St Paul's Bay, Malta, where the ship that Paul was sailing on probably ran aground.

KEY
¹ Acts 21:18
² Acts 22:25
³ Acts 23:23–35
⁴ Acts 27:14
⁵ Strabo, *Geography*, 2.5.20
⁶ Acts 28:1
⁷ Acts 28:13–14

As daylight came, the ship struck a sandbar in a bay with a sandy beach. The whole company got safely to shore, those unable to swim using planks from the ship as floats. It was only when they were ashore that they realized they had landed on Malta.⁶ St Paul's Bay on the north-east of the island or the adjoining Mellieha Bay are the most plausible sites.

Malta

The island of Malta had been settled by Phoenicians in the seventh century BC. Indeed 'Malta' means 'refuge' in Phoenician. It had come under Roman control in 218 BC. Luke records two miracles that took place on the island.

Paul suffered no ill effects when a viper fastened itself on his hand, and he healed the father of Publius, the island's chief official. Incidentally, Luke's term 'chief official' was used on a Greek inscription found on the island. The shipwrecked sailors spent three months on the island, before being put on an Alexandrian ship for Syracuse (modern Siracusa) in Sicily, amply furnished with supplies by the hospitable islanders.

In Rome at last

From Syracuse Paul and his companions sailed for Rhegium (modern Reggio di Calabria), on the Italian mainland side of the Straits of Messina, opposite Sicily. Sailing again, they disembarked at Puteoli (modern Pozzuoli) and journeyed northwards towards Rome along the Appian Way, the road that ran from Brindisi on the heel of Italy to Rome.⁷ At the wayside towns, the Forum of Appius and the Three Taverns, Luke notes, they were greeted by 'brothers' who had come from Rome to meet them. The book of Acts closes with a record of Paul staying two years in Rome under house arrest in his own rented house and welcoming all who came to see him. 'Boldly and without hindrance he preached the kingdom of God and taught about the Lord Jesus Christ' (Acts 28:31).

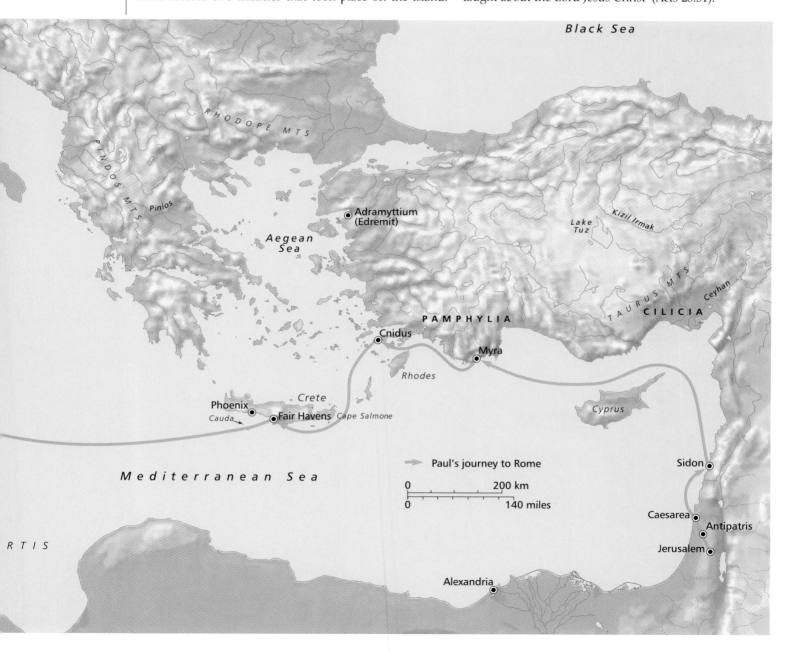

THE LETTERS OF THE NEW TESTAMENT

(AD 48–95)

LETTERS FROM THE ROMAN EMPIRE

Many letters from the Roman empire have been preserved. The letters of the Roman statesmen Cicero (106–43 BC) and Pliny the Younger (AD 61–112) have now been augmented by, among others, papyrus letters from Oxyrhynchus (Behnesa) in Egypt and wooden writing boards from Vindolanda (Chesterholm), near Hadrian's Wall in the north of England. Many of the letters from Egypt were written in the common Greek spoken by the ordinary men and women of the eastern half of the Roman empire. These letters have shed light on numerous words and expressions employed by the writers of the twenty-one letters now preserved in the New Testament.

Paul's last journey
The map shows a conjectural route of a journey made by Paul around AD 63–65, following his first release from prison in Rome.

Paul's letters
The map shows where Paul wrote his various letters, now preserved in the New Testament.

THE NEW TESTAMENT LETTERS

The Chester Beatty
Papyrus II, c. AD 200,
showing the beginning
of Paul's letter to the
Ephesians, with the words
'in Ephesus' missing.

The twenty-one New Testament letters were written by apostles and other authoritative church leaders to churches and individuals. The letters to the seven churches of the province of Asia are also preserved in the book of Revelation. The thirteen letters of Paul form the largest single group. The apostles Peter and John wrote two and three letters respectively. The exact identity of James and Jude is uncertain, but it is highly probable that they were both brothers of Jesus. The writer of the letter to the Hebrews is completely unidentified; with stylistic criteria seemingly ruling out Paul, some suggest Barnabas or Apollos.[1] Hebrews is the most artistic piece of writing in the New Testament, following a pattern laid down by Greek rhetoricians.

Many of the letters of the New Testament were more than just letters, they were 'epistles', a new type of biblical literature, where the key doctrines of the Christian faith are set out in a detailed and closely argued manner.

THE LETTERS OF PAUL
Paul's letters are presented in modern Bibles, with the exception of his letter to the Galatians, in descending order of length. This does not reflect the historical order.

- Paul's first letter would appear to be his letter to the Galatians. Although it is not accepted by all scholars, we take the view that it was written in AD 48–49 to the churches of Pisidian Antioch, Iconium, Lystra and Derbe that Paul had founded on his first journey.[2]
- Paul wrote 1 and 2 Thessalonians to the church in Thessalonica in northern Greece while at Corinth on his second journey.[3] This is to be dated to AD 51.
- In AD 55, towards the end of his three-year residency at Ephesus, during his third journey,[4] Paul wrote the first of his two letters to the Corinthians. In 1 Corinthians 10:25 Paul urges the Corinthian Christians to eat anything sold in the meat market without raising questions of conscience. The term for 'meat market' has been found on a fragmentary Latin inscription near the Lechaeum road north of the Corinthian *agora*. Paul wrote his second letter to the Corinthians from Macedonia the same year.[5]
- Later in his third journey, in AD 57, Paul wrote his letter to the Romans while staying at Corinth. At the end of his letter he passes on greetings from his friend Erastus, the city treasurer.[6] Near the theatre at

Corinth a slab was found with a Latin inscription: 'In commemoration of his office of commissioner of public works Erastus laid this pavement at his own expense.' It is quite probable that Erastus later became the commissioner of public works and marked his promotion by donating to the city the pavement of which the inscribed slab formed a part.

- In AD 60, while under house arrest in Rome,[7] Paul wrote to the churches of Philippi and of Colosse and also to his friend Philemon at Colosse concerning a runaway slave named Onesimus. The church at Colosse (modern Koyun Aliler Köyü, near the Turkish town of Denizli) is of interest since it was established by Epaphras, who had come to faith in Christ through contact with Paul at Ephesus.
- Paul also wrote a letter that we now know as Ephesians. It is perhaps significant to note that in the oldest manuscripts of this letter the words 'in Ephesus' are missing. The letter might have been a circular letter sent to all the churches and may be the letter from Laodicea mentioned in Colossians 4:16.
- In Paul's remaining letters reference is made to places mentioned neither in his journeys recorded in Acts nor in his other letters. References to Crete and Nicopolis[8] suggest that Paul was released from prison and able to make a fourth and final journey, the exact course of which remains speculative. Paul wrote his first letter to Timothy and his letter to Titus on this journey, AD 63–65.
- Paul then returned to Rome and wrote his last letter, his second to Timothy, while imprisoned under the emperor Nero AD 66–67. Paul senses that his time is almost up: 'For I am already being poured out like a drink offering, and the time has come for my departure. I have fought the good fight, I have finished the race, I have kept the faith. Now there is in store for me the crown of righteousness, which the Lord, the righteous Judge, will award to me on that day' (2 Timothy 4:6–8a).

OTHER NEW TESTAMENT LETTERS
It is more difficult to work out a chronology for the remaining New Testament letters. James is probably the earliest, being written before AD 50 and the three letters of John the latest, perhaps written AD 85–95. Only 1 Peter has a specified destination: 'to God's elect strangers in the world, scattered throughout Pontus, Galatia, Cappadocia, Asia and Bithynia' (1 Peter 1:1) – all in what is now Turkey. Only 3 John has a named recipient: 'my dear friend Gaius, whom I love in the truth' (3 John 1). The Greek of 2 Peter is commonly considered to be inferior to that of 1 Peter, but interestingly in his first letter Peter acknowledges the help of Silas.[9]

The significance of the New Testament letters cannot be overstated. It is here that the doctrines of the Christian faith are set forth in their clearest and most detailed expression.

KEY

[1] Acts 4:36; 18:24
[2] Acts 13:14–14:21
[3] Acts 18:1–18
[4] Acts 19:8, 10; 20:31
[5] 2 Corinthians 2:13
[6] Romans 16:23
[7] Acts 28:16, 30
[8] Titus 1:5; 3:12
[9] 1 Peter 5:12

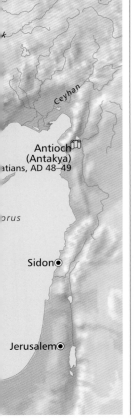

Ceyhan

Antioch
(Antakya)
atians, AD 48–49

orus

Sidon

Jerusalem

ROME

PAUL AND PETER IN ROME

In AD 57, while staying at Corinth, Paul wrote to those in Rome who believed in Jesus. It was a further three years before he was able to visit them. He spent two whole years in Rome, AD 60–62, under house arrest[1] and it is likely that he suffered a further period of imprisonment under the emperor Nero, AD 66–67, when he wrote his last letter, 2 Timothy. Tradition records that Paul was beheaded in Rome, by the Ostian Way.[2] The Church of the Three Fountains near the third milestone marks the site of his execution and the church of St Paul Outside the Walls, about 1.5 km (c. 1 mile) nearer the city, marks the site of his burial. According to tradition Peter was to meet a similar fate, except that he was crucified.[3] The world-famous church of St Peter on the Vatican hill marks the traditional site of his burial.

ROME IN PAUL'S DAY

Rome grew up around the first crossing point of the River Tiber, some 20 km (13 miles) from the sea. Seven hills – the Capitol, Palatine, Quirinal, Viminal, Esquiline, Caelian and Aventine – were enclosed by the so-called 'Servian wall' dating from the fourth century BC and enclosing an area of 426 hectares (1,053 acres).

Athough fire destroyed half of the centre of Rome in AD 64, a number of the monuments in existence in Paul's day have survived, if not always in their original form.

Rome's forum was the original market place of the city in a valley between five of the hills. It was about 175 m by 60 m (574 ft by 197 ft). As the city grew, the shops were relocated elsewhere and the forum took on a ceremonial role, being adorned with victory pillars and statues and surrounded by porticoes and colonnades. The original forum was augmented by the forums of Caesar and Augustus. Remains of several temples are still preserved. Augustus's mausoleum, an immense stone cylinder 88 m (289 ft) in diameter and 44 m (145 ft) high, planted with trees and crowned by a bronze statue of Augustus, is partly preserved by the River Tiber to the north of the city. Augustus boasted that he had found Rome in brick and left it built of marble.[4]

The Theatre of Marcellus dates from 23–13 BC and seated some 11,000 spectators. Two of its three tiers are still partially preserved.

The Circus Maximus occupied the space between the Palatine and Aventine hills. It was originally built by Julius Caesar in 46 BC. In its heyday it was over 600 m (1,970 ft) long, nearly 200 m (656 ft) wide and could seat 255,000 spectators. Down the length of the track was the *spina*, racing around which four quadriga chariots did seven laps (8.4 km or c. 5 miles). In the fourth century the centre of the spina was graced by a 32 m (105 ft) red granite obelisk of Ramesses II (1279–1213 BC) now in the Piazza del Popolo.

A number of Roman bridges that spanned the Tiber – Sublicius, Fabricius and Mulvius – are still in use.

Fourteen aqueducts brought an estimated 1 billion litres (264,172,800 gallons) of water a day into the city. The great Aqua Claudia, begun in AD 38, brought water to Rome from Subiaco, 72 km (45 miles) away. Some of its surviving arches are over 30 m (98 ft) high.

A huge brick-built barracks for the Praetorian guard was constructed on the north-east side of the city.

According to early fourth-century records Rome had 1,797 private houses, and 46,602 tenement blocks or *insulae*. In Rome several tenement blocks have partially survived, but those at Ostia, the port of Rome are better preserved. The tenements rose to five or more storeys high until Augustus limited their height to 20 m (66 ft) and Nero to 18 m (59 ft).[5] Built of concrete faced with bricks, they often had continuous balconies. Numerous large windows faced the street and often the central courtyard or light-well. Window glass was rare, folding shutters must have been used. Water was not available for residents of the upper floors. Baths and latrines were communal. The ground floor was often used for shops. Not surprisingly, fires were frequent.

Outside the city many tombs have been preserved. Perhaps the most remarkable is the pyramid of Gaius Cestius dating from 12 BC. A concrete core is faced with white marble.

ROME AFTER PAUL

Many of the most significant buildings of ancient Rome – such as the baths of Caracalla, Diocletian and Constantine, the mausoleum of Hadrian (Castel San Angelo), the forum of Trajan, the columns of Trajan and Marcus Aurelius and the arches of Titus, Septimus Severus and Constantine – date from after the visit of Paul to the city. Three structures are worthy of further comment.

The Colosseum is an immense, elliptical amphitheatre 189 m by 156 m (620 by 512 ft) in the valley between the Esquiline and Caelian hills. It was built between AD 70 and 80 and could seat some 50,000 spectators. The Colosseum, which had seventy-six entrances, was inaugurated with a hundred days of games, involving five thousand animals on a single day. It was also the scene of gladiatorial contests and mock naval battles. The fact that many Christians were martyred there ensured its preservation by the Catholic Church.

The Pantheon dates from AD 120–124. It is a round temple, dedicated to all the gods, made of concrete faced with brick, with a height and a diameter of 43 m (141 ft). A circular opening in the middle of the dome, 8 m (26 ft) in diameter, provides the only lighting.

Plan of Rome
Capital of the empire, a city whose population reached a million.

KEY
[1] Acts 28:16, 30
[2] Jerome, *On Illustrious Men*, 5.8
[3] Jerome, *On Illustrious Men*, 1.2
[4] Suetonius, *Life of Augustus*, 28.3
[5] Strabo, *Geography*, 5.3.7; Tacitus, *Annals*, 15.43
[6] Revelation 18:10

The forum, looking towards the Colosseum.

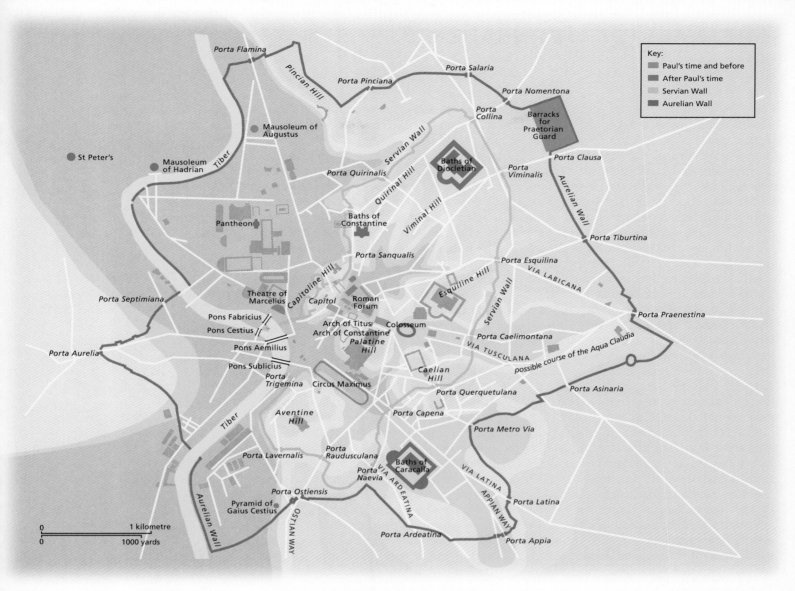

Key:
- Paul's time and before
- After Paul's time
- Servian Wall
- Aurelian Wall

Under the empire Rome expanded far beyond the original 10-kilometre-long (6 miles) fourth-century BC walls. It was not until AD 271 that, following an incursion of Germanic tribesmen into the Po Valley, the emperor Aurelian commissioned new walls. The 3.5-metre-thick (11 ft 6 in), brick-faced, concrete walls took ten years to build and extended for 19 km (11¾ miles). There were eighteen main gates and about every 30 m (98 ft) there was a square tower. These walls enclosed an area of 1,372 hectares (3,390 acres).

CAPITAL OF THE EMPIRE

Rome was the capital of an empire that in the second century AD stretched from Hadrian's Wall in northern England to the River Euphrates in eastern Turkey, and from the River Danube to the Sahara Desert. The estimated population of the empire is some fifty to sixty million, perhaps one fifth or one sixth of the world population at that time. It is estimated that at its height the population of Rome reached a million, with 400,000 being slaves.

In 20 BC Augustus had set up a 'golden milestone' in the Roman forum. In fact it was a stone column, embellished with plaques of gilded bronze, which recorded the distances to all the main cities of the empire, measured from Rome. Rome was the hub of a network of some 85,000 km (52,800 miles) of roads.

Products from all over the empire and beyond flooded into Rome. Huge granaries were built on the south side of the city near the river Tiber to store grain from Egypt. It is estimated that Rome consumed 150,000 tons of grain per year, 75 million litres (20 million gallons) of wine and some 20 million litres (5,280,000 gallons) of olive oil. This was used for cooking, washing and lighting. Near the Tiber an eighth hill (Monte Testaccio) was created from broken Spanish amphorae (olive oil containers). It is 30 m (98 ft) high and some 800 m (half a mile) in circumference. It is estimated it contains 53 million smashed amphorae, which once held 2,000 billion litres (over 528 billion gallons) of olive oil.

BEYOND ROME: THE NEW JERUSALEM

The apostle John was exiled to the Greek island of Patmos, probably under the Roman emperor Domitian (AD 81–96). John provides a detailed description of the trade-products of Rome in the book of Revelation: 'Cargoes of gold, silver, precious stones and pearls; fine linen, purple, silk and scarlet cloth; every sort of citron wood, and articles of every kind made of ivory, costly wood, bronze, iron and marble; cargoes of cinnamon and spice, of incense, myrrh and frankincense, of wine and olive oil, of fine flour and wheat; cattle and sheep; horses and carriages; and bodies and souls of men' (Revelation 18:12–13)

Actually the city is referred to as 'Babylon', whose doom comes in a single hour.[6] Whether John has Rome specifically in mind is uncertain, though a reference to the seven hills in Revelation 17:9 lends some credence to this. It may be more likely that he is ultimately looking ahead to the fall of the entire world system. What is clear is that John is looking beyond Rome, to Babylon's replacement, the New Jerusalem. 'I did not see a temple in the city, because the Lord God Almighty and the Lamb are its temple. The city does not need the sun or the moon to shine on it, for the glory of God gives it light, and the Lamb is its lamp' (Revelation 21:22–23).

THE FALL OF JERUSALEM

(AD 66–73)

JESUS PREDICTS THE FALL OF JERUSALEM

After Jesus' triumphal entry to Jerusalem his disciples remarked on how the Temple was adorned with beautiful stones and gifts dedicated to God. Jesus' reply must have surprised them: 'As for what you see here, the time will come when not one stone will be left on another; every one of them will be thrown down' (Luke 21:6).

Jesus also listed the signs that would precede his own return with power and great glory,[1] but mixed into this discourse are clear warnings about the impending destruction of Jerusalem: 'When you see Jerusalem surrounded by armies, you will know that its desolation is near. Then let those who are in Judea flee to the mountains, let those in the city get out, and let those in the country not enter the city' (Luke 21:20–21).

REASONS FOR THE REVOLT

In AD 6 Augustus removed Herod's successor in Judea, Herod Archelaus, and abolished Judea's status as a client kingdom. It became a province of the Roman empire under an imperial governor, who commanded a body of troops and who exercised judicial powers. This was to continue until AD 66 apart from the brief interlude provided by the client king Agrippa I, AD 41–44.

Roman taxes, and the dominance of the Roman fortress of Antonia over the Temple in Jerusalem, fomented Jewish resistance to Roman rule. Even the high priest's vestments were kept under Roman control in the fortress of Antonia, and the Jews had to defer execution to the Romans.[2] In numerous petty disputes the Romans usually took the side of the non-Jew against the Jew. Eventually the Temple priests built a high wall to stop the Roman soldiers in the Antonia fortress from peering over into the Temple.

Simmering tensions came to a head in May AD 66 when the Roman governor Gessius Florus confiscated seventeen talents (nearly 600 kg or 1,323 lb) from the Temple treasury. The people rioted, cutting the communications between the Antonia fortress and the Temple. Florus withdrew, and in September AD 66, when the mob captured the Antonia fortress, the remaining Roman soldiers in the city surrendered.

THE REBELLION SPREADS

Soon rebels stormed the fortress of Masada, near the Dead Sea. Across Palestine Jews and non-Jews set about killing each other. The historian Flavius Josephus (AD 37–100) noted that the whole of Palestine was in hopeless confusion and every city was divided into two camps, the survival of one depending on the destruction of the other.[3] Rioting even broke out in Alexandria in Egypt.

Josephus had been appointed governor of Galilee, but at heart he had no stomach for war with Rome. In the summer of AD 67, when Josephus was beseiged at Jotapata in Galilee, he surrendered to the Roman general Titus Flavius Vespasianus, the future emperor Vespasian, apparently prophesying his elevation to the throne.[4] Thereafter Josephus adopted a pro-Roman stance as is evidenced in his account, *The Jewish War*.

Vespasian continued to crush the Jewish resistance in Galilee. Particularly fierce was the resistance that he encountered at Gamala, to the east of Lake Galilee, in the autumn of AD 67. In the spring of AD 68 Vespasian severed Jerusalem's communications with the outside world, occupying Samaria, Peraea, Idumaea and the Mediterranean coast. By the summer only a few isolated fortresses, such as Herodium and Masada, remained in rebel hands. But as Vespasian was preparing for the final attack on Jerusalem, news came of the suicide of Emperor Nero in his villa outside Rome on 9 June AD 68.

The Jews were quick to take advantage. Simon bar Giora took Hebron, another rebel leader, John of Gischala, made himself master of Jerusalem. The Christians, remembering Christ's words, fled to Pella in Peraea.

In the spring of AD 69 Simon entered Jerusalem. Other rebel leaders would not recognize him. This led to different parts of Jerusalem being controlled by different leaders, Simon occupying the Upper City, his son Eleazar the Temple, while the rest of the city including the Antonia fortress was in the hands of John of Gischala. Disputes between these leaders led to the reserves of grain in the city being destroyed.

THE SIEGE OF JERUSALEM

In June AD 69 Vespasian returned to reoccupy Hebron. He did not stay long, since he was proclaimed emperor. He transferred the command to his son Titus, who began the siege of Jerusalem in the spring of AD 70. The countryside for some 15 km (9 miles) around was stripped bare of trees.[5] In Jerusalem internal quarrels intensified, with John of Gischala gaining control of the Temple and removing Eleazar. However, when the Romans attacked the third and outermost wall, John and Simon buried their differences. In May both the third and second walls fell quickly.

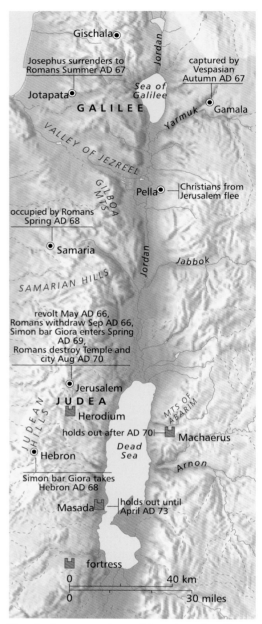

Two legions were brought against the Upper City and two against the fortress of Antonia. Josephus, now on the staff of Titus, vainly urged those in the city to surrender.

In three days the Romans threw up a seven-kilometre (c. five-mile) wall around the city to prevent all supplies from reaching the city.[6] Many inside the city perished with hunger. Putrefying bodies piled up in the streets. In June the Antonia fortress fell and siege was laid to the Temple. As famine raged on, cannibalism was reported.

THE TEMPLE IS DESTROYED

On 27 August AD 70 the Roman troops burnt the gate of the Temple and broke in. The Roman generals debated whether or not to set fire to the Temple. On 29 August a Roman soldier tossed a piece of blazing wood through

Scene from the Arch of Titus (AD 79–81), Rome. Roman soldiers carry off the golden lampstand from the Temple in Jerusalem.

LEFT: **The Roman War against the Jews** AD 66–73
The Roman armies captured Jerusalem in AD 70. Jewish resistance was finally crushed by the assault on Masada in AD 73.

The mountain fortress of Masada near the Dead Sea. It was the scene of the last Jewish resistance to Rome, finally succumbing in April AD 73. The Roman siege ramp can be seen on the right.

KEY
[1] Luke 21:27
[2] John 18:31
[3] Josephus, *The Jewish War*, 2.462
[4] Josephus, *The Jewish War*, 3.401; Suetonius, *Life of Vespasian*, 5.6
[5] Josephus, *The Jewish War*, 6.151
[6] Josephus, *The Jewish War*, 5:508–9
[7] Hebrews 8:13

the inner gate, setting the Sanctuary ablaze. Titus's pleas to extinguish the flames went unheeded. The Romans, judging it useless to spare the remaining parts of the Temple, set them ablaze too. The great stones of Herod's temple were prized apart to get the molten gold. A terrible, indiscriminate massacre ensued.

Pockets of resistance held out in other parts of the city until September. The city was razed to the ground, but a stretch of city wall and the three towers of Herod's palace were preserved. Titus returned to Italy with his spoils, among which was the table of the shewbread, the *menorah* or the seven-branched lampstand and the silver trumpets. These were depicted on the Arch of Titus in Rome, erected after his death.

THE SIEGE OF MASADA

The fortresses of Herodium and Machaerus held out. But it is the exploits of Eleazar, son of Jairus, and his nine hundred and sixty followers at the fortress of Masada in

the desert near the Dead Sea that are the most famous. Reservoirs, fed by flash floods and huge enough to hold 4,000 million litres (1,057 million gallons) of water, kept the defenders supplied with water. Stores were stocked with grain and dates. For three years they held out as a Roman siege-ramp piled against the great cliff rose higher and higher. Covered siege engines were pushed up the steep slope. Huge stone ballista balls were catapulted into the fortifications. Battering rams hammered the outside wall. By April AD 73 this was breached, but behind it the defenders built another wall of huge wooden beams. The repeated action of the battering rams only served to strengthen it.

Fire proved a more effective force. Seeing that the next day the Romans would finally triumph, the defenders appointed ten executioners, who killed the whole company and burned their bodies. Then on 21 April, after drawing lots, one of the ten executioners put his fellows to death before killing himself. An old woman and five little children who had hidden in an underground water conduit survived.

JUDAISM IN THE AFTERMATH

With the destruction of the Temple, sacrifice and offering ceased, as predicted by the writer to the Hebrews.[7] The Sanhedrin and high priesthood were abolished. Even the schismatic temple at Leontopolis in Egypt was abolished to prevent it from becoming a rallying point for Jewish resistance. Of all the Jewish sects only the Pharisees were to survive. Jewish worship that could no longer be met centrally through the Temple continued locally through synagogues in an ever-widening diaspora.

THE SEVEN CHURCHES OF ASIA: EPHESUS, SMYRNA, PERGAMUM

(End of first century AD)

JOHN ON PATMOS

The John who wrote the book of Revelation is commonly identified with the apostle John. He wrote it while exiled to the small Aegean island of Patmos. 'I, John, your brother and companion in the suffering and kingdom and patient endurance that are ours in Jesus, was on the island of Patmos because of the word of God and the testimony of Jesus' (Revelation 1:9). The island of Patmos is some 60 km (37 miles) off the modern Turkish coast and probably served as a Roman penal settlement.

John is then instructed to write on a scroll what he saw and send it to the seven churches in the Roman province of Asia: to Ephesus, Smyrna, Pergamum, Thyatira, Sardis, Philadelphia and Laodicea.[1] There then follows a series of seven letters, in which the risen Lord Jesus addresses the angel of each respective church.

Some have advanced the view that in addressing the angel of the church he is addressing the leader of the church, but in the New Testament churches had shared or collective leadership, rather than a single leader, so it seems more likely that the angel is a personification of the church as a whole, since John certainly hopes that his letters will produce change in the spiritual life of his hearers.

We should bear in mind that in addressing the seven churches, the risen Jesus through the instrumentality of John was addressing people, not buildings or institutions. No traces of the meeting places used by the believers in Jesus of John's day have survived, nor should we expect them to come to light. From the letter of Paul to Philemon we know of a church that met in Philemon's home.[2]

EPHESUS

The risen Lord begins with a commendation of the church at Ephesus. He praises their hard work, perseverance and their intolerance of false apostles – perhaps members of a harmful, unidentifiable sect called the Nicolaitans, alluded to in Revelation 2:6.

'Yet I hold this against you [says the risen Lord]: You have forsaken your first love. Remember the height from which you have fallen! Repent and do the things you did at first. If you do not repent, I will come to you and remove your lampstand from its place.'
REVELATION 2:4–5

We have already considered the part that Ephesus played in Paul's journeys.

SMYRNA

The second church addressed is that of Smyrna. Like Ephesus, Smyrna is on the sea and has a venerable history. Perhaps Smyrna is Tishmurna, mentioned in the tablets from the Assyrian colony of Kanesh in central Turkey which ceased trading c. 1780 BC. The risen Jesus is full of praise for the church at Smyrna, but warns them of coming persecution. They are exhorted to be faithful even to the point of death, and they will gain a crown of life.[3]

Today Smyrna is the modern Turkish city of Izmir, situated at the head of the 50-kilometre-long (31 miles) Gulf of Izmir and an important port. The most impressive ruin

ABOVE: The Greek island of Patmos, where the exiled apostle John saw his Revelation.

RIGHT: **Plan of Pergamum** Pergamum is a town built on several different levels. The cone-shaped acropolis rises some 300 m (984 ft) above the surrounding valley. The second-century Temple of Serapis in the valley has the River Selinus running under its precinct.

FAR RIGHT: The seven churches of the Roman province of Asia.

LEFT: The heavily restored library of Celsus, Roman governor of Asia, Ephesus, AD 110.

KEY
[1] Revelation 1:10–11
[2] Philemon 2
[3] Revelation 2:10
[4] Pliny, *Natural History*, 13.70
[5] Plutarch, *Life of Antony*, 58.6

of ancient Smyrna is the market place (or *agora*), built in the middle of the second century, but devastated by an earthquake in AD 178. It was rebuilt by Faustina, the wife of the Roman emperor Marcus Aurelius. It has an impressive series of underground vaults.

PERGAMUM

We now move inland to the third church, that of Pergamum, the modern Turkish town of Bergama. The citadel of Pergamum was built on a cone-shaped hill rising some 300 m (984 ft) above the surrounding valley. The citadel area contains the palace and arsenal of the so-called Attalid kings of the third and second centuries BC. It was here too that the famous library was established early in the reign of Eumenes II (197–159 BC). It originally contained some 200,000 scrolls. There was intense rivalry between

RIGHT: The theatre at Pergamum. The altar of Zeus was located beneath the tree towards the top of the picture.

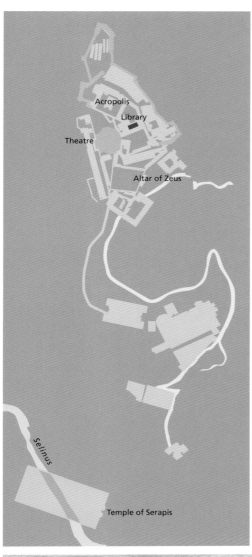

Acropolis

Library

Theatre

Altar of Zeus

Selinus

Temple of Serapis

Pergamum and the famous library at Alexandria in Egypt, established by Ptolemy I c. 295 BC. When the rulers of Hellenistic Egypt banned the export of papyrus, Pergamum developed its own writing material by splitting the skins of sheep, goats and other animals into thin sheets and polishing them with lime. Thus the name Pergamum gave rise to the term 'parchment'.[4] The contents of the library were presented as a gift by Antony to Cleopatra in 41 BC to replace books from the library at Alexandria burned during Julius Caesar's campaign.[5]

In 133 BC Attalus III died childless and bequeathed the entire kingdom to the rising power of Rome, who made it the capital of their new province of Asia. Pergamum was to remain capital of Asia until Hadrian transferred the capital to Ephesus c. AD 129.

The theatre at Pergamum was built during the reign of Eumenes II (197–159 BC). Cut into the side of a hill, it seated 10,000 spectators arranged in eighty rows of seats and was the steepest theatre in the ancient world.

Churches mentioned by John

0   150 km

0   100 miles

Pergamum

Thyatira

Sardis

Philadelphia

Smyrna

Aegean Sea

Ephesus

Laodicea

The citadel was the site of the celebrated altar of Zeus, built by Eumenes II to commemorate Attalus I's defeat in 230 BC of the invading Gauls (who were perhaps to become the Galatians of the New Testament). The 36 by 34 m structure, which had a frieze 120 m long by 2.3 m high (394 ft by 7$^{1/2}$ ft) showing battling giants and gods, has now been re-erected in the Staatliche Museum in Berlin.

In the middle of the modern town is a structure with an uncanny resemblance to a Victorian railway station. The so-called Kızıl avlu 'red courtyard' is an immense, red-brick building dedicated to the Egyptian god Serapis. It dates from the early second century and originally it was faced with marble of various colours. This is the largest building from antiquity to have been found in the province of Asia. The River Selinus (Bergama Çayı) runs under the 200 m by 100 m (656 ft by 328 ft) temple precinct in two vaulted canals.

Some have identified this structure with 'Satan's throne' mentioned by John in Revelation 2:13, but it was not in existence in John's time. Others propose the altar of Zeus, as a candidate for Satan's throne. Probably the reference is more generally to the whole city, which was the official centre of emperor worship in Asia and the site of the first temple erected to Rome and Augustus in 29 BC.

THE SEVEN CHURCHES OF ASIA: THYATIRA, SARDIS, PHILADELPHIA, LAODICEA

(End of first century AD)

THYATIRA

We now move to the site of the fourth church – Thyatira, the modern Turkish town of Akhisar. It is perhaps ironic that the longest of the seven letters is addressed to the city that we know least about.

In antiquity Thyatira was famous as a centre for the manufacture of purple cloth. This dye, obtained from the madder root, was still used in Akhisar in the late nineteenth century. Lydia, whom Paul met at Philippi in northern Greece,[1] was from Thyatira. She was a dealer in purple cloth and it seems likely that Lydia was her nickname, reflecting the area of the province of Asia where she came from.

Another important industry was the manufacture of burnished bronze, alluded to in Revelation 2:18. Apart from in that verse in Revelation, the word occurs nowhere else in Greek literature, but it seems that a refined alloy of copper or bronze with traces of metallic zinc is in view here. Other trades are known to have flourished in the town. Membership of trade-guilds would have involved an attendance at guild meetings with their paganism and accompanying immorality. The risen Lord seems to address this by rebuking the church at Thyatira for tolerating the wicked woman Jezebel, who calls herself a prophetess. By her teaching she misleads the church into sexual immorality and the eating of food sacrificed to idols.[2]

Very little of ancient Thyatira survives. A ruined Byzantine church is the only witness to a Christian past.

SARDIS

The fifth church is Sardis. This is the modern Turkish village of Sart, bestraddling the Izmir–Ankara road, near Salihli in the province of Manisa. An inscription in Lydian and Aramaic found at Sardis and dating from the fourth century BC spells the name Sepharad, as found in Obadiah 20. Incidentally, this term has given its name to the Sephardic Jews – Jews of Iberian and North African origin who were considered like Sardis as being to the north-west of Jerusalem.

Sardis was the capital of the ancient kingdom of Lydia. During the reign of the Lydian king Gyges (c. 680–644 BC) gold was discovered in the Pactolus River (Sart Çayı), which runs through Sardis, and Lydia introduced the world's first coinage in gold, silver and electrum (an alloy of silver and gold).

John records the words of the risen Jesus to the church at

The temple of Artemis at Sardis. Although begun in c. 300 BC, most of the surviving masonry is Roman.

Fourth-century mosaic pavement in the courtyard of the synagogue of Sardis.

KEY
[1] Acts 16:14
[2] Revelation 2:20
[3] Herodotus, *Histories*, 1.84
[4] Colossians 4:13

Sardis: 'If you do not wake up, I will come like a thief, and you will not know at what time I will come to you' (Revelation 3:3). This may be an allusion to the surprise capture of the seemingly impregnable acropolis of Sardis by the Persian King Cyrus II in 547 BC. The Persians scaled the citadel by a neglected path, down which a Lydian soldier had been seen to descend in search of a helmet which had rolled down the hill.[3] Sardis was the terminus of the 2,680-kilometre-long (1,665-miles) Persian 'Royal Road' from Susa in southern Iran. A section of this road can be seen in Sardis.

In the last couple of centuries BC there was considerable Jewish settlement in the area. The synagogue at Sardis, the largest ancient synagogue known, has been restored by the largesse of American Jews. It was probably established c. AD 166, the restored structure being built between AD 220 and 250. An inscription on the marble synagogue wall reads: 'I [name lost] with my wife Regina and my children from the bounties of the Almighty God gave the entire marble cladding and painting.'

PHILADELPHIA

The sixth church addressed is that of Philadelphia, the modern Turkish town of Alaşehir. Philadelphia was established as a frontier fort of Pergamum in 189 BC. The name means 'brotherly love', commemorating the love of Eumenes II (197–159 BC) of Pergamum for his younger brother, Attalus. Once again a ruined Byzantine church is the only witness to a Christian past.

LAODICEA

The last church to be addressed is that of Laodicea. The ruins of Laodicea are located near the village of Goncalı, north of Denizli. The city was named by the Seleucid king Antiochus II after his wife Laodice, whom he divorced in 253 BC. Its ruins are poorly preserved. The risen Jesus rebuked the church at Laodicea: 'I know your deeds, that you are neither cold nor hot. I wish that you were one or the other. So because you are lukewarm – neither hot nor cold – I am about to spit you out of my mouth' (Revelation 3:15–16).

The rebuke for being lukewarm – neither hot nor cold – may have a particular reference to the problem that Laodicea had in antiquity of securing drinkable water.

Looking north from Laodicea, you cannot help seeing at some ten kilometres' distance the spectacular white travertines of the hot springs of Hierapolis.[4] The curtain of stalactites and shallow pools is now the tourist attraction of Pamukkale 'Cotton castle'. The risen Jesus' 'hot' may be a reference to the hot springs of Pamukkale. Today they come out of the ground at 36° C (97° F). To the south-east is the imposing Honaz mountain. This provided 'cold' water to the city of Colosse. Laodicea lacked any natural water supply and so had to bring water by an aqueduct, from hot mineral springs some 8 km (5 miles) away at Denizli. By the time this water reached Laodicea it was 'lukewarm'.

Once in the city the water was distributed through square, stone water pipes about 1 metre (3 ft) across, a number of which litter the site. These were bored through the centre lengthwise and cemented together.

In antiquity Laodicea had an important pharmaceutical school, hence the risen Jesus' allusion to 'eye salve' in Revelation 3:18.

The hot springs of Hierapolis (modern Pamukkale) glow in the evening sun.

THE SPREAD OF CHRISTIANITY

(AD 33–337)

THE SPREAD OF THE GOSPEL

In Paul's last letter, 2 Timothy, he notes of his colleagues that Crescens had gone to Galatia and Titus to Dalmatia.[1] Galatia is central Turkey and probably included the churches Paul had founded in the vicinity of Pisidian Antioch: Iconium, Lystra and Derbe. Dalmatia is modern Albania and parts of Serbia and Montenegro. Clearly Paul's colleagues were continuing his practice of preaching Jesus where he was not known.[2]

The New Testament is silent on where many of the apostles and other church leaders went to preach the gospel. Later tradition places the apostle John living his latter years at Ephesus and the apostle Philip at Hierapolis (Pamukkale) in Turkey.

Later tradition also associates the apostles Thomas and Bartholemew with India, but what is meant by 'India' is not clear; any land bordering the Indian Ocean might be so described.

How Christianity spread throughout the Roman empire and beyond remains a largely untold story. Certainly the 85,000-kilometre (52,800-mile) network of roads and sea communications throughout the empire facilitated its propagation. The following three examples illustrate different aspects of the spread of Christianity:

- In AD 79 the volcano Vesuvius erupted and buried the city of Pompeii in southern Italy. Here was found a Latin inscription comprising five five-letter words arranged in a square. The meaning of the word-square is cryptic, but it contains the words 'PATER NOSTER' ('our father'), the first two words of the Lord's prayer in Latin,[3] together with two extra A's and O's, perhaps standing for the Greek letters Alpha and Omega, used as a name of God in Revelation 1:8. If, as seems most likely, it was a Christian secret sign, a device with which Christians would recognize others of the same faith, it is evidence that Christianity had reached Pompeii before the fateful year of AD 79. Copies of this word-square have also been found in distant parts of the Roman empire and beyond.
- In AD 112 Pliny the Younger, the Roman governor of the province of Bithynia in north-west Turkey, alarmed at the spread of Christianity in his province, wrote to the emperor Trajan. He noted with some consternation that even the religious conservatism of the villages was being overcome and that pagan shrines were being neglected. Pliny, who sought to

execute all those who professed the new faith and would not publically recant, gave the following testimony: 'They were in the habit of meeting on a certain fixed day before it was light, when they sang an anthem to Christ as God, and bound themselves by a solemn oath not to commit any wicked deed, but to abstain from all fraud, theft and adultery, never to break their word or deny a trust when called upon to honour it' (Pliny, *Letters*, 10.96.7).
- At Dura Europos (as-Salahiya) in Syria a house dating from AD 232–233 was adapted soon after its construction to make a hall holding a hundred people. The walls have painted scenes from both the Old Testament and the Gospels and imply the building was used for Christian worship.

PERSECUTION AND MARTYRDOM

Even a cursory reading of the Acts of the Apostles shows that the early church faced periods of persecution. Divine intervention allowed Peter to escape from prison,[4] but at the same time, AD 44, the apostle James, the son of Zebedee, was put to death by Herod Agrippa I. Later tradition has Andrew being crucified in Achaia in Greece, and Peter at Rome.

In the letters of the risen Lord Jesus to the seven churches in Revelation each of the churches was exhorted to overcome.[5] Some such as Smyrna were warned of specific persecution,[6] indeed much of the rest of the book of Revelation (however precisely it is to be interpreted) is about the church standing firm under persecution. At the end of the book 'Babylon' – some of the details of which fit Rome, but which is more likely to be the entire world system – falls and the New Jerusalem comes down out of heaven from God.[7] 'Now the dwelling of God is with men, and he will live with them. They will be his people and God himself will be with them, and be their God. He will wipe every tear from their eyes' (Revelation 21:3b–4a).

Such a hope gave the early Christians great courage in the face of death. Even within the New Testament period there were many martyrs whose deaths are unrecorded by the New Testament itself. In AD 64 when much of Rome was destroyed by fire, the emperor Nero blamed the Christians. He conducted mass arrests and had his victims covered in the skins of wild animals and torn to death by dogs, crucified or set on fire.[8] Further persecution broke out under Domitian (AD 81–96). John's imprisonment on the island of Patmos, during which, it is commonly believed, he wrote the

book of Revelation, was under this persecution.

Persecution of Christians continued under the emperors of the second and third centuries. Thus in briefest summary:

- In AD 156 Polycarp, the aged bishop of Smyrna, refused to recant his faith before a pagan mob. 'Eighty-six years have I served him, and he has done me no wrong, how can I blaspheme my Saviour and King?' was his reply.[9]
- In AD 177 Marcus Aurelius directed severe persecution against the churches of Vienne and Lyon in the Rhône Valley of France.
- In AD 202 Septimus Severus issued an imperial edict explicitly forbidding conversion to Christianity. Thousands died, particularly in Egypt and Carthage.
- In AD 250 Decius issued an edict that everyone in the empire must sacrifice to the state gods and get a certificate to say they had done so.

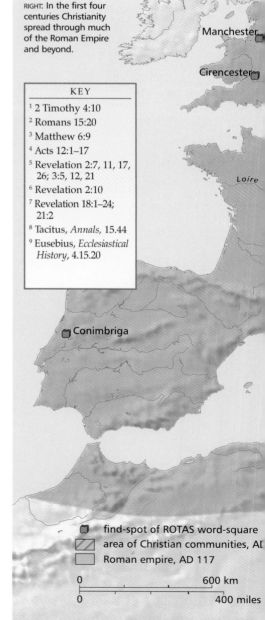

RIGHT: In the first four centuries Christianity spread through much of the Roman Empire and beyond.

KEY
[1] 2 Timothy 4:10
[2] Romans 15:20
[3] Matthew 6:9
[4] Acts 12:1–17
[5] Revelation 2:7, 11, 17, 26; 3:5, 12, 21
[6] Revelation 2:10
[7] Revelation 18:1–24; 21:2
[8] Tacitus, *Annals*, 15.44
[9] Eusebius, *Ecclesiastical History*, 4.15.20

Manchester

Cirencester

Loire

Conimbriga

⬜ find-spot of ROTAS word-square
▨ area of Christian communities, A
⬜ Roman empire, AD 117

0   600 km
0   400 miles

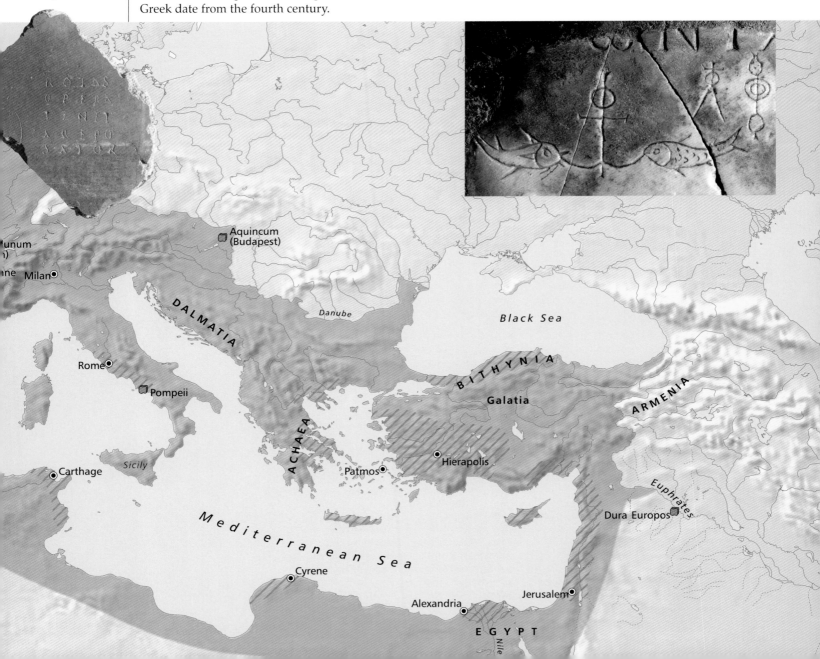

- In AD 257 Valerian banned Christians from holding public meetings and denied access to their cemeteries.
- In AD 303 Diocletian ordered the destructions of church buildings and copies of the Bible.

OFFICIAL RECOGNITION OF CHRISTIANITY

Official recognition played a part in the spread of Christianity. Abgar IX (AD 179–216), ruler of the kingdom of Edessa (the modern town of Urfa in south-east Turkey), converted to Christianity. In AD 301 King Tiridates and his family, of Armenia on the eastern border of the Roman empire, were baptized as Christians.

At Milan in AD 313 the Roman emperor Constantine issued an edict of toleration in favour of Christians. Although this did not immediately end persecution, it at least gave Christianity official recognition. In the year of his death, AD 337, Constantine was baptized. Whether imperial endorsement of Christianity was good for the church remains debatable, but with a few exceptions it at least brought to an end state-sponsored persecution of Christians.

Up until the end of persecution there had been too great a risk of books being destroyed for a complete set of biblical books to be gathered into one place. So it is no coincidence that the first complete manuscripts of the whole Bible in Greek date from the fourth century.

AN ONGOING STORY

Until the invention of printing in the mid-fifteenth century all manuscripts, whether Bibles or any other type of literature, had to be labouriously copied by hand. In total 3,286 manuscripts of part or all of the Greek New Testament have been preserved. No other ancient book has so many manuscript copies preserved of it. A very distant second is Homer's Iliad at 665 copies.

The New Testament was also translated into a number of vernacular languages. Syriac, two dialects of Coptic (the successor to ancient Egyptian), Latin (two versions: the so-called Old Latin and the Vulgate of Jerome), Gothic (a Germanic language), Armenian, Georgian, Old Slavonic (the ancestor of the Slavic languages), Ethiopic and Sogdian (an Indo-European language of central Asia) all had translations before the end of the first millennium. Today the Bible is the world's most translated book. It has been translated in total into 392 languages and the New Testament into a further 1012. The impact and influence of the Bible's message is worldwide, something perhaps glimpsed by the Old Testament prophet Habakkuk: 'For the earth will be filled with the knowledge of the glory of the Lord, as the waters cover the sea' (Habakkuk 2:14).

Glossary

Words marked with an asterisk provide a cross-reference to head-words in the Glossary.

Akkadian

The Semitic* language spoken in Mesopotamia* (modern Iraq and eastern Syria) by the Assyrians and Babylonians. It was written in the cuneiform* script.

Anatolia

A name sometimes given to the peninsula now occupied by modern Turkey, called Asia Minor in Roman times.

apostle

A title derived from a Greek word meaning 'one sent out'. The apostles were the authoritative leaders of the early church. Jesus himself selected twelve of his disciples and designated them apostles (Mark 3:14; Luke 6:13). When Matthias was selected as an apostle to replace the traitor Judas, he was required to have been with Jesus from the beginning of his ministry and to have been a witness of his resurrection (Acts 1:21–22). The title 'apostle' was most famously given to Paul, but was also used of Barnabas (Acts 14:14), Silas, Timothy (1 Thessalonians 1:1; 2:6) and the unknown Andronicus and Junias (Romans 16:7). Such designations suggest that the term was sometimes used more widely than just for the original twelve.

ark of the covenant

An acacia wood chest, overlaid inside and out with gold. It held the two stone tablets inscribed with the Ten Commandments and was surmounted by a gold atonement cover and a pair of gold cherubim with outstretched wings. It was deposited in the Most Holy Place* of the tabernacle* and later of Solomon's temple in Jerusalem.

Asherah pole

A representation of the Canaanite mother-goddess Asherah, its exact form is uncertain.

centurion

A commander of a hundred men. Although originally the term was used to designate a rank in the Roman army, it was also used to designate a rank in the army of Herod Antipas (the Tetrarch), which was organized in Roman fashion.

Corinthian

An order of Greek architecture, characterized by capitals with stylized acanthus leaves. This was the latest order to be developed, first attested on the Choragic Monument of Lysicrates in Athens, c. 334 BC.

covenant

An agreement between two parties, but (unlike a treaty) not limited to the political sphere. In the Old Testament the Lord makes several covenants with selected individuals and with his people, the Israelites.

cuneiform

The wedge-shaped writing system of Mesopotamia*.

Doric

The simplest and earliest order of Greek architecture. Its capitals consist of a circular disc tapering outwards, supporting a square top.

high place

An unauthorized cult centre where the Lord or pagan deities or both might be worshipped.

Holy Place

The middle of the three rooms in the centre of both the tabernacle* and the Temple of the Lord in Jerusalem. The golden shewbread table, golden lampstand (*menorah*) and altar of incense were placed here.

Indo-European

The language family comprising most European and some Iranian and Indian languages.

Ionic

An order of Greek architecture developed in the sixth century BC in Ionia, the Aegean coast of modern Turkey. The capitals have a volute or spiral scroll.

Israel

The name that God gave to Jacob – meaning 'he struggles with God' (Genesis 32:28) – was also given to Jacob's descendants, the Israelites. Its first occurrence outside the Hebrew Bible is in the stela* of the Egyptian king Merenptah c. 1209 BC. In this *Atlas* the usage 'Israel' is reserved for the kingdom of Israel established by Saul and the northern kingdom of Israel established after the death of Solomon in 930 BC. This kingdom came to an end in 722 BC when the Israelites were exiled to Assyria.

Mesopotamia

A Greek term meaning 'between the rivers' used to designate the region between the Tigris and Euphrates rivers, corresponding to modern Iraq and eastern Syria.

Most Holy Place

The name given to the innermost of the three rooms in the centre of both the tabernacle and the temple of the Lord in Jerusalem. This room, traditionally called the Holy of Holies, housed the ark of the covenant* and was only entered by the high priest once a year on the Day of Atonement (Leviticus 16:12–17).

Mycenaean

A civilization that developed in Greece in the Bronze Age. It is named after Mycenae, one of its most important sites, and came to an end in c. 1200 BC with the invasion of the Dorian Greeks.

ostraca

Broken pieces of pottery that were used to record short messages.

patriarch

The name given to the ancestors of the Israelites: Abraham, Isaac and Jacob.

Pentateuch

The first five books of the Old Testament – Genesis, Exodus, Leviticus, Numbers and Deuteronomy – traditionally ascribed to Moses.

proconsul

The title given to governors of Roman provinces administered by the Roman senate. Such provinces did not have Roman military garrisons stationed in them.

prophet

Someone who delivers the words of a deity to the people. In the Bible the making of predictions was only part of the ministry, not the whole. The term is primarily used in an Old Testament context but was also used to designate a ministry in the early church (Acts 11:27–28; 21:10).

Ptolemaic

A term given to the dynasty of Greek-speaking kings, all called Ptolemy, who ruled Egypt from 323 to 30 BC.

satrap

Officials who ruled over one of the twenty administrative units of the Persian empire from the reign of Darius (522–486 BC) to 330 BC.

the (bronze) Sea

The name given to a huge, bronze, hemispherical water-tank used for ceremonial purification, described in 1 Kings 7:23–26.

Sea Peoples

The name given to a coalition of peoples, primarily of Aegean and Anatolian* origin, who attacked Egypt and may have contributed to the fall of the Hittite empire in c. 1180 BC. The Philistines were a Sea People.

Seleucid

A term given to the dynasty of Greek-speaking kings, who from 311 to 63 BC ruled Syria and parts of the former Persian empire further to the east.

Semitic

The language family to which many Near Eastern languages belong, including Hebrew, Arabic and Akkadian*.

stela

An inscribed upright slab or pillar.

tabernacle

The traditional English name (from the Latin for 'tent') given to the portable worship-tent and its surrounding courtyard that Moses erected in the desert. Once the Israelites had settled in Canaan, it was pitched at Shiloh (Judges 18:31; 1 Samuel 1:9). Objects from it, such as the ark of the covenant,* the table for the shewbread and the lampstand (*menorah*), were installed in Solomon's temple in Jerusalem.

vassal

A ruler who had pledged loyalty to a greater king.

BIBLIOGRAPHY

Abegg, M., Flint, P., and Ulrich, E.,*The Dead Sea Scrolls Bible* Harper, San Francisco, 1999.

Akurgal, E., *Ancient Civilisations and Ruins of Turkey* Türk Tarih Kurumu, Ankara, 1973.

Baly, A. D., *The Geography of the Bible* Lutterworth Press, London, 1957.

Bright, J., *History of Israel* (Fourth edition) Westminster John Knox Press, Louisville / London, 2000.

Bruce, F. F., *The Books and the Parchments* (Third Edition) Pickering and Inglis, London, 1963.

Bruce, F. F., *Israel and the Nations* Paternoster, Exeter, 1963.

Bruce, F. F., *Paul: Apostle of the Free Spirit* Paternoster, Exeter, 1977.

Douglas, J. D. (editor), *The Illustrated Bible Dictionary* 3 vols Inter Varsity Press, Leicester, 1980.

Freedman, D.N. (editor), *The Anchor Bible Dictionary* 6 vols Doubleday, New York, 1992.

Grant, M., *Herod the Great* Weidenfeld and Nicolson, London, 1971.

Heidel, A., *The Gilgamesh Epic and Old Testament Parallels* Chicago University Press, Chicago, 1946.

Hoffmeier, J. K., *Israel in Egypt. The Evidence for the Authenticity of the Exodus Tradition* Oxford University Press, 1997.

Kitchen, K. A., *On the Reliability of the Old Testament* William B. Eerdmans,Grand Rapids, Michigan, 2003.

Millard, A. R., *Discoveries from Bible Times* Lion, Oxford, 1997.

Millard, A. R., *Reading and Writing in the Time of Jesus* Sheffield Academic Press, 2000.

Murphy-O'Connor, J., *Oxford Archaeological Guides: The Holy Land* (Fourth edition), Oxford University Press, 1998.

Roux, G., *Ancient Iraq* (Third Edition) Penguin, London, 1992.

Smith, G. A., *The Historical Geography of the Holy Land* Hodder and Stoughton, London, 1895.

Thiele, E. R., *The Mysterious Numbers of the Hebrew Kings* (Third edition) Chicago University Press 1986.

Wiseman, D. J., *Nebuchadrezzar and Babylon* Oxford University Press, 1985.

Yamauchi, E. M., *The Stones and the Scriptures* Inter Varsity Press, London, 1973.

Yamauchi, E. M., *Persia and the Bible*, Baker Book House, Grand Rapids, Michigan, 1990.

INDEX

Page numbers refer to the left-hand page of the spread on which the reference occurs.

GAZETTEER

SCRIPTURE REFERENCE INDEX

Picture Acknowledgments

Maps and plans

Cosmographics (*draft cartography*): pp 15, 17, 18. 20 (both), 21 (both), 22, 25 (right), 27, 39, 68, 77, 86, 96, 98, 100, 105, 107, 113, 119 (top), 148 (bottom).

NASA, MODIS Rapid Response Team at GSFC (*satellite images*): pp. 39 (centre), 125.

Richard Watts (Total Media Services): pp. 10/11, 15, 17, 18, 20 (both), 21 (both), 22, 25 (bottom left, right), 26, 27, 29 (left), 30, 33, 34, 36, 39 (top), 42, 43, 44, 46, 47, 48 (top centre, top right), 51, 52 (bottom left, centre, right), 53 (left, centre), 55, 57, 58, 59 (bottom), 60, 61, 63, 65, 67, 68 (both), 70/71, 73, 77, 78, 81, 82, 84, 85, 86, 87, 89, 90, 91, 92, 95 (centre), 96, 98, 100, 103, 105, 106/107, 110, 113, 114, 119 (both), 120, 122, 126, 127 (left), 129, 130, 134 (all), 137, 139, 140, 144, 148 (both), 150/151, 153, 154, 156 (top), 161, 162/3, 164 (top), 164/165, 168, 171 (centre), 174/175.

Simon Emery (Aqua Design): pp. 23 (bottom left), 48 (bottom left), 77 (right), 95 (below), 99, 104, 109 (top), 116, 124, 133 (top right), 143, 146, 156 (centre), 157, 167, 171 (left).

Illustrations and diagrams

Andy Rous (*photography and image manipulation*): pp. 1, 3, 5.

Jonathan Adams (*panoramic illustrations*): pp. 40/41, 74/75, 88/89, 108/109, 132/133, 140/141, 158/159.

Martin Sanders (MapArt) (*battle plans*): pp. 45, 59 (top, centre), 62.

Stephen Conlin (*illustration*): p. 23 (bottom right).

Todd Oliver (Lion Hudson) (*diagrams*): pp. 25 (top), 29 (right), 52 (top), 53 (top), 54, 79, 127 (right).

Photographs

AKG-Images: pp. 3 (far left and second right), 31 (bottom), 33, 35 (below), 66 (top), 94 (below), 99, 118 (below), 123 (below), 159 (Erich Lessing); p. 36 (below) (Archives CDA/Guillo); p. 117 (right) (Gérard Degeorge).

Alamy: pp. 16 (above) (© E.J. Baumeister Jr.), 26 (© Images&Stories), 31 (middle) (© Royal Geographical Society), 50 (© Mark Boulton), 80 (above) (© Edward Parker), 136 (© Eitan Simanor), 152 (above) (© Kevin Lang), 152 (below) (© Westend61), 154 (© Robert Harding Picture Library Ltd), 155 (above) (© ALIKI SAPOUNTZI / aliki image library), 160 (above) (© DIOMEDIA), 160 (below) (© Peter Horree), 170 (above) (© terry harris just greece photo library), 172 (above) (© Sean Burke).

Bridgeman Art Library: pp. 28 (both) (Egyptian National Museum, Cairo, Egypt); p. 32 (above) (Valley of the Nobles, Thebes, Egypt, Giraudon); pp. 37, 96 (Egyptian National Museum, Cairo, Egypt, Giraudon); p. 87 (below) (British Museum, London, UK); pp. 113 (inset), 116 (National Museum of Iran, Tehran, Iran); 115 (Persepolis, Iran, Giraudon); 118 (above) (Archaeological Museum, Thessaloniki, Greece); 128 (below) (David Lees, Florence).

British Museum: pp. 31 (top), 89, 111 (below) (© The Trustees of The British Museum).

Chester Beatty Library: p. 165 (Reproduced by kind permission of the Trustees of the Chester Beatty Library, Dublin).

Corbis UK Ltd: p. 175 (right) (Araldo de Luca).

Corinium Museum, Cirencester: p. 175 (left).

David Alexander: pp. 27, 43, 66 (middle), 83 (middle), 110, 128 (above), 132, 138 (below), 146, 147 (bottom), 155 (below), 163.

Hanan Isachar: pp. 44, 45, 49 (above), 52, 63, 85, 100, 130 (above), 145 (below), 147 (top), 169 (below).

John Rylands University Library of Manchester: p. 121 (below).

Jon Arnold Images: pp. 32 (below), 35 (above), 38, 59, 80 (below), 142, 151 (above), 152 (below), 156, 157 (above), 166, 170 (below), 171, 172 (below), 173.

Lion Hudson: pp. 36 (above), 57, 83 (bottom), 135 (above), 139, 145 (above), 147 (middle) (David Townsend).

NASA: p. 14.

Network Photographers: p. 104 (Georg Gerster).

Paul Lawrence: p. 21.

Rex Features: p. 149 (Sipa Press).

Superstock: p. 113 (main) (© age fotostock).

Scala: pp. 3 (second left) (Paris, Louvre. © 1995. Photo Scala, Florence), 3 (far right) (London, Ann Ronan Picture Library © 2004, Photo Scala Florence/HIP), 23 (Baghdad, The Iraq Museum © 1990, Photo Scala, Florence), 24 (below) (London, British Museum © 2003, Photo Scala Florence/HIP), 49 (below) (London, Spectrum, HIP112005 © 2005 Photo Scala Florence/HIP), 73 (London, © 2004, Photo Scala Florence/HIP), 88 (Paris, Louvre © 1995 Photo Scala, Florence), 94 (above) (London, British Museum © 2003 Photo Scala Florence/HIP), 114 (London, British Museum © 2003 Photo Scala Florence/HIP), 120 (Vatican, Egyptian Museum © 1990 Photo Scala, Florence).

Stéphane Compoint: p. 124 (©stephanecompoint.com).

Werner Forman Archive: pp. 19 (below) (Egyptian Museum, Turin), 24 (above) (British Museum, London), 40 (Egyptian Museum, Cairo), 76, 162.

West Semitic Research: p. 13 (below) (Photograph by Bruce and Kenneth Zuckerman, West Semitic Research, with the collaboration of the Ancient Biblical Manuscript Center. Courtesy Russian National Library (Saltykov-Shchedrin)).

www.HolyLandPhotos.org: p. 157 (below).

Zev Radovan: pp. 12, 13 (above), 16 (below), 19 (above), 39, 46, 47 (both), 60, 61 (both), 65, 66 (bottom), 69, 72, 74, 78, 82, 83 (top), 87 (above), 93, 95 (both), 101, 102 (both), 107, 111 (above), 112, 121 (above), 122, 123, 130 (below), 131, 135 (below), 138 (above), 150, 151 (below), 161, 169 (above).

Lion Hudson

Commissioning editor: Morag Reeve

Editorial team: Catherine Giddings, David Bygott (*freelance*), Liz Evans (*freelance*), David Hutchison (*freelance*)

Designer/Cartographic editor: Nicholas Rous

Picture researcher: Juliet Mozley

Production manager: Kylie Ord

All Lion books are available from your local bookshop, or can be ordered via our website or from Marston Book Services. For a free catalogue, showing the complete list of titles available, please contact:

Customer Services
Marston Book Services
PO Box 269
Abingdon
Oxon
OX14 4YN

Tel: 01235 465500
Fax: 01235 465555

Our website can be found at:
www.lionhudson.com